This is the first one-volume survey in English of religion and devotion in Europe between the fourth and fifth Lateran Councils. Intended primarily as a student textbook, it provides essential background for a proper appreciation of medieval western society.

Avoiding the history of institutional structures, the book concentrates on the spirituality which the medieval church sought to promulgate and control. After an outline of the basic beliefs of catholicism in the period, there follows a series of thematic chapters which detail and analyse the nature and significance of various manifestations of religious concern. Underlying the discussion are basic questions about the format of medieval religious experience, ranging from the nature of authority to the relationship between priests and laity, and how far it is actually possible to talk of a monolithic catholicism. The book also responds to recent historiographical debates, about whether there was a divorce between 'élite' and 'popular' religion, whether medieval catholicism was deep rooted or superficial, and the relationship between catholicism and other Christianities and non-Christian faiths.

Cambridge Medieval Textbooks

RELIGION AND DEVOTION IN EUROPE,
c. 1215–*c.* 1515

Cambridge Medieval Textbooks

This is a series of specially commissioned textbooks for teachers and students, designed to complement the monograph series Cambridge Studies in Medieval Life and Thought by providing introductions to a range of topics in medieval history. The series combines both chronological and thematic approaches, and will deal with British and European topics. All volumes in the series will be published in hard covers and in paperback.

For a list of titles in the series, see end of book.

RELIGION AND DEVOTION IN EUROPE,
c. 1215–*c.* 1515

R. N. SWANSON

University of Birmingham

CAMBRIDGE
UNIVERSITY PRESS

Published by the Press Syndicate of the University of Cambridge
The Pitt Building, Trumpington Street, Cambridge CB2 1RP
40 West 20th Street, New York, NY 10011–4211, USA
10 Stamford Road, Oakleigh, Melbourne 3166, Australia

First published 1995
Reprinted 1997

A catalogue record for this book is available from the British Library

Library of Congress cataloguing in publication data
Swanson, R. N. (Robert N.)
Religion and devotion in Europe, *c.* 1215–*c.* 1515 / R. N. Swanson.
p.   cm – (Cambridge medieval textbooks)
Includes bibliographical references and index.
ISBN 0 521 37076 0 (hard). – ISBN 0 521 37950 4 (pbk.)
1. Europe – Church history – 600–1500. 2. Europe – Religious life
and customs. 3. Religion and culture – Europe – History.
4. Europe – Religion. 5. Church history – Middle ages, 600–1500.
I. Title. II. Series.
BR735.S93 1995
274'.05–dc20   94–35211   CIP

ISBN 0 521 37076 0 hardback
ISBN 0 521 37950 4 paperback

Transferred to digital printing 2004

For Heather

CONTENTS

ILLUSTRATIONS

PREFACE

To cover 300 years in the religious history of the whole of catholic Europe in one volume has proved a daunting task. The aim in writing has been precisely to provide a textbook, a general survey of religion and devotion. The obvious terminal events for any analysis of late medieval Christianity are arguably major turning points in the history of the medieval church: the Fourth Lateran Council of 1215 and the Reformation. The first poses no problems. However, to avoid entanglement in the debate about the outbreak of the Reformation, I have deliberately ended the discussion slightly before the problems of the Lutheran challenge became apparent, at the opening of the Fifth Lateran Council in 1512. As well as making the project more manageable, that date provides something like a convenient symmetry to the overall perspective.

The book is intended as an outline survey. Many of the specific instances cited reflect the focus of my other work in being drawn from England; but I hope that I have maintained sufficient balance to provide a fully European perspective. Since many of the texts used in England also had a continental circulation, the seeming English emphasis is in some cases merely illusory. As most readers will probably be best acquainted with England, a bias in that direction may also be excusable. However, I would certainly not claim that English experience was normative for all of catholic Europe, and I trust that that is evident in the chapters. I have tried to assume an ignorance of Christianity among readers; but also sought not to be patronising. As the cultural baggage of Christianity becomes increasingly a thing of the past, it is necessary to start from a relatively basic level if the volume is to be of any real and general utility (readers who already feel sufficiently catechised may therefore be tempted to skip chapter 2). At the same time, religion has to be set against a wider social context. In its totality, that cannot be done here; at least, not in detail. I have obviously alluded to the background where appropriate, and sought to illustrate how it affects the religious developments (or was affected by them) when necessary. The format is intentionally thematic, which inevitably entails some duplication in the description of historical circumstances. Where that occurs, I hope that it does not appear as padding – nor too repetitious.

As the book is primarily intended to serve as an outline, even as an introduction, I have deliberately eschewed extensive footnoting. For someone who actually enjoys writing footnotes, this has frequently been frustrating. However, to give full referencing would have made the text immeasurably longer, and also required acknowledgement of and involvement in debates which are beyond the book's main concerns. The outcome would have been a very different volume: much more daunting to construct and, I suspect, to read. Incomplete and seemingly random and inconsistent noting I personally find infuriating and unsatisfactory; but footnotes cannot be completely excluded. As a policy, therefore, references are provided only for cross-references, for quotations, or when individual historians are directly mentioned or alluded to. I may have slipped occasionally, but that is the policy. Often I rely on citations made by others; where a quotation's original language is not English, I have silently translated for inclusion in the text.

A book such as this cannot be exhaustive. Life is too short to deal with all the material fully, especially as the presses continue to produce books and articles which would make valuable contributions. A halt must be called somewhere, and arbitrarily. A glance around the publishers' bookstalls at the Kalamazoo congress in May 1993 – when I foolishly thought I had almost finished – produced an extensive list of possible additional material which had not yet reached this side of the Atlantic (some because it is still in press), and which would improve the coverage even if not necessarily expanding the argument. I am conscious of the amount of reading which could still be done, of the nuances which could be added; but I hope that such deficiencies are not too obvious in the final work. Needless to say, any remaining imperfections are solely my fault and responsibility.

Research these days progresses in a series of fits and stops. The first draft of the text was completed over three years ago, but then had to be set aside as the changing burdens of university life made other demands. The interval was, as such gaps tend to be, beneficial: the final version is massively altered and massively improved. I am grateful to Bill Davies of the Press for his forbearance with a delivery date which constantly receded into the future: I hope he feels the wait was worthwhile. Almost every library I have visited over the past few years has contributed to the contents. Necessarily, I have relied primarily on the University Library at Birmingham, which has had to put up with a constant flurry of recalls and inter-library loan requests; borrowing rights at Cambridge University Library also proved invaluable. Colleagues, friends, and students, too numerous to mention, have stimulated my thoughts – perhaps unwittingly – and all contributed to the final format. They may recognise specific debts: I am afraid that after all this time, and all the rewriting, my ability to identify them has become rather blurred. Christopher Brooke's comments on what I hoped was the final draft provoked some last-minute emendations (and gave the opportunity for further additions and nuancing). The whole text has benefited greatly from the assiduous criticism of Heather Swanson, who as ever has forced me to rethink and clarify my ideas and expression . . . and cut out excessive references to Margery Kempe. Authors usually acknowledge a spouse for emotional support and carrying an unfair share of domestic responsibilities. My debts certainly fall under that umbrella; but to be married, in addition, to a historian who can judge a book from the joint perspectives of reader and teacher is an incalculable bonus. There are, accordingly, no prizes for guessing the identity of the dedicatee.

I

INTRODUCTION

———— • ————

In 1302, in the midst of his second major conflict with the French King Philip IV, Pope Boniface VIII issued one of the most ringing statements of papal headship over the church. The first substantive statement of the bull *Unam sanctam* was a forthright declaration of the nature and comprehensiveness of the Christian church:

That there is one holy, catholic, and apostolic church we are bound to believe and hold, our faith urging us, and this we do firmly believe and simply confess; and that outside this church there is no salvation or remission of sins.[1]

The unity and unicity of the church were constant concerns throughout the middle ages; but in fact the church was almost equally constantly divided from the mid eleventh century, principally between the Orthodox and Catholic traditions. For western Europeans, and for Boniface VIII, however, there still remained only one real church: that headed by St Peter's successor, at Rome or wherever he happened to be in exile, as was often the case. The church – *the* church – was for them essentially a western institution, Latinate, dependent on Rome. The Christianity to be considered in the following chapters is similarly Latinate, Rome-centred in the sense that it was linked to an administrative and jurisdictional structure which acknowledged its links with the papacy, in a hierarchy of authority stretching from the pope down to the parish priest.

---

[1] B. Tierney, *The crisis of church and state, 1050–1300* (Englewood Cliffs, NJ, 1964), p. 188.

LATIN CHRISTENDOM

Defining the geographical area to be covered in the following chapters presents some problems. The papal church never accepted its restriction to western Europe; and to some extent was not actually so restricted. Just as Christ was *dominus mundi*, Lord of the world, so was his Vicar: to quote *Unam sanctam* again,

> If the Greeks or any others say that they were not committed to Peter and his successors, they necessarily admit that they are not of Christ's flock . . . [I]t is altogether necessary to salvation for every human creature to be subject to the Roman Pontiff.[2]

Those who were not for the pope were necessarily against Christ, and therefore excluded from the church outside which there was no salvation. The following chapters concentrate on developments primarily within western Europe, in territories ruled by catholics; but catholicism as such expanded far beyond the frontiers of those lands.

The more precise definition of the church which existed within western Europe obviously demands some consideration. The period under survey contains centuries during which there was effectively only one western church which, with few exceptions, continually accepted papal authority even if there were times, notably during the Great Schism of 1378–1417, when exactly who ought to be exercising that authority was unclear. The terminal dates are to some extent self-explanatory. In 1215 Pope Innocent III presided over the assembly which can be considered the culmination of his pontificate, the Fourth Lateran Council. The largest of the medieval church councils, it adopted a wide-ranging programme which has been characterised as effecting a pastoral revolution, intended to move the church into the forefront of personal experience and individual existence. At the other end of the period, after three centuries during which the church confronted institutional challenges, internal tensions, and the problems of relating to a world which refused to conform sufficiently precisely to the Christian precepts which the church decreed, there occurred the Fifth Lateran Council. In session from 1512 to 1517, that gathering to some extent marks the height of lost opportunities, for the church and the world both then needed reform of comparable breadth to that provided by Lateran IV; but the required leadership was not forthcoming. Lateran IV started a process of change, initiated a dynamism which was to be spread – with admittedly varying degrees of effectiveness – throughout the western world, and

---

2 Tierney, *Crisis of church and state*, pp. 188–9.

beyond. Lateran V suggests that that dynamism was played out. It is not that the church lacked dynamic individuals and schemes for reform which need not have destroyed the old structure – manifestly there were such individuals, and such schemes – but the ability, possibly the will, to implement them was apparently lacking. Lateran IV reflects papal leadership and inspiration, a determination to overcome obstacles. Lateran V reflects the stultifying effects of institutionalisation, of lack of enterprise at the top which feared to move for concern about the consequences. In the end, failure to move proved the more costly option: extensive reform could not be held back indefinitely, and in this case the failure to offer a lead from the top provided the opportunity for a more damaging Reformation.

That Reformation terminated the era of the unitary western church, and began the era of denominations. Between 1215 and 1515, western unity was never seriously undermined. Although heretical groups did develop, few had sufficient strength and organisation to pose an effective challenge. The Cathars were a significant threat in the twelfth century, and had some success in creating a rival church, or churches, in southern France and parts of Italy. But papal authority had responded vigorously in the thirteenth century, and the Inquisition and the Albigensian Crusade put paid to that rivalry. Later, the only serious structural threat was offered by the Hussites in fifteenth-century Bohemia. Their creation of a nationally organised ecclesiastical structure outside the catholic system, with its own doctrines and practices, was again a significant rival. After decades of warfare, which witnessed the eradication of the more threatening doctrinal stances, the Hussite challenge was neutralised by the *Compactata* of Basle of 1436, which reintegrated the moderate Hussites into the catholic whole in a compromise which gave the traditionalists the upper hand without totally annihilating the Hussite system. Nevertheless, the unwillingness of most Hussites to move totally outside the doctrinal system of the universal church meant that their challenge to catholicism as a system was rather limited.

Shorn of these two episodes, the geographical scope of the western church – and with it, of this book – ranged over most of western Europe throughout the period. Yet it was not a static structure. For Europe itself, there were frontiers to be pushed backwards. In the west, the Spanish Reconquest continued throughout the thirteenth century, and into the fourteenth, pushing the Christian–Islamic frontier in Iberia ever southwards. A lull after the 1340s was ended in 1492 when a brief campaign completed the expulsion of Moorish political authority from the peninsula by the capture of Granada. The Spanish Christian kingdoms had meanwhile retained substantial Islamic and Jewish populations throughout, so that the coherence of 'Christian' Spain was to some extent compromised. Elsewhere in the western Mediterranean, the conquests of the Balearic Islands in the thirteenth century also extended Christian territory, and Alfonso X of Castile even schemed to extend Spanish rule into Africa. (Friars were actually nominated to bishoprics in Morocco, but their life expectancy was rather short if they sought to make reality of their titles.) In the late fifteenth and early sixteenth centuries, more secure north African footholds were established, with the Portuguese on the Atlantic coast and in Ceuta, and the Spaniards acquiring the coastal towns which they still hold.

In the east, changes were more extensive. In 1215, catholic Christians still had a foothold in the Levantine Crusader states – the principality of Antioch, kingdom of Jerusalem, and county of Tripoli. These Palestinian states maintained a pathetic existence throughout the thirteenth century, surviving more by chance than judgement, being slowly whittled down until the conquest of Acre in 1291 drove the Latins from their final toeholds, eliminating their political and colonising presence and, despite continued dreams of crusading revival, rendering them thereafter merely tourists or tolerated residents of Jerusalem and the Holy Places. The final Christian state in the Near East – the kingdom of Cilician Armenia – was of Orthodox inclinations, although the proclamations of unity between its autonomous local church and the papacy brought it essentially within the catholic fold, even if doubts were sometimes expressed, especially in the early fourteenth century, about the completeness of its doctrinal integration. That kingdom, too, was overwhelmed in the Islamic advance, falling to the Turks in the 1370s.   The other main area of concern was south-east Europe and the Balkans, particularly centring on Constantinople. In 1215 the brilliance of Lateran IV was partly due to the fact that this second Rome was held by Latin Christians: with the capture of Constantinople by the Fourth Crusade in 1204, the establishment of the Empire of Romania and its satellite states gave the Latins control of the city and its dependent territory – although without actually converting the majority of the subject populations. Areas of Greece and the Balkans remained within the Latin Christian ambit for some time thereafter: Constantinople itself until its recovery by the Byzantines in 1261, and minor principalities in Achaea and the Greek Islands, which were gradually eroded away in a rather piecemeal fashion by Greek recovery on the one hand and the Turkish advance on the other – the latter in the long term taking over everything. Even by 1515, however, this process of erosion was incomplete: a number of island principalities, such as the Duchy of Naxos, remained under Latin rule; the slowly retreating commercial empires of Genoa and Venice retained most of the

Aegean islands (and Venice had recently taken over Cyprus on the extinction of the Lusignan dynasty); while the Order of St John maintained a more than symbolic presence on Rhodes.

Despite such tenacity, in the eastern Mediterranean Latin Christendom was realistically in retreat – politically at least – for most of the period, with even Italy facing threats (the Turks occupied Otranto in 1480–1). There was also political retreat in central Europe by the early sixteenth century, most dramatically evident in the Turkish conquest of Hungary following the battle of Mohacs in 1526. Just as the Latins had not converted the Greeks when they took Constantinople, however, the Turkish advance could not extirpate Christianity, whether Greek or Roman, in the territories it conquered. Moreover, even while the central and southern Slavic lands were under attack, the papacy secured a major success with the implantation of catholic Christianity on Europe's north-eastern frontier. This chiefly occurred in the later centuries, although the slow eastward advance of the German frontier and the establishment of the Teutonic Knights along the Baltic coast was a continuous process throughout. The major success was the formal adoption of Latin rather than Greek or Russian Christianity by the Grand Prince of Lithuania and his subjects in 1386, thereby bringing vast areas of eastern Europe under the oversight of the Christian missions. As the Polish–Lithuanian state expanded, a catholic ecclesiastical structure was established as far east as Kiev. Missionary activity also occurred under the Teutonic Knights in their territories, in what are now the Baltic states, although they were accused of not being as missionary as they ought to be.

Despite such expansion, the overall identification of Roman Christianity as a western European religion during this period is tenable; but it was not exclusively western European. The world-wide claims of the papacy, and of Christianity, found expression in many ways. Missionary activity continued in the Middle East – St Francis of Assisi had actually sought to convert the Sultan of Cairo – while yet further east there were high hopes of conversion of the Mongols in the late thirteenth and early fourteenth centuries. The last years of the thirteenth century actually saw the nominal establishment of a series of catholic bishoprics along the route to China, terminating at Peking which was elevated to the status of an archbishopric in 1294. However, this ambitious missionary campaign seems to have fizzled out in the fourteenth century. Much closer than China there were continued efforts to expand catholicism among the Tartar realms and in the area around the Black and Caspian Seas, which continued well into the fifteenth century and met with some degree of temporary succes. However, these successes were eroded by

Islamic expansion and continued vitality among local non-catholic Christian traditions. Although successions of resident bishops were maintained in some places into the fifteenth century, the reality of this failed missionary activity is epitomised by the extensive use of episcopal titles for sees now 'in the regions of the infidels' (*in partibus infidelium*) to identify suffragan bishops in western Europe. Eastern titles conferred episcopal status on those workhorses among the suffragans who ensured the continuity of diocesan sacramental activity in dioceses whose nominal bishops were otherwise engaged in secular and ecclesiastical government.

Yet the aspirations crystallised in the creation of an archbishopric of Peking, while ultimately doomed, were not quenched. The last years of the period under review saw the start of a new era of expansion, in new directions, whose repercussions were to be incalculable. To the south began the tentative Roman penetration of sub-Saharan Africa, with the conversion of the king of Kongo (now in northern Angola), who under Portuguese influence ruled as Afonso I from 1506. Much more significant in the long run was the westward expansion. Columbus may have been searching for the terrestrial paradise; he found the New World. The Christianisation of the Americas was to pose its own problems, and present major challenges, which fortunately do not have to be considered here.

DEFINING 'THE CHURCH'

The church was more than a geographical construction, and to have begun with the geographical discussion may have given a misleading impression of it. Its principal justification, and motivation, lay in the religion which it propagated. That religion entailed the creation of a complex jurisdictional and administrative system, comprising a series of courts, a system of taxation (of various kinds, and at all levels of the church), and an extensive bureaucracy. The jurisdictional and administrative pyramid headed by the papacy – wherever the papacy was, for although usually associated with Rome the centre of government was with the popes and the *curia Romana* wherever located – reached right down to the smallest of localities, through archbishoprics and provinces to the individual dioceses and their components of archdeaconries, deaneries, parishes, and chapelries. Alongside that basic system, which had its own regional variations, there was also the structure of the religious orders, many (but not all) exempt from the hierarchical jurisdictional structure of the 'secular' church and directly dependent on the papacy. Monks, canons, and friars could thus create autonomous structures, often overlapping, and not infrequently in conflict with, that of the secular church, but integrated into the complex totality by their subjection to the universalist papacy.

Although it generated this jurisdictional and administrative organis-ation, that was not the defining force of the church – at least, not completely. The middle ages maintained two definitions of the church; as there still are. On the one hand, there was the restricted, institutional definition, which segregated the 'ecclesiastical' from the 'secular', insofar as that was possible. On the other hand, there was a wider definition, which encompassed the whole company of baptised Christians who acknowledged the papacy as their earthly head, and which might be extended to incorporate other Christians who had fallen into heresy or error (although the degree to which this occurred varied very much depending on circumstances). It is the wider definition which is the more significant for present purposes: that body of the faithful which made up the mystical body of the church which was also the body of Christ. The main focus of concern in the following chapters will not be with the institutional relationships, but with the reactions of the widely defined Church to the demands and dictates of Christianity. The institutional side cannot be ignored: it was, after all, the institution which actually decided on the nature of the demands and dictates of Christianity, for the most part; the attempts to enforce the disciplinary aspects of the resulting relationship will obviously demand comment. Where there was formal rejection of that disciplinary and doctrinal oversight – through defection to heresy, most blatantly – then the heretics fall outside the scope of discussion. The attention is deliberately focused primarily on the orthodox: heterodoxy may reflect differing responses to similar imperatives, but still produces a different relationship between institution and individuals, which cannot be examined here in detail.[3] Problems of heresy cannot be totally excluded from consideration, however, and the unorthodox obviously played a part in the development of numerous religious practices; but they are not intended to be a prominent feature of the following chapters.[4]

Equally importantly, the disciplinary relationships under review are those which explicitly affected spiritual life. The ecclesiastical institutional and jurisdictional structure brought within its purview a whole range of contacts between 'ecclesiastical' and 'secular' life, which involved conflict over economic activities like tithes, fees, and other demands; sought to influence extensive areas of domestic life through jurisdictional claims

---

[3] The most recent general survey is M. Lambert, *Medieval heresy: popular movements from the Gregorian Reform to the Reformation* (Oxford, 1992).

[4] See also below, pp. 272–5, and index.

over matrimony, implementation of wills, and suchlike; and integrated clerics into the wider structure of benefice holding which brought in issues of lay patronage and support. While all of these spheres are important for a proper understanding of the complex relationship between the church and lay society in the middle ages, the church as spiritual director of the laity provides more than enough material for present purposes. The concern here is more to consider the church's attempts to satisfy and direct the religious and devotional desires of the laity, to meet their scruples, and to answer their questions. To some extent, also, it is a matter of examining the clergy's ability to maintain control of the church as a spiritual force.

This demands more comment, for a major strand in recent consideration of medieval Christianity – perhaps of all Christianity – has highlighted the linguistic conveniences which historians adopt in dealing with 'the church' and 'religion'. Given the existence of the institution hierarchically organised up to the papacy, and the concomitant administrative structure, it is extremely easy to fall into the trap of seeing medieval Latin Christianity as a monolith, spiritually regimented and strongly controlled, with all of western Christendom subscribing to an identical set of beliefs and engaging in identical religious activities. But that perception is largely invalid. In an important contribution, Gavin Langmuir has recently proposed a distinction between 'religion', the system of beliefs prescribed by the ecclesiastical authorities, and 'religiosity', the format in which individuals construct a spiritually satisfying enactment of that religion.[5] This pinpoints one of the key tensions which will become apparent as this survey progresses: that while there was something which can be labelled 'western Christianity', the more closely it is examined the less solid it becomes. Because Christendom contained millions of individual Christians, whose responses to the defined religion would vary with space and time, then Christianity as such becomes increasingly atomised, right down to the level of the individual engaging in practices which were found individually satisfying. That need not entail an individualistic approach to spirituality – especially if, as will be argued, a major imperative in medieval Christianity was a doctrine of charity, which generated manifestations of spirituality which were social and socially oriented. But it does mean that 'western Christianity' must be seen very much as an umbrella term, a generalisation encompassing an almost infinite variety of regional, parochial, familial, and individual Christianities which were subject to constant change and development in

---

[5] G. I. Langmuir, *History, religion, and antisemitism* (Berkeley, Los Angeles, and Oxford, 1990), especially chapters 7, 9, 10.

response to a wide range of forces. Yet this collection of interlocking and overlapping segments, did somehow make up a whole. Christendom might then be portrayed as a series of 'discourse communities' (in the terminology of rhetorical theorists), sharing perceptions, aspirations, and vocabulary, and operating independently at a variety of levels; but all cohering in the umbrella discourse community of 'orthodoxy'.[6]

Such a situation would obviously generate reciprocal relationships between 'institution' and 'individuals', just as there is implicit tension between 'religion' and 'religiosity'. Moreover, how far the authorities could prescribe – or, by extension, proscribe – in their defining of religion, was affected and limited precisely by that tension.

In the early thirteenth century, there is much to be said for the argument that the authorities had to initiate a programme of instruction to provide the basics of Christianity. Yet that same period, which witnessed the spread of the mendicants and the burgeoning of lay pietistic movements such as the Beguines and the mendicant Tertiary associations, also revealed one of the major problems which constantly confronted the church: it rarely had the power effectively to limit the ways in which popular spirituality actually developed. Its role was normally responsive, reacting to developments among the populace. Sometimes control and redirection were possible; but often the church's spirituality was generated at a 'grass roots' level, in cults, in devotions, in demand for indulgences and privileges. The institution could rarely initiate a totally new direction in spirituality; it might try to redirect movements after their inception, encourage them if it saw fit, or even crush them entirely; but often it had no option but tolerance, and protest against over-enthusiasm and misdirection. Ultimately, the devotional practices of the medieval church were demand-led, by the spirituality and desires of the laity. That, of course, provoked a good deal of uncertainty within the institution, and weakened its ability to present a unified, monolithic orthodoxy. Investigation of the resulting intricate relationships, of the complexities above all of what people did and felt, needs no justification.

---

[6] See B. A. Rafoth, 'The concept of discourse community: descriptive and explanatory adequacy', in *A sense of audience in written communication*, ed. G. Kirsch and D. H. Roen, Written communication annual, 5 (Newbury Park, London, and New Delhi, 1990), pp. 140–53; B. A. Rafoth, 'A discourse community: where readers, writers, and texts come together', in *The social construction of written communication*, ed. B. A. Rafoth and D. L. Rubin (Norwood, NJ, 1988), pp. 131–46.

2

THE FAITH AND
ITS DEMANDS

·

Although it is no longer the habit to refer to the pre-Reformation centuries as the 'Age of Faith', nevertheless religion and devotion presupposed a foundation of faith, defined and made accessible. That definition has to be the first area of analysis; its format and formulation must be understood if the practices which it generated are to make any sense and be properly appreciated.

BACKGROUND TO A DEFINITION: THE RELIGIOUS FERMENT OF THE TWELFTH AND THIRTEENTH CENTURIES

When it met in Rome in the summer of 1215, the Fourth Lateran Council marked the apogee of the papacy of Innocent III, himself one of the most dynamic and influential of medieval pontiffs. The fourth general council summoned in the west by the popes, and continuing the tradition of the Lateran assemblies of 1123, 1137, and 1179, it was the most impressive and important thus far. Following the Latin Conquest of Constantinople of 1204 it could be claimed that it – unlike previous western councils – was truly representative of the universal church, with over 1,200 ecclesiastics in attendance.

The Council assembled at a critical point in the development of the Latin church. Since the period of 'Gregorian Reform' of the late eleventh century, western religious life had been in a state of almost unrelieved turmoil. New religious movements – notably the proliferation of regular orders like the Cistercians, Carthusians, and Augustinians – had shattered the former Benedictine monopoly of institutionalised religious life. Even though many of the new orders were based on interpretations of the Benedictine Rule, they consciously offered different responses to the demands of their members. But the Benedictine Rule's monopoly of regulation had been formally broken with the evolution of the Rule of St Augustine, and the consequent development of the Augustinian canons and associated orders such as the Premonstratensians and (in England alone) the Gilbertines. The evolution of Military Orders like the Templars and Hospitallers to assist the crusading effort in the east, offered a novel religious version of knighthood. This expanded with the creation of additional Iberian orders to assist the Spanish Reconquest, and with the establishment of the Teutonic Knights and other groups in the Slav lands of central and north-east Europe. Women's religious aspirations had also been addressed, to varying effect, by a proliferation of nunneries. These were sometimes parts of double houses containing both monks and nuns, as in the Order of Fontevrault; they often sought to follow the rule of one of the reformed orders, particularly the Cistercians.

But the twelfth century's transformation of religious life – what has been labelled 'the Medieval Reformation'[1] – was not just a matter of seeking new forms of monasticism. The apostolic life, the *vita apostolica*, was also redefined, to remove the necessity for the formal profession associated with a regular life. A new definition of the search for Christ reduced the significance of retreat from the world, and emphasised existence within it. Following Christ came to mean two things: preaching, and the adoption of poverty. The pastoral and edificatory roles had to be constructed within the world – preachers did, after all, need an audience – and might not be exclusively restricted to those whom the church authorities considered 'clerics'. The laity increasingly sought to share in the reform movements, more and more undertaking and participating in religious lives which had a Christian inspiration. The best documented movements of this kind were the early Waldensians, who originated at Lyons in the 1170s, and the north Italian movement of the Humiliati. Both adopted a life of poverty – of relative poverty, that is, which allowed them to exist on a sufficiency earned by their own labours, rather than the total renunciation which was associated with 'apostolic poverty' in the thirteenth century. Both also sought to preach and expound the gospel, demands which, among other things, necessitated access to a translated Bible.

The laity here approached the limits of the tolerable. There was, technically, no ecclesiastical obstacle to either ambition of poverty or preaching, but the latter would need to be constrained within the

---

[1] B. M. Bolton, *The medieval Reformation* (London, 1987).

disciplinary framework of the church. In particular, the content of preaching had to be restrained, to prevent the laity embarking on discussion of doctrinal matters, with its attendant risks of misinterpretation and misinstruction: the untrained should not aim to train the untrained, although they might inform them of Christ's impact on their lives. The rejection of the controls on preaching, particularly by the Waldensians, led to their condemnation by the papacy, and their being considered heretics after 1179.

Waldensianism was markedly different in nature from other contemporary heresies, its original condemnation by the catholic hierarchy having little to do with doctrine and much to do with discipline. However, once condemned it gained a doctrinal identity, which evolved and changed, and as it spread across Germany and central Europe acquired regional characteristics. As an essentially underground movement, although one with its own clergy and some degree of organisation, Waldensianism survived the middle ages to merge into the reformist movement of the sixteenth century.

In its twelfth-century origins, Waldensianism offered one manifestation of the tensions which produced the first serious western confrontation for centuries between mass heresy and the ecclesiastical establishment, and certainly the first major encounter of the later middle ages. The Gregorian Reform movement of the late eleventh and early twelfth centuries had stimulated an upsurge of questioning on the status and activities of the church and its ministers. This questioning had, to a large extent, been promoted by the reformers themselves, as they inveighed against simony (the buying – not necessarily for money – of spiritual powers and privileges) and clerical marriage, and came close to a formal denial of the sacraments performed by priests whom they considered unworthy. Advocacy of that stance would itself have been heretical, smacking of the arguments of the Donatists against whom St Augustine had argued in the sixth century; but the leading Gregorian Reformers stopped short, just, of such formal heresy. Their followers had greater problems with the dividing line between heresy and orthodoxy, and in the twelfth century the hyper-Gregorianism of some led to formal condemnation. Among these the most obvious were Henry of Lausanne, against whom St Bernard was active in the 1150s, and Peter of Bruys.

But that was not the limit to heresy. Other movements also challenged the church. The twelfth-century's intellectual activity, with its intense vivisection of the faith in the search for a definition of the relationship between God and the world, instigated a continuous conflict between reason and faith. The intellectual urge to understand the incomprehensible – God – forced thinkers to the frontiers of the faith, and sometimes over them. The first flickers of such conflict appeared in the late eleventh century, in the dispute between Berengar of Tours and Archbishop Lanfranc of Canterbury over precisely what happened at the moment of consecration in the mass: what was meant by the words of consecration; what effect did they have on the bread and wine being consecrated? For Berengar, they consecrated, but could not alter: bread and wine stayed bread and wine, even if Christ was somehow infused into them. For Lanfranc, consecration fundamentally changed the nature of the bread and wine: they might retain all the accidents (shape, colour, texture, taste, and so on), but their substance, their essential 'breadness' and 'wineness', had been replaced by the physical body and blood of Christ. At consecration, bread and wine were thus altered to make Christ physically present. This was the revival of a long-standing debate, which remained unresolved in the twelfth century; but the decisions taken on it by the Lateran Council in 1215, seen as a dogmatic assertion of this 'transubstantiation', had an impact throughout the later centuries.

The debate over eucharistic consecration was but one feature of the guerrilla warfare between reason and faith which occupied much of the twelfth century. The struggle was further stimulated as ancient philosophy (especially Aristotelianism, and particularly as mediated by Arabic thinkers) took new roots in the nascent schools and universities, and the linguistic logic which was a critical element in intellectual development was applied (some would have said misapplied) to the science of the knowledge of God, theology. Contemporaries appreciated the problems associated with using a humanly constructed language to tackle a non-human problem like the divinity; but human language was the only mode of expression available. The resulting tensions were epitomised in the crisis which erupted over the teaching of Peter Abelard at Paris in the 1140s. Abelard, one of the most brilliant minds of his day, sought to tackle theology simply through linguistic analysis. But the application of such tools to the doctrine of the Trinity – that consubstantial, co-eternal, Three-in-one-and-one-in-three of Father, Son, and Holy Ghost – dismayed his contemporaries, especially St Bernard. Abelard was condemned: too rigorous an application of linguistic logic, particularly by a non-theologising mind, would either make the three into one, so denying the Trinity as Three-in-one, or fragment the one into three distinct entities and deny the One-in-three.

If theology was difficult for intellectuals, its orthodox comprehension posed greater problems for those not embroiled in academic debates. Lay rationalisation could itself produce a theology for a religion consonant with experience, regardless of what the church might direct. In the twelfth century the main strand in this direction erupted as Catharism in

southern France. It is perhaps best seen as a rationalisation of the problem
of evil in a world created by a God who was by definition incapable of
evil: to replace the unitary religion of Christianity, the Cathars developed
a dualist creed, based on the eternal battle between good and evil, with
God (as good) as one basic principle in opposition to the world (which
was bad, and diabolical). The resulting theology, transmuted by contacts
with eastern heretics, especially dualists from the Balkans, produced a
purely spiritual Christ, denied the need for a church (or, at least, for the
papal church, as the Cathars developed their own organisation with a
ministerial hierarchy), and solved many of the intellectual and moral
tensions implicit in the demands of Christianity. By 1200, Catharism was
well entrenched in southern France and northern Italy, although
doctrinal divisions quickly shattered any unity in the movement,
especially in Italy. Catharism was one possible solution to the problem of
twelfth-century reform: like the orthodox apostolic life, it advocated a life
of poverty and simplicity, rejecting an institutionalised church which
appeared incapable of living according to its own precepts. Catharism was
a real threat, one which Catholicism confronted forcefully, if at first rather
tentatively. Programmes of conversion through preaching were
attempted; but in 1208 Pope Innocent III, reacting to the murder of Peter
of Castelnau, his legate in Languedoc, instituted the first anti-heretical
crusade, which developed into the Albigensian Crusade and eventually
resulted in the conquest of southern France by troops from the north.
That, and the Inquisition, operating in both France and Italy, were major
forces which contributed to the suppression of the Cathar threat; although
contemporary changes in catholicism – the preaching missions of the
Dominicans and Franciscans, and the new place found for lay spirituality
in the thirteenth-century church – were important for reducing the
heresy's appeal. Despite the multi-faceted challenge, the last traces of
Catharism were not eliminated until the early fourteenth century.

It was against this background of fervour and ferment that the Lateran
Council met in 1215. Innocent III had already shown his hand against
some of the challenges. He had authorised the assault on the Cathars. He
had accepted the validity of the new definition of the *vita apostolica*,
provided that its followers accepted papal authorisation, by reintegrating
into the church some of the groups which had earlier been driven out.
Some Waldensians were reconciled, but the success was only partial:
Waldensianism survived as a heresy throughout the middle ages, to the
Reformation and beyond. Greater success was achieved with the
Humiliati, who were fully reintegrated as a religious order in their own
right. Given a variation of the Augustinian Rule, they were established
as a threefold order of clerics, sisters, and married laity who had not

withdrawn from the world. In some ways, the reconciliation of the Humiliati provided a blueprint for the treatment of the most dramatic expression of lay spirituality in the thirteenth century, the foundation of the mendicant orders – so called because they were originally meant to live by begging – and their offshoot Third Orders. In this movement the Franciscans, or Friars Minor, were undoubtedly the most dynamic force. Although rapidly clericalised, the Franciscan Order was a truer reflection of the lay movement than the Dominicans, whose ethos and role was always clerical and 'church-centred'. Bible-based, and founded on personal conviction, the apostolate of Francis of Assisi was legitimated only through the personal intervention of Innocent III and his successors. Papal approval of Francis' search for a new way of life *c.* 1210 thus showed that the pope at least was willing to embrace and aid the spiritual developments born of the twelfth century, and to encourage the creation of a church which, adapting to meet new demands, would be able to take the lead in the process of Christianising lay society.

For that process, the decrees of the Fourth Lateran Council were to have a pivotal role, maintained throughout the centuries. But what was the Christianity which was to be imposed?

DEFINITIONS: CREEDS, CHURCH, AND CHRISTIANITY

Fundamentally, Christianity claimed to offer Truth. Founded in Christ, the church which proclaimed His message declared itself to be 'one, holy, catholic, and apostolic' – a claim incessantly repeated no matter how fragmented the ecclesiastical body actually was. As such, the church was conceived as unitary and unsullied in its faith, brought together by participation in the revelation of Christ which it had a duty to transmit to the rest of the world. Moreover, although itself in time, the church was timeless: it was not just a collection of people in the world, it was all Christians throughout time, for whom time was merely accidental. The church would always exist, somehow.

While the church could articulate its ideals, their full implementation proved virtually impossible. Unity was difficult to maintain, and fragmentation was common. Doctrinal and other differences produced divisions, for the western church the most significant occuring in 1054, to divide the Greek and Latin churches for the foreseeable future. That rupture was not meekly accepted; there were several attempts over the centuries to secure its resolution. Some involved force, like the western conquest of Constantinople in 1204; others negotiation, as at the Councils of Lyons (1274) and Florence (1439). Reunion was formally proclaimed at both, only for the wound to reopen within a few years.

Generally speaking, western, Latin, catholicism developed along its own
course after 1054, and it is that course which has to be followed here.

Despite differences and divisions in the universality, there was also
some remembrance of unity. This was manifested in the Creeds, the
shared declarations of the faith. Two of these were particularly important:
the Apostles' Creed, and the Nicene Creed. Of these, the former was the
simpler, and was known, or meant to be known, by all layfolk throughout the period. According to tradition, it had been drawn up by the
apostles themselves (with the Virgin Mary in the background), each
contributing one phrase. It summarised the beliefs of the church in a
highly succinct form:

I believe in God the Father almighty, maker of heaven of earth; and in Jesus Christ
his only Son, Our Lord, who was conceived by the Holy Ghost, born of the
Virgin Mary, suffered under Pontius Pilate, was crucified, dead, and buried; he
descended into Hell. The third day he rose again from the dead; he ascended into
Heaven; and sits on the right hand of God the Father almighty; from thence he
shall come to judge the living and the dead.

I believe in the Holy Ghost, the holy catholic church, the communion of saints,
the forgiveness of sins, the resurrection of the body, and the life everlasting.

This basic list of the tenets of required belief was the keystone of most
people's awareness of the faith throughout the centuries. It had an
unrivalled place in the formulation of belief, providing the outline which
would be tested at confessions, and when the time came to prepare for
death.

More 'intellectual' in content, and less popularly diffused, was the
Nicene Creed, the statement of faith produced in 323 at the Council of
Nicaea. This was integrated into the format of the mass, recitation being
mainly restricted to priestly performance as the 'mass creed'. Concocted
in response to doctrinal conflict, it gave greater precision on aspects of
the complex relationship between the Persons of the Trinity and the
Incarnation, but still retained a fairly summary form:

I believe in one God, the Father almighty, maker of heaven and earth, and of all
things visible and invisible; and in one Lord, Jesus Christ, the only-begotten Son
of God, begotten of his Father before all worlds: God of God, Light of Light, Very
God of Very God, begotten, not made, being of one substance with the Father,
by whom all things were made. Who for us men, and for our salvation, came
down from heaven; and was incarnate by the Holy Ghost of the Virgin Mary; and
was made man. And was crucified also for us under Pontius Pilate; he suffered; and
was buried. And the third day he rose again, according to the Scriptures;
and ascended into heaven; and sits on the right hand of the Father. And he shall
come again with glory to judge both the living and the dead; whose kingdom shall
have no end.

And I believe in the Holy Ghost, the Lord and giver of life; who proceeds from the Father and the Son [although this procession from the Son – the *filioque* clause – was not accepted by the Greek church, so that here the two churches differed in their credal statements]; who with the Father and the Son together is worshipped and glorified; who spoke through the prophets.

And I believe one catholic and apostolic church; I acknowledge one baptism for the remission of sins; and I look for the resurrection of the dead and the life of the world to come.

The third major statement of the faith considered definitive by the western church was the so-called Creed of St Athanasius, also known from its opening words as *Quicunque vult*. This in fact had nothing to do with the saint on whom it was fathered, having originated probably in the late fifth or early sixth century, in all likelihood in what is now southern France. Nor, technically, was it a creed, never being formally adopted as an ecclesial statement of faith – Thomas Aquinas declared that it had not been compiled as a Creed, but as an exposition of doctrine. Nevertheless, it was accepted by the western church, incorporated into Psalters and service books, and regularly recited during the divine office, generally on Sundays at Prime. Being mainly a doctrinal exposition, concerned to elucidate the problems of the Trinity and the relationship of its Persons, and the combination of Natures in Christ, it was primarily aimed at the clergy, receiving considerable comment in the twelfth century. Only then does it appear to have been accorded credal stature; its general standing alongside the Nicene and Apostles' creeds in the trinity of summaries of the universal faith was secured only in the next century. Once established, however, it was not lost.

While the Creeds provide the basis for comprehending late medieval Christianity, they cannot summarise its totality. Faith, and perceptions of faith, changed considerably over the centuries – there were great differences between the faith promulgated in a somewhat pioneering spirit in the twelfth and thirteenth centuries, and the Christianised ethos of fifteenth-century Europe. The sophistication of lay perceptions was altered, the demands made of the faith changed. Christianity was not a simple religion, to be summarised exclusively in a few bold sentences. Instead, because of the problems which it confronted, it would be totally wrong to envisage it as a monolith, as disciplined and secure as preconceptions based on post-Tridentine Roman Catholicism or on post-Reformation Protestant polemic might suggest it should be. Precisely because Christianity was much more than just the Creeds, which served as foundations on which understanding was to be built, there was considerable scope for uncertainty, for analysis, for varying interpretations. Rather than being unified and monolithic, concrete and static, medieval Christianity was incessantly fluid and evolving, often uncertain, unwilling to be certain, and plagued with doctrinal pluralism approaching individualism. Indeed, it could be argued that there was no such thing as *the* Christian faith − even if Christendom is confined to the area of the Latin rites − but a multitude of definitions of faith which for convenience can be lumped together as Christianity, but which either voluntarily or by imposition shared a good deal of identity. Acceptance of the kernel, the basic statements of the Creeds, was generally what was tested; individual reconciliation of those statements with an understanding of what surrounded the kernel was rarely investigated by the authorities, except among academics.

That opportunity for individual interpretation and reconciliation clearly offered scope for the creation of 'religiosities'; but some basic formulations of the faith did exist, and were essentially unchanging. They were primarily theological, not explicitly concerned with a Christian's earthly existence. But Christianity had to exist within the world; as a religion which acknowledged the existence of sin it needed a morality which would tie together the earthly and the other-worldly, directing Christians to the life ahead. The definition of that morality operated in two distinct ways. Firstly, because Christianity was a continuation and development of Judaism, Christians were bound by the Mosaic Law. The Ten Commandments therefore defined much of what was acceptable in the Christian way of life, suitably adapted for the specific circumstances altered by the Incarnation − like the movement of the Sabbath to Sunday; or the retention of images provided that they did not actually receive true worship. The Commandments defined the relationship with God, and with other humans. Beyond that, however, there were the greater injunctions derived from the New Testament, and Christ's two Great Commandments which summarised the Old Law whilst defining the New:

You shall love the Lord your God with all your heart, and with all your soul, and with all your mind, and with all your strength. This the first commandment. And the second is like it . . . You shall love your neighbour like yourself. There is no other commandment greater than these.[2]

The second of these injunctions generated a basic moral doctrine, the idea of *caritas*, charity in a widest sense, to regulate life within the world. This notion gave an assurance of fraternity or co-operation, which in theory prevented exploitation and imposed mutuality on relationships to prevent excess. On the basis of this Christian definition of the charitable society,

---

[2] Matthew, 22: 34–40.

human life was to be regulated to secure everyone's place within this world, and assist in securing a place in the next.

The emphasis on *caritas* is crucial, for while Christianity focused on Christ, it could be argued that it centred on Mankind. It was, essentially, an attempt to provide the means whereby a defective creature could achieve perfection. Man was defiled by the Fall, and by the Original Sin incurred when Adam succumbed to temptation. Eve may have been responsible for the Fall by allowing herself to be beguiled by the serpent, and beguiling Adam in her turn; but according to some, Adam's sin was greater than Eve's, for he had refused to accept responsibility for his actions in tasting the forbidden fruit, and sought to transfer the blame to Eve. Whoever was to blame, Mankind had fallen, had lost Eden. Christianity held out the prospect of its recovery, but not in this world. To that end, the penalties of original sin, latently expunged by Christ's Incarnation and Crucifixion, were actually expunged by baptism. Thereafter, it was for individuals, following the precepts of Christ and the church, to live out the pilgrimage of this earthly life, hoping to merit eternal presence with God after the final judgement. Human existence was thus only part of a lengthier life of the soul, which continued after bodily death, and might lead to eternal felicity in participation in the timelessness of God. But that felicity had to be earned, or at least merited. Life, then, was but a pilgrimage in search of salvation, with an unworldly goal. Thanks to the Incarnation, Redemption had become possible; but only the final judgement would clarify whether it had been granted.

This long-term perspective affected the definition of 'the church'. It was not merely the Christians alive on earth at any given moment; it was all Christians who had ever lived. According to legends, it included a few others as well, like the righteous judge whose body had been miraculously preserved uncorrupt from centuries before the birth of Christ, and revived to be baptised by St Erkenwald. They constituted a unified body which anticipated the eventual final judgement. The long-term existence of this church made it convenient to define it as three separate entities: the Church Militant, which consisted of living Christians; the Church Dormant, containing those who had died but awaited judgement; and finally the Church Triumphant, comprising an unknown and essentially unknowable number – the saints – who were already experiencing God face-to-face. The long-term ambition was to join the Church Triumphant; the difficulty lay in getting there. Life had to be endured, and even after its end there were problems: sin and Hell stood in the way. Life on earth might be controlled, with difficulty; but death had to be faced, and what happened after death. This last was the most problematic, because no one really knew what it entailed. Visions, revelations, and ghostly visits might provide some indication; but the period between death and the finality of the Last Judgement was an area of considerable doctrinal uncertainty throughout the period.

The idea of a triune church – militant, dormant, triumphant – and of the progression or pilgrimage through to eternal union with God after the Last Judgement, created alongside the basic statements of the faith a cluster of additional concerns and means to fulfil that desire. The morality of the Christian life provided the model for meriting salvation; but humanity meant that many would need more than mere prescriptions. Assistance would be needed from Christ himself, and from other sources. The ambiguities of doctrine also confused matters: just how much control did individuals have over the destiny of their souls, in a Creation which incorporated time, but was created by a timeless entity aware of all creation throughout all time? For centuries, the church had debated issues of free will and predestination. If the former operated then humans might seek and, perhaps, by acts of will merit, eternal life. But if the future was already mapped out in the divine wisdom, then all was already predestined – perhaps especially worrying, individuals might be predestined to Hell as well as heaven. Or, if predestination applied only to those foreknown as achieving heaven, could those not initially predestined thereto nevertheless gain sufficient merit by earthly works to aspire to salvation? Officially the church accepted both free will and predestination, without providing an effective reconciliation between the poles. However, the implications of predestination were serious: if the elect were elect regardless of their actions, and the damned likewise, then what was the function of the church? If such double predestination applied, and only God knew who fell into which category, were the church and Christianity nothing more than a sham, in which God was merely using humanity as playthings? The ultimate nihilism generated by such speculations, based on the impossibility of any sense of security except by personal revelation, never considered the most trustworthy source of knowledge in matters theological, forced the church to step back from total dogmatic acceptance of predestinarian beliefs. But to deny either extreme was to go too far; the resulting fudged compromise to some extent pushed the issue under the carpet, except when it was forcibly raised by such as the fourteenth-century Oxford academic, John Wyclif. It could not, however, be completely ignored. The opposition between free will and predestination, the problem of the degree of control which individuals had over their earthly and *post mortem* lives, continued as an undercurrent which occasionally rose to the surface.

BEYOND THE CREEDS: EXPANDING DEFINITIONS IN THE THIRTEENTH CENTURY

The vagueness of definitions of the faith beyond the Creeds was a vital element in the development of medieval Christianity. There were, however, many attempts to offer more precise summaries the faith. The Fourth Lateran Council itself sought to do so, its legislation being prefaced with a resounding statement of its perception of the content of the faith. This provides an appropriate starting point for discussion of the faith as experienced and defined in the centuries between 1215 and 1515:

We firmly believe and simply confess that there is only one true God, eternal and immeasurable, almighty, unchangeable, incomprehensible and ineffable, Father, Son and holy Spirit, three persons but one absolutely simple essence, substance or nature. The Father is from none, the Son from the Father alone, and the holy Spirit from both equally, eternally without beginning or end; the Father generating, the Son being born, and the holy Spirit proceeding; consubstantial and coequal, co-omnipotent and coeternal; one principle of all things, creator of all things invisible and visible, spiritual and corporeal; who by his almighty power at the beginning of time created from nothing both spiritual and corporeal creatures, that is to say angelic and earthly, and then created human beings composed as it were of both spirit and body in common. The devil and other demons were created by God naturally good, but they became evil by their own doing. Man, however, sinned at the prompting of the devil.

This holy Trinity, which is undivided according to its common essence but distinct according to the properties of its persons, gave the teaching of salvation to the human race through Moses and the holy prophets and his other servants, according to the most appropriate disposition of the times. Finally the only-begotten Son of God, Jesus Christ, who became incarnate by the action of the whole Trinity in common and was conceived from the ever virgin Mary through the cooperation of the holy Spirit, having become true man, composed of a rational soul and human flesh, one person in two natures [i.e., both divine and human], showed more clearly the way of life. Although he is immortal and unable to suffer according to his divinity, he was made capable of suffering and dying according to his humanity. Indeed, having suffered and died on the wood of the cross for the salvation of the human race, he descended to the underworld, rose from the dead and ascended into heaven. He descended in the soul, rose in the flesh, and ascended in both. He will come at the end of time to judge the living and the dead, to render to every person according to his works, both to the reprobate and to the elect. All of them will rise with their own bodies, which they now wear, so as to receive according to their deserts, whether these be good or bad; for the latter perpetual punishment with the devil, for the former eternal glory with Christ.

There is indeed one universal church of the faithful, outside of which nobody at all is saved, in which Jesus Christ is both priest and sacrifice. His body and blood are truly contained in the sacrament of the altar under the forms of bread and wine, the bread and wine having been changed in substance, by God's power, into his body and blood, so that in order to achieve this mystery of unity we receive from God what he received from us. Nobody can effect this sacrament except a priest who has been properly ordained according to the church's keys, which Jesus Christ himself gave to the apostles and their successors. But the sacrament of baptism is consecrated in water at the invocation of the undivided Trinity – namely Father, Son and holy Spirit – and brings salvation to both children and adults when it is correctly carried out by anyone in the form laid down by the church. If someone falls into sin after having received baptism, he or she can always be restored through true penitence. For not only virgins and the continent but also married persons find favour with God by right faith and good actions and deserve to attain to eternal blessedness.[3]

Most of this declaration was reasonably traditional. The requirement for, and profession of, such statements was not novel at the time: during the previous century, similar summaries had been demanded from, imposed on, or volunteered by several people accused of heresy or deviation. Peter Abelard issued a personal *credo* at the time of attacks on him at the Council of Sens in 1140; while before breaking with the church Valdes, the 'founder' of the Waldensians, had proffered a declaration of faith. Indeed, much of the Lateran decree can be paralleled in the statement issued by Durand of Huesca and his colleagues when reconciled from Waldensianism in 1208.[4] Nor were such statements unknown after 1215: almost every later Council issued a similar document, frequently in response to challenges which confronted the faith in contemporary Europe.

The declaration of Lateran IV thus responded to challenge and crisis, seeking to define and declare the orthodox position. Its emphasis on the identification of the Trinity, with its statement on the Procession of the Spirit, both replied to the logical challenges of twelfth-century academics and affirmed Latin doctrine against that of the Greeks. Statements about the relationship between the spiritual and the carnal in man, and on Christ's double nature, answered Cathar challenges; as did the insistence that the devil was a creature. The insistence on a dual spiritual and corporeal creation may also have been a response to heresies.

Following discussion of the Trinity and Christ, however, the decree reflects more than mere development, and becomes more overtly innovatory. Its insistence on a unitary church was unexceptional; but

---

[3] N. P. Tanner, ed., *Decrees of the ecumenical councils* (2 vols., London, 1990), I, pp. 250–1.

[4] Compare W. L. Wakefield and A. P. Evans, *Heresies of the high middle ages* (New York, 1968), pp. 222–5.

the affirmation that the bread and wine were 'changed in substance' at consecration, had been 'transubstantiated', was. In settling the Berengarian question by a formal declaration in a general council, the only body capable of declaring articles of faith, the Lateran assembly hoped to end conflict. In fact, the question of how the decree should be interpreted caused problems for centuries: it satisfied neither academic intellectual analysis nor common-sense experience. Although it asserted that the elements were transubstantiated, the nature of that process remained without definition. Until the sixteenth century, theologians differed over whether the process was one of instantaneous replacement of one set of substances by another, or whether the substances were actually transformed. The only certainty was that both sets of substances did not co-exist. Where theologians could not agree, it is small wonder that the laity were generally not expected to have a technical understanding. For them it was enough to accept the presence of 'the body of Christ in form of bread'. Despite the uncertainty over the mechanics, the assertion of a mystery of transubstantiation, which could be effected only by a duly ordained priest, was crucial for the elevation of the priesthood which was a feature of the late medieval church.

The only other sacrament treated in the declaration of faith issued at Lateran IV, baptism, was also a response to Cathar and Waldensian challenges, asserting that sacrament's status as a rite of incorporation against their alternatives, and declaring that it remained effective given repentance after sin. This also fits into the context of contemporary changes in appreciations of the nature of penance. The final assertion that even the married might merit eternal life, while perhaps seeming peculiar, again responded to challenges to sexuality from the heretics, and had its own importance for the later development of religious and devotional life. It opened the way to salvation explicitly to those not tied by a regular life, or any formal commitment to withdrawal from the world. It can be no coincidence that the pontificate of Innocent III had in 1199 seen the first canonisation of a lay married man, Homobonus, who had not been linked to a religious order. The possibility of developing a lay spirituality, one which, by exploiting other sections of the Lateran decrees, could be a spirituality of works as well as faith, was now greatly enhanced.

While Creeds and confessions like that of 1215 were intended mainly for use within Christendom, Christianity had to appeal beyond its frontiers as well. Doctrinal clarification would not necessarily explain Christianity; it did give extra particulars about how the religion should be approached. Throughout the ages a key element in Christianity has been an emphasis on conversion, ultimately aiming at worldwide reception of its truth. Truth here must be the operative concept, for without the insistence on an acceptance of its truth as a precondition for discussion, Christianity remained highly vulnerable. Its origins and theology generated the assertion that it definitively superseded Judaism; its message to the Gentiles gave it claims to worldwide validity. Yet, Christianity, as the final revelation of divinity, could not in turn be replaced, either by heresies (although to use the label of 'heresy' is to use the language of the ultimate victors in particular doctrinal struggles) or by subsequent revelations such as Islam which sought to incorporate but demote the status of Christ.

The resulting assertive language used for propagandising the faith and for self-assurance reveals what those who considered themselves the leaders of western Christendom perceived their truth to be. This particularly applies to statements made for purposes of conversion. Although the frontiers of Christianity advanced considerably in Spain and north-east Europe during the period under consideration, the main deliberately missionary effort was aimed, odd as it may seem, at the Mongols. Numerous missions were sent to them, not without some flimsy successes. The envoys to the khans regularly carried summaries of what were considered the essentials of the faith; these were strikingly different in style from the bold affirmations of the Creeds and conciliar statements. The effort to convert the Mongols began with the papally sponsored journey of the friars Lawrence of Portugal and John of Piano Carpini to the Great Khan in 1245–7. In a letter commending his emissaries, Pope Innocent IV included a statement of belief which merits attention precisely because it is so different from the credal statements, stressing Christ's function to redeem the Fall through his Incarnation. The pope also emphasised the papacy's centrality in the structure and faith of the church, evoking the Petrine commission and his own inheritance of Peter's role. While the profession considers the Virgin Birth and the relationship between Christ and the Father, the Holy Spirit is barely mentioned, nor is the Final Judgement. Considering the letter's destination – to a ruler whose subjects included Nestorian Christians whose stance on the union of the divine and human natures in the person of Christ differed from that of Latin Christianity – the omission of any discussion of the relationship between Christ's two natures, except perhaps by allusion, is also rather surprising:[5]

God the Father, of His graciousness regarding with unutterable loving-kindness the unhappy lot of the human race, brought low by the guilt of the first man, and desiring of His exceeding great charity mercifully to restore him whom the devil's envy overthrew by a crafty suggestion, sent from the lofty throne of heaven down to the lowly region of the world His only-begotten Son, con-substantial with

⁵ C. Dawson, *The Mongol mission* (London, 1955), pp. 73–4.

Himself, who was conceived by the operation of the Holy Ghost in the womb of a fore-chosen virgin and there clothed in the garb of human flesh, and afterwards proceeding thence by the closed door of His mother's virginity, He showed Himself in a form visible to all men. For human nature, being endowed with reason, was meet to be nourished on eternal truth as its choicest food, but, held in mortal chains as a punishment for sin, its powers were thus far reduced that it had to strive to understand the invisible things of reason's food by means of inferences drawn from visible things. The Creator of that creature became visible, clothed in our flesh, not without change in His nature, in order that, having become visible, He might call back to Himself, the Invisible, those pursuing after visible things, moulding men by His salutary instructions and pointing out to them by means of His teaching the way of perfection: following the pattern of His holy way of life and His words of evangelical instruction, He deigned to suffer death by the torture of the cruel cross, that, by a penal end to His present life, He might make an end of the penalty of eternal death, which the succeeding generations had incurred by the transgression of their first parent, and that man might drink of the sweetness of the life of eternity from the bitter chalice of His death in time. For it behoved the Mediator between us and God to possess both transient mortality and ever-lasting beatitude, in order that by means of the transient He might be like those doomed to die and might transfer us from among the dead to that which lasts forever.

He therefore offered Himself as a victim for the redemption of mankind and, overthrowing the enemy of its salvation, He snatched it from the shame of servitude to the glory of liberty, and unbarred for it the gate of the heavenly fatherland. Then rising from the dead and ascending into Heaven, He left His vicar on earth, and to him, after he had borne witness to the constancy of his love by the proof of a threefold profession, He committed the care of souls, that he should with watchfulness pay heed to and with heed watch over their salvation, for which He had humbled His high dignity; and He handed to him the keys of the kingdom of heaven by which he and, through him, his successors, were to possess the power of opening and of closing the gate of that kingdom to all . . .

Clearly, Innocent IV's statement is an incomplete enunciation of the faith, intended for propagandistic purposes, as the first step towards conversion. That being the case, the emphasis on redemption – to secure adherence – and on the Petrine commission – to secure subjection – stand in an intriguing juxtaposition. (It must also be emphasised that there is no suggestion here of papal infallibility: although the matter was debated throughout the late medieval period, the dogma of papal infallibility dates only from the nineteenth century.)

FAITH FOR THE PEOPLE: INSTRUCTION FOR THE LAITY

While missionary popes and general councils offered verbal definitions of the content of the faith, Christianity had to be more than a matter of words. To move on to definitions of religious obligations and expectations provided for the ordinary parishioners is to shift from theology to reality, from theory to practice.

For the practicalities of medieval spiritual life, perhaps the most important decree of the Fourth Lateran Council was *Omnis utriusque sexus*, demanding annual confession and communion. In consequence of this, the laity's main spiritual contact with 'the church' as an organised disciplinary and regimenting body would come in the annual Easter confrontation between priest and (supposed) penitent. The demands of confession offered the clergy the opportunity to test the laity's religious knowledge. Such testing is presented as preliminary to confession in many of the confessional tracts of the period. John Mirk's *Instructions for parish priests*, written in England in the early fifteenth century, thus examined knowledge of the Creed, the Ten Commandments, and other matters before the private inquisition which was to reveal the faults requiring penance. Instructive as such confessional tracts are, even more informative on the nature of the faith demanded of ordinary Christians are the manuals of instruction repeatedly issued by the clergy for the laity in the centuries after 1215. Such manuals are generally important for allowing assessment of the dissemination and comprehension of the faith; for present purposes they also set out what people were expected to accept as the rudiments – indeed, something beyond the rudiments – of their faith.

In the early fifteenth century John Drury, a schoolmaster of Beccles (Suffolk), drew up a tract in preparation for the annual confession, as the basis for instruction during Lent.[6] This offers the overall definition not of what a Christian was expected to believe, although that comes into it, but of what a Christian was expected to *do*. In order for Christianity to be effective within the world, that was probably the more significant side to the coin. A critical aspect of late medieval Christianity is the emphasis on practicality: the religion of the great majority was not one of consideration and comprehension of deep theological matters, but action and reaction to secure salvation. Agreed, there was intense devotion and a strong streak of contemplative religion which could become mysticism, but the emphasis is on action, on *living* the Christian life. This distinction between action by the people as against analyses of doctrine and theology (which could be left to the learned) has stimulated much of the recent debate about the distinctions between 'learned' and 'popular' religion, although the validity of the distinctions is highly

---

[6] R. N. Swanson, *Catholic England: faith, religion, and observance before the Reformation* (Manchester, 1993), pp. 53–8.

questionable.[7] From the perspective of the authorities, what mattered for the majority was that they should willingly accept the definitions provided by the church, and be ready to believe what the Church defined as requiring belief (overall, even if idiosyncratically), rather than become confused or be lost by seeking to penetrate what were essentially mysteries.

Drury's work fits into this world of action, the whole tract being directed towards the requirements of penance. The three demands of penance (contrition, confession, and satisfaction) are first stated, with a preliminary declaration that contrition required one to be 'repentant and sorry for all your sins you have done'. The process of confession is more long-winded, examining the heart against the manifold requirements of the faith. First come the Ten Commandments, summarised rather abruptly. Contained in the Old Testament Book of Exodus,[8] these provided the outline for the legal order of life, and for the relationship with God. Against Drury's abruptness, others discussed them at considerable length. The author of the English tract *Dives and pauper*, written *c.* 1410, provided an translation of each commandment before its discussion:

You shall . . . have no other strange gods before me. You shall make for yourself no graven image, no idol, no likeness of anything that is above in heaven, nor below on earth, or of anything that is in the water under the earth. You shall not worship them outwardly with your body, nor inwardly with your heart . . .

In the second commandment, God orders that we should not take his name in vain, for whosoever does so . . . shall be [judged] guilty, and shall not go unpunished . . .

In the third commandment, God orders that you should think and hold well in mind to hallow the holy day. Six days . . . shall you labour, and do all your own work. On the seventh day is the Sabbath, that is, the rest of your Lord God. On that day you shall do no servile work, neither you, nor your son, nor your daughter, nor your servant (man or woman), nor your beast, nor the stranger within your gate . . .

These first three commandments defined the relationship between Man and God. The others, the commandments of 'the second table', defined the relationships between people, which were no less a part of Christian responsibility, social as well as religious:

'By the first commandment of the second table we are taught: . . . honour your father and your mother . . .

The fifth commandment is . . . you shall not kill; in which precept God forbids to us all forms of unlawful manslaughter, both physical and spiritual . . .

---

[7] See pp. 184–8.   [8] Exodus, 20: 2–17.

The sixth commandment is . . . you shall do no lechery, nor interfere with
anything carnally other than your lawful wife [or husband] . . .

The seventh commandment is . . . you shall do no theft, neither in will nor
deed . . .

The eighth commandment is . . . you shall speak no false witness against your
neighbour . . .

The ninth commandment is . . . you shall not covet your neighbour's goods
wrongfully, whether house or land . . .

The tenth commandment is . . . you shall not desire your neighbour's wife, nor
his servant, nor his handmaiden, nor his ox, nor his ass, nor anything belonging
to him . . . [9]

The analyses of the individual commandments contained in the tract were
wide-ranging, including as breaches a whole variety of activities which
might not immediately spring to mind. Thus, when dealing with theft,
offences were taken to include

all forms of false receipts, and all forms of false withholding or extraction of other
men's goods against their will. And all the means that lead to theft are also
forbidden by this commandment, such as false weights, false measures, false oaths,
tricky speech, deceit in workmanship and deceit in selling, false workmanship and
lazy labour in labourers who take great wages and do little therefor. Also ravin,
extortions, false withholding of debts and men's wages, and false withholding of
men's and women's rights and obstruction of their rights . . . [10]

extensions which brought under review a good deal of contemporary
economic practice.

To return to Drury: after demanding rehearsal of the Ten Commandments, he also requires the penitent to consider his commission of the
Seven Deadly Sins – of pride, covetousness, sloth, envy, wrath, gluttony,
and lechery. Clearly here there is considerable overlap with breaches of
some of the Commandments, as is apparent from comparing the analysis
of failure to keep the commandments in *Dives and pauper* with the
meticulous dissection of the various aspects of each of the Deadly Sins in
Chaucer's *Parson's Tale*. For Drury, there is a precise opposition between
these sins and the chief Christian virtues, which are to be encouraged, for
'Pride destroys meekness; envy destroys charity; wrath, patience; sloth,
spiritual activity; lechery, chastity; covetousness, generosity; and gluttony
destroys abstinence.' These seven virtues were highly important – the cult
of chastity, and the asceticism of abstinence, were major elements in late

---

[9] *Dives and pauper*, ed. P. H. Barnum, Early English text society, o.s. 275, 280 (1976–80), I,
pp. 81, 221, 263, 304, II, pp. 1, 58, 130, 211, 253, 295.

[10] Barnum, *Dives and pauper*, II, p. 130.

medieval piety – but there was an obvious antipathy between sin and virtue, which any penitent had to consider.

As if the names of the sins are not enough – and Drury, unlike Chaucer's Parson, makes a point of not analysing them – the means to sin have to be considered. The five senses are 'five towers or five gates to save or lose your soul: if they are well kept, your soul is safe, if badly, insecure'.

In opposition to sin, there were the opportunities to do good, the Seven Corporal Acts of Mercy. Six of these derived from the instructions given by Christ in Matthew's Gospel, the seventh being added from the Book of Tobit.[11] Christian charity, and Christ's precept, required that the hungry be fed, drink given to the thirsty, the sick visited, the naked be clothed, the imprisoned be visited, the homeless accommodated, and the dead buried. Not everyone was physically capable of such acts – notably, for Drury, members of the religious orders, the poor, those living in their parents' households, and others lacking a sufficiency of material goods for such purposes. However, there were also the Seven Works of Spiritual Comfort, which anyone could perform. These (counsel, correction, comfort, forgiveness, endurance, prayer, and instruction) were to be considered as part of the process of justification which could eventually earn heaven.

Only having got this far does Drury turn to the Creed and to demands explicitly of faith rather than morality. The Creed is here more than usually compressed (and in Latin) to emphasise the essentials of the faith. In the process of explication, Drury lists the sacraments: baptism, orders, confirmation, matrimony, Eucharist, penance, anointing (or extreme unction). The discussion of these and their impact is perhaps the most explicit discussion in the tract, emphasising their cleansing quality. Thus, baptism 'cleanses . . . from original and actual sin', while matrimony 'excludes deadly sin from the act of generation between man and woman'.

The roll-call continues, for beyond the sacraments, there were the theological virtues to be inculcated. Principal are the requirements of faith, hope, and charity – faith self-explanatory in terms of the Creed, hope for spiritual benefits, and charity as a love of God. The four cardinal virtues, etymologically defined as cardinal because they are the hinges which justly govern human life, comprised righteousness or justice, prudence, strength or fortitude, and temperance (the avoidance of excess). The remaining seven virtues had already been discussed in opposition to the Seven Deadly Sins, and so received no further discussion.

The overall impression given by Drury's tract differs from that derived from discussion of the Creeds and other doctrinal statements. Here the

---

[11] Matthew, 25: 35–40; Tobit, 1: 19–21, 2: 3–9.

doctrine is given a context, making it only one element in the totality of 'the faith'. The requirement was not simply to believe in something, but to be fully a Christian, with all the implications and demands of that label. The total package was perhaps most succinctly summarised by the Portuguese friar, Pelagius Parvus (d. *c.* 1250) in one of his sermons: 'Sincerity of faith; charity to God and neighbour; clarity of contemplation; unity of concord; saintliness of mind and mind; generosity in alms; completeness in confession; true humility; chastity of mind and body'.[12] Translating such ideals into reality produced what could be an extremely demanding programme, which established aspirations, and social rules, even if not everyone would actually attain the goals.

SACRAMENTS

The demands of the faith as set out by John Drury, the search for membership of the Church Triumphant which was the goal of earthly existence, imposed considerable obligations on the members of the Church Militant. In demanding perfection, Christianity may have asked too much: the programme was too hard to fulfil without assistance. There was the constant problem that the road to God was an uncertain journey. For most people, hope of ultimate success had to lie in some degree of Free Will, of being able to strike a bargain with God. Here again the emphasis lay on action, on personal commitment – but with some dangers. Too much stress on personal responsibility, or on the possibility of a contractual relationship between the individual and God based on the former's actions and obliging God to grant salvation smacked of the heresy of the Pelagians; yet some suggestion of such Pelagianism was all-but unavoidable in a spiritual climate which emphasised works as a means to salvation.

Nevertheless, beyond the possibility of influence, there remained the frailty of humanity. The spirit might be anxious, but the flesh remained weak. Moreover, there were other forces to take into account, forces which seemed to conspire against the feeble attempts of humans to improve their lot. While the ecclesiastical authorities were adamant that belief in fate and the fates was anti-Christian, nevertheless malefic forces did affect mankind. The devil and all his works were built into Christian

---

12 M. C. Pacheco, 'Exégèse et prédication chez deux auteurs portugais du XIIIᵉ siècle: saint Antoine et frère Pelagius', in *De l'homélie au sermon: histoire de la prédication médiévale. Actes du colloque international de Louvain-la-Neuve (9–11 juillet 1992)*, ed. J. Hamesse and X. Hermand, Université catholique de Louvain, publications de l'institut d'études médiévales: Textes, études, congrès, 14 (Louvain-la-Neuve, 1993), p. 179.

cosmology, as part of the Creation, even if in no sense equivalent to the Creator. As parts of that totality, witchcraft and sorcery were accepted amongst the reality, as were ghosts and other manifestations of evil. But demonic forces were antipathetic to the divinity, and could not be accorded any claims to divinity or to appeasement – evil was there to be crushed, not pacified.

The devil was fairly easily put in his place, in theory if not in practice. But sin, and the temptation to sin, remained, and the devil was always ready to take advantage of it. On the other hand, God punished sin, and humanity alone was incapable of fighting effectively against it. Additional help was therefore needed to counteract sin's threat. Alongside the church's basic theology there developed a mass of beliefs and practices – all included within the general concept of 'the faith' – which sought to relieve the gloom which a definitive judgement of individual failings might entail.

A critical defining feature of medieval Christianity was the special significance it gave to certain actions or stages in the progress of the Christian life: the seven sacraments of baptism, confirmation, ordination, confession, communion, matrimony, and extreme unction. The exact number of sacraments was defined only at the end of the twelfth century (when, for instance, it was decided that royal coronation would not be included); from then it was fixed until the Reformation, when the whole issue was revived.

The sacraments had several functions. They demonstrated and confirmed membership of the Christian body and adherence to the Christian life; they also marked stages in spiritual development, and in human relationships.

Baptism was the initiation rite, admitting to the body of the universal church, with the rejection (at least in theory) of human proclivities to sin, and acceptance of Christ's offer of salvation. Except in cases of conversion to Christianity, baptism almost invariably occurred soon after birth – often on the birth day. It swept away the penalty of Original Sin which was the inheritance from the Fall, and made the baptised a potential entrant to Heaven. (Infants dying unbaptised went to an ill-defined Limbo.) Baptism was the means by which individuals entered the church, and were said to become imbued with the faith even if they did not comprehend it; hence the notion that baptism was itself the sacrament of faith. It was indelible, establishing a life-long obligation which could not be revoked without becoming liable to the penalties of apostasy. Baptism was vital, and consequently it could be administered in emergency by anyone – technically, even by a non-Christian. As long as the correct words were said, it was effective.

Confirmation, unlike baptism, had to be performed by a bishop. It was a reaffirmation of the baptismal vows, undertaken by the candidate in person. Where it was administered, however, confirmation generally occurred in childhood, even in infancy. Between the ages of five and seven seems to have been the usual time for reception. However, as confirmation added nothing to the effect of baptism, it may be that many people simply omitted it, despite priestly injunctions. The true position is unknowable: there are no formal records of confirmations, although anecdotal evidence suggests that it was routinely administered by bishops as they toured the areas in their charge.

Every Christian had to receive baptism, and might receive confirmation. Every Christian would also hope to receive extreme unction, the final preparation for death. This rite of departure was a final affirmation of faith, and attempt at reconciliation with God and the world, to permit unhindered access to Purgatory at least. As the centuries passed, the point of death became increasingly important: the rituals associated with the deathbed, a preparation for death which included assurance of and in the faith of the dying, generated a special literature, the *ars moriendi* (the 'art of dying') which became ubiquitous in the fifteenth century.

In between birth and death, the number of sacraments taken by any individual would vary. Ordination, for instance, could not be received by women; and would not be undertaken by all males. Equally, the frequency of its receipt varied: large numbers of men received the so-called minor orders in their various gradations. Up to the rank of acolyte, these did not critically affect status within the world, as they did not preclude marriage. Minor orders could offer qualification for receipt of the privilege of benefit of clergy – the avoidance of the death penalty in serious criminal cases – but it is unlikely that that was the actual reason why so many people received them. Beyond acolyte, in the 'holy' orders of subdeacon, deacon, and priest, there were fewer recipients, but most of them probably received all three grades if they could. Clearly, only a small minority would receive the highest order, of bishop, given the restricted number of dioceses and demand for suffragan assistance. Receipt of orders, especially the holy orders, would reflect the various pressures of contemporary life – economic and population changes, for instance, and changes in inheritance patterns, as well as changing attitudes to the priestly life itself.

The commitment to celibacy demanded by holy orders had some effect on the numbers submitting to the sacrament of matrimony. (This does not mean that those in holy orders never experienced marriage: orders might be taken on the cessation of a marriage by death of the wife, or by mutual agreement which required her to enter a religious life of some kind; while a few priests did marry and thereby forfeit their ordered status.) Matrimony was an oddity among the sacraments, the only real justification for its inclusion being its sanctification by Christ's presence at the Feast of Cana, and the allegorical interpretation of Christ's relationship with the church as akin to a marriage. Marriage as a sacrament did not require priestly participation, although the church authorities sought disciplinary control by trying to insist that every marriage be solemnised by a priest. It acquired its binding force from the freely willed consent of the parties: once that had been given, the contract was almost indissoluble, except by death. There was no concept of divorce as now known, only an extremely legalistic interpretation of the marriage rules which could produce annulment and total invalidation of the agreement.

Important as these five sacraments were, their impact on daily life paled into insignificance in comparison with the remaining two: confession (or penance), and the Eucharist. To some extent they were inextricably entwined, for the consecration of the elements made them available for communion, which officially could only be received after confession. The link was made explicit in the decree *Omnis utriusque sexus* of Lateran IV, which imposed on everyone the duty of confession to the parish priest at least once a year and communion at least at Easter, on pain of exclusion from churches and the denial of Christian burial.

The act of consecration was obviously the highpoint of the mass, the focus of the sacrificial rite which commemorated and re-enacted Christ's redemptive self-sacrifice in a restatement of the words of the Last Supper. Because the re-enactment was actually performed by Christ, it being His power which effected the consecration, the character and suitability of the priest were irrelevant – except that he had to be a priest and have received proper ordination. Like the other sacraments, because consecration became effective by the correct performance of the rite – *ex opere operato* – rather than from the personal qualities of the human performer – *ex opere operantis* – there could be a mental distinction between attitudes towards the clergy (who might well be considered unworthy, indeed unfit, for the task), and towards the consecrated elements which, unavoidably, became the Body and Blood of Christ by the words of consecration and process of transubstantiation. The split between appreciation of the clergy, and appreciation of the Host, underlies much of the problem of late medieval 'anticlericalism', exacerbated by a natural tendency to exaggerate the capacities of the priest, so that he might be seen, with all his faults, as a 'God-maker'. Meanwhile the consecrated elements, especially the bread-made-flesh in the Host, could become the focus of a cult, Corpus Christi, which formed a major element in medieval spirituality.

The purification needed to receive communion, to be more than a spectator at the rite of consecration (the status accorded to most of the laity for most of the time) had to be obtained through confession and absolution. By the thirteenth century the consensus was that the absolution was the sacramental act – that Christ working through the priest removed the stain of the confessed sin. Confession, however, was a necessary preliminary to absolution, and to penance, with the whole process being seen as a unity.

Confession was integral to the constant process of purification and repristination necessitated by a continuous rejection of sin and acceptance of Christian morality – even though at the same time its repetition acknowledged man's inability to achieve immunity from sin. Sin, the constant challenge, had to be fought by acknowledging faults in repentance to a priest who could then grant absolution. That power to absolve was inherent in priesthood. Absolution, like consecration, was effective *ex opere operato*. It, too, tended to heighten perceptions of clerical power, and raised similar difficulties about the quality of the clergy in relation to the import of their sacramental actions. (Some commentators permitted confession *in extremis* to a lay person, but whether this was sacramental was uncertain, with assertions that only a blessing could be offered in response in such circumstances, and not full absolution.) Mere acknowledgement of sins was not enough: proper confession – as Drury had noted – had three distinct components, contrition, repentance, and satisfaction. A real sense of remorse was needed for the confession to have meaning; contrition implying also the intention not to fall back into sin. Acknowledgement had also to be made through punishment, both earthly and other-worldly. Sin carried two penalties: guilt (*culpa*), which the priest could alleviate by granting absolution, and punishment (*pena*), which was less straightforwardly expunged, but would be worked off through the penance imposed by the priest here, and hereafter in Purgatory. The rise of the notion of Purgatory, and the assurance of the effectiveness of absolution, eased some of the pressures of penance: whereas until the late twelfth century the penances imposed by priests had often been extremely arduous, these new doctrinal developments were less demanding. Priest-imposed punishments could now be lighter and more tolerable – in part to ensure that they were performed (for it was pointless to impose harsh penances which would simply be ignored, and were a disincentive to further confession). Earthly penance had to be sufferable on earth, but was recognised as only a partial satisfaction of the punishment due. The penances to follow death would be of a totally different order, and totally unavoidable.

Confronted with this unavoidability of *post mortem* punishment, and burdened by sin, human beings clearly needed assistance in this world as much as the next. Christ was the major hope, and the Christo-centric character of much devotion was a constant thread during the middle ages. But Christ, while able to provide the assistance, might be too remote. More human and humane intercessors were needed, a need which generated the cult of the saints, those who, going beyond life into life, already had audience of God, and so could be advocates and deliver miracles. The definition of sanctity was, of course, uncertain – the church could not claim dogmatically that it had recognised all the saints, nor that all the saints whom it accepted were considered such by God. Nevertheless, those who were apparently outstanding Christians (however defined) had an aura of sanctity, and if that aura could be confirmed by miracles and other proofs of divine favour, then it appeared a reasonable possibility that they were actually saints.

Devotion to the saints became a major aspect of medieval catholicism.[13] Despite centralisation of the procedures for canonisation, making proclamation as a saint a papal prerogative, there were many who were still treated as saints without papal approval. Local cults and devotions flourished, while the unquenchable desire for access to divine power through saintly intercession and assistance produced cults for many 'saints' of doubtful provenance and historicity. This potent body of heavenly intercessors were useful support troops in the battle against evil, and to make life tolerable by assuming responsibility for specific illnesses or misfortunes, such as toothache (St Apollonia) and plague (St Sebastian, and later St Roche). Their invocation led, not unnaturally, to reverence of their relics, and the erection of images and statues which often served as foci for devotion. However, the saints and their images were not actually to be worshipped: only God deserved that honour. Images and relics might be treated with reverence (*dulia*, rather than *latria*, in the technical language of theology), but that was all: idolatry was not condoned, no matter what the manifestations of the cult of saints might suggest.

---

[13] Sainthood and its appeal are considered at greater length below, at pp. 145–70.

Saints could assist on earth, by performing miracles, strengthening resolve, and preserving and protecting so that mere humans might retain some control over their lives and complete preparations to meet their Maker. That confrontation would still occur after death; and the question of life after death posed other problems in defining the faith, and working out how to ensure that as many people as possible did benefit from the Christian promise.

The crucial question was: what happens after death? The twelfth and thirteenth centuries had evolved an answer, adding another facet to the agglomerate of Christianity which was built into the faith and rapidly became a major aspect of it. Until around 1200, the choice had been solely between Heaven and Hell: the good went one way, the bad the other. Sometimes there were nuances to the ideas, with numerous suggestions of a possibility that not everyone would be immediately saved, but some might yet attain salvation through some form of *post mortem* expiation or purification; but on the whole the categories were well defined. Most of the laity were considered automatically condemned, while those who renounced the world for Christ were automatically saved – they might improve the earthly lot of their contemporaries, but not their *post mortem* destination. Heaven was populated chiefly by monks, nuns, and saints. However, by 1300 this perception had changed. The validation of Christian lay life – manifested in the acknowledgement by Lateran IV that even the married laity might gain salvation – attested a major change of stance, not simply towards laity in the world, but towards the afterlife. No longer was there a straightforward choice based on this-worldly track records. Purgatory had appeared, as a formal locality rather than an undefined state of being.

Purgatory served many useful purposes. In confessional theory, although a priest might offer absolution from sins, only God could determine whether there had been sufficient satisfaction to annihilate the punishment due for sin. Until the theology of Purgatory emerged, it was widely assumed that if full satisfaction was not made by the point of death (and how could one tell?), then Hell was the only possible destination. With the identification of Purgatory as a distinct location, that changed. It was still necessary to be relieved of the sin before death, through confession and absolution; but Purgatory offered the experience of Hell-like pains without being in Hell, thus completing the required satisfaction for sins to purge the soul and allow it, repurified, to merit judgement. That judgement, because full satisfaction had been made, was guaranteed to be favourable. This was a crucial change: hitherto, the immediate hope had been Heaven, but as an all-or-nothing aspiration. Now, with

Purgatory, it was enough not to be so bad as to merit immediate damnation: admission to Purgatory in fact secured eventual admission to Heaven. However, the precise timetable for these events remained unclear. Generally it was believed that Purgatory was entered immediately after death, or, at least, immediately after the preliminary judgement which followed death, so allowing adequate time for the completion of its experience and contemplation of the divinity even before the Last Judgement. However, there are signs of the continuance of another tradition, derived from the exegesis of St Augustine, which placed the process of purgation directly in the context of the Last Judgement, to follow immediately after the general resurrection of the bodies and the entrance to eternity.

The possibility of purging sins after death offered new incentives to prepare for the after-life, which were rapidly exploited. Assurances that Purgatory was a transient stage in the expiation of earthly sins were not enough. Even though Purgatory was technically outside time, the only way in which it could be quantified as an experience was in units of time. Treating Purgatory as an experience which could be quantified not unnaturally led to attempts to make it less threatening, by actions undertaken by the living on earth. Prayers and masses for the dead would assist the soul by reducing its torment, providing the basis for the whole movement of *post mortem* commemoration in the later medieval period, and for the currency of prayers and masses which underlay much of medieval 'charitable' activity. Such prayers emphasised the mutuality of living and dead which integrated all Christians into a continuum uniting the three elements of the church. Alongside, indulgences were also developed, allowing individuals to dock time off Purgatory by actions in this life. The idea of the Treasury of Merits was formally adumbrated by Pope Clement VI in 1343; although it had been partially worked out by others earlier. The saints, and pre-eminently Christ by his Passion, had built up a super-abundance of merit before God which the church could direct to other causes; a theory which allowed the hierarchs, primarily the pope, to distribute indulgences which remitted the pains to be incurred after death. The idea of indulgences grew massively, haphazardly, and almost spontaneously, from what seems to be its first appearance in Pope Urban II's proclamation of the First Crusade in 1095. Indulgences were marketed as remissions of both guilt and satisfaction, although the doctrine of indulgences was rather more complex than that. (Precisely what it was, though, and exactly how it operated, took some working out, and remained a matter of debate.) The collecting of indulgences, including the full-scale remissions of plenary indulgences, eventually allowed individuals to accumulate massive stockpiles of time off Purgatory

— although as time in Purgatory functioned differently from time on earth, the system was probably misunderstood by most recipients of indulgences. However, it was only in the mid fifteenth century that it was officially agreed that indulgences could be bought to aid the souls of those already dead.

The development of Purgatory and its ancillary elements provides a splendid illustration of the problem of defining the Christian faith between 1215 and 1515. Purgatory was obviously a major element in contemporary spirituality – many of the major manifestations of piety were predicated on its existence and on making due preparations for it; yet precisely what Purgatory was lacked formal definition throughout most of the period. Although it was discussed magisterially by Pope Innocent IV in 1254, and its acceptance was implicit in the profession of faith submitted by the Byzantine emperor Michael VIII in 1274 as part of the process of reunification of the Greek and Latin churches after the Second Council of Lyons, it was only at the Council of Florence, in 1437, that Purgatory's existence was decreed as an article of faith for the whole church (once more in the context of plans for reunification with the Greeks). Given contemporary circumstances, with a rival council meeting at Basle, the impact of the Florentine decree might be considered uncertain. This delayed definition of Purgatory exemplifies the relatively vague and evolutionary nature of much of the faith. It also demonstrates a critical aspect of many developments in late medieval spirituality: that the institutional church had to follow popular demand. The theologians' formulations on Purgatory actually post-dated the development of a widespread acceptance that there had to be some third alternative to the stark choice of Heaven and Hell. Prayers for the souls of the dead and ghost-stories attesting their effectiveness in securing salvation from torments (which, logically, contradicted ideas of eternal condemnation) pre-dated the theological definitions on which Purgatory as a doctrine was to be founded.

Much Marian doctrine was equally unclear, its development responding both to popular demand and to theologians' debates. One of the greatest of those debates in the period centred on the issue of Mary's Immaculate Conception – whether she had been generated in sin or not. Rivalry on this even extended to the promulgation of different points of view by the rival pontiffs in the Great Schism of 1378–1417. Similarly, although the church calendars included a Feast of the Assumption, the doctrine of Mary's Assumption was not actually an article of faith – and did not become one for catholics until 1950. The dogma of the Immaculate Conception is only a century older, having been proclaimed in 1854.

TENSIONS AND AUTHORITY

Christianity's developing complexity over the centuries required the creation of authorities and disciplinary machinery to ensure its maintenance and continued refinement. Because the faith was not rigidly defined and monolithic, but undetermined and evolving, it had to be interpreted and teased out of the available sources. The prime source was obviously the Bible; but the weight to be allowed to the Bible as authority was problematic. Although it contained divine injunctions, it was essentially a human, indeed ecclesiastical, compilation; as such it could not demand total and unqualified adherence.[14] The gaps in its analyses left room for individual ideas, academic debate, and intellectual mindgames in the search to comprehend and elucidate what Christianity actually was and entailed. However, although Christianity – specifically, here, Latin Christianity – was not a monolith, there obviously had to be some restrictions on what could legitimately be debated: there were some points which could not be rejected, could not be annihilated through argument. Interpretation had its limits, and a machinery was needed to define and hold those boundaries.

Yet, because it retained opportunities for interpretation and variation in responses, Christianity could not be static. As it claimed to offer the only truth for the rest of time, it had to be always changing and developing in reaction to the pressures of the times, either positively or negatively. The faith and its content were not only defined during time, as the pendulum of emphases swung back and forth (between, say, the poles of free will and predestination); it was added to and expanded as the questions and anxieties which arose from its inconsistencies and apparent irrationalities called for resolution. Christianity always had to provide answers, no matter how frequently the questions changed. That, again, raised the problem of authority, of the validation of accretions. Here the idea of the church as a tradition, a handing-on, came into operation. In the thirteenth century, the church itself, as a collectivity, became the validating force, authoring, authorising, and determining the definition of faith which identified 'Christianity'.

The need for answers to ever-changing questions lay at the heart of another major difficulty with Christianity as a system of belief. Fundamentally, the whole edifice rested on faith, not human reason. It was not that Christianity was actually considered irrational, but that the rationality needed to comprehend it fully was beyond human resources.

---

[14] On this, see also below, pp. ooo.

The first crusaders had responded to Pope Urban II's sermon at Clermont in 1095 with the cry '*Deus vult*' – 'God wills it' – and the divine will was the first mover of all creation. By definition, the divine will could not be irrational; rather it was the fount of rationality, no matter how incomprehensible to humans. Faith had to seek understanding, while recognising that comprehension would not – could not – be attained within the limitations of human mental, linguistic, and conceptual resources. On the other hand, human self-confidence meant that God had to be brought down to a human level in some respects: people would ask questions, and would seek answers, in terms of their own rationality, of their own limited ability to comprehend and analyse. Here, in the tension between human ability and divine ineffability, lay opportunities for error and for heresy, for challenges to the faith made in the attempt to understand the faith, in acts of human will which (in the eyes of the ecclesiastical establishment in opposition to them) contradicted the divine will. The tension between the two starting points for the approach to God had been stated bluntly in the twelfth century. St Anselm had argued for faith as the only route to full appreciation, for belief as the foundation of understanding, so that 'unless I do believe, I shall not understand'. In the opposite corner, Peter Abelard had demanded rationalism, a doubt which led to inquiry, and investigation which led to the truth.

These opposing and essentially irreconcilable positions imposed a dual task on the ecclesiastical authorities in relation to the world. They had, firstly, to ensure that the truth of Christianity was spread and taught to all potential Christians, with prime responsibility for those actually under their jurisdiction, and that once received it was reinforced and upheld. They also had to defend the Christianity which was defined as orthodox against the challenges of attack and deviation derived from misdirected inquisitiveness. Yet, in a situation where there was so much scope for debate, such lack of definition on many aspects of the doctrine, clearly both tasks would be difficult. In such circumstances it is not surprising that there was so much laxity about the varied manifestations of faith, laxity which almost amounts to a deliberate refusal to investigate what most people actually believed. Inquisitions and heresy trials may suggest a contrary impression, but the authorities generally seem to have been remarkably tolerant, acting only when individuals or movements became manifestly deviant. To catechise, to instruct in theological details, might raise more questions, and more pernicious questions, than the effort was worth. The tensions which are often apparent within religious practices and devotion over the centuries to a great extent derived from the irreconcilability of the various extremes. Yet, for all its imperfections, Christianity as a faith did exist. The theory of what being a Christian was

was there to be drawn on; but merely stating it was not enough. It had to be offered in practical terms. This was the preliminary task of the fathers of the Lateran Council of 1215, a task followed in later centuries: the formulation of a programme to disseminate and inculcate the Christian faith and Christian way of life.

3

ACCESS TO THE FAITH

Intellectuals and general councils might seek to define Christianity, but ensuring that their definition was effectively promulgated was a very different matter. Throughout the middle ages, the dissemination of Christian ideals and beliefs was a two-way process: on one side the provision of instruction and information; on the other the reaction to that provision, the reception of the message. Demand was also problematic: whether the forms of belief being supplied were those which the believers actually wanted, and would accept. What was perceived as being provided might not, therefore, be what was perceived as being received; and difficulties were encountered in retaining control over the means of reception. Yet the process of spreading awareness, of ensuring and obtaining access to the Christian message, was a major aspect of religion and devotion – indeed, a precondition for them. Obviously, the issues raised varied over time and space: reactions depended on local conditions, while the increasing permeation of Christianity meant that Europe's culture was more recognisably a Christian culture in 1500 than in 1200.

The spreading of Christian beliefs was dependent on the creation of a structure of authorities through which it could be done, able to authorise actions and legitimise manifestations of faith. The nature of authority within medieval Latin Christendom presented a number of problems. Fundamentally, authority was not just a matter of creating an ecclesiastical hierarchy; it was also a question of textual authority, of the basic sources on which the beliefs were to be constructed.

STRUCTURES OF AUTHORITY AND CHANNELS OF COMMUNICATION

The church and its hierarchy

The skeleton of an administrative and authoritarian hierarchy had largely been established by 1200, although it needed some tinkering, and reinforcement, throughout the centuries. From the twelfth to the sixteenth centuries, the church was dominated by the monarchical papal system, and a process of centralisation which made its efficient functioning as a universal entity dependent on the *curia Romana* (although until the mid fifteenth century that 'Roman' court was frequently peripatetic, its longest period of stability being the years spent at Avignon from 1309–67).

At root, and as increasingly interpreted from the eleventh century, papal authority depended on the Bible, being derived from the commission given by Christ to Peter as recorded in the Gospel of Matthew:

Thou art Peter, and upon this rock I will build my church; and the gates of Hell shall not prevail against it. And I will give unto thee the keys of the kingdom of heaven; and whatsoever thou shalt bind on earth shall be bound in heaven; and whatsoever thou shalt loose on earth shall be loosed in heaven.[1]

By exploiting these and other verses, plus a heady mixture of ideas derived from Roman law and wishful thinking, an almost irrefutable logical schema was constructed, establishing the pope's status as virtually Christ-on-earth. But there was an ambiguity in the construct. The purpose of the commission itself was unclear: was it really addressed solely to Peter, or to the church as a whole as represented by all the apostles? This uncertainty meant that papalism was always subject to the restraints of challenge.

The Gregorian reform movement had so encouraged the development of papalism that from 1100 the power and authority of Peter's heir was felt throughout the western church to an unprecedented degree. The creation of a central administration, acknowledged as authoritative by those over whom it claimed power, made great progress during the twelfth and thirteenth centuries, perhaps reaching its apogee during the Avignonese period of the fourteenth. The acknowledgement of rule was crucial, for papal authority, whatever canonists might proclaim, was essentially built on acquiescence: without collaboration and acceptance of the papal claims in the localities, the whole edifice was very insecure. The concession of

[1] Matthew, 16: 18–20.

authority, and the recognition of the primacy of the Bishop of Rome as exercising a vicariate from Christ which was unlike the powers exercised by other bishops and hierarchs, allowed the papacy to dominate the church for centuries. However, domination was rarely tyranny. The papacy might arrogate to itself a centralising role within the church, but it was contingent precisely on recognition and acceptance. In the devotional field, this tension was perhaps most critically reflected in issues of canonisation. From about 1200 the popes enjoyed exclusive authority to determine who had actually entered the ranks of the Church Triumphant by control of the process of canonisation; but the nominations of potential saints were usually put forward by the localities, and numerous local, unapproved, cults flourished across the continent. Nevertheless, although these local cults existed, acceptance within the calendar of the universal church was totally dependent on papal approbation.

While the papacy was accorded a primacy, the precise nature of papal authority was never fully agreed. Popes were not infallible. Some people sought to erect a barrier of infallibility around their pronouncements, most dramatically in the crisis afflicting the Franciscan order between 1250 and the 1330s which saw attempts to limit papal freedom of action in the controversy over apostolic poverty; but the popes themselves never claimed such status – or if they did, soon let it slide. They were not, therefore, unerring. They had no individual definitive role in the development of doctrine; they might make mistakes – might even fall into heresy – and had to be open to correction. Had Pope John XXII been infallible, his pronouncements on the Beatific Vision in 1331–2 would have made it an article of faith that the blessed would be denied the sight of God until the Final Judgement, in contrast to the view that the saints and those purged of their sins enjoyed the vision before then. As the infallible recipient of divine illumination, the pope could not be other than right. But John XXII was not infallible; his discussion of the Beatific Vision was simply an attempt to analyse doctrine in a speculative rather than definitive statement. He could, therefore, be contradicted, was actually accused of heresy, and in due course was persuaded to retract his ideas.

If the papacy, although authoritative, was not definitive, where did doctrinal power actually lie? Obviously, somewhere in the church, which by definition was indefectible, even if individual members (who might constitute almost all of the whole) could err. Thirteenth-century authors conceded magisterial authority to the Roman church as a universal entity whose pronouncements as a church were *ipso facto* binding; but without cutting the Gordian knot of ambiguity. The precise locus of supreme doctrinal authority on earth remained undetermined. Christianity was constantly undergoing doctrinal refinement and definition, and was therefore constantly mutable, within limits; such processes could continue without having to appeal to a basic authority or to resolve the fundamental question of who decided what the church should believe. Heresy trials and other approaches to theological and doctrinal refinement often appear backward-looking, dependent on a perceived precedent, without actually seeking to understand or appreciate changes over time. Thus, Wyclif was attacked for reviving Donatism and Berengarism; Luther for reviving Wycliffism. Rarely were the key questions asked: why is this wrong, who says so, and by what authority?

While the pope could not introduce major doctrinal changes alone, some machinery had to exist for such evolution. Formal pronouncements which actually produced a dogmatic statement had to be made in a general council. The approach to such statements is hard to define; they seem to have been consensual as much as legislative, although the degree of debate about individual proposals varied greatly (and whether those of Lateran IV were actually debated at all remains doubtful). Nevertheless, that an assembly like Lateran IV could decree that the body and blood of Christ were truly contained in the consecrated elements (something which would gradually harden into a doctrine of a 'Real Presence', although the decree was inexplicit about the mechanics of the process of 'transubstantiating'), and that a consensus of the church could be held to be reflected in the pronouncements of a general council, obviously raised issues of the source of authority and sovereignty within the church. After all, the Nicene Creed originated in a council. Conciliarism, the notion that Christ's commission to the church and His promise to be perpetually present within it were manifested in a general council, operated as a counter-weight to the more extreme papalist ideas. The thirteenth century developed the idea that the council fully reflected Christ's authority within the church, reducing the pope and cardinals to the status of ministers who provided a sort of permanent secretariat or executive which was accountable to the wider body, even if that body met infrequently. The inherent threat to papal monarchy and its determinative authority was obvious, but matured slowly. Conciliarism peaked between 1380 and 1450, when the Councils of Pisa (1409), Constance (1414–18) and Basle (1431–47) tried to impose a new ecclesiology which would seriously limit papal scope for action. The challenge to the papacy was put most forcefully at Constance and Basle, in the affirmations and reaffirmation of the decree *Haec sancta* as promulgated on 6 April 1415, in which it was asserted that the council 'has power immediately from Christ; and that everyone of whatever state or dignity, even papal, is bound to obey it in those matters which pertain to the faith.' Alongside the blunt statement, penances and punishments were threatened against anyone who should reject such conciliar authority.[2]

Momentous as this challenge was, it proved ephemeral. The sheer practicalities of conciliarism were incompletely thought through; the papalist counter-argument that conciliar decrees gained their force only from papal approbation effectively undercut hopes for a 'democratic' ecclesiology. The papacy existed continuously, councils did not – and those attending them frequently worried about how they were to meet their bills. Pisa and Constance were considered successes. They had made a major contribution towards terminating the Great Schism, a division in the catholic church created in 1378 by the rival elections of Urban VI and Clement VII as popes and effectively ended by the election of Martin V at Constance in 1417. Both councils also stimulated hopes of extensive reform, in the end imperfectly realised. The Council of Basle generated a head-on clash between the two standpoints, in which conciliarism's weaknesses were fully revealed. Basle eventually proved to be a disaster, and in 1460 the notion that such gatherings had authority over popes was explicitly condemned by Pope Pius II. Nevertheless, conciliarist ideas lingered. They were invoked against Pope Julius II in 1509, and more seriously, but ineffectively, in the early stages of the Reformation, when there were still aspirations to retain the unity of the church.

Although the theoretical issue of the earthly headship of the church under Christ was never properly solved, effectively the pope was head. Papal spiritual headship was rarely contested, although practical, administrative, headship was a rather different matter, especially on matters affecting relations between church and state. With these the attritive erosion of papal sovereignty continued unremittingly from the later thirteenth century. It often led to formal concordats with the secular governments, especially in the fifteenth century. Yet, on the spiritual level, the papacy's authoritative claims, justified by the Petrine inheritance, allowed it to claim a definitive role within the church, and to oversee the dissemination of the faith.

From the papacy at its head, assisted by the cardinals whose pivotal role within the church became of increasing significance as the centuries passed, authority permeated downwards through the hierarchy. Until the late thirteenth century, archbishops and bishops continued to uphold notions of collegiality of authority among the episcopate based on their own apostolic succession, a view which gave the papacy a primacy of honour, but not of jurisdiction. In reality such collegiality was extinct by

---

[2] N. P. Tanner, ed., *Decrees of the ecumenical councils* (2 vols., London, 1990), I, p. 409.

1300, although intellectuals sometimes sought to uphold it even later, and notions of episcopally directed diocesan autonomy may have had something of a revival in fifteenth-century England. To use papal terminology, Peter's successor had the *plenitudo potestatis* (the fullness of power), while other bishops had only the *pars solicitudinis* (a share in the obligations of caring and responsibility). When access to high ecclesiastical office became dependent on papal support and provision, ideas of collegiality were the first victims. Only as kings increased their control over national episcopates, and papal headship seemed little more than titular recognition, would local ecclesiastical authorities recover their prerogatives, although in a much mutated form.

Within the localities, the provincial authorities and their subordinates responded to the pressures imposed by their superiors, and sought to retain control over the religious beliefs of their spiritual subjects. An ecclesiastical structure existed by 1200 throughout most of Europe; although a diocesan and inferior hierarchy remained to be established in those lands where Christianity was still expanding. The system was always subject to occasional modifications, such as the creation of new dioceses in southern France by Pope John XXII, which responded to the region's history of heretical leanings by seeking to bring it under more immediate and effective ecclesiastical government. Below the metropolitans and their suffragan bishops were the lesser geographical jurisdictions of the archdeaconries, below them the deaneries, below them the parishes. Like the diocesan system, the parochial structure was largely in place by 1200, bringing almost all of western Europe within a pattern of cures of souls which allowed the church to exercise spiritual and administrative authority over its flocks. The system's effectiveness obviously varied from place to place; in England it seems to have ossified by 1300 and become almost incapable of responding to changing needs as the population fluctuated in later centuries. There were some modifications: smaller chapelries were created within parishes, and might gain some sort of independence; while other parishes lost their congregations and economic foundations, and were amalgamated.

The pyramidical structure of the local churches and the spread of a parochial system within which individual clerics with cure of souls had specific responsibility for their subjects provided reasonably clear routes for divulging instruction and information to the populace. Provincial and diocesan synods of the clergy were enjoined as part of the programme of Lateran IV to discuss and promulgate the latest notions on the content of the faith, and establish an educational programme to heighten awareness of it. This was particularly important in the thirteenth century, when there is widespread evidence of diocesan synodal activity to implement

and encourage the 'pastoral revolution' required by the decrees of Lateran
IV. In many cases the codifications produced in the thirteenth century
retained their validity for much of the later middle ages. The Le Mans
codification of 1247 was still in use in 1489, subject to slight modifications.
Such diocesan activity continued in later centuries, becoming increasingly
legalistic but never losing its concern with the faith and its reinforcement.
Sometime provincial synods determined what was acceptable as faith, by
dealing with matters considered heretical. Decrees and legislation would
be issued to encourage new devotions and reinforce or abolish old
practices. Thus, in 1281, Archbishop John Pecham issued his Lambeth
Constitutions, which had legislative effect throughout the province
of Canterbury; while the fifteenth- and sixteenth-century Archbishops of
York codified their provincial legislation, largely based on Canterbury's,
to strengthen the local church and clergy. Instructional legislation
provided for clerical and lay education, and for its control. In this context,
some of the most significant of the English decrees were those issued by
Archbishop Arundel of Canterbury in 1409, which restricted access to
religious books in the vernacular, and limited the scope of unauthorised
preaching by requiring every preacher to have a licence, and by limiting
the subject matter of sermons.

A key means of maintaining disciplinary oversight, as much in matters
of faith as administrative practice, was visitation. It was to episcopal
visitation that the papacy had originally turned in its drive against heresy
– the decree *Ad abolendam* of 1179 envisaged the creation of a Europe-
wide structure to counteract heretical tendencies. This was over-
ambitious, being in due course replaced – but not everywhere – by the
heresy-hunts of the Inquisition. (The famed registers of early-fourteenth-
century proceedings against heresy in southern France, covering
Montaillou and its neighbourhood, resulted from the episcopal visitation
of Jacques Fournier – later Pope Benedict XII – as bishop of Pamiers;
while heresy proceedings in late medieval England were likewise based on
a system of episcopal inquiries.) In more routine matters, visitation was
central. Archbishops could visit during vacancies of suffragan sees, and
were entitled to visit their whole province once in their pontificate to
ensure that all was operating smoothly. Bishops were canonically required
to hold regular visitations of their dioceses; archdeacons or their
equivalents were to tour their jurisdictions annually. Of course, this
system was never entirely effective: English evidence suggests that it
was rarely implemented in full. Nevertheless, there is enough evidence,
both in England and on the continent, to say that visitations remained
important, perhaps becoming even more significant as reforming
currents revived in the fifteenth century. The available evidence rather

concentrates on the physical and moral aspects of administration, although references to the spread of new feasts and concern for the provision of sermons and the maintenance of services reflects a sense of pastoral responsibility. Even below the archdeaconries, the rural chapters – for which, admittedly, evidence is very patchy – could have operated as educational and instructional bodies, to spread ideas and check on the activities of the clergy.

The administrative pyramid provided channels for communication both upwards and downwards. Bishops could issue decrees to be read out in parish churches; the system of visitation allowed instructions to be issued and complaints received. The exploitation of the church's structure as a means of communication is most eloquently revealed with the ordering of prayers and processions in response to particular events – intercessions for a king's recovery from illness; thanksgiving for a recent military victory. Indeed, the most blatant use of the pyramid was by political authorities for their own propagandistic purposes. This was notably the case in England during the Hundred Years War, when prayers, processions, and information disseminated via the pulpit were used to stir up nationalist fervour and patriotism. But it is not difficult to envisage the church using the structure for its own purposes – that was, after all, why it existed.

In addition to the local hierarchies, the papacy had its own agents operating in the localities, who played a crucial role in spreading the programme envisaged by Lateran IV and in later developments. The evolution of an organised system of papal legates was a feature of the thirteenth century, refining and building on earlier experience and precedents. It gave the popes access to the localities, and some degree of direct control. The status of papal legate superseded all local ecclesiastical authorities, importing what was in effect a local papacy to enforce whatever changes might be considered necessary. In the implementation of the Lateran IV programme, the use of papal legates was highly significant. In the Spain of the 1220s, the legate John of Abbeville struggled – admittedly, in the end, relatively ineffectively – to transform local structures and create a church consonant with the aspirations of Innocent III. His failure indicates the strength of local forces which reformist disciplinarians always encountered; but he probably sowed the seeds for later thirteenth-century Spanish complaints against ecclesiastical maladministration and over-weening royal interference. By simply publishing the Lateran decrees in Spain, Abbeville ensured that a model for the development of the church was known, even if it could not immediately, or fully, be followed.

Not all legations were as ineffective as Abbeville's: even in Spain, the legatine council held at Valladolid in 1322 was more successful. In the England of Henry III, the two legates Otto and Ottobono established basic rules of ecclesiastical organisation which lasted throughout the period. The regulations affecting vicarages, and insisting on personal residence, were particularly important for securing a permanent pastorate, although they could be circumvented by evasion and dispensations. Until such by-passing became common, the Constitutions of Otto and Ottobono demonstrated the effectiveness of papal authority, working to achieve the aims of Lateran IV.

While legates had great powers, they not unnaturally faced local opposition. Authorities in church and state resented the prerogatives and protocol attached to their visits. Subjection to the papacy was all very well – as long as it was to a distant pope, not some quasi-pope in close proximity. After the early fourteenth century, the English government usually managed to prevent the admission of formally appointed papal legates; but there were nuncios and other visitors with almost legatine powers, yet without the crucial title and status. The papal legates in England were generally only the local archbishops, whose odd standing as *legatus natus* (a standing shared with many continental metropolitans) made them effectively legates *ex officio*, without the formal powers or status of a *legatus missus* (who would not be a cardinal) or a *legatus a latere* (who would be). The full impact of a papal legation in England was best revealed in the 1520s when Thomas Wolsey, as Cardinal-archbishop of York and papal legate *a latere* for life, united both English provinces under his local popedom, and sought – but lacked time to effect – a full-scale reformation of the organisation and rationale of the *ecclesia Anglicana*.

The force of thirteenth-century papal legations owed much to the fact that the popes and their emissaries were working to the same programme. By the fifteenth century, things had changed. Then, the papacy's dependence on local support rather upset the relationships and the unity. Nicholas of Cusa, despatched as legate on a reforming mission in Germany in the 1450s, sought strenuously to fulfil his charge, challenging local disciplinary failings and the more outrageous displays of religious exuberance. But his attempts at reform faced local opposition – especially when he opposed one of the most popular and profitable of contemporary pilgrim cults, the Precious Blood of Wilsnack – and led to complaints to the pope. A papacy anxious to secure its position in Germany after the Council of Basle could not afford to alienate local opinion; Cusa's appeals for papal support were consequently ignored, for purely pragmatic reasons, and the reform programme failed.

Authority and uniformity

The church's hierarchical structure and administration, with its apex in the papacy, clearly aided centralisation. The concentration of authority generated machinery to assist the regulation of religion, but could not itself dictate what the faith was. Perceptions of the faith were also a matter of authority. Obviously, papal authority was significant; but the activities of the councils revealed alternatives. Moreover, as faith was often a matter of interpretation, determinative authority might also be conceded to those with the appropriate skills, to intellectuals and academics. None of these individually had sufficient authority to identify the faith, they could merely posit possibilities; but the personal authority conceded to some of them, such as Thomas Aquinas (d. 1274) – the Angelic Doctor – and Bonaventure (also d. 1274), was highly influential. Perhaps more significant was the context in which intellectuals generally operated, the universities. Not all universities had faculties of theology, but those which did grew in numbers from the mid fourteenth century, partly from the creation of new faculties in pre-existing universities, partly from a major increase in the number of universities, and claimed some sort of determinative role in theological issues and matters of faith. Universities would condemn dubious theological propositions, prohibiting their further discussion and spread, and claimed to be able to define heresy. Such claims reached a peak during the Conciliar Movement, as the universities sought to establish their credentials as the fountainheads of orthodoxy in the crisis confronting the church, even seeking independent representation at the general councils of the time. The University of Paris was particularly strident in its claims, with its chancellor, Jean Gerson, at one point almost claiming for it a determinative role above that of the council.

The intellectuals' activities were confined to a small group; but much of the determination and debate was eventually reflected (or perceived by the ecclesiastical authorities as being reflected, which might be rather different) in more widely held beliefs. Among the general populace, however, the main means of determination and dissemination were less high-flown, and the concerns rather different. For most the required attitude was of receptivity rather than inquisitiveness, of submission to authority rather than a desire to comprehend and understand. Authority among the people was again localised: the main contact would be with the local incumbent or his stand-in, possibly with a visiting preacher and confessor – perhaps a friar. Archdeacons and bishops might occasionally put in an appearance, perhaps more often than might be supposed if the activities of peripatetic suffragan bishops are added to the picture. The main access to the faith was through the local structures, and the multitude of ancillary modes of instruction which it could be argued that the laity created for themselves, although with some clerical oversight: the fraternities, plays, and private possession of books and images.

Such accretions might be tolerated, but the critical task for the ecclesiastical authorities was to ensure uniformity in faith. Not a total uniformity, not the imposition of an absolutely identical scheme of actions and reverence throughout Europe, which would have been unattainable in practice, but a uniformity which worked at its heart and around which local traditions and usages could build. While 'the faith' had to be considered as a universal, and therefore a uniformity, manifestations of the faith did not have to be identical: the Fourth Lateran Council had recognised this, although probably without intending it to apply to western Europe, when it ordained that provision should be made for the varieties of regional rites and ceremonies. Uniformity lay in acceptance of the basics, and their implementation as a social construct. Ultimately, then, the laity had to be instructed, be brought under authority and into the wider Christian body through an educative process which, beginning in the thirteenth century but building on earlier foundations, would allow them to meet the demands imposed on them by the decrees of Lateran IV. That was only one side of the problem. Their instructors also had to be instructed. The most important channel for spreading the faith was the parish clergy; although the friars ran them a close second for much of the period. Friars, however, were mainly urban creatures – given their dependent way of life as mendicants, they tended to be town-based – and were also highly mobile. Friars might not be a rare sight in rural areas, but they would usually be no more than visitors. It was the beneficed parish clergy with cure of souls (theoretically but not always in reality stabilised in their parishes) and their assistants, who would be the mainstay of any programme for lay instruction. Other clerics not directly involved in the parish system – friars acting as confessors and preachers, private chaplains, and hermits – would also play a part, which could be significant. However, their involvement brought problems of their integration into the overall pattern, and of controlling the message which they were issuing, to ensure that the laity were not confused by contradictions or over-sophistication.

The clergy as instructors: training

That the parish structure was already planted in the heartlands of western Christendom by 1200 – in France, England, and Italy – was a necessary precondition for using parochial clergy as instructors. The appointment of the clerics to hold such livings varied considerably from area to area, depending on local power relations and the effects of patronage; but they would generally be priests. Their intellectual quality and qualifications for their task are often uncertain. Nevertheless, as the pivotal link between the church's higher authorities and the parish, as the local embodiment of authority in issues of faith, they had a crucial place in the structure.

From the available evidence, ensuring the quality of the parish clergy was one of the most persistent and fundamental problems facing the western church throughout the period. Actually ensuring continuity in the supply of priests was the preliminary hurdle; for priesthood was but one of many possible careers open to individual males. Recruitment rates therefore fluctuated over the years, and geographically, as local circumstances dictated. As Christian Spain expanded in the thirteenth century, the movement of the frontier and creation of new dioceses and their parochial infrastructure increased the need for priests, without guaranteeing their supply. As one major problem encountered in the Spanish Reconquest was a lack of Christian inhabitants for the conquered territories, the external economic pressures on males to become priests would be limited. Elsewhere, in England for instance, the situation was different; but England may provide a model for elsewhere in Europe. There, in the thirteenth century and first half of the fourteenth, priesthood was apparently a highly popular career, but not necessarily a vocation. The impact of the Black Death in 1348–9, with a massive fall in population and consequent social and economic transformations, changed this. Parochial cures were perhaps less remunerative, although there was a great demand for priests to serve non-parochial functions in chantries or as household chaplains. Clerical recruitment declined considerably, reaching its nadir in the 1420s and 1430s. By then, the provision of parochial clergy may have been reaching crisis point, at least in areas like the south-west. However, from 1450, as the social and economic balance began to tilt back, entry to the priesthood increased. By 1530 recruitment of secular clergy in England (i.e., ordinands who were not already members of religious orders) had reached levels not seen since before the Black Death.

The problems encountered with the parish clergy were not confined to recruitment. Many other pressures affected their careers and the control which the ecclesiastical authorities exerted over them. The development of patronal rights often excluded bishops from direct influence over employment patterns: their ability to reject nominees for specific posts was extremely limited, especially when kings and governments became involved. Patronal control over careers – often explicitly lay control – reduced clerical independence and hierarchical disciplinary authority.

Over the centuries sermons and satires castigated the clergy's intellectual, moral, and pastoral failings, their abuses of their parishioners and their posts. While such evidence runs the risk of creating stereotypes, and some attacks were mere commonplaces demanded by the circumstances of their delivery, clearly there were problems in ensuring the quality of the clergy. The demanded standards were applied from two sides: the ecclesiastical authorities, and the recipients of clerical ministrations. Lay perceptions of the obligations of priesthood might differ from the obligations which the church authorities considered appropriate. Equally, the clerics could be ground between their responsibilities to both their superiors and their subjects, and the need to exploit their livings to guarantee a livelihood.

The attacks on the clergy show a strong awareness of their faults; but there were also attempts to resolve the problem. Clerical standards were indeed often poor, as is especially attested by reports of early visitations – in the 1220s the papal legate John of Abbeville uncovered a quite scandalous situation in Spain; while in mid-century Eudes de Rigaud's visitations in his archdiocese of Rouen reveal similar faults. The litany of local conflicts and failure to fulfil duties is almost interminable, being recited throughout Europe. The danger with these sources is that, because complaints are expected, they are noticed: it is also notable that serious complaints are generally few. Only failings – alleged, not necessarily real, faults – are reported; there are no appraisals of clerics who were doing their jobs properly.

The stereotype of the 'typical medieval cleric', who can be identified as the antithesis of Chaucer's Poor Parson, is therefore probably misleading. Not all the clergy were bad, and even those with failings were probably not all bad. Faults were unavoidable, but were there to be remedied: the intention behind the sermon literature, when addressed specifically to the clergy, is precisely to encourage a maintenance of standards by a process of reformation. The stance is evident in two major English sermons of the early sixteenth century. One was delivered to prospective ordinands by William Melton, chancellor of York Minster, in which he urged them to confront their consciences regarding their suitability for promotion; the other was an oration by John Colet, dean of St Paul's, to the convocation of the province of Canterbury in 1512, urging moral reformation of the clergy and maintenance of clerical dignity and standards as the prelude to a wholesale reformation of society.

The ecclesiastical authorities recognised their obligation to provide a means whereby the clergy could fulfil their duty of providing access to the faith for their parishioners. From the early thirteenth century there are signs of a programme to guarantee the educational standards of the parish clergy, even if its full implementation had to be delayed until after ordination.

The provision of clerical education was built into the decrees of Lateran IV. But the distribution of those injunctions throughout Europe – a slow, piecemeal process, still improperly elucidated, but clearly dependent on the personal contacts of those who attended the meeting who would promulgate its requirements in their own dioceses and neighbouring regions – resulted in local synodal injunctions defining how the clergy were to be instructed, and what they were to be taught. The creation of standards for ordination and admission to a benefice permitted an examination of educational qualifications and theological awareness at two of the critical points in a cleric's career, even if the hurdles could sometimes be side-stepped. In mid-fifteenth-century Cracow, the bishop restricted ordination to major orders to those who had studied for at least three years in the cathedral or collegiate schools; a similar insistence that any men ordained without reaching the required intellectual standard should continue their education appears in the Gniezno ordination lists of 1482. Equivalent concern is shown by the frequent insistence in English ordination lists that candidates spend more time in the schools before being allowed to undertake full parochial responsibilities (presumably here emphasising their ability to instruct their parishioners effectively), and by references in various licences to the testing of a cleric's *scientia*. What this entailed for the would-be priest is sometimes indicated by synodal legislation. That of Tuy in 1482, for instance, insisted that deacons (the order next below priests) should 'know how to read well and to sing and pray the canonical hours'. Intended priests should also 'know how to pray the canonical hours and conduct them themselves', and know how to confer baptism and extreme unction. As for *la sacra* (presumably the mass), that 'they should know by heart, and should read it slowly, without any doubt about it, with the pauses and to the letter'.[3]

Where were the clergy to acquire their education? More particularly, how were they informed of the requirements of them *as clerics*, whether pastorally or theologically? Obviously, there were opportunities for formal education, but the late middle ages had not yet developed the seminary. Most clergy received an elementary education prior to ordination, and could construe some Latin. Theological abilities are less clearly demonstrated – perhaps it was merely a matter of being able to recite the basic elements of the faith without difficulty; yet after 1215 theological demands were being made. According to the Lateran decrees,

---

[3] A. García y García, ed., *Synodicon Hispanicum, I: Galicia* (Madrid, 1981), p. 357.

cathedral chancellors were to provide some theological instruction for
their diocesan clergy, although the extent to which this worked is
problematic. Sermons directed at the clergy, *ad cleros*, would presumably
supplement this official instruction; as would sermons and other
discussions at synods. Such assemblies, besides providing opportunities
for spreading the latest theological news, were also the occasions for
issuing legislation regulating clerical discipline and behaviour. Notable
among such legislation is the frequent requirement, in French texts at
least, that the clergy should possess copies of the synodal codifications,
which they were to produce on demand, usually at later synods.
Sometimes, as in the Le Mans requirements, these synodal decrees
were also to be expounded at quarterly meetings of the rural chapters.
Although this legislation had to respond to local needs, nevertheless there
is often an overlap. The Salamancan code of 1410 clearly reveals the
complex inter-relationships affecting this synodal material, for it has
much in common with the *Liber synodalis* produced by an assembly at
Nîmes in 1252.

While decrees were issued from the synods, their real impact is hard to
determine. The evidence of testing of theological awareness at institution
to a benefice is limited; and if formal theological examination occured
only then, perhaps only at admission to the first benefice with cure, most
of the clergy – the unbeneficed chaplains who shouldered much of the
routine burden of running a late-medieval parish – were left largely to
their own devices. There is no sign that the unbeneficed were required
to attend diocesan synods, so even the limited amount of instruction given
there would have been unavailable to them. Quite possibly most of the
clergy received no structured training at all: if the suggestions of some
individual careers are any guide, the majority may have gained the
required knowledge simply through a form of apprenticeship, by
working with their local priest before and after ordination, and thereby
picking up what was needed.

The most formal training in theology was offered at the universities;
but it is important to make a distinction between different types of
theology. In practical terms, the most useful theology for ordinary priests
would concentrate on their pastoral responsibilities, being needed
especially to determine the disciplinary relationship between priest and
penitent so that the priest could fulfil the obligation to care for the souls
of his flock. For such purposes canon law and its analyses were of most
significance, as reflected in the production of instructional manuals for
clerics which summarised and tabulated their responsibilities by offering
digests of appropriate material. That faculties of canon law existed
in virtually every European university was therefore an important

consideration for the production and distribution of such works, and a significant factor affecting the extent to which ordinary priests could be made aware of developments in this field.

Purely doctrinal theology was in a different category. As taught at the universities, it was a rarified discipline, which raises the issue of how the clergy in general became aware of the latest developments in theological thought. In the thirteenth century only three universities possessed theological faculties – Paris, Oxford, and Cambridge, with the first undeniably dominant. With the growing number of such faculties and of universities from the mid fourteenth century, opportunities to acquire a theological education also expanded. A corollary of this might be an increase in the regionalisation of the religion: more sources of theological instruction would increase the variety of theologies. As the universities' 'catchment areas' became more regionalised, so the impact of their theologies would similarly become more localised.

Even though the opportunities for studying it at university increased, theology still demanded a major commitment. The subject was only available at postgraduate level – that is, after acquiring the initial arts degree. As it took seven years to become an MA, proceeding to a doctorate in theology could take a total of fifteen years of study. Most students at medieval universities lacked that commitment, or the resources to fund it: formal theology was always a minority subject. Yet many clerics and would-be clerics did attend universities, even if they did not take degrees; most could have acquired some 'theological' awareness. The Arts course, although essentially a matter of linguistic philosophy, nevertheless had a religious context: the functions of a university were at root ecclesiastical, their members (outside Italy, at any rate) were usually aiming to pursue ecclesiastical careers. Probably most general theology would be assimilated through the arts course, with its discussions of the properties of terms in relation to the Creation, and through university sermons. The major 'theological' trends of the late middle ages derive from philosophical movements; and these changing philosophies would be spread through the careers of their recipients, through the operation of the patronage system which secured posts for individuals who might then preach locally. Thus, theological innovation would percolate to the laity; but was probably neither rapidly nor widely spread. Late-fourteenth-century Prague was certainly affected quickly by the emergence of Hussitism, but there the circumstances were decidedly peculiar; and there is little concrete evidence for the rooting of the Hussite theological message in the countryside until some years later. Access to sermons, which would be common in university towns, might make the laity there more immediately aware of theological drifts; but how effectively the laity alone could spread ideas is not clear. Where there are signs of this, as with the connections established between some Lollard groups in fifteenth-century England, the links are not exactly tenuous, but are certainly fragile.

The almost accidental rural dissemination of university thought meant that most theological ideas remained élitist. To that extent, 'popular' religion might justifiably be treated as something distinct from 'educated' or 'élite' religion. But the distinction is false, especially in cutting off the educated from the popular – the educated were merely one layer of the populace. That new thought was spread is suggested by what is perceived as a major change in religious temperament in the later middle ages, after William of Ockham had emphasised the need for revelation and the insecurity of simple trust in God, forcing individuals to look more to the security of the own salvation. Even with this transformation, actually tracing the development and the distribution of ideas is problematical. By definition historians can use only the available evidence, but the problem with a lack of change, as opposed to a deliberate resistance to change, is that it rarely leaves positive evidence.

The establishment of the orders of friars – the 'mendicants', so called because they were originally meant to live by begging – in time added to the sources of theological knowledge. The orders' internal development meant that they created their own educational structures. These *studia* were a possible alternative to universities as sources of theological awareness. The Dominican and Franciscan schools were essentially training grounds for preachers from those orders; how far their lectures were open to others is not clear. As training grounds they had to provide theological instruction; they needed libraries; they produced thinkers. It is striking how many major preachers and thinkers of the period were actually members of the mendicant orders – from Thomas Aquinas (Dominican) and William of Ockham (Franciscan) through Vincent Ferrer (Dominican) and Bernardino of Siena (Franciscan) to Luther (Augustinian) himself. Because such people were trained in both theology and preaching, they were ideally equipped to spread new theological ideas, among clerics as well as laity. Although there is extensive evidence of rivalry between the secular clergy and the mendicants, this can be overstated. There was considerable interplay between the mendicant and secular structures, with the seculars often borrowing books from the friars, joining their confraternities, and maintaining relations with individuals, with houses, and with orders, which could offer access to the theological developments occurring among them. Correspondingly, mendicants preached in diocesan synods, and provided instructional manuals for the clergy.

Something similar could probably be argued for the monastic houses, whose libraries were presumably not closed to the secular clergy. Monks were often sent to universities for study, and so contributed to theological development: at Oxford, for example, the Durham monks had their own college, while Osney abbey provided a base for members of the Augustinian order. The larger houses, like Durham, also maintained large libraries which kept them well aware of theological arguments, even if not always the most up-to-date.

Religion for the laity: manuals for clergy and laity

High-level theology filtered down through channels such as these; but purely doctrinal theology was always élitist. The crucial issue remains to determine how far down it did penetrate in a pure form, before being diluted, accommodated within the existing structure, and reconciled to it. General trends can be interpreted in terms of the perceived intellectual movements, but those might not be the movements which actually influenced general developments. The evidence for theological speculation is always more concrete, because it is written down, than the evidence for its impact on belief.

As few clergy received direct 'academic' theological training or formal pastoral instruction, other ways were needed to prepare them as channels to communicate the Christian faith and message. The adopted solution was in fact addressed equally to clergy and laity: the production of instructional manuals. From the thirteenth century, texts appeared to aid clerics in their tasks as preachers, teachers, confessors, moral overseers, and pastors, with the academics providing for the non-academic. While mainly addressed to the clergy, and often in Latin (although a fair number became available in vernaculars), the mere fact of being written allowed their potential consultation and possession by literate laypeople. The instruction might thus be aimed at the clergy, but received by the laity. This may apply particularly with the more theological and moral treatises; those dealing with canon law, or confessional practices, would probably be less widely distributed – although confessional manuals which catalogued sins could still find lay audiences: the discussion of sin and its remedies in Chaucer's *Parson's Tale* is derived from just such compilations.

The instructional material aimed at the clergy reflected their role as intermediaries who were to pass on the teaching and injunctions to their parishioners. Much of the conciliar and synodal legislation also counts as instructional material; certainly the Lambeth constitutions, issued in 1281 by Archbishop Pecham of Canterbury (himself a Franciscan friar), would fall under that heading – especially that on *Ignorantia sacerdotum* ('the ignorance of priests'). Those constitutions in fact inspired a whole series of pastoral manuals in later medieval England, and were themselves put into English in the fifteenth century. In this they are matched by a wide range of continental productions, all at root stimulated by the pastoral requirements of the Fourth Lateran Council, as moderated by local legislative assemblies.

Decrees such as Pecham's, while setting standards for the clergy, also made demands of the laity. The process which transmuted clerical instruction into lay teaching is epitomised in the creation of the so-called *Lay folks' catechism*, produced in the diocese of York in 1357. Under the auspices of Archbishop John Thoresby a provincial council drew up a Latin statement of the essentials of the faith. This was directed at the parochial clergy, to inform them of their pastoral responsibilities and help them to avoid inciting heresy (even unwittingly) in their preaching. A second stage followed: Thoresby commissioned John Gaitrik, a monk of St Mary's Abbey, York, to produce an expanded vernacular version of the text, with the intention, according to the provincial decision, that the clergy should read it out to their parishioners every Sunday. By thus informing them directly of the basics of the faith, the hearers would be able to avoid the temptations to error which occasionally arose from the confusion induced by contradictory preachers. Gaitrik in fact greatly expanded the Latin work, drawing extensively on Pecham's *Ignorantia sacerdotum* constitutions. To ensure an audience, an indulgence of forty days was offered to the hearers. Whether the scheme for weekly recitation actually worked cannot be tested – it seems unlikely – but the vernacular *Lay folks' catechism* survives in several manuscripts, and remained popular for over a century, subject to frequent adaptation and amendment. In fact it passed into the general stream of devotional and instructional works, the manuscript tradition indicating that it was used as much by the laity as by the clergy, if not more.

The *Lay folks' catechism* gives a good illustration of the stages whereby instructional material became available to the laity, and may reflect a fairly common pattern. Spain provides strong evidence of similar developments, particularly after the Council of Valladolid of 1322. Here again, clerics were instructed to inform their parishioners of the basics of the faith. The synod of Salamanca in 1396, for instance, ordered them to write out summaries of various aspects of the faith, which would be made publicly available in the church. The clergy were to expound them on appointed days; but between such expositions the texts would remain available for consultation. Here, however, the system seems not to have worked; that at least was the complaint in 1410, when a much more elaborate statement was centrally produced and distributed. Initially in Latin, a Castilian version appeared later in the century. Spanish instruction after 1322 seems, however, to have been only imperfectly organised: there was no formal catechitical instruction for the laity. That only seems to have been instituted after the 1480s, to ensure fuller awareness of the content and demands of the faith.

The clergy also needed more detailed and specific handbooks for their own 'official' use. These tended to be more legalistic in nature, more concerned with tackling problems of penance and confession than simple recitations of the faith. The confessional concern possibly received increasing emphasis from the fourteenth century onwards. Such works were numerous, the legal emphasis in their citations of authorities (necessarily derived mainly from canon law) perhaps diverting attention from the fact that they were in essence practically motivated attempts to address real concerns at the heart of a cleric's pastoral responsibilities. In England, the most influential example was undoubtedly William of Pagula's *Oculus sacerdotis*, compiled in the 1320s. This was abstracted *c.* 1384, emphasising its canon law content, by the Cambridge chancellor, Johannes de Burgo, as the *Pupilla oculi*; it was also partially Anglicised by John Mirk, an Augustinian canon, as the *Instructions for parish priests*. Both later recensions had a lasting impact. The usefulness of the *Pupilla oculi* is reflected by its being printed *c.* 1512. The *Instructions* are of more immediate significance for providing contact with the faith, emphasising the essentially sacramental functions of the priest. There is a great concern with baptism, and some discussion of the provision of masses and the ritual of extreme unction. It is, however, sin and confession which occupy the bulk of the tract, placing it in the genre of confessional writings produced across the centuries and throughout Europe – works like the *Manipulus curatorum* of Guido de Monte Rocherii, and Jean Gerson's *Opus tripartitum*.

Sin as a social force is shown by Mirk's inclusion in the *Instructions* of the Great Curse, the roll-call of failings which incurred automatic excommunication and so required speedy confession and reconciliation beyond the annual confession and communion enjoined by *Omnis utriusque sexus*. It is the annual cleansing and communion, however, which occupies most space. Confession is clearly considered preliminary to communion, and the preparation included an examination on familiarity with the basic contents of the faith. With confession itself, the concern is to winkle out the sins. Perhaps more important than eliciting information on wrong-doing was the function of the process to communicate awareness of Christian morality by defining behaviour which was socially unacceptable, a feature again shared with other confessional

tracts. Possibly confession should be seen more as social act than private
concern: the sins to be repented were those which fractured the social
body, fragmenting the cohesion of the Christian fraternity, rather than
necessarily affecting the conscience in its direct relation to God (although
it was acknowledged that some people would have such consciences,
which would require appropriate treatment). The confessional was
concerned with sins which primarily affected others and disturbed the
requirements of *caritas*. This confessional concern to instil a social ethic
which bound Christendom together is demonstrated in the massive
summae for confessors which appeared throughout the period, with their
detailed analyses of what was or was not permitted. These compilations
pose problems, for the scale of their conception suggests that they were
not widely accessible, even though there were to be among the earliest
printed books. Their principal function may have been magisterial, for use
as a teaching aid for theologians and penitentiaries, who would pass on
suitable bits of the material to the local clergy. The impact of the *summae*
ought perhaps to be sought mainly in the abstracting of a text like Mirk's
Instructions, which considered confessional procedure in great detail, but
said little about the kinds of sins which might be revealed, or appropriate
penalties.

The motivation for the production of such compendia is problematic.
The *summae* for confessors, for instance, have been categorised as a means
of ensuring social control, by limiting the scope for licit lay activity and
encouraging the creation of a culture based on guilt. Confessors may
have sought to instil a sense of guilt, but their primary concern was to
stimulate remorse, and with it contrition; and the very fact that penances
became less severe over the centuries suggests that the moves for 'social
control' (whatever that phrase actually means in this period) were not very
strong. Given that religious activity was 'demand led', and that personal
contact with Christ became increasingly important in devotions, the only
way to ensure that confession and penance occurred was to make them
tolerable by lightening the burdens in this life with light penances and
absolution from immediate penalties and holding out hope of a reduction
in *post mortem* punishment by other means.

Instruction was not limited to confession and penance. The volume
of vernacular material produced in the late middle ages is emphatic
testimony of a developing lay literate culture. The content of the faith had
to be elucidated, which required more than simple statements of
Christian beliefs, actions and morality. Access also meant some understanding and appreciation, but not too much. Hence, perhaps, the
translations of the Our Father and Apostles' Creed which proliferated
across Europe. Even if recited in Latin, the critical elements of popular

involvement in the faith had to be understood in the native language if they were to have any meaning.

Not only did the laity need instruction in and translations of the basics of the faith, they also needed expositions of what they should do and what was going on during the services themselves. This especially applied to the mass: that peculiar rite in an arcane language during which by means of the priest Christ entered into the bread and wine, and could there be directly experienced. To this end, descriptive and devotional tracts on the mass were produced, providing an outline of understanding, encouraging devotion, and offering a choreography which the spectators could engage in in syncopation with the proceedings at the altar. The *Lay folks' mass book*, for one, was originally prepared in French in the twelfth century, and later translated into English. It offered guidance on how the laity should react to the priest's performance, with their own susurration of prayers and devotions as a counterpoint to the order of the mass. Later writers also provided instruction, some (like Clement Maidstone in the fifteenth century) insisting on a contemplative approach, imagining the procession of the mass as a re-enactment of Christ's Passion and sacrifice. This development of inspirational works on the mass reached a height in Gherit vander Goude's *Dat Boexken vander Missen*, first printed in Antwerp *c.* 1507. Accompanying its woodcuts showing the stages of the service were directions to the reader explaining the events and their meaning. A highly allegorical analysis gave every act and every piece of clothing a special significance, all of which was to be absorbed and appreciated by the lay spectator in order to receive the full benefits of the celebration.

The information imparted by such instructions for the laity rarely had great theological depth. But such depth was not considered necessary – which does not mean that the laity did not seek it. Instruction was to inculcate the basics, defined for one set of godparents as essentially teaching no more than the Creed, the Paternoster, and the *Ave*; a list often supplemented by adding the *Salve Regina* in praise of the Virgin. The demand for unenquiring acceptance of the faith necessarily limited the amount which it was felt appropriate for the laity to know, to prevent their misunderstanding and misapplying doctrines. Unsurprisingly, therefore, most instruction offered to the laity in 'official' sources dealt with the morality of Christianity and the afterlife rather than with issues of theology proper, with exhortation more than explanation. The mutuality of Christendom, and lay involvement therein, was central to much of the preaching and pastoral care of these centuries: the notion of Christianity as fraternity and community, as society.

Religion for the laity: sermons and preaching

Such concern with the social body permeates the second main mode of direct theological instruction, the sermons. These, in their multiplicity, provide massive amounts of material for study, reflecting social concern, theological development, linguistic achievement, criticisms of laity and religious, and much more. But perhaps because of their proliferation, medieval sermons are problematic. Question marks hang over much of the available material, regarding date, ascription, and the extent to which it reflects actual preaching. Although numerous manuscripts contain what purport to be sermons, the mode of their delivery and the precise function of the extant texts are often unknown. Some sermons can clearly be both dated and located – as for example with the sermon diary of Archbishop FitzRalph of Armagh, recording preaching in Avignon, England, and Ireland, or the extensive series attributed to the Dominican Giordano da Pisa, delivered in Florence in 1303–9. Others were preached, but audience, location, and date are hard to elucidate, as with some of the sermons of Bishop Thomas Brunton of Rochester. Many 'sermon' manuscripts, however, fall into a different category: although some may reflect actual preaching, were all the models provided by John Mirk in his *Festial* really used by him? What of the famed Lollard sermon cycle, extant in many manuscripts but with no clear evidence of formal delivery? How should the Latin 'sermons' of Philip Repingdon be approached: as devotional reading, as real sermons, or as material from which others could quarry their own smaller nuggets?

A major difficulty with medieval 'sermons' is that they purport to represent an oral act trapped in amber by literary transmission. Their function therefore changes, by being written up for an audience. While a sermon notebook has an immediacy, a reality as a sermon, which is undeniable (but may be misleading: the transcriptions of Giordano da Pisa's sermons apparently omit the funny stories and retain only the heart of the matter), compilations like Mirk's *Festial* or some of the Franciscan sermons are different. They then acquire literary characteristics and functions, and are perhaps unrepresentative of the reality of contemporary sermonising. Indeed, the evidence of the *Festial* suggests that texts were deliberately changed in transmission. Any unrepresentativeness depends, obviously, on function: the odd sermon transcribed among a mass of devotional material retains a devotional function for its reader because of its context – but more as a basis for meditation, perhaps, than a recollection of an aural experience. On the other hand, some of the Franciscan collections, although written up, may serve an aural function, providing models for development in different circumstances.

The task with these texts is to break through the written to the unwritten, to the oral and to the audience. Here sermons as recorded pose two main problems. First, many do not fit modern preconceptions of a sermon, and there are strange gaps in the material; second, there is the difficulty of assessing the audience and their receptivity to the messages. With the latter there are sometimes hints – the so-called *ad status* sermons, common in the thirteenth century, categorise the hearers as 'women', 'clerks', 'townspeople', and so on, tempering their content and delivery to the supposed audience. This particularly applies with sermons for the clergy, for whom the niceties of doctrine were considered more appropriate than for the laity. But often there is no concrete evidence, of either audience or reactions. The congregation is usually missing in anything other than a token form – analysis has to be founded on the text, rather than its reception. Yet sermons were delivered, and heard. In fifteenth-century England, Margery Kempe's 'autobiography' records her attendance at them, and her responses; and she seems to have deliberately sought out opportunities to hear them. The account books of the Willoughby family of Sutton Coldfield in the early sixteenth century also indicate presence at sermons – but as the record is only of payment to the preacher, there is no indication of content or reaction. Elsewhere, the impact of preachers such as Savonarola, or Bernardino of Siena, is more directly attested. The scale of attendance obviously varied; but the popularity of sermons is clear. Famed preachers could attract large crowds – numbering thousands, according to chronicle reports – from a wide area. The dangers of such great gatherings of people were keenly appreciated in times of plague. At Châlons-sur-Marne in 1467, and at Grenoble in 1523, the city magistrates banned gatherings for sermons in order to reduce the risk of spreading the infection.

Uncertainties arise when considering the function of sermons and their records in providing access to the faith. Here the simplistic category of 'sermon' may be inappropriate, as too large. There does, for instance, seem to be a real distinction between the academic expositions, produced within and intended for a learned milieu, and the more straightforward texts – maybe better described as homilies – addressed to a wider audience. The evidence suggests that sermons to develop lay theological awareness were rare. The communication of doctrine, and assurance of comprehension, is rarely indicated. This does not mean it never occurred: possibly such expositions were so commonplace that they were not recorded. The existence of the clerical instruction manuals, and the ascription of such inculcation to the parish clergy rather than the 'trained preachers' may mean that such sermons were almost doomed to oblivion. Perhaps, also, there was concern to restrict the recording of sermons about doctrine, to prevent their getting into the wrong hands. In 1242 the Dominican chapter general banned the recording of sermons in the vernacular for fear that the laity might start thinking beyond their capabilities on dangerous issues.

Although infrequently recorded, theological concerns do appear in sermons. Repingdon's, for instance, incorporate discussions of the nature of priesthood, and of the significance of the Eucharist; and the theological content of supposedly heretical sermons was often what attracted the attention of the ecclesiastical authorities. Repingdon again serves here: it was a sermon at Brackley in 1382, in which he declared his support for Wyclif's theories on the consecrated elements in the Eucharist (effectively a denial of transubstantiation), which brought down the hierarchy's wrath against him.

Most non-polemical sermons which survive seem linked to the church's confessional and penitential functions, concerned with the Christian brotherhood and the demands of *caritas*. They therefore define sins, castigate the sinful, call for repentance, urge penance and a return to something like pristine innocence by the rejection of sin, and offer hope of salvation by acceptance and enactment of the requirements of the Christian life. Discipline and devotion are to the fore, rather than theology: the bases are the Ten Commandments and the lives of saints. The aim was not to expand understanding of the faith, but to encourage acceptance and reinforce acquiescence, by stressing discipline and providing models and encouragement. To achieve this effectively it was necessary to target the discussions. One key feature of late medieval sermons has been highlighted as the way in which mendicants used the language of contemporary economic life, supposedly to mitigate the guilt induced by money, and produce a reconciliation between the church and wealth; legitimising the money economy by assuaging the guilt induced by usury and money-making, and so Christianising proto-capitalism. There is doubtless something to this view, especially given the regions and precisely urban contexts of much recorded mendicant preaching; but the reconciliation of Christianity and money was only one aspect of preaching, and the extent to which merchants and tradesmen were actually the precise targets of a preaching campaign is questionable. Not all mendicants found the reconciliation easy: the sermons of Giordano da Pisa continually show the tensions between the fraternal demands of Christianity and the individualism of proto-capitalism, reconciled only by emphasising responsibility towards God. Moreover, opposing reconciliation, the force of preaching against wealth could be considerable. Radical preaching such as John Ball's during the English Peasants' Revolt of 1381 had a significant impact at least on perceptions of what that revolt was about, even if its precise influence on the rebels is unclear. Even more dramatic was the outcome of Savonarola's preaching in Florence in the 1490s: there, hostility to wealth and conspicuous consumption was revealed in an outbreak of virulent puritanism, and the forced destruction of fripperies. There was a clear trend towards the reconciliation of Christianity and wealth; but this was a reconciliation which stressed mutuality, emphasising the responsibilities and rights of both rich and poor, as forcefully expressed in the tract *Dives and pauper*.

The sheer comprehensiveness of the basic genre of 'sermon' makes assessment dangerous. Much was polemical, even political. Anti-heretical sermons might be more theological, although they could degenerate into mere diatribes, but their preachers had to ensure that their condemnation of heresy was not the occasion for its propagation. Alongside the lengthy sermons which survive, there were the regular (or seemingly regular) sermons unconcerned with deep theology or current politics, which sought to stimulate immediate devotions, and repentance. These fall somewhere between the theology of the mendicants and the doctrinal instruction of the *Lay folks' catechism*, with more affinities to the latter than the former. They may be the type of sermon envisaged in the *Instituta* of Roger Weseham (bishop of Coventry and Lichfield from 1246 to 1257), which were to develop from an exposition of the Apostles' Creed. Providing a breakdown of that Creed, he listed material appropriate for consideration in sermons addressed to the populace, 'simply and without discussion', giving example rather than 'subtle reasoning or investigation or discussion'. Thus, in dealing with the Creed's seventh article, 'that on the third day he rose gloriously from the dead', the preacher 'could turn to the glorification of the body and soul of Jesus Christ, and the victory over death, and suchlike'; while to consideration of the twelfth article 'pertains that he will repay the just beyond their merits, and on account of their merits will punish those to be damned, maintaining justice and mercy in all things'.[4] Spanish evidence on the requirements for exposition suggests similar concerns: the programme decreed by Bishop Alonso de Cartagena of Burgos in 1443 sets out the aspects of the faith which were to be treated on the successive Sundays of Lent.

Such straightforward sermons, which merely described the content of the faith and admonished the congregation to adhere to its precepts, seem to be ill-represented in the extant sermon material (or, at least, in that so far edited). This may be precisely because they were so much the norm. The sermons which do survive are often presented as cycles – a structure which raises questions about the method and reason for their compilation,

---

[4] C. R. Cheney, *English synodalia of the thirteenth century* (Oxford, 1941), pp. 149–52.

and whether they represent 'real' sermons. Many of the French series do
seem to do so; but the English material is more problematic. Thus, John
Mirk's *Festial*, produced in the late fourteenth century, provides a series
for the year, often as forewarnings and foretellings of saints' commemorations. Some of the contents were apparently delivered, but why issue
them as a group? And why, as a group – and, even more so, one from
which individual sermons could be extracted – were they so popular?
Were they to be treated as no more than mere homilies, narratives and
exhortations to a better life? Were they cribbed by other preachers
and issued from other pulpits? The evidence is insubstantial and
inconclusive. Yet these brief sermons, with their pathetic descriptions,
emotive tales of the saints, and insistence on the withdrawal from sin, may
well have been the typical fare offered by ordinary preachers. Certainly,
they bear comparison with other published sermon series, where the
format is similar.

Such relatively undemanding sermons – undemanding of preacher and
listener – may suggest that the church was inadequately fulfilling its
edificatory duties. But that misrepresents the sermons' function. While
medieval sermonising had contemporary critics, among them John
Wyclif, who complained about the inclusion of unlikely tales and mere
story-telling without any really 'religious' message, such criticisms missed
the point. Sermons were not there to spread doctrine but the wider
message of Christian morality and *caritas*, through exhortation, through
tales of the saints which provided good examples and showed prospective
rewards, through reports of miracles, and with horror stories to warn
against following a bad example and the penalties for those who neglected
their duty. The stories, the *exempla*, each had a message, and like modern
advertising, the message had to catch the attention and stick in the mind.
The Christianisation of the mundane which is reflected in many of the
shorter sermons was, in those terms, highly effective for spreading
the basic message and expanding awareness of doctrine alongside the
requirements of the Christian life. The inclusion of popular songs in
sermons, reinterpreted as Christian allegories, and the provision of new
words for popular tunes, generated associations and memories to carry the
sermon's message after its delivery was over.

Perhaps equally important, the non-doctrinal content of the sermons
may have reflected perceptions of preachers' abilities, and fears about
misinformation through sermons. Both were matters of concern,
especially in the twelfth and thirteenth centuries.

The twelfth-century redefinition of the apostolic life, the *vita apostolica*,
as a combination of preaching and poverty, raised the problem of those
among the irregular and unordained who wished to assume a preaching

ministry within the church. The general expansion of the demand for preaching in that century had coincided with an explosion in the numbers wishing to preach. But what sort of preaching? How could an unlettered layman hope to communicate the complexities of a developing theology, and *get it right*? The first real test case came in the 1170s, with the Waldensian movement in southern France. Their demand for papal confirmation of a preaching ministry achieved limited success: they would be allowed to bear witness, but not to discuss matters of theology. These were outside their province. The rejection of that limitation was among the factors which led the church to condemn the Waldensians as heretics, for denying papal authority over preaching. But that did not close the issue, as laity continued to demand – and usurp – the right to preach. The Humiliati in Italy acted like the Waldensians, and suffered like them until reconciled by Pope Innocent III; and that pope also had to deal with an outbreak of lay preaching in Metz. The distinction between mere witness and calls to repentance, which could be part of the lay ministry, and more abstruse doctrinal discussion, was consistently maintained, nevertheless: the first Franciscans had to work within its confines, limitations which perhaps gave their earliest preaching missions their distinctive form. Although the content of legitimate lay preaching was limited, there was no blanket ban. (Precisely what the verb 'preaching' entailed is not always clear: it may simply have involved discussion of religious matters in small groups, like Margery Kempe's table-talk, or recapitulation of a sermon, as sometimes enjoined in household rules of religious observance.) The persistence of those laity who felt they had a real preaching vocation is evident across Europe throughout the middle ages, often combining with some sort of religious life. It is likely that many hermits and beghards – effectively laymen – also engaged in preaching activities.

The dangers of uncontrolled preaching were well appreciated. One of the few strands of heresy visible in England before the outbreak of Lollardy in the fourteenth century was associated with preaching by hermits. If their supposedly 'non-theological' preaching had that effect, with the unlearned applying themselves to matters for which they were untrained, how much more serious might be deviations caused by access to doctrinal intricacies? Archbishop John Thoresby's commissioning of the *Lay folks' catechism* was in part intended to dispel the confusion caused among the laity by the contradictory arguments of preachers; who themselves may have been insufficiently educated in doctrine. Clerics lacking theological awareness would not be able to cultivate the theological appreciations of their parishioners. That may be why most parish sermons were restricted to mere exhortations to *caritas* and repentance, and expositions of saints' lives. In 1409, Archbishop Arundel of Canterbury confirmed this perception of the dangers in his restriction on the content of sermons and attempt to ensure theological conformity.

Meanwhile, the growth of the mendicant orders after 1215 created a task-force capable of working effectively for the Christianisation of the world, with a verbal mission to enforce the faith. Theoretically, the mendicants' right to preach was unrestricted, and apart from minor limitations imposed at the end of the thirteenth century after long conflict with the secular clergy over their respective rights, which indeed continued in succeeding centuries in lesser forms, they retained that notional right to preach unhindered. But local organisations could impose limitations. The bull *Super cathedram* of Pope Boniface VIII was intended to enable diocesans to control the confessional activities of mendicants within their dioceses; but in England the resulting episcopal licences were seen as also licensing those entitled to preach. It is also notable that preaching licences for non-mendicants in pre-Reformation England were limited largely to university graduates – some of whom were specifically funded as preachers by bequests. Preaching on doctrine and theology, at least in fifteenth-century England, seems to have become increasingly rare.

Regardless of depth, preaching remained a Christianising force. The Christianisation of the mundane was essential for maintaining the Christian ethic and morality. The morality's integration with the cosmology and theology created a whole which, despite seeming inconsistencies, was coherent. At the same time, the question of access to 'faith', because of the lack of detailed theological instruction, meant that 'Christianity' as a generalisation had to be largely self-enforcing and self-reinforcing, and have its own means of development. The lack of any precisely drawn authoritarian structure for identifying the faith permitted accretions as a result of popular developments, allowing 'faith' to incorporate both anachronistic and mythical elements. Thus, the English mystery plays could unabashedly portray Herod as a Moslem, and in showing the Nativity add midwives to the *dramatis personae*, one of whom miraculously suffered a withered hand for doubting the Virgin Birth. This process of accretion was not restricted to 'popular' religion: the theologians' construction of the Marian tradition was wholly unBiblical, but none the less valid. Moreover, the lack of an authoritative system for the definition and dissemination of the faith, for integrating Christianity into the overall world-picture, meant that there were many ways of receiving the faith besides the formal instruction delivered by those within the ecclesiastical hierarchy; ways therefore of bypassing the priest and the sermons. All the verbal and plastic arts contributed; there seems to have been little which could not somehow be interpreted for religious purposes. Books, and the 'books for the unlearned' provided by pictures, images, and plays, all contributed to the spread, maintenance, and vitality of medieval western Christianity.

MODES OF ACQUISITION

For lay access to the faith the establishment of the programme of Lateran IV as a cultural norm was of the utmost significance. The prime medium for cultural transmission was unavoidably the family, and this would apply to Christianity no less than to other contemporary cultural assumptions. The most basic context for upholding the faith would therefore be the household. Although it is the area for which there is least concrete evidence, the importance of familial continuity of faith cannot be understated. Its significance is well-attested in heretical circles across the centuries; there is no reason to suppose that orthodoxy fared any differently. Given medieval domestic divisions of responsibility, such a household context may mean that while the church had a patriarchal structure, the strongest formative influence on spiritual development would be maternal. Christianity might, then, be considered almost as a matrilineal religion, which makes the available evidence for female literacy and cultural transmission through books and their ownership even more significant.

Beyond such processes of miasmic cultural acquisition, there were more specific means of providing indirect 'non-priestly' instruction. In a mainly non-literate society a process of oral transmission was clearly vital. Here, popular songs could provide a means for reinforcing both awareness and devotion. In Catalonia, devotional vernacular songs – the *goigs* – are known from the late fourteenth century, perhaps a reflection of mendicant influence. In Bohemia, songs were used by both the Catholic and Hussite parties in the fifteenth century as reinforcement and identification of their rival stances. The use of songs also provided a bridge between priests and people: as has been noted, one gambit in mendicant preaching was to use and reinterpret secular songs in sermons, giving them a Christian meaning which would thenceforth affect responses to them.

The most important source of indirect instruction would, however, be books. Given the absence of mass literacy, even in the sixteenth century, such an emphasis may seem odd; but the nature of Christianity, and the means of ensuring a common core to the inheritance, validate it. Christianity as a religion depends on books: as Moslems acknowledged,

Christians were 'people of the Book', and the religion's Biblical foundations impel consideration of that particular compilation above all others. Books also provided continuity and similarity: textual traditions ensured reasonable (but not always complete) agreement between copies of manuscripts; liturgical complexity required the constancy which only books could provide; and when printing made books more widely available in the fifteenth and sixteenth centuries, access to doctrine and devotional instruction, and to debate, was greatly increased.

The concern here is primarily with explicitly instructional works rather than those which were mainly 'devotional'. That distinction is admittedly artificial, perhaps inept; but is essentially between books defining the content of the faith and liturgical actions, and those ordaining mental spiritual reactions to the religion. Yet all books dealing with religious matters contained elements of the faith, which might stimulate and confirm belief: a classic case might be *The book of the craft of dying*, which in seeking spiritual preparation for death also imparts a good deal of doctrine. The didactic concern could produce even more esoteric texts. One work which became increasingly popular from the thirteenth century was *Barlaam and Josophat*, a Christianised version of the life of Buddha originally drawn up in the sixth century. This became widely available in vernacular versions in the late middle ages, offering an idealised model for Christian ascetic experience. Equally eclectic, by being influenced by Islamic Sufism, was Ramon Llull's 'novel', *Blanquerna*, written in the 1280s. That offered a Utopian model of spiritual reformation and worldly evangelisation carried out by a saintly individual whose progression through the ecclesiastical hierarchy culminated in abdication of the papacy and withdrawal to a hermitage.

The overlap between categories means that devotional works some-times encountered problems: the faith to which they gave access was at times questionable. Meister Eckhart's German sermons, speedily distributed in manuscript, were suspect in places; mystical works encouraged individualism which could get out of control. The ambiguity, and the need for oversight, are shown in reactions to Marguerite Porete's *Mirror for simple souls*. That had originally been considered heretical; indeed, it caused its author's death, as she was burnt for heresy in 1310. However, the spirituality which was considered so dangerous was also appreciated for its depth, those approving it even included Pope Eugenius IV. The text circulated widely in orthodox circles in the following centuries, being translated into several vernaculars. Yet the need for careful handling was recognised, and made explicit in the fifteenth-century English translation, which was carefully furnished with glosses to water down latently heretical statements: the faith which the text conveyed had to be rendered orthodox, even if it was not so to start with.

The Bible

The Bible, the combination of the Old and New Testaments, was pre-eminent in Christian literature. It had a unique status, and a peculiarly authoritative role within Christianity. However, the Bible's precise standing remained ill-defined. While authoritative, as the authentication of Christianity and its church, its own authentication was based on a circular argument, being in turn derived from the church. Circulating alongside the accepted canon (which included Old Testament books now considered apocryphal in the Protestant tradition) were several texts with an appeal of their own, like the *Gospel of Nicodemus*. Their authority was always uncertain, but they clearly contributed to the understanding and acceptance of the faith.

The Bible's authority was also made problematic by the form of its existence. The Latin text which became identified (from the sixteenth century) as the Vulgate was not the original version. As a translation, for the most part into a slightly demotic language adopted by St Jerome (d. 420) when producing his new translations and revisions of preceding texts, it lacked the authenticity of a direct Word of God which might have been claimed for its original version. Whatever the claims about the degree of revelation received by the translators, the fact remained that the Vulgate was not, in the direct sense, a Divine Revelation. The Latin text could not be granted that degree of literal fundamental authority to which other Holy Books – notably the Koran – laid claim. Supporters of such fundamentalism were rare, and rather misplaced the Bible in the context of medieval Christianity by giving it an authoritative and prescriptive status not consonant with its role as foundation and inspiration to a religion which was still receptive of ensuing revelations. That the normative Biblical text was in Latin also had an impact, although this varied regionally. In much of northern Europe, the absence of a vernacular translation denied direct acquaintance with the text to most people. Further south, the varying proximity of the Romance languages to Latin affected the comprehensibility without translation; the evidence suggests that most interchangeability of vernacular and Latin had been lost by 1300. Even Italian vernacular Bibles appeared in the thirteenth century; the need for them attests the unintelligibility of the Latin text by that date. Those Italian translations also attest a desire to comprehend and have access to the scriptures: alongside the Latin, there was throughout Europe a varying and variable tradition of translation, of the full Bible or segments of it. By 1500, most of the dominant vernacular languages had their own texts of the Bible, although the existence of such translations was not always welcomed by the ecclesiastical authorities.[5]

Primarily in Latin, and of uncertain authority, the Christian Bible also suffered the vicissitudes facing any medieval manuscript tradition. The text itself was largely established by the mid thirteenth century, the version used at Paris providing a standard which was to be generally accepted (but not universally used) until Erasmus' retranslations in the 1520s fundamentally challenged the Vulgate's standing. It was at Paris that the now traditional division into chapters and verses was first adopted, around 1200. The spread of the Parisian Bible over the next half century did not completely displace previous formats: old divisions of chapter and verse, old numberings of the Psalms, were sometimes continued, often being evidenced only in vernacular versions. There were even texts of 'the Bible' which did not derive from Jerome – a Latin version of Tatian's *Diatessaron* (compiled *c.* 170 AD as a harmony of the four gospels) circulated in limited numbers, again providing the basis for vernacular translations. Yet, because it was essentially a working tool, assisting in the understanding of the Christian world and its Creator, the Bible's text was constantly being abused. Glosses, miscopying, interpolation, all took their toll. Although textual similarity might be maintained with considerable success, precise universal textual identity was unattainable. Nor, surprisingly, does there appear to have been a great concern to attain such uniformity. A major outburst of Biblical textual criticism occurred in the thirteenth century, largely exploiting Hebrew scholarship in another attempt to get back to the original text and remove accretions. Thereafter, there is virtually nothing until the fifteenth and early sixteenth century, although there are signs of textual comparison in some of the translations, particularly the acknowledged work of collation which underlies the late-fourteenth-century English Wycliffite Bible (so-called because of its association with the Lollards, the followers of the Oxford reformer John Wyclife (d. 1384)). The culmination of the late-medieval endeavours was, on the one hand, the new translation of the New Testament prepared by Erasmus and published in 1519, and on the other, the Complutensian Polyglot, published in 1514–22, which insisted on the supremacy of the Vulgate but made available parallel texts in Hebrew and Greek. The labours of the late-medieval revisers of the Latin text, using linguistic skills in the search to create a more perfect Latin version from the Greek and Hebrew originals, brought to the fore the questions of authority inherent in treatment of the Bible. The emerging challenge

5 On translation, see also, pp. 75-8.

to Jerome's Vulgate, and the insistence of many clerics that that version be retained as the authoritative text, heightened the tensions over the nature of authority in western Christendom. Fundamentally, these developments raised the question of whether the Bible authorised the church, or *vice versa*; although it was rarely put that bluntly. Recognition of this symbiotic relationship, this mutual under-pinning, between church and Bible is a feature of Pierre d'Ailly's *Letter to the new Hebrews*, written in 1378. That work also points to the dangers of the symbiosis: by making its approval of the specific Vulgate text one of the fundamentals of its own claim to authority, the church was thrown onto the defensive when the imperfections of that text came under attack. The way the hierarchs responded to that challenge would help to determine the fate of western Christianity in the succeeding centuries.

Given that the Bible existed, with all its imperfections, how much access did people have to it? The notion of a Bible-less church may appear odd, but it is likely that full Bibles – despite the many surviving manuscripts – were rarely encountered. In some circumstances they would be absolutely essential: in universities with theology faculties, and in teaching establishments of the regular orders. But most places did not need them: church service-books would provide all the bits required for such purposes, as they still do, thereby easing access for the priests and excluding the unwanted chunks.

Yet, although the full text might be rarely encountered, its constituents were still around. Individual books, or collections of books, were available to varying degrees. The gospels were usually found together, as distinct compilations; while of the Old Testament books the Psalter clearly led the field until the proliferation of the more portable Books of Hours from the fourteenth century onwards. The Psalter remained popular thereafter, but probably to a reduced degree. Apart from the Latin texts, access to 'the Bible' could be obtained in several ways. Sermons built on the texts; abbreviated forms made the key features visible in picture-books, glass, and images; various vernacular treatments also made the text available – in mystery plays like those of the York cycle, whose coverage extended from the Creation to the Last Judgement, or in verse adaptations like the thirteenth-century English *Cursor mundi*, a sort of world history narrated by the Tree of Knowledge which, shattered by experience in the Garden of Eden, provided the wood for Noah's Ark, the lintel of Solomon's Temple, and finally the Cross of Jesus. Deliberate translations of the whole or of individual books also contributed.

Translation was the most obvious way to make the Bible's contents generally available. Again, the availability of individual component books is as significant as access to the whole, and the Psalter again dominates. But translation of the Bible presented major problems. For one thing, it impeded the traditional method of dealing with the text. Because the Bible was a working text, whose function was to encourage spiritual and devotional development, its contents were generally approached to that end. But Christianising all the texts, and reconciling their contradictions, was hard work. Simple acceptance of the letter was insufficient: something like the *Song of Songs* was clearly not explicitly Christian, or even explicitly religious; while the value of the mere history in several Old Testament books was uncertain, and may explain why much of it was omitted in the abridgements. The Bible had to be tackled at more than the literal level; and from at least the time of St Augustine, three other modes of interpretation had been applied, all intended to sustain and encourage a spiritual interpretation in accord with the Christian tradition. In a sense, those modes had to be accepted before the Bible could be 'correctly' appreciated – to believe in order to understand. Christian morality was therefore read into the Bible at a second level of meaning, sometimes known as the tropological sense. The third and fourth senses – the allegorical and anagogical (or mystical) interpretations – were especially applicable to the Old Testament as prefiguring the Christian revelation. The allegorical thus allowed the Old Testament to be interpreted to apply to the Christian message, as presaging the later revelation. The anagogical sense sought the ultimate truth hidden in the depths of the words, again presupposing a connection with the Christian revelation, but at a more mystical level. This complex process of interpretation clearly could not be learned overnight; hence the development of a science of theology. Clearly, also, it was highly dependent on language and the rules for its use. But language, being human, was fallible – even as the science of theology developed in the twelfth century, theologians accepted and recognised the human tongue's inability to contrive words adequate for the immensity of the divinity and related subjects. In Biblical scholarship, Latin was therefore a critical medium: it controlled the interpretation, by either its rigidity or its ambiguity. The technicality of the language, universally applicable, defined the content of the faith; a situation which would create difficulties when wider access to the scriptures facilitated individual interpretations to define individual faiths.

A vernacular Bible posed fundamental problems. The text had to be accessible, but its use had to be controlled: faith should not be perverted by losing something in translation. This realisation possibly developed slowly, as the clergy lost their monopoly of preaching, and perhaps as theology became more technical. Certainly the earliest translations, from before 1000 AD, seem to have aroused no objections. But after 1200 the climate changed. There was no specific ban on making the Bible available in the vernacular, but there was wariness about the nature of any translations and their use.

As with the Latin Bible, production of vernacular texts was limited, but not exactly small-scale: there are over 200 surviving copies of the English Wyclifite Bible. Individual books and paraphrases were also available. The creation of the translations rarely seems to have been a deliberate policy – except with the Wyclifite text. In France, the development of a complete text in the *langue d'oeuil* was a slow process. What eventually emerged had taken almost a century to assemble and still lacked some books, reflecting a mishmash of translations of varying levels of competence. Other translations reflect different traditions: the thirteenth-century Flemish 'Bible' was based not on the Vulgate, but on the *Diatessaron*. In some areas the vernacular came late, or not at all.

But translation was not indiscriminate. A move from Latin to another tongue necessarily involved a transmutation not just of words but of meanings. Where the ambiguity of the Latin might be lost, and a different precision imported, qualms might be justified. Unsurprisingly, therefore, the church sought to retain control over some aspects of Bible production. When asked about vernacular Bibles at Metz, Innocent III did not ban them, but did order that the translations be checked for orthodoxy. Similarly in England, Archbishop Arundel's constitutions of 1409 did not actually prohibit translation (in fact, they tacitly legitimised pre-Wycliffite versions, and held out the possibility of the legitimation of Wycliffite and later texts through episcopal licences); but they did aim to control access. The meaning was to be preserved, or if not fully retained, at least upheld by ensuring that the vernacular versions were considered subsidiary to the Latin. The existence of parallel translations, or parallel use, ensured that Latinate spirituality was not lost. (Richard Rolle's translation of the Psalter into English was thus intended to be used by nuns alongside the Latin text, so that they would know the meaning of the words otherwise recited by rote.) Latinity remained important: the language of spirituality and theology remained highly Latinised, so that some translations in fact became more Latinate in the search for greater precision. The similarity of Romance languages and Latin was one source of difficulties – there the possibilities of mistranslation through wrongful assimilation were obviously worrying. With the Germanic tongues, the difference from Latin posed other problems: precise translation might then produce misdirection. Mistranslation could only be avoided by a conscious – self-conscious – retention of Latinisms. The resulting neologisms to paper over the problem of the lack of a vernacular spiritual language would undoubtedly have been obscure in meaning to at least some readers of the vernacular texts, but they did retain the technicality of the traditional terms. The desire to retain such technicalities became most apparent in the furores over some of the sixteenth-century translations into English, like the dispute between Thomas More and William Tyndale over using certain English words in place of Latin because of their specific connotations (as with 'congregation' for *ecclesia*, and 'minister' for *presbyter*). At the other extreme the conservative scheme for an officially sanctioned English Bible in the early 1540s, precisely to retain the original meanings argued for the retention of some hundred Latin terms – including *ancilla*, *ecclesia*, and *presbyter* – which were not to be translated, although they might be 'Anglicised'.

One region where Bible translation may have caused specific doctrinal and emotional problems was Spain. Translation of the Old Testament was necessarily dependent on the separate Biblical tradition of Judaism, as recognised by the Christian exegetes of the twelfth and thirteenth centuries who had exploited Hebrew scholarship extensively. By 1350, however, the Jews had been expelled from much of Europe, with flourishing communities left only in Spain and Italy. Both regions retained a distinct Jewish tradition of Biblical interpretation; but in Spain after 1350 that tradition came into striking contact with the Christian tradition following the mass conversions of Jews after the pogroms of 1391 and later years. The fifteenth-century Castilian vernacular Bible has one strand which includes translation from Hebrew originals, based on elements of Jewish exegesis and translating some passages accordingly. This tradition probably retained a hold among the *conversos*, the Christianised ex-Jews and their descendants, thereby encouraging their feelings of separateness from the rest of the Christian population. If the distinctions between *conversos* and Old Christians included different approaches to the Bible and its exegesis it would explain both the Old Christians' fears of the *conversos* as a disrupting force, and the apparent ease with which *conversos* continued to mingle with their Jewish friends and relatives. It would also help to explain why the Spanish church was seemingly particularly fearful of a vernacular Bible: the first major Spanish translation which was actually printed (made by Boniface Ferrer in the early fifteenth century, but printed only in 1484) was fairly effectively rooted out by the Inquisition, so that only a few pages of one copy now survive.

Books and literacy

The strictures regarding the Bible apply to most books. Yet to deal with books raises the question of literacy, and the fact is that medieval European society was not one of mass literacy. In the twelfth and thirteenth centuries, reading and writing, especially writing, were restricted skills, although they became more common later. Reading may have been more widespread than writing, and would inevitably increase as vernacular literatures themselves developed. The society may always have depended on a considerable amount of what might be labelled 'passive literacy', an awareness of the value of the written and receptivity to texts even if direct access was limited. Certainly, Christianity could operate on that basis: priests could recite texts on behalf of their flocks, who themselves might well acquire texts by memory, and even be able to recognise them when written as cues for particular actions. This would certainly apply with requests for prayers inscribed on tombs: the significance of '*orate pro anima*' would probably be acquired almost instinctively and responded to, even if the rest of an inscription was indecipherable. It could, indeed, be argued that the 'pastoral revolution' of the Fourth Lateran Council was predicated on the existence of passive literacy.

The availability of formal education to teach reading and writing, especially education in Latin, was limited, but expanded considerably over the centuries. There were major regional differences: literacy in Italian cities was almost certainly greater than in rural areas; while the proportion of Italy's population who could be considered literate was probably greater than in England. However, precise figures cannot be calculated, and only impressionistic assessments are possible. Even so, literacy clearly increased everywhere after 1300. In England, the number of schools grew in the fourteenth and fifteenth centuries, many as formally endowed grammar schools, several established by guilds and non-clerical associations specifically for lay education. Education also expanded elsewhere, with many of the pietistic and devotional movements of the age – from the *Devotio moderna* in the Rhineland to the Hussites in Bohemia – taking advantage of the spread of literacy. This was, though, education mainly for males: women and girls had to depend on less formal modes of instruction. Nevertheless, women were not universally illiterate: as work progresses, so the scale of their book possession seems to become increasingly important not just for themselves, but for their role in cultural transmission.

Critical for the spread of literacy was the creation of a vernacular literature, lacking the esoteric overtones of Latin and more readily understood. Such literature was not necessarily provincial, much of it comprising translations from Latin (or, if from one vernacular to another, via Latin). However, a vernacular literature was necessarily addressed to a local audience, especially in a period when dialects had particular identities. Texts restricted to a particular vernacular thus had an isolated

Figure 1 Comic strip religion. A woodcut depicting the Ten Commandments, produced in Germany (possibly Strasbourg) c. 1460. Usually breaches of the precepts are shown, with a devil fluttering to seize the errant sinner. The first and second (and perhaps the fifth) contrast obedience and disobedience; the fourth shows only obedience. The appearance of the Commandments in German presupposes some degree of vernacular literacy; the use of woodblock technology would allow relatively wide distribution. (Munich, Staatsbibliothek, Inv. Nr. 81528 (s. 1846))

existence and impact. Failure to incorporate other devotional movements through translation would also increase isolation – producing the apparent paradox of a vital northern French vernacular spiritual literature in the fifteenth century which was seemingly uninformed by awareness of external movements like the *Devotio moderna* or Italian mysticism by access to the appropriate texts through translations.

The mechanics of book production greatly restricted the spread of a literate book-based religion before the advent of printing. In a world of manuscripts, difficulties of access to texts limited the influence of particular developments. This would only reinforce the regionalism of medieval religion, from differences in calendars to the impact of movements like German mysticism. It would also affect the social distribution of movements, with religious trends dependent on literacy being largely confined to the middle and upper ranks of society. Unless assisted by official commendation, individual texts would have to spread rather by trial and error, while old texts would retain their validity because it would be hard to challenge their written and therefore (to an extent) authoritative stature. This persistence of the old, and the dependence not on what was most recent, but on what was available, also accounts for some of the eclecticism of medieval developments.

The rise of printing in the fifteenth century changed that situation, in several ways. Firstly, printing on cheap paper meant a manifold increase in production. Prices of books fell, the time taken to prepare them was reduced. This does not mean that Europe was then swamped by books: print runs were small, but reprinting was possible. Not only did production increase, but the stability of the text improved. Manuscript production was always liable to distortion, and no two texts would be exactly alike unless an extremely rigorous checking process was applied, of which there is little sign. Printing made available a form of text which, precisely because it was available in numerous identical copies, could be more readily considered as authoritative and be reproduced as such. It might not be a 'correct' text by modern editorial standards; but any required corrections could be relatively easily publicised in new editions. The incorporation of changes in successive editions still precluded absolute uniformity; but the goal of a correct and uniform text did become a possibility. This applied both to vernacular and Latin texts; perhaps especially to Latin, as new humanist principles of textual criticism encouraged the search for an authentic text. The wider availability of Latin works – whether the base texts of the Fathers, or current theological speculation like Luther's – allowed a greater spread of theological awareness and of specific doctrinal strands among the Latinist élite in the universities and elsewhere; and also provided new texts for translation and

popular consumption. It is no coincidence that the early sixteenth century
first reveals Europe-wide acquaintance with many of the major doctrinal
and devotional works of earlier centuries: although manuscripts had their
own histories, it was only with printing that tracts like the English
translation of the *Imitation of Christ* would have more than a purely
localised impact. Printing also ensured the continued validity of many
older canonistic and instructional works. The printed confessional
material of the early sixteenth century thus included texts going back to
the thirteenth century; but the fact of being printed made them contemporary works. One last aspect of printing needs emphasis: manuscript
distribution was easier to control than book production. If a manuscript
work incurred disapproval, there would probably be few copies to be
tracked down; but the elimination of the complete run of a printed book
would be much harder. Thus, Wyclif's theological works were almost
completely eradicated in England (most of the principal surviving
manuscripts are Bohemian), while of the condemned writings of Bishop
Reginald Pecock only some now exist, in unique copies. Although many
printed books have been lost, their disappearance probably owes more to
the fragility of their paper than to a deliberate policy of destruction.

Even in an age of manuscripts, the spread of literacy was significant.
The changing format of books in the thirteenth century, with the
increasing numbers of small portable volumes (including the Books of
Hours), attests the widening of access. The increasing availability of books
also increased access to books among the non-readers. The publicity of
reading, as an aural activity, was vital: Margery Kempe owed her
acquaintance with a surprising range of devotional material to the reading
skills of her parish priest. The emphasis on the aural which accompanied
public reading also encouraged memory: fifteenth-century heresy trials
record individuals memorising whole epistles and other tracts for
recitation. Memory brought further problems for textual transmission,
threatening corruption, and would almost necessarily be restricted to
vernacular works; although those committed to a religious life would
have to know the Psalter off by heart, which was no mean task, and
Thomas Aquinas was credited with phenomenal textual recall.

Drama

Remaining at the literary level, the use of drama to inculcate the faith and
provide mass access to it also demands comment. Drama developed in its
own ways throughout Europe, with the different traditions in turn
contributing to the regionalisation of religion. Even in England, although
most emphasis is on the great mystery cycles, the plays from Cornwall –

written in Cornish – have been considered more akin to the French dramatic tradition than that of the rest of England.

The development of medieval drama is intimately linked with the transmission of the Christian message. Its roots have been traced to developments from liturgical celebrations, and to some extent the liturgy retained a theatrical element, especially with the intense allegorisation of some of the services. However, drama was not solely connected with such transmission, nor was that always considered drama's main function. With civic mystery plays, for instance, local pride and the development of a tourist trade were significant forces; for individual parishes, a play was a good means of fund-raising, regardless of content, and on the same level as the church-ale.

Nevertheless, the conveyance of Christianity through drama was important, and the clear links between clerics and the production of many late-medieval plays justify thinking of these as dramatised sermons. From the earliest liturgical dramas, usually associated with the Easter Resurrection ceremony, the church had elaborated the year's major ceremonies. The popularisation of the Christmas crib – a thirteenth century phenomenon usually associated with St Francis, but apparently not invented by him – also added emotion and visual impact to the message of the Nativity. The undercurrents which stimulated such acts were complex, but two main strands begin to appear at the end of the thirteenth century, developing further between then and the Reformation.

First, there were plays which recited the Biblical story. In that sense, plays were another type of Bible, although often containing apocryphal elements and highly selective in what they portrayed. During the fourteenth and fifteenth centuries, the major cycles were being created throughout Europe, although the extant texts mainly date from towards the end of the period. The Bible provided the basis for enactments of events from Creation through to the Last Judgement, incorporating key vignettes of redemption history along the way. Some – like the Harrowing of Hell – were not strictly Biblical; but the Harrowing did have Credal support, and was supported by apocryphal narratives like the *Gospel of Nicodemus*. The function of the plays, with their anachronisms, their comedy, and their social comment, was also didactic: the message was both historical and spiritual, with frequent asides of religious instruction and explanation to stress the nature of the faith and the parallels to be drawn between the various events. Indeed, the plays may have provided the main popular access to appreciation of the manifold levels of Biblical interpretation.

Alongside the Biblical cycles there were other types of play. These, for want of a better label, can be lumped together as morality plays; but a more nuanced classification is perhaps needed. On the one hand, there were the specifically doctrinal plays; on the other, the moralities and dramas. The doctrinal plays dealt with specific aspects of the faith: in York, for instance, the *Paternoster Play* dealt with that prayer, going through the clauses to reflect their message. Similarly at York, the *Creed Play* – an extremely lengthy piece – documented the Apostles' creation of the Creed, and expanded on the significance of the individual clauses. Other plays, such as the Croxton *Play of the Sacrament*, have been seen as deliberately constructed to refute heresy and proclaim orthodoxy (in this case asserting the veracity of transubstantiation against Lollard attacks). On the continent, the Spanish *Mystery of Elche* reflected the development of Marian doctrine, with the production of a mystery (centred on an image) which helped to spread acceptance of the doctrine of the Assumption – even when that Assumption was not dogmatic.

The morality plays differ in content, but were equally didactic. Here the emphases were on Man's dependence on God, and on individual and social responsibility. Everyman's history was told, his temptations, his falls, his victory. Virtues received their reward, and the means to crush sin were expounded. Some of the plays were in fact cycles – at Beverley, for instance, they dealt with the Deadly Sins. But many were single (or apparently single) dramas, often allegorical, the parts being allotted to personified qualities. Thus, the main characters in the English play of *Wisdom* are Wisdom, Soul (*Anima*), Will, Understanding, and Lucifer, with walk-on parts for various Sins and Senses.

The spiritual reaction to such plays is usually unrecorded. Their teaching function was clearly appreciated, and there was great concern to ensure that the text was followed correctly, the play taken seriously, and the right message conveyed. Should a play provoke the wrong response, it would be altered. The clearest such instance with the York plays affected the *Play of Fergus*, one of the apocryphal productions which dealt with events at the burial of the Virgin. This had degenerated into little more than a burlesque; its performers therefore requested its omission from the cycle and that they be allowed to amalgamate their acting with another company. As a result, *Fergus* has disappeared from the text of the cycle. On the other hand, the teaching element was also to be controlled. This is indicated in the way in which clerics apparently retained oversight of the plays' textual development; but the need for it was most clearly shown during the swings in religion in sixteenth-century England, when their old message proved unacceptable, and the whole tradition was killed off.

For many among their audiences, the plays were doubtless seen more as entertainments than religious instruction. The growth of drama as entertainment, and its secularisation, have to be built into the picture. Nevertheless, even entertainments might contain and convey a message, or reinforce a pre-existing awareness of doctrinal requirements; and if they succeeded in that, little more could be required.

The fragmentation of the play cycles merges in with the other dramatic entertainments of the period. While the content of parish plays is largely unknown, the reference being usually to the sums collected when a play was performed, there were many opportunities for drama to reinforce religion and devotion. Processions often had a dramatic element, reflecting a saint's life for instance. Major spectacles like a royal visit, which would be accompanied by pageants and histrionics, were much rarer. The successive pageants of a royal entree naturally said much about the town being visited, and about perceptions of royalty; but they would also reinforce the concept of the virtues, of links between God and Man, and of the social relationships of Christianity, even if in a deliberately political manner. When King Francis I of France entered Rouen in 1517, the carefully constructed sets operated on a multiplicity of levels. Their ambiguity may have obscured some of the meanings, but the meanings were there to be found. Moreover, just as members of the religious orders were responsible for the preparation of plays, so clerics (often mendicants) organised the solemn entries of high officials and royalty. At Amiens in 1466 the Dominican Michel le Flamenc arranged the reception of Charles the Bold, Count of Charolais (soon to become Duke of Burgundy); while at Grenoble in 1507 a canon and a Dominican jointly prepared for the royal entry of King Louis XII of France.

Icons and iconography

Beyond the verbal, more concrete forms of representation must have made them a major channel for reinforcement of individuals' appreciation of the content of the faith. The ubiquity of such representations, the varied types and styles of artefacts, preclude adequate assessment of this material in a short space. All that can be attempted is a brief survey of the material and possible responses to it.

The most obvious survivors in this field are the ecclesiastical buildings themselves. Their decoration provided a means whereby the 'books for the unlearned' of wallpaintings, glass, and statuary could be displayed in all their colour. Just what the intention behind much of the decoration was is sometimes unclear – although a concern to spread the faith is unavoidable, nevertheless physical inaccessibility, the impossibility of identifying images at great heights, the darkness of many buildings, and sheer ignorance, must have prevented full appreciation. Churches were

primarily built *ad majoram Dei gloriam* – to the greater glory of God – so
that while the instructional and devotional features of their decoration
were important, they would be subsidiary to the basic glorification of the
House of God.

Yet, even though subsidiary, they had an impact. The whole decorative
scheme of glass, images, statues, and painting, served an instructional
purpose. Sometimes, admittedly, this would not be directly concerned to
communicate dogmas – representations of saints perhaps fall into that
category, although they clearly reinforced the doctrine of saints, of
miracles, especially if linked to a shrine, and may have reinforced ideas
of Christian morality. The complexity of decorative schemes also needs
consideration. An individual statue of a specific saint would not necessarily convey much immediately, but would still be a reminder of that
saint's full story, and so lead to wider considerations and reflections. Just
as the crucifix could stimulate meditation on the full story of the Passion
and the idea of Redemption when discussed in devotional works, so other
images would generate specific emotional responses. However, some
caution may be needed. Images reflected demand as well as control.
Appreciations of saints might not be purely doctrinal. The ubiquitous
images of St Christopher – encountered from small country churches like
Hailes in Gloucestershire to cathedrals like Toledo in Spain – were there
presumably mainly to satisfy the belief that a sight of the saint was an
assurance against sudden death, rather than anything else.

Important as individual images might be in communicating aspects of
the faith (as fifteenth-century alabaster images showing the Trinity, or
souls resting in Abraham's bosom, clearly were), the cyclical depictions
were most important for instructional purposes. Here, functions varied.
Much glass and sculpture dealt with merely historical issues, depicting
Bible stories, the lives of the saints, and suchlike. They were probably a
major means for the laity to acquire knowledge of Biblical texts. But
greater sophistication also operated: not merely was the Bible depicted,
but its several layers of meaning were also shown. The tropological
interpretation could be set out by cunning juxtapositioning of sculptures,
as in several of the major French cathedrals; or in the arrangement of
stained glass, as in the windows of Canterbury cathedral. The busy
sculptures and paintings of judgements, whether over church doorways or
chancel arches, conveyed not merely the fact of a Final Judgement, but
also the need to prepare for it in this life.

The directly Biblical elements were only one facet of the use of the
decorative arts within churches. They could also convey more 'theological' teaching. Glass and paintings often showed the Seven Sacraments,
showing their connection with the truly Christian life. Similar decorations

presented the morality of Christianity; as in the Corporal Acts of Mercy window in All Saints, North Street, York, where the obligations of a Christian life and the mutual dependence of rich and poor are vividly illustrated.

Many of these images and teaching aids could also be used outside the church. The alabaster figures which proliferated during the later middle ages were often privately owned; while one major means of reinforcing the faith during this period came from possession of a rosary. Ownership of rosary beads is commonly recorded in late medieval wills. Private houses and other buildings might also be furnished with instructive wall paintings, or hangings. As domestic background their impact is obviously uncertain; but their presence cannot be ignored.

Printing greatly extended the scope of acquaintance with the faith through pictures. Woodblock prints, often with indulgences attached to them, provided objects for meditation, and the means to make people aware of the Passion, and other events. Some were very simple, such as a Pietà (the depiction of the dead Christ in his mother's arms); but others were very complex, like the print produced by Wolf Traut of Nuremberg in 1510, which includes the Seven Sacraments among an overwhelming wealth of other allusions. The didactic rather than devotional inspiration appears in some of the 'comic strip' blockprints, like those of the Seven Deadly Sins, or of the Ten Commandments, produced in Germany in the fifteenth century. Such prints might well be privately owned, alongside the books, the relics, and other accoutrements of private religion. Indeed, domesticated woodblocks may provide a better guide to devotional concerns than wall-hangings, because of their cheap production. The decorative urge is less likely to apply to the undemanding act of sticking a devotional print on the wall of a house, as depicted in an Annunciation painting of *c*. 1430. The Christian faith was all around, was literally all-encompassing, especially if its allegorical elements are taken into account. Where almost everything could be taken to mean or represent something else, opportunities for the reinforcement of the faith were immense.

The opportunities might exist, but the mechanics are hard to delineate. Perceptions of the faith are less readily revealed than the artefacts defining it. Alabaster images of the Trinity, for instance, might confirm a particular appreciation of that doctrine: a patriarchal Father, a suffering (or victorious) Son, and a dove-like Holy Spirit, giving concrete form to much more complex theological relationships. Yet there is little evidence of how people did react to such images. Depictions of the Crucifixion might emphasise the humanity and physicality of the dying Christ, emphases reinforced by portraying Mary as the grieving Mother in the increasingly popular Pietà imagery, and by the rather gory urge to share

in the spectacle and agony of Christ's death which appears in the
devotional literature, but this could be at the expense of a full appreciation
of Christ's divinity. The complexity of the imagery could also be self-
defeating: elaborate iconographic schemes might actually increase
obscurity. The code had to be known before it could be broken, and it is
impossible to tell how many people did crack the cyphers. The readiness
and willingness to see things at various levels of meaning may mean that
the depictions were better understood then than now; but even so, the
system was hard to appreciate without an interpreter. Mutual instruction
between lay people could fit in here, although with the dangers of
misinterpretation. Readings might differ, or change over time. At Moissac
in France, the Christ of the Apocalypse on the abbey portal was being
popularly interpreted by the mid fourteenth century as a depiction of St
Clovis, the first Christian king of France, whose unofficial cult was then
receiving considerable encouragement. A feature of the later middle ages
is that many pictures are accompanied by texts – the classic case being the
printed *Biblia pauperum*, with its woodblock illustrations and their
tropological interpretations (although whether this was intended for
popular consumption is debated). Other devotional prints similarly had
explanations and indulgences attached to them; while the *Prick of conscience*
window in All Saints, North Street, York, has panels depicting the signs
of the last days accompanied by couplets from the poem, in English.
These lines offer explanation, and were clearly intended to be read. This
might be a comment on spreading vernacular and Latin literacy; it
might also reflect increasing sophistication in popular appreciations of
theological and doctrinal matters.

The multiplication of the images, the varying fashions which affected
the portrayals, necessarily affected understanding of the events. The
intellectual impact of images and pictures may have been greater during
the 'missionary' stage of the thirteenth century, than in the fifteenth,
when their decorative role was perhaps more important and their attached
stories had become part of the society's cultural baggage. The overall
ethos had transformed between 1215 and 1515, with Christianity
becoming more embedded in the system. By 1500, indeed, the function
of the images and pictures may have changed, from historical to more
affective and doctrinal concerns. Many of the 'sacramental' images
date from the fifteenth century, when the Pietà came into its own.
Conversely, there are signs of a spreading revulsion against over-
decoration and gaudiness: Lollards and others complained about the
misleading and superstitious impact of images, demanding a reduction in
ecclesiastical decoration which distracted worshippers from the building's
main function. Such blasts probably had some justification. By 1500 a

Figure 2 Continuity and change in interpretation. The south porch of Moissac abbey, in southern France, constructed in the twelfth century. The sculpture of Christ of the Apocalypse (surrounded by the signs of the four evangelists and the twenty-four elders) conveyed a message to those who looked at it throughout succeeding centuries. However, from the mid fourteenth century it was locally interpreted as portraying Clovis, the first Christian king of France, surrounded by his court. The abbey laid great emphasis on its links with Clovis, whose cult as a putative saint was encouraged by the monks.

considerable mythology had accrued around some images and pictures –
like those of St Christopher; while the association of images with
miracles, especially those of the Virgin, had produced real rivalries
between the shrines, even though they were only statues, and all of the
same person. In such circumstances, one task for the interpreters may have
been not to instruct but to demythologise.

Yet to amalgamate all these means of spreading the faith into a 'system'
runs the risk of making the whole structure too solid. To consider access
to 'the' faith presupposes considerable definition, but the rigidity of a
definition is highly debatable; that it changed is not. Moreover, the
effectiveness of the means for dissemination remains largely untestable.
The church certainly hunted heretics, but it appears generally reluctant to
inquire too closely into precisely what people believed and how they
understood it. Acceptance of the basic principles was sufficient; deep
insight was unnecessary, and was even inappropriate for those not called
to serve in the priesthood (sometimes even for those who were). There
was an ambivalence in attitudes towards doctrinal instruction, similar to
the ambivalence about confessional procedures: too many searching
questions, especially leading questions, were dangerous, because they
might teach people the wrong things.

Localism

A final issue which affects the question of dissemination goes beyond the
universalism of the faith to the fact of the existence of a multiplicity of
local variants. In many respects, particularly aspects which accreted
around the kernel of the faith, western catholicism was created from the
bottom upwards, not merely imposed. In some cases, as with particular
cults, the spread was therefore from and among localities; it might even
have an 'imperialistic' element, as particular forms of worship expanded
to crush local variants.[6] On the other hand, localities might reject, ignore,
or be unaware of changes elsewhere, thereby confirming the regionalism
of interpretations of the faith. This permitted relatively localised
movements like the *Devotio moderna* in the Rhineland, or the early
beguines in Flanders, alongside the faith's universal elements.[7] The
importation of feasts and suchlike could be a slow process: the devotion
to Corpus Christi, for instance, began as a local celebration in the
Netherlands in the early thirteenth century, and acquired papal approbation in 1264. However, it was almost another century before it really
took off, to become one of the dominant elements in late-medieval

---

[6] Below, pp. 95–6, 150, 154.   [7] Below, pp. 109–16.

devotion. Other feasts similarly spread slowly: many of the fifteenth century's more mystical feasts were only incompletely integrated into English liturgical life on the eve of the Reformation. The logistics of producing copies of the new services in sufficient numbers, the difficulty of cramming new celebrations into local calendars, meant that not all would or could be adopted with equal enthusiasm.

Regardless of the distinctions and differences, most people would be aware of the faith's demands, and could respond to them. That response might necessitate some reconciliation with a wider sense of religious activity, involving superstition, witchcraft, astrology, and other influences – a reconciliation almost necessitated by Christianity's personification of devils and acceptance of ghosts. The response to Christianity also varied over time. In the earlier centuries, the concern was to Christianise, to spread awareness of what being a Christian entailed, beyond an omnipotent God who condemned the majority to Hell. This process had been completed for most of western Europe by 1350, but was still under way in more remote or recently converted areas like northern Scandinavia and Lithuania.

Even if appearing somewhat mangled, the Christian message was available, through a structure established to spread it, and through numerous ancillary modes of communication. The promulgation of the programme of Lateran IV had been a major concern and achievement of the thirteenth century; by the end of the fourteenth, at the latest, the redefined Christianity had been securely planted, and had become largely self-reinforcing. Of course, having its own momentum it tended to pursue routes which were less easily controlled than when in a missionary situation. Moreover, while it is possible to reconstruct the channels available for communication, assessment of the degree of communication is another matter. Some at least failed to receive the message completely, and there are instances of quite abysmal ignorance. Levels of comprehension of the faith can only be derived tangentially, by considering what devotional activity entailed, and popular presuppositions of the way the faith functioned. But these were critical, for while Christianity did exist as an academic exercise, it was its practices which ruled people's lives.

4

RELIGIOUS LIFE

——— • ———

Christianity imposed a morality and ethic on all its adherents, no matter how nominal their involvement. Through its disciplinary and penitential structure, its preaching and promises of Hell, Purgatory, and Paradise, the church both oversaw the continuance of the moral structure in this world and tried to cajole people into self-regulation. The detailed organisation of the Christian life was an important element in the totality of the Christian experience.

Over the centuries, many adopted specific lifestyles which showed commitment in a degree of regularisation. The extent to which this happened might be very slight, and very personal. A brief survey of so varied and diffuse a range may leave a feeling of incoherence; but here perhaps the concept of Christianity as a conglomerate of 'discourse communities' is useful, for all the varieties are subsumed within the unity of 'the church'. Even if regulation was not voluntarily adopted by everyone, everyone was subject to some degree of regulation, if only by the liturgical round. While the more explicitly 'religious' lives carried detailed regulation of many aspects of existence and demanded a very personal commitment, the liturgical sequence was institutionally imposed by the ecclesiastical establishment: reception was not voluntary. The liturgy established the timetable for the religious and spiritual Christian life; it dictated the opportunities for worship, the means of achieving contact with God. Liturgy, in a real sense, defined devotion.

LITURGICAL EXPERIENCE

Calendars, conformity, and particularism

The medieval church's liturgical round had three main forms. First was the divine office, the series of daily prayers and praises which defined the hours and was especially important for those committed to a formal regular existence. The monastic horarium split the day into a series of celebrations, from Lauds (initially held at midnight, but increasingly put back towards dawn), through Mattins, Prime, Terce, Sext, and Nones, to Vespers and then Compline. In each service there would be chanting of psalms and Biblical readings: the function of the hours was to praise God and meditate on His word, not commemorate Christ's sacrifice. These services were not a daily repetition of the same material. The psalms changed according to a set pattern, so that all 150 of them were recited over the course of a week; the readings aimed to complete the whole Bible during the year. Use of this horarium was not confined to those bound to the regular life: secular clerics were meant to recite the daily hours; lay people could also participate – there is plenty of evidence for lay attendance at such services, either when visiting religious houses, or in their private chapels. Not everyone participated in full celebration of the office, although it would be wrong to under-estimate its impact: the ringing of bells to announce the hours would have made people aware of their recital, permitting some form of equivalent commemoration like the Paternosters enjoined on illiterate fifteenth-century English hermits.

The divine office functioned on both weekly and annual rounds, as did other liturgical celebrations. The weekly round clearly focused on Sunday, the day specifically dedicated to God. Then there would be the full range of services in every parish church; except in cases of dire need all work and trading had to cease; entertainment opportunities were limited. While Sundays were prominent, other days had their own spiritual restrictions. Saturdays came to be dedicated to the Virgin, with celebrations of her masses occurring then. Fridays also had a special significance, in recollection of Good Friday, with meat-eating being banned although fish was permitted. Wednesdays were also considered important, but less so than Friday. This fragmented week did not make specifically spiritual demands, except on Sunday; but it demonstrated that the church did not accept that spirituality should be confined to that one day.

Above the weekly round was the annual calendar. Over each year the church recollected Christ's ministry and its after-effects, especially the reception of the Holy Spirit. The seasons began with Advent in

November, moving through Christmas and Lent, to the great climax of Easter with its commemorations of the Crucifixion and Resurrection. Then came a lull until the celebration of the Ascension, the receipt of the Holy Spirit at Pentecost, and the final acknowledgement of the triune God on Trinity Sunday. After that there was rather a hiatus: having crammed so much into little more than six months – if, in fact, so long – the long period between Trinity and Advent, the unimaginative succession of Sundays after Trinity, apparently had no function other than to be Sundays after Trinity.

This superficial division of the year into holy and quiet halves has been used to argue for other chronological and perceptual divisions, between ecclesiastical and secular portions, especially in the towns of late medieval England. But to concentrate solely on the seasonal calendar would be wrong: the church's year contained much more. A multitude of other feasts interrupted the round, increased the demands of devotion, and had their own impact on daily life, often in a ban on trade and labour. Many of the commemorations were international, but their local impacts varied to some extent depending on their significance for more secular purposes. In England, for instance, four feasts had particular significance as the days on which accounts were settled. In most of England (where the official calendar year began on the feast of the Annunciation, 25 March) the quarters were celebrated at St Michael the Archangel (Michaelmas, 29 September), Christmas (25 December), the Annunciation or Lady Day (25 March), and the Nativity of St John the Baptist (Midsummer, 24 June). In other parts of the country the quarters differed: St Martin in winter (11 November, Martinmas), the Purification of the Blessed Virgin Mary (Candlemas, 2 February), Pentecost or Whitsun (with all the nuisances of being a moveable feast falling anywhere between mid-April and early June), and St Peter *ad vincula* (1 August). Similar arrangements presumably applied elsewhere, although few regions can have been as idiosyncratic as northern France. The expansion of Capetian power there during the thirteenth century was accompanied by the adoption of the royalist administrative calendar, according to which the year began at Easter. This was (and is) a moveable feast, producing years of variable length which might contain the first fortnight of April twice over.

Celebrations over a year were many and varied, with differing local significances. The linking of Midsummer with St John the Baptist, and harvest with Michaelmas, doubtless strengthened their commemoration, but possibly also limited their spirituality. The start of November saw the joint festival of All Souls and All Saints, when Christians commemorated their dead. Lent, although a period of abstinence and repentance, was also a period of spring-time renewal and positive activity. While it was the season of confession and self-denial, its processes of purification in preparation for Easter communion had very positive associations. One French preacher described Lent as

the fair of things good for the soul. For the churches are open, indulgences are given, masses and prayers are multiplied and preaching takes place frequently, the confessors sit ready to remit sins. Truly this is the time in which all things are renewed, and the vines and trees make themselves ready to bear fruit.[1]

While the standard calendar was long-established, it was not immutable. With the passage of time, the yearly timetable became increasingly crowded: new spiritual concerns generated new officially sanctioned holy days; local unofficial cults added to the pressures. This cluttering caused concern: there was intermittent debate on reform to limit the number of holy days, most pertinently at the Council of Constance, but nothing was actually done beyond occasional local adjustments. The piecemeal processes of adoption (or non-adoption) of new commemorations – especially the more mystical Christocentric feasts which arose from the fourteenth century – could only emphasise the regionalism within the universalism of the catholic church. Even so, some celebrations were universally adopted, most spectacularly the cult of Corpus Christi. After a false start in the mid thirteenth century, that mushroomed in the fourteenth, becoming one of the most potent elements in late medieval spirituality.

Although there was a standard liturgical round, this did not produce liturgical uniformity. If the geographical fragmentation of the medieval Latin church is anywhere made explicit, it is in the regional liturgies of the several 'Uses'. These differing formats for what were essentially the same rites began as diocesan arrangements, often enforced in the thirteenth century by synodal legislation. (The reality of that enforcement is often questionable, however: the liturgical possibilities of a cathedral greatly exceeded those of an ordinary parish church, where practicalities must have led to considerable pruning of the ceremonial.) The various regular orders also devised their own liturgical forms, adding both to the confusion and the variety. Greater standardisation did gradually evolve, essentially through a process of 'liturgical imperialism'. Thus, in England, several 'Uses' existed at the start of the thirteenth century – of Sarum (Salisbury), York, Hereford, St Paul's (London), and perhaps others. By 1500 the Sarum Use was dominant, although both York and Hereford retained sufficient vitality to go into print. The Roman liturgy naturally

---

[1] H. Martin, *Le métier de prédicateur en France septentrionale à la fin du moyen âge (1350–1520)* (Paris, 1988), p. 389 n117.

claimed pre-eminence in Italy, but faced resistance. Although the distinctiveness of the rite of Aquileia (near Venice) was constantly being eroded, it retained a hold until the sixteenth century. The variety of Uses, and the relative freedom of choice among them, meant that individual institutions might stand as liturgical islets in a surrounding tradition. The Use of Hereford found an unexpected enclave in Savoy at the collegiate church of St Catherine, Aiguebelle, where it was established by the church's founder Peter of Aigueblanche, then bishop of Hereford, in 1267. Despite the opposition of the bishops of Maurienne, this outpost – increasingly anachronistic and divorced from the Hereford tradition – survived until the late sixteenth century. On a smaller scale, Richard Kyngeston, dean of St George's chapel, Windsor, received permission from Pope John XXIII in 1413 to continue to abide by the Hereford Use even though he held a prebend in Salisbury cathedral, the fountainhead of the Sarum rite. As for the uses of the regular orders, the 'little old mass book . . . of friars' use' which appeared in the inventory of Thomas Kebell, an English lawyer in 1500, may have been used in his private chapel and been destined in his will for the chantry chapel in his local parish church.[2]

The liturgical standardisation which is obvious by the late 1400s could only be assisted by the power of print. Uses left unprinted were effectively condemned to extinction – even those printed depended on market forces for their replication. The standardisation of texts which printing provided was a potent weapon: by 1600 the Roman church had a liturgical standard following the promulgation of the new Roman Breviary (1568) and Missal (1570) as base texts for the whole church.

The feasts and seasons of the Christian calendar were not just dates: they impacted on daily life in dietary and other restrictions – the abstinence from meat on Friday and Lent; a ban on sexual activity at certain seasons (notably during Advent and Lent) or on particular days, prohibitions on trade and labour, the halting of judicial processes. The superaddition of other features gave individual feasts particular greater local significance, whether in payment of rent or the termination of periods of office.

The localism of many commemorations must also be stressed: individual parishes celebrated their own dedication dates; the major offering days might be affected by local customs; local cults claimed their days in the calendar. Religious associations (notably guilds and fraternities) emphasised particular saints and their commemorations. Individuals and groups, even nations, identified patron saints with whom they claimed

[2] E. W. Ives, *The common lawyers of pre-Reformation England* (Cambridge, 1983), pp. 445, 414.

a special relationship, which would be reflected in their increased prominence in devotions.[3]

While liturgy to some extent presupposes ceremony and participants, the laity's status primarily as spectators in most celebrations, especially of the mass, meant that their actual participation was limited. This was compensated for by the evolution of what might be considered a 'private liturgy', most highly developed in Books of Hours. However. these were not universally accessible, and were often more elaborate and demanding than most people would have been able to cope with. The fifteenth-century Franciscan preacher Louis Peresi envisaged a much more basic daily liturgical round which every Christian was bound to undertake, of five recitations of the Our Father in honour of the Five Wounds of Christ, seven *Aves* in honour of the Seven Joys of the Virgin, and one Creed. Failure to do this each morning was to be considered a mortal sin. Similar schemes were proposed by other clerics across the centuries.

Even if they presuppose certain levels of literacy and perhaps social status, the Books of Hours demonstrate the desire for the creation of a personal liturgy which was not necessarily church-centred. The books themselves proliferated from the thirteenth century onwards, and were guaranteed best sellers when versions of the *Horae* went into print. While often lavishly illustrated, as with the several volumes produced for the Duke of Berri in France between 1380 and 1416, their primary function was for prayer. They offered sequences of psalms and prayers, including the Office for the Dead, and various devotions to the Virgin, which could be consulted in private or used to bolster devotions during church services. It was this use of the books which a Venetian envoy to England around 1500 alluded to in an oft-quoted remark about church attendance, with 'any who can read taking the office of Our Lady with them, and with some companion reciting it in church verse by verse in a low voice, after the manner of the religious'.[4]

The Books of Hours clearly encouraged a private devotional tradition; their utility for giving greater formality and a liturgical form to a personal religious life needs no underscoring. As the Venetian envoy hinted, they were a development from the old monastic rounds, reformulated for consumption within the world: an equivalence which sets them alongside *The abbey of the Holy Ghost*, a tract which itself sought to provide a 'monastic' context for lay spirituality. They may also have another feature worth

---

[3] See further below, pp. 145–6, 168–70, 293.

[4] C. A. Sneyd, *A relation, or rather a true account, of the island of England, with sundry particulars of these people and of the royal revenues under king Henry the seventh, about the year 1500*, Camden society publications, 1st ser., 37 (1847), p. 23.

stressing. There is considerable evidence to associate many of these volumes, especially those from the thirteenth century, with women, and so with the creation of a domestic female spirituality.

The private liturgy reflected in Books of Hours was capable of extension by other means, through the development of individual cycles of prayers which did not have to be confined within the liturgical round established by the church. Beyond the threefold standard of the Our Father, Creed, and *Ave*, private prayers proliferated throughout the late medieval period. Sometimes they might be little different from incantations; others (notably those addressed to Christ) were more passionately lyrical. The integration of prayers into personal spiritual lives in a quasi-liturgical manner allowed for the preparation of instructional books and tracts dealing with prayer, the development of what might almost be called an *ars orandi*, an art of praying.

The mass

The most important liturgical celebration was the mass, the re-enactment of Christ's sacrifice in which the consecrated bread and wine became His Body and Blood, made available to his believers. How it fits into a liturgical round is not easily considered, for masses were celebrated with almost mind-boggling regularity and in incalculable quantities, especially with the rise of votive masses and masses for souls. Each parish church was meant to have one mass a day, but local circumstances and the assiduity of the clergy would vary the arrangements. In extensive parishes, dependent chapelries might have masses on only a few days a week; in collegiate churches the priests' masses might be arranged according to a timetable to satisfy demand. Chantries and other institutions for *post mortem* commemoration, not to mention priests simply available for hire by the day, could also increase the daily total. Attitudes reflected in the numerous private masses raise some questions: those for souls clearly fit into the concern for a speedy journey through Purgatory, whilst also reinforcing links between the living and the dead as members of the same body of believers; those for good weather or to deflect the threat of plague may be seen as reflecting a concern to assuage God's displeasure; but masses to recover lost hunting dogs, such as Alfonso V of Aragon had celebrated, seem much more problematic.

Although the words matched, the mass as a priestly celebration is not the same as the mass as communion. The former, particularly when masses were commissioned or endowed for private reasons, falls into its own category of devotion. As communion, the mass became a necessary part of every Christian's liturgical experience when the Fourth Lateran

Council made annual communion (at least) a general obligation. That annual communion normally occurred at Easter, as the climax of the process of confession and penance. By 1300 only the priests received both bread and wine. Lay communion was in one kind only, the Host alone being received, and this remained the case through to the Reformation. There were a few striking exceptions: at their coronations, the Holy Roman Emperor and King of France took communion in both kinds, but only then. Wine might be taken from a chalice, but it was not consecrated wine. Only in the fifteenth century was there a partial return to lay reception in both kinds, as a result of the Utraquist movement among the Hussites of Bohemia. Their insistence on receiving the chalice was recognised but not allowed to spread by the agreement between catholics and Hussites in the *Compactata* of Basle of 1436.

Annual communion probably sufficed for most people. Whether it was the norm is impossible to say. Detailed Flemish evidence on consumption of hosts and payment of offerings has been used to argue for large-scale non-attendance at parish masses and non-reception of communion;[5] but it is hard to evaluate what this actually means in terms of spirituality, or how far that picture is applicable to the rest of catholic Europe. The lack of specific complaint of non-reception elsewhere (and the evidence for close oversight of reception in some visitation returns) suggests that few could have escaped detection as absentees for long. The synodal decrees of Tournai in 1336 certainly did complain that some people throughout the province of Rheims had abstained from confession and communion for ten years and more; on the other hand, at least one proclaimed excommunicate deliberately adopted false identities to deceive priests into giving him communion. Doubtless there was some deliberate non-reception of communion; doubtless detection as an abstainer was more easily avoided in towns than in the countryside. But, ultimately, the scale of the problem – if it was a problem – remains obscure.

If most people would have been content with communicating only once a year, more frequent reception was usually a sign of special devotion. Indeed, several of the female ascetics of Italy, Germany, and the Low Countries developed almost insatiable cravings for frequent communion as part of their eucharistic devotion. But the desire for regular reception need not be so extremist: several of the more notably devout individuals in late medieval England, ranging from Margery Kempe to Lady Margaret Beaufort, were not satisfied with merely annual reception. There were occasionally regional campaigns to increase the

---

[5] J. Toussaert, *Le sentiment religieux en Flandre à la fin du moyen-âge* (Paris, 1963), pp. 128–41, 160–94.

frequency of communion: in late-fourteenth-century Bohemia, the reform movement led by Matthias of Janov was marked by insistence on frequent, even daily, communion. Similar concern for regular reception appears among the thirteenth-century beguines and the later *Devotio moderna*.

For the laity, the mass was usually a spectator event, for all its abundant celebration. Priests performed an essentially private rite addressed to God: the presence of an audience was an accident, although audiences were encouraged. Yet the mass was a public event: although church layout meant that the main parish celebration took place in the chancel, and was therefore somewhat removed from the congregation, celebrations at side altars allowed much greater proximity. There was certainly great popular demand to witness the celebration, to see God present in the Host, even if it was not actually consumed. The desire to see the consecrated elements led in the twelfth century to a widespread development in the ritual, which became standard practice in the thirteenth: the elevation of host and chalice. Immediately after the consecration the priest would raise the transubstantiated blood and wine for adoration. In this brief period, accompanied by the raising of candles and the ringing of the sacring bell, the laity would be in the direct presence of Christ, might therefore perceive and communicate directly with Him. For some this spiritual communion was a major element in their devotions; others had a more mechanistic approach. The elevation soon became a focal point of the mass: people tried to ensure that they were present precisely then, so much so that there are tales of people rushing in and out of churches for the sight, abandoning preachers in mid-sermon when the sacring bell rang and dashing off to see the elevation, even speeding from church to church to see as many elevations as possible. A charitable interpretation would see this as a sign of real adoration of Christ in the Host; more cynically it might be linked to the practice of totting up repetitions of the Paternoster during the elevation as a means of curtailing time in Purgatory.

From the clerical perspective, the laity as spectators had little direct involvement in the process of celebration, even though the enactment itself was a major devotional focus, which provoked a variety of responses.[6] While the priest performed the rites, they simply watched, perhaps reciting their own liturgy of *Aves*, Creeds, and Paternosters, but not as an integral part of the proceedings. The clerical notion that the lay role should be purely passive, and spectative, may not have been matched by lay attitudes. Especially at the communal parish masses, and even where

[6] See further below, pp. 137–42.

there was no communion, the laity may have seen the rites as entailing a more active and inter-active approach, where the celebration was 'less sacrifice and sacrament than a communal rite of greeting, sharing, giving, receiving, and making peace . . . the establishment of social and spiritual solidarity among God, the Church, and the lay community'.[7]

Beyond such considerations, the power of the mass as a force securing divine intervention, and as a means of worship, was keenly appreciated. Here there was an implicit difficulty in human relations with the divinity which the church does not seem to have resolved: how much was God obliged to respond to the celebrations and invocations? The causal efficacity of the mass was often asserted, yet in other circumstances theologians condemned celebrations and actions which tried to tempt God, or seemed to constrain the divinity's freedom of action. Regardless of any such reservations, the hunger for celebrations had many associations. The mass was a semi-magical force: it was a life-preserver; it could evoke miracles; it might secure better weather and good crops. As a world-influencing event, it was keenly encouraged; as a soul-saver after death it was desperately sought. Masses for souls were perhaps the most numerous celebrations in the later middle ages, growing alongside appreciations of Purgatory. The development of votive masses, of masses for special celebrations (of the Five Wounds, of the Holy Name, of the Virgin, of the Holy Spirit, and so on), filled the missals and the churches. It was easily possible to create a liturgical week with different commemorations on each day; or even to concentrate on one particular type of mass. Provision of masses was not just a means of gaining private benefit, but a public benefaction, which itself merited reward from the prayers of those present. The endowment of a mass, while often a search for a private reconciliation with God, was also a means of establishing a memorial.

The consecration and elevation were the focal points of the rite. The presence of Christ was the vital element; the insatiable hunger to see the consecrated elements had its offshoots in other devotional practices: the reservation of the sacrament, and the growth of the eucharistic cult of Corpus Christi. It also had more down-to-earth consequences. Hence the development of timetables for masses in those churches with sufficient priests. Hence the concern in visitation reports when priests failed to say the mass at a regular hour, so that people missed the celebration. Private chapels gave some people the opportunity to privatise the mass: in them hired priests would say masses at convenient times. King Henry VIII

---

[7] V. Reinburg, 'The liturgy and the laity in late medieval and Reformation France', *The sixteenth-century journal*, 23 (1992–3), pp. 532, 542.

of England would not have been alone in witnessing several before breakfast.

Most churches would, necessarily, have to make do with a fairly simple celebration: in this respect the rubrics of service books like the Use of Sarum, based on the requirements and clerical resources of larger cathedral churches, must often have been a dead letter. But as devotion to the mass itself grew in the middle ages, so the arrangements for the celebration became more complex. From the mid fourteenth century there are increasing signs of a movement to increase the 'beauty of holiness' surrounding the service. This applied not merely to the physical surroundings – with many churches being rebuilt and redecorated, from cathedrals to relatively lowly guild and chantry chapels – but to the emotional response evoked by the event. The liturgy itself became richer, with the Sarum missal being almost wholly transformed between 1300 and 1350 in a manner which provoked some of the Wycliffite counter-blast to the elaboration of ceremonies. Even if the words were not altered, there were other opportunities for change. The choreography became more complex; the interpretation of the actions and vestments more precise and esoteric. Above all, there were the opportunities presented by greater use of music, as the development of polyphonic chant added a further layer to the spiritual reactions. To the swirl of incense and the guttering of candles and torches was now added the complexity of the motet. Where voices and funds were available, choirs came into their own, with specially composed celebrations of the mass for important occasions and the development of the anthem. All done to the greater glory of God, this emphasis on the background to the celebration helped focus attention on the priest's actions, so heightening the emotional response to the climax of consecration.

A STRUCTURED LIFE

The potential for a lay religious life

The liturgy gave a framework to religious experience; but non-liturgical activities and extra-liturgical opportunities for the expression of devotion were perhaps equally (if not more) widespread and important. The liturgy ordered time, but it could not provide the format for all of life. Attendance at mass demanded a different commitment from, say, taking a vow of chastity; and many clerics complained about the way the laity ignored everything except the elevation, and generally misbehaved in churches. (Churches were seemingly little appreciated as specifically holy buildings – they might be houses of God, but they were clearly open houses.) For most people religion was but one element – even if important – in life as a whole, something to be fitted in with everything else. For a minority Christianity offered a distinct mode of living, a more formalised code of action and experience to be followed as closely as humanly possible. The concept of 'medieval religious life' almost inevitably conjures up visions of monasteries, nunneries, and friaries, of those formally committed to such regular lives which marked them off from 'ordinary' people. Such visions are too restrictive. Almost by definition any medieval life was religious if it seriously attempted to meet the demands of Christianity and follow the pilgrimage of this world through to its conclusion. Twelfth-century writers such as Gerhoh of Reichersberg (d. 1169) had made this clear in their reactions to the expansion of the *vita apostolica*. Gerhoh proclaimed that

Whoever has renounced at baptism the devil and all his trappings and suggestions, even if that person never becomes a cleric or a monk, has nonetheless definitely renounced the world . . . Whether rich or poor, noble or serf, merchant or peasant, all who are committed to the Christian faith reject everything inimical to this name and embrace everything conformable to it. Every order and absolutely every profession, in the catholic faith and according to apostolic teaching, has a rule adapted to its character; and under this rule it is possible by striving properly to achieve the crown of glory.[8]

The Fourth Lateran Council's formal confirmation that even the married laity might attain salvation merely clarified matters against heretical assertions: it did not of itself mark a major transition.

Just what a regulated Christian life entailed was not precisely defined by 1215, and varying ideas developed thereafter. Yet a crucial point about medieval life – if taken at its widest possible definition – was that a religious element was unavoidable. To separate the religious from the ordinary, to compartmentalise the everyday, imposes a distinction which is often false. Because Christianity provided one of the contexts against which normality was set, that normality was often defined in relation to Christianity as a religion and a set of social practices. Ways of speech, actions, and daily routines, provided a context which integrated Christianity's demands and practices into the normal; so much so that in Sestairol in southern France in the thirteenth century a woman in childbirth was suspected of heresy because she transgressed the cultural norms by invoking the Holy Spirit to ease her labour pains rather than the customary appeal to Christ or the Virgin.

[8] M. D. Chenu, *Nature, man, and society in the twelfth century: essays on new theological perspectives in the Latin west* (Chicago and London, 1968), p. 222.

The search for a tighter definition of 'religious life', as something
beyond the ordinary, had initially been restricted to those prepared to
make the total commitment demanded by monastic regulation. However,
between 1100 and 1250 monasticism's monopoly was shattered. As
Gerhoh of Reichersberg indicated, the concept of 'order' was greatly
expanded, allowing many to assume spiritual commitments previously
unavailable. This produced a major efflorescence of formal and informal
organisations to cater for the expanding demand. The format and
development of these organisations altered over time, but all aimed to
make some degree of spiritual satisfaction almost universally available.
Contemporaries certainly accepted this widening of the definition of a
'religious'. In his *Summa aurea* of *c.* 1255 the great canonist Hostiensis
could state that

> in the wide meaning, a 'religious' is so called who lives holily and religiously in
> his own house, even though not professed . . . such a one is called a 'religious' not
> because he is tied to any specific rule, but on account of his life, which he leads
> more strictly and holily than other secular people.[9]

The key developments between 1100 and 1250, to impose rough
limits, stressed the apostolicity of the Christian life. The search for the *vita
apostolica*, for a re-experiencing of the *vita Christi*, became identified with
a life dominated by two features: poverty and preaching. Even if the
church was cautious about lay preaching, the poverty of renunciation was
acceptable, so that the theme of the sanctified status of apostolic poverty
became almost a commonplace in and after the thirteenth century. 'To
follow, naked, the naked Christ', was almost an obsession with many, of
whom Francis of Assisi and Mary of Oignies (the 'foundress' of the female
beguines) were merely two dramatic examples. Intermittent instances of
people acquiring the stigmata, the marks of Christ's suffering at his
Crucifixion, gave even greater justification to the quest. The desire for full
physical imitation of Christ could reach disconcerting proportions. That
Gerard Segarelli of Parma (eventually burnt as a heretic in 1300) should
attempt a literal re-enactment of Christ's early life – even being swaddled
and suckled, although himself an adult – seems over-dramatic; but such
ambition to re-experience the life of Christ also demonstrated the
extremity of devotion.

The union of poverty and preaching, the redefinition of the apostolic
life which was completed by the early thirteenth century, could only
be enjoyed by a limited number. Few had the determination and

---

[9] P. Biller, 'Words and the medieval notion of "religion"', *Journal of ecclesiastical history*, 36
(1985), p. 358 n24.

commitment to maintain so demanding a life; a life, moreover, which was predicated on a species of élitism. Logistics required that it be restricted to a few, while the many provided the charity from which the perfect poor derived their sustenance. Indeed, the definition of the type of poverty which was perfect was also paradoxical: it required renunciation. Those with nothing to renounce could not be 'perfectly' poor, although their poverty would be meritorious if patiently endured. But if not everyone could be poor, not everyone had to be. The idea of the individual apostolate did not demand the adoption of poverty. Preaching of some sort remained an option, as did the demonstration of a holy life: teaching by example. Christ might therefore be imitated without going to extremes.

The apostolic life, and the imitation of Christ through re-enactment of His physical experiences (something rather different from later ideas of Imitation of Christ, which laid greater stress on emotional participation in His experiences rather than their physical repetition), represented only one of several versions of the religious life as it developed during these centuries. Other options were also available, and were to some extent competitive. From the time of Augustine at the latest there had been regular debate about the relative superiority of the so-called 'active' and 'contemplative' lives. The paradigm for this debate was provided by the sisters Martha and Mary when visited by Christ at Bethany.[10] Martha had busied herself caring about the necessities of life; while Mary let her sister do the work as she sat at Christ's feet. Which was the more commendable? The gospel suggested Mary, the retreat into contemplation; but Martha, and living the Christian life within the reality of the world, surely had some justification?

The tension between Mary and Martha was constant within medieval Christianity. It was initially a tension within the clerical order – between the 'regulars' who withdrew from worldly contact into a life of worship and contemplation, and the 'seculars' who undertook an active ministry, feeding the sheep. Developments between 1100 and 1250, notably the evolution of the Augustinian canons and the rise of the mendicants, altered but did not eliminate this tension among the clerics. There were now disputes between monks and canons about whose was the more perfect form of life; more vitriolic were debates between the mendicants and seculars over the relative merits of their definitions of the active life, with the friars enhancing their claims by their conscious apostolicity and holy poverty.

The debate over the active and contemplative lives also affected the

---

[10] Luke, 10: 38–42.

laity. As opportunities for lay spiritual experience expanded, so there developed the possibility of lay contemplation. The tension between a life in the world – even an avowedly Christian life – and a life dedicated to quiet meditation, even participation in God, was intense. For those who did not want a total renunciation of this world, or were tied to it by unbreakable obligations and responsibilities, the tension had to be reconciled. Accordingly, a compromise was evolved: the mixed life, allowing retention of worldly status and obligations alongside a life of devotional practices, personal retreat, and contemplation, without formal profession or regularisation. This was best defined in the late fourteenth century by the English Augustinian Walter Hilton. He offered advice on achieving spiritual fulfillment without formal withdrawal from the world, requiring his addressee to fulfil his obligations to the world as part of his spiritual quest. For Hilton, to cling to the rewards of contemplation to the detriment of social obligations was actually unChristian, a dereliction of duty to one's fellows.

The laity and the regular orders

While generalisations provide some of the definitions, greater precision is possible. Many versions of late medieval spirituality entailed specific forms of living, which can be described and to some extent assessed. They reflect notions of personal commitment, of social grouping and organisation, of social discipline and control, even of individualism, adding to the kaleidoscope of activities contained within the religious life of the period.

The starting point for any discussion of the regularised life has to be with the religious orders. Here there is room only for a brief consideration, for the very fact of their regular status to some extent shifts the orders outside the main concerns of this book. Their institutionalisation, and their transformation from the twelfth to the sixteenth centuries, demand more detailed treatment than is possible here, and their histories raise questions beyond the scope of the present survey.[11] Yet they cannot be completely ignored, and their limited attention does not imply any invalidation of their spiritualities or their contributions to the religious life of the period.

Until the twelfth century the life of a monk or nun had been almost the only form of regular life available (although it could be undertaken individually, by people wishing to be hermits rather than full monks). The regular life was primarily one for men; opportunities for women

---

[11] Unfortunately, despite a plethora of histories of individual orders and national surveys, no adequate general treatment of the late medieval religious orders is yet available in English.

were limited. The Viking invasions in England and the collapse of the Carolingian empire on the continent had led to the virtual eclipse of female monasticism in Britain and Francia, although nunneries remained relatively numerous – and certainly influential – in tenth-century Germany. The revival of nunneries through a wave of new foundations was especially a feature of the twelfth and thirteenth centuries. The religious transformation of the twelfth century greatly increased the available options for the regular life, as did the rise of the orders of friars in the thirteenth. The changing format of the regular life, with the proliferation of orders providing a range of alternative lifestyles, and for a time the system of *conversi* or lay brethren permitting the unlearned to dedicate themselves to God, widened the scope for membership; the numerous foundations of nunneries, and of double houses of men and women, also specifically enhanced opportunities for women.

The impact of the regulars on religious and devotional life was immense. While they were popular, and recruitment continued over the centuries, their form of religious life put them in a category of their own. (At least, it was meant to: all too frequently in later years there were complaints that the regulars were much too involved in the world.) Yet the orders were intimately connected with religious and devotional practices. Liturgically they were *par excellence* the celebrants of the divine office. They had a major influence outside the walls of their convents, as preachers, by encouraging mysticism and producing devotional writings, in provision of pastoral care, and so on. The regulars affected various strands of contemporary piety: their houses sheltered pilgrims, offered charity, served as mausolea and the sites of chantries; their members became saints and confessors, encouraged cults, and offered religious and devotional instruction. This applied universally, regardless of which order was concerned.

The overlaps between lay and regular experience are often noticeable. Only in the twelfth century was monasticism thoroughly clericalised, in the sense that monks and canons regular would be expected to become priests. The tradition of laypeople joining religious orders at the point of death lingered on, although not as obviously as in the twelfth century. In later centuries it is perhaps most noticeable in connection with the friars and related orders. King Robert of Naples (d. 1343) thus became a Franciscan in his final days; his Queen Sanchia was associated with the Clarisses from 1317, being finally allowed to retreat to a convent after her husband's death. Others simply required burial in a habit as a sign of confraternity, as did Sir John Meaux of Yorkshire in 1377. Monasteries and nunneries were also places of fairly regular retreat (if that is the right word) by laity. Members of religious orders addressed writings to lay

people. The fifteenth-century Carthusians were particularly notable for
the dissemination of spiritual tracts and encouragement of translation.
Nicholas Love, prior of Mount Grace in Yorkshire, produced one of
the most significant religious texts of late medieval England, the *Mirror of
the blessed life of Jesus Christ*, derived from the *Meditationes vitae Christi*
which were falsely ascribed to St Bonaventure. The concern to make texts
widely available is shown in the production of Latin versions of works by
Richard Rolle and Walter Hilton, intended for continental distribution.

It is as representatives of devotional movements, as foci and locations
for pious works, that the religious orders, their houses and members, fit in
here, rather than as a specific form of the religious life. The regular life of
monks, canons, friars and nuns, with their vowed commitment to
poverty, chastity, and obedience, was the formal model for all forms of
religious life; but it was the unvowed religious life, or one which did not
demand the full triple vow, which was the more widespread. The
required distinction is not a crude one between laity and clergy, but
between ordered and unordered. Monasticism and mendicancy did not
demand priesthood: although he respected priests highly, St Francis had
been avowedly lay and egalitarian in his vision, and never received priestly
ordination (although he did become a deacon, one rank lower than priest
in the hierarchy of orders). The clericalisation of monasticism was part of
the changes of the twelfth and thirteenth centuries, confirmed by the
virtual disappearance of lay brethren (*conversi*) in most orders by 1330. (It
was not total: there were still some even in the sixteenth century.) By
1300 the friars were also equated with priesthood. Even so, before their
ordinations friars, monks, and canons were laymen; the fighting members
of the military orders were always laymen (the Prior of the Order of St
John in England accordingly sat in the House of Lords as a lay peer).
Nuns, as women, could not become priests. For all these groups, their
formal commitment to a shared and regulated life separates them from the
other laity and the secular clergy. However, it is those others, outside
the formal orders, who demand most attention here.

Quasi-regular lay movements

Alongside the flourishing of the fully regular orders, several lay groups had
also developed a structured religious life by the late twelfth century,
establishing a thread which lasted throughout the period. The main
exponents of the trend were the Humiliati in Italy, and the men and
women established as beguines and beghards in Germany and the Low
Countries. The former provide the best outline of the structures.
Although originally pushed outside the church for rejecting papal

authority, they were reconciled by Pope Innocent III in 1201 and reintegrated into the church in three gradations. Their first order consisted of clerical men, fully bound to a regular life. Then came the second order, of women living in their own communities as regulars. Finally, as the group which demands most emphasis here, there was the third order, or tertiaries. This consisted of lay people not formally bound by vow but living under a voluntary rule either in groups or in their own houses, recognising and submitting to some form of association. They adopted a form of voluntary poverty which obliged them to live from their own labours, usually within the textile industry, but which by no means reduced them to indigence. Such a life of restraint rather than complete renunciation allowed for membership from a wide cross-section of society. Widespread in north Italy, the tertiaries were allowed to continue their tradition of preaching – although with limitations – and so supplemented the activities of the local clergy.

The beguines of the Netherlands and western Germany followed similar lives. Here, the main concern is with the women: the men, the beghards, had a rather different organisation, perhaps more akin to the unenclosed hermits to be considered later, and seem to have developed more erratically. Nevertheless, some beghards were stabilised in their own houses, although this seems to have happened later than with the beguines and affected fewer people. In Basle, for instance, there were only two beghard houses; while the five at Mainz contained only thirty men in the mid fifteenth century. Several of the beghard houses in the Low Countries later adopted the rule of the Franciscan tertiaries, a status increasingly formalised in the fifteenth century.

The first beguine groups appeared towards the end of the twelfth century, adopting a life of voluntary renunciation and prayer. They burst into view with the striking personality of Mary of Oignies (d. 1213), as part of the penitential movement of the time; but their origins went back farther into the twelfth century. Although scholarly attention focuses on their development in the Netherlands and the Rhineland, they exemplified a spiritual trend across Europe. Similar pious women are also attested in Italy, there known as *bizoca*, and in Iberia.

The beguines did not embrace total 'apostolic' poverty, but maintained a subsistence economy, some of them being supported from rents and pensions, others from begging and self-employment. Some of them lived alone, others in groups sharing a house and generally categorised as 'convent' beguinages even though not formally affiliated to a regular order nor bound by permanent vows. The Low Countries saw a specific further development of '*curtis*' beguinages, containing from twenty to several hundred inhabitants, which was a much more elaborate institution and 'a virtual women's town'.[12] It was these which in due course became separate ecclesiastical parishes, a change which helped to establish their 'regular' credentials. The beguines' religious life was one of simplicity, prayer, and contemplation; but despite close similarities (including the recitation of psalters for the souls of the dead) it was not the life of a nun. For many women the years in a beguinage were only a phase in their lives: the vows bound only so long as an individual wished to remain bound; there was no stain of apostasy for anyone who left. Many therefore became beguines only for a while, eventually leaving to marry. The spiritual motivation for assuming the life was often pre-eminent, and it was to them that the cult of Corpus Christi mainly owed its origins. The movement's spread may also have owed something to the problem of surplus women in the population in the thirteenth century: beguinages, rather like twelfth-century nunneries, were a relatively cheap way of relieving the problem. Given the spiritual focus, many beguines did eventually move into the fully regular life. Mechtild of Magdeburg (d. 1282–97), writer of the mystical *Flowing light of the Godhead*, moved in her old age from the Magdeburg beguinage to the nunnery of Helfta, itself a hothouse of mystical devotion. Whole houses might change their vocations: two at Metz transformed in the thirteenth century, one becoming Dominican, the other Augustinian.

The beguines spread rapidly, although precise numbers are rarely available. They were a notable presence in Cologne by 1250, sufficiently so to be mentioned in English chronicles. Elsewhere, their presence at Metz may be hidden under the appellation of '*vaudoise*' – a label which might otherwise suggest Waldensian heretics, in itself a striking reflection on perceptions of their way of life. The 'ripple effect' of a new movement is well-shown by the chronology of foundations, where the peak period moves up the Rhine in a discernable flow. At Cologne and Mainz this occurred before 1300; but in Basle was delayed until *c.* 1350–60. As the life's attraction declined, so the ripple went into reverse. Houses were still being founded at Cologne at the end of the fifteenth century, when there were 169 for about 1,500 beguines within the city. At Mainz there were also continued foundations into the sixteenth century; but elsewhere the situation was less lively. The houses in Strasbourg declined fairly consistently after 1415. Those in Basle were dramatically extinguished by episcopal decree in 1411; as the last foundation had been in 1388 the

---

[12] J. E. Ziegler, *Sculpture of compassion: the Pietà and the beguines in the southern Low Countries, c. 1300–c. 1600*, Institut historique belge de Rome, études d'histoire de l'art/Belgisch historisch Instituut te Rome, Studies over Kunstgeschiedenis, 6 (Brussels and Rome, 1992), p. 72.

movement may already have passed its peak. The beguines continued in the Netherlands, although there increasingly regulated by urban authorities as the establishments merged into hospitals.

The main difficulty with the beguinages was one of status. The ambiguity of the beguines' position – neither fully regular not straightforwardly lay – made the church's response uncertain: although they had powerful advocates like Jacques de Vitry, they also had detractors. Beyond the institutional uncertainty there was the issue of sex. Women together, driven only by their own religious aspirations, were perplexing. Any group of laity seeking spiritual consolation from their own resources, outside the formal structures of the church, raised the spectre of deviation. There were signs of this with the beguines in the late thirteenth century. These were partly due to assimilation to the tertiaries of the mendicant orders, especially the Franciscans, who in southern France were also called beguins (without an 'e'). The question of their response to their own meditations (one encountered with all introspective and contemplative groups) also played a significant part. The contemplation of Christ, the losing of the self in Him through a process of abnegation which was the ultimate attainment of contemplative devotion, carried with it the danger of misperception: that the loss of the self in Christ produced complete identification with the Godhead and liberation from the effects of sin; that the freed spirit was so liberated that it became incapable of sin. This 'heresy of the Free Spirit' was felt to encourage libertinism and misrepresent the relationship between Man and God. Doubtless some among the beguines and other religious groups did fall into its trap; others were perceived to have fallen, although whether there was anything which could be called a Free Spirit sect remains debated. Marguerite Porete, writer of *The mirror of simple souls*, was a beguine; the accusations of Free Spirit heresy against her in 1310 were framed in terms supposedly extracted from her book. The linkage made between Free Spirit heresy and the beguines in the late thirteenth and early fourteenth centuries, even if the heresy was largely a figment of the accusers' imaginations, led to a campaign against both beguines and beghards, until in 1318 Pope John XXII recognised the need to offer protection to those who had not fallen into error. After these tempestuous experiences came something of a lull, until a further wave of persecution erupted in the later fourteenth century. By then the main beguine moment may have passed, with alternative ways to gain spiritual satisfaction gradually proving more attractive.

The crisis over the beguines in the fourteenth century highlighted the issue of control over groups outside the church's normal structure. Their reintegration was therefore vitally important. Pope Innocent III had

succeeded with the Humiliati; the response to the beguines was slightly
different. Making the beguinages separate parishes was one answer,
creating an administrative system in which priests retained some
disciplinary control. Attempts were also made to ensure control by
subjecting the houses to the Cistercians and the mendicants; but none of
the male orders actively sought the responsibility, and tried to slough it
off. The demand for Cistercian and Dominican oversight also reflected
the spirituality which the beguines themselves wanted – just as many
nunneries had earlier desired links with the Cistercian Order when they
adopted its practices, but had their advances rejected. Some houses did
formally change their status, and were absorbed into a proper order.
Others did not go quite so far, becoming 'tertiaries' of the mendicant
orders.[13] Thus the community associated with St Agnes at Tongeren
(Holland), founded in 1418, was permitted to adopt the rule of the
Franciscan tertiaries in 1438. They were then placed under the oversight
of the male beghards of Zepperen, who were likewise Franciscan
tertiaries. Such changes were not always beneficial: in the Rhineland
association with the Franciscans dragged the beguines and beghards into
the conflicts between the mendicants and the secular clergy.

Movement from an amorphous lay status to formal integration with a
regular order was not limited to the beguines. In Italy, similar households
of women joined the Clarisses, although this was not always done
without opposition to the change. In 1406–7, for instance, Bernardina
Sedazzari established the house of Corpus Domini in Ferrara, living under
a vaguely Augustinian regime but without vows. This was maintained
even after her death, until 1431 when something like to an internal coup
secured the house for the Clarisses. (An earlier attempt to enforce the
Augustinian status had been foiled, with those defeated departing to
establish a nunnery of their own.)

Similar transformations occurred in the second major devotional
movement which arose in the Netherlands, that of the Brethren and
Sisters of the Common Life. They were a major impetus behind the
spiritual trend identified as the *devotio moderna*, which had wide-ranging
impact. It emerged in the late fourteenth century, under the inspiration
of Geert Groote of Deventer (d. 1384). He was himself a cleric, a
Carthusian, but secured a widespread following for his reformist
preaching. His followers adopted a common life of prayer and meditation
based on renunciation and a quasi-monastic office, supported by their
own labours. The sisters were obviously lay; the men seem to have been
mainly priests and prospective priests. They were at first attacked precisely

---

[13] For tertiaries, see p. 113–14.

as beguines and beghards, but their association of houses soon grew, centring mainly on the northern Netherlands but extending to Rostock and Cologne. Pressures for regularisation were strong. As early as 1386, some of the men formally adopted the status of Augustinian canons at Windesheim. (This generated a major reformist force among the Augustinian canons of north Germany, which was an inspiration for much of the re-purifying 'Observant' movement in that and other orders.) While the original common life was maintained in some houses, the attractions of a formally vowed and regular life often proved irresistible. Both males and females adopted the status of Franciscan tertiaries; in due course several of those houses changed again by formally assuming the Augustinian rule and canonical status.

Most of these lay movements were inspired by the penitential trend which developed in spirituality from the late twelfth century. The Italian strand which emerged as the mendicant tertiaries gradually expanded its influence over much of continental Europe, but seemingly never penetrated the British Isles, despite the existence of some English versions of their rules. The earliest groups, whose programme is reflected in a series of regulations given papal approval in 1221, were from the same background as Francis and his first disciples. Indeed, the first Franciscans should be seen as penitents as much as mendicants. Unlike the mendicant orders, the penitential movements retained a fully lay status. The Franciscans' and Dominicans' penitential mission stimulated the further foundation of brother- and sisterhoods dedicated to penitential good works, whose members eventually ordered their lives by versions of the two mendicant rules (and, later, that of the Augustinians). As, technically, the friars refused formal ownership of real property as incompatible with their apostolic poverty, and needed an arrangement whereby others administered the possessions on their behalf, this may also have stimulated such associations, although that was often done through more formally established fraternities. The growth of the lay penitential groups was largely spontaneous, not explicitly connected to the mendicant structures. Although an 'Order of Penitents of St Francis' existed in the mid thirteenth century, the institutionalisation of a lay penitential movement as the third branch of officially-recognised mendicancy only really began with the promulgation of a bull of Pope Nicholas IV in 1289. The structured pattern of mendicancy thus proposed in the late thirteenth century was very similar to that of the Humiliati: the first order of male clerics, the second of nuns (the Dominican sisters, and the Clarisses for the Franciscans), and a third lay movement (the 'tertiaries').

The tertiary life essentially involved the adoption of a religious round based on the divine office or recitations of the Paternoster and Ave, and an attempt to meet the charitable and penitential demands of Christianity. To some extent the tertiary groups merge into the fraternities and guilds which were so ubiquitous an aspect of contemporary life; but they merit some emphasis, their function being primarily to define a way of life rather than encourage particular religious and devotional practices. Requiring a more formal vow than many other associations, their 'regular' status was more assured. Their chief motivation was the fulfillment of the Seven Corporal Acts of Mercy; the tertiaries therefore appear providing hospitals, arranging for burials, caring for the poor, and overseeing charitable activities which were not limited to their own members (this perhaps being the main difference between them and some of the other associations). They clearly provided a means for individuals to achieve some, but probably not all, of their spiritual aspirations, and were a vital element in religious life. They also provided a model which, as in the case of the beguines, could be imposed to ensure conformity with the demands of the established church. However, tertiary status was sometimes no less problematic than that of the beguines. Tertiaries adopted a more formal commitment than most other laity, but remained non-regular. The Franciscan tertiaries showed particular concern with adherence to apostolic poverty. In southern France, it was they who provided the backbone of the beguin movement condemned for heresy because of its attachment to apostolic poverty and the writings of Peter John Olivi (d. 1298), a writer whose apocalypticism and assertions of the Christ-like status and authority of Francis and his Rule posed a significant challenge to the contemporary church. In the Rhineland, the tertiaries were sometimes accused of the Free Spirit heresy.

Finally, beyond these fairly institutionalised arrangements, it was also possible for people to commit themselves solely as individuals. Indeed, the development of the third orders and other groups ought perhaps to be seen as emerging from a former stage of personal commitment. Although *conversi* are primarily associated with the reformed religious orders of the twelfth century, notably the Cistercians and Carthusians, the status of *conversus* could be assumed in other ways, as a statement of individual commitment and association. That status seems to have lingered longest, at least under that name, in northern Italy, although its occurrence perhaps declined after the thirteenth century. Individuals, or couples, would donate themselves and their possessions to an institution to receive the spiritual and practical benefits of association, and adopted a quasi-regular status in consequence of that link. In northern Europe people in this position seem to be encountered less frequently, although the title of *conversus* was applied to those living on alms in English monasteries from the late thirteenth century, as a new type of 'lay brother'. Perhaps the

Italian *conversi* can be more strictly paralleled to some of the corrodians associated with northern religious institutions, who similarly gave at least their possessions, or substantial donations, in return for something like pensionary status within the house. The extent to which such people were subjected to the institution's religious regime is, however, generally unknown.

The nature of the commitment undertaken by the Italian *conversi* does, however, raise questions about their motivations. Association with the institutions and the adoption of a form of clerical status also conveyed the temporal privileges of that status. The immunity from prosecution and from the demands of communal citizenship was for some undoubtedly more attractive than the spiritual rewards. Communes and prelates sought to limit such exploitation of status for the wrong reasons: in the early fourteenth century, Enrico del Carretto, as bishop of Lucca, issued synodal statutes against

Conversos and *conversas* . . . who remain as before in their houses and concerned with secular business and duties, even though they offer themselves and their possessions to God and the churches with their lips. This, however, they do solely so that when they offend they may elude the punishment, and to evade the burdens of the Luccan commune, both real and personal.

He also instructed religious institutions not to receive as *conversi* 'any man or woman . . . who is burdensome or useless or who is not of good reputation, or who is in fraud of the Luccan commune or of any community of the Luccan district, or . . . who is obligated in any lawsuit', including among these those 'who, remaining in their houses just as before, do not properly wear the habit of a *conversus*, or who immerse themselves in secular business and affairs just as before'.[14]

Their adherence to poverty beyond the confines of a formal rule perhaps proved the undoing of many of these lay movements. The validity of their way of life was fundamentally questioned in the fifteenth century. The very existence of such 'sturdy beggars' came under review. By then, too, perhaps little distinction was being made between the various types of lay life. In 1400 at Basle the Franciscan friar Rudolf Buchssmann wrote 'in defence of lollards, beghards and beguines living as much within the third order of St Francis as without, to the effect that they are allowed to provide for themselves by begging, even though they might be sturdy laypeople and capable of working with their hands'.[15] His

---

[14] R. Manselli, 'La sinodo lucchese di Enrico del Carretto', in *Miscellanea Gilles Gérard Meersseman, Italia sacra*, 15–16 (2 vols., Padua, 1970), I, pp. 220–1.

[15] J.-C. Schmitt, *Mort d'une hérésie: l'Église et les clercs face aux béguines et aux béghards du Rhin supérieur du XIVe au XVe siècle* (Paris, 1978), p. 206.

argument was vigorously refuted by a Dominican in 1405, on the grounds that these groups were not bound by a formal rule, although the regular mendicant structures were justified. (Such arguments against continental 'lollards' are strikingly similar to those used against the mendicant orders by English Wycliffites.) The bluntest rejection of lay mendicancy came in 1449, in the canonist Felix Hemmerlin's glosses to Eugenius IV's bull of 1431 which reaffirmed the distinction between orthodox and heretical beguines and beghards. Hemmerlin denied any validity to the beguine and similar movements because of the incompatibility between their claims to apostolic poverty and their lay status. Whether such polemical challenges affected recruitment cannot be tested; increasing unease with the presence of 'sturdy beggars' and a move away from indiscriminate charity may have been more significant.

Guilds and fraternities

Movements such as the beguines and the mendicant tertiaries stand out because of their claims to quasi-regular status. The most ubiquitous religious organisations of the period, the devotional and charitable associations known as guilds or fraternities (or by other localised names, as with the *scuole* of north-east Italy), were similar to them in some ways – especially to the tertiaries – but were not identical. As 'the most characteristic expressions of late medieval Christianity',[16] it is difficult to deal with them summarily. The simple term, 'fraternity', applies to such a variety of forms and functions that it loses meaning: the individual organisations need to be categorised, their functions dissected. But even doing that is perplexing, for the functions of these ritual brotherhoods (and sisterhoods, although most of the evidence concerns male groups) evolved and varied over time. Very little was needed to create a fraternity: a decision to pray together, and perhaps hire a priest once a year, would be enough. Yet some fraternities grew into extensive organisations; several in England, like the Palmers' Guild of Ludlow, had nationwide membership. Their wealth and prestige also made them important features of local social and administrative identities. In Venice the leading associations, the *Scuole grandi*, were closely supervised by the government, and made a significant contribution to the city's pageantry.

A major problem in assessing the fraternities lies in finding an acceptable definition for them. To cover them all may require something as wide as 'a voluntary association of people who come together under the guidance of certain rules to promote their religious life in

---

[16] J. Bossy, *Christianity in the west, 1400–1700* (Oxford, 1985), p. 58.

common';[17] but that needs the immediate qualification that it excludes members of the regular orders, membership of which was, after all, voluntary. The terms for them across Europe varied greatly, with the danger of using a label which gives the wrong impression. Some commentators seek to differentiate between 'fraternity' and 'confraternity', applying the latter only to the way in which religious orders and institutions shared the spiritual benefits they could confer with lay (and clerical) supporters.[18] Some associations with dispersed membership might be considered more as 'prayer unions': 'inter-regional institutions whose members would not know each other, or would know of each other only by name, unless they lived in the same town'.[19] That limitation can perhaps be applied to the 'confraternities' of St Ursula at Strasbourg, Tulln, and Braunau, which were exclusively prayer-based and whose 'membership fee' was the simple recitation of three Our Fathers and three *Aves*. The inter-regionalism and lack of knowledge among the membership would also apply to the Ludlow Palmers' Guild, but the membership fee for that had to be paid in cash.

The cash element may be what distinguishes the fraternity proper from the prayer-union, but dogmatism is inappropriate. The fraternities which were not inter-regional existed primarily for mutual support. When not assuming other responsibilities, their main concern was with reciprocal benefits, usually provision of a reasonable funeral and guaranteed *post mortem* remembrance. This was the common characteristic of groups from England through to Germany, Italy, and Spain. Some fraternities, such as that of St Jacques at Apt, or the guild of harness-makers and painters at

---

[17] C. F. Black, *Italian confraternities in the sixteenth century* (Cambridge, 1989), p. 1. The definition as 'voluntary groups of laymen who met together at regular intervals to do pious and charitable works in honour of a patron saint' (J. Henderson, 'Piety and charity in late medieval Florence: religious confraternities from the middle of the 13th century to the late 15th', unpublished PhD thesis, University of London, 1983, p. 2, cited and adopted as a working definition in R. MacKenney, *Tradesmen and traders: the world of the guilds in Venice and Europe, c. 1250–c. 1650* (London and Sydney, 1987), p. 44) has the advantage of stressing the role of works, but the disadvantage of asserting exclusively lay (and perhaps male) membership. The insistence on a patron saint would seem to exclude groups with more 'mystical' affiliations, like those for the Souls in Purgatory at Avignon, or of the Five Wounds at Geneva.

[18] C. M. Barron, 'The parish fraternities of medieval London', in *The church in pre-Reformation society*, ed. C. M. Barron and C. Harper-Bill (Woodbridge, Suffolk, 1985), pp. 17–18.

[19] A. Schnyder, 'Unions de prière patronnées par sainte Ursule en Allemagne du sud à la fin du XVe siècle', in *Le mouvement confraternel au moyen âge, France, Italie, Suisse: Actes de la table ronde organisée par l'Université de Lausanne avec le concours de l'École française de Rome et de l'Unité associée 1011 du CNRS 'L'institution ecclésiale à la fin du moyen âge', Lausanne 9–11 mai 1985*, Collection de l'École française de Rome, 97 (Rome, 1987), p. 264.

Barcelona, even had their own burial vault. However, while the funerary provision may have been the basic function, and remained so in many cases, that was not necessarily exclusively the case. In many respects parochial life was meant to reflect the ideals of fraternity, and it was as a fraternity that the parish was meant to operate, through officials like the churchwardens. This parochial fraternalism is often obscured, but is shown in the way in which the inhabitants of the Staffordshire chapelry of Keele organised the administration of their chapel via a guild comprising all the households, which paid for the provision and maintenance of the chaplain. Similarly, in some Italian *pieve* through to the fifteenth century, the parish priest was elected by the parishioners rather than being appointed by a patron. The election of parish officials maintained the relic of the old concept of the lay fraternity within the parish; but further fraternities, within and transcending the parishes, also had a part to play.

The extent to which fraternities created a religious life is hard to assess. In part it would depend on the relative strength of the parish as a religious unit. Italian urban fraternities may have effectively supplanted the parish as the basic ecclesiastical force by the fifteenth century; although evidence from Venice to Florence suggests that this was a lengthy evolution, in which originally the fraternities had tended to reinforce and augment parish identity. In Spain the *hermandades* also apparently held aloof from the parish. The small parish associations maintaining a light in honour of a particular saint clearly had a devotional significance; so did those which maintained whole chapels. The fraternities linked with specific devotions, such as those associated with Corpus Christi, were equally responses to evolutions in spirituality. The multiplicity of fraternities within one place is also striking: Geneva listed thirty-eight in 1487, Florence had at least a hundred in the later fifteenth century, while in England Great Yarmouth had around eighteen in the century before the Reformation. This is significant. While some guilds may have restricted their membership, there must often have been some choice about which any particular person would join. Multiple fraternity membership was not uncommon, sometimes, as for several Londoners, of guilds scattered over a fairly wide area.

The demands and impositions of membership obviously varied: a member of the guild of Boston who resided in London could not be a very active member. Indeed, the distances beyond which membership became purely nominal are likely to have been quite small: the guild at Knowle (a small town in Warwickshire) had a scattered and wide-ranging membership including royalty and nobility, as well as several prelates who, as in their links with other guilds, were obviously honorary members.

Most members came from the surrounding countryside, where even ten miles might make a real difference between active and inactive involvement. Where membership was bought for the dead to earn participation in the guild suffrages and *post mortem* indulgences, clearly it was purely nominal.

For those who did more than pay their subscription and actually attended services and other events, membership made greater demands. Fraternities often had strict regulations about attending meetings and maintaining moral standards, the ultimate sanction being expulsion. Their primarily spiritual objective could take many forms; their charitable activities, as a means to good works, were by definition also spiritual. Those charitable fraternities which were joined mainly by wealthier members of society were thus part of the process of reconciling wealth with the demands of Christianity. The returns to the great English inquest into guilds in 1389 mention fairly frequent gatherings for prayers, attendance at funerals, meals, and suchlike. The benefit-society or funeral club element was to the fore. Many fraternities may have experienced a somewhat cyclical history of rise, decline, and reincarnation: if outgoings exceeded income, the association would simply fold up, or change its rules and its religious functions. Change might equally happen if the association became very wealthy. Social fashion might also affect membership, particularly when a choice of fraternities was available: if one was apparently in decline, it would no longer attract new members. Generally, an important factor was the evolutionary pressures affecting the fraternities, both in their membership (particularly changing ratios between the sexes) and in their social and spiritual roles.

In the typology of fraternities, the Italian experience is perhaps most revealing, offering a clear distinction between the categories. The charitable and primarily devotional associations (*misericordia*) constitute one type, and perhaps fit the pattern most commonly encountered elsewhere in Europe. Two other formats are more distinctive.

The more public manifestation was in the groups of *laudesi*, which sprang up from the middle of the thirteenth century and can be associated with the burgeoning of 'mendicant' spirituality. Their function was primarily devotional, in the public singing of praises to the saints, especially to the Virgin. The social range of their membership varied: at San Sepolcro, in the upper Tiber valley, the Confraternity of Santa Maria della Notte consisted mainly of agriculturalists, who according to later tradition sang their *laudes* on their way to the fields in the morning.

Markedly different, and more private, were the groups of *disciplinati*, penitential associations which were founded mainly in the years after the Black Death. These groups were usually smaller than the *laudesi*, although some of the large Venetian *scuole grandi* contained *disciplinati*. As penitential groups they were characterised by a Passion-centred devotion which manifested itself in flagellation. This was not the violently extrovert flagellation of some of the more hysterical religious movements of the period, but a more controlled – indeed at times almost token – beating, usually performed in the fraternity's own quarters.

These *disciplinati* were marked by the confessional and moralistic nature of their obligations. Their penitential regime, with its insistence on confession to the fraternity's leader, can be viewed as directly challenging priestly cure over souls. It is unclear whether that situation was appreciated in quite those terms, by either priests or brethren. There is certainly no sign of the *disciplinati* being anti-ecclesial, or anti-sacerdotal: many of the companies established chapels within their parish churches, and so explicitly announced their acceptance of and integration with their surroundings.

The fraternities' development beyond their spiritual roles was important, for many groups which became major social forces can be tied to the fraternity movement. Thus, the urban craft guilds originated as religious associations, bringing together members of one trade to commemorate a saint and worship at a particular church. As convenient organisations onto which other responsibilities could be grafted, their 'craft' associations were expanded, with regulations concerning manufacturing and trade being foisted on them which obscure but cannot totally obliterate the underlying religious fraternity. Admittedly, the religious side of things may also have declined in significance. Certainly the creation of a 'religious fraternity' might be considered a socially divisive action, its members disguising an economic pressure group as a spiritual association. But the potential for diversion existed in other circumstances as well. In many towns (in England, York, Norwich, and Coventry spring immediately to mind) identification as a member of the urban élite was linked to membership of particular guilds; and rivalry between fraternities might reflect partisan divisions within the city government. Participation in processions such as those of Venice, or the English Corpus Christi parades, was also a public statement of status; while in many Italian towns the most sumptuous and impressive funerals were those organised by the fraternities, as they were exempt from communal sumptuary regulations on such matters. Although fraternities often transcended parochial boundaries in Italian towns like Venice and Florence, elsewhere they gave a basis for local loyalties and partisan actions which affected the development of communal institutions and provided a machinery through which patronage could operate. Partisanship also inspired some of the belligerently 'anti-heretical' associations of thirteenth-century Italian towns. There the quarrels between the Guelphs and the Ghibellines (respectively, if nominally, supporters of the papal and imperial sides in the long-running Italian wars) could be portrayed as a sort of crusade, with individuals flocking to the banner of the Church in danger.

The complexities which embroiled the fraternities in the contemporary world were not always extreme. The simple desire to forge connections – perhaps primarily in trade – or the wish to retain links with a region after moving away, also played a part. Fraternity membership could be important in establishing or maintaining an identity – perhaps especially in late medieval towns dependent on constant immigration which deprived incomers of their old securities. 'Outsiders' in a society certainly did establish their own associations, like that of the Hanseatics in London, or the Slav confraternity set up in Venice in 1451. In Toledo, the *conversos* reinforced their identity in a fraternity, until tensions between it and a fraternity of Old Christians became so intense that the two were amalgamated by royal decree in 1465.

One aspect of the fraternities requires emphasis. Several positively encouraged passive membership by selling indulgences. Some of the great associations in pre-Reformation England owed their nominal size to such sales, which inflated the inactive membership while concentrating funds for the fraternity's religious activities. The importance of the indulgences to the members is hard to assess: with the Boston guild, the extensive privileges which were acquired (over £3000 was spent on obtaining the indulgence from Rome in the early sixteenth century) were almost certainly important; but the mere hundred days offered by Knowle to distant donors (visitors received rather more) seems insufficient to account for more than a fraction of that guild's large membership, unless the habit of collecting indulgences extended to collecting guild memberships for precisely that reason.

It is impossible to test the impact that membership of any particular fraternity – or fraternities – had on any individual's daily religious life. The most direct influence was probably in social matters, in instilling and encouraging a spirit of charity and solidarity. The guilds' moralistic regulations may have had an effect; there were some expulsions for breaches of them. At the other extreme, the fraternities served to fund and administer almshouses, provide education, pay pensions, provide a primitive form of social security, and other good works. Often these benefits were directed solely to fellow members of the particular fraternity, but in some areas – notably Italy – they developed into assistance groups for the poor in general, maintaining hospitals and arranging burials. Such activities may have sought to assuage the guilt of wealth surrounded by poverty; as attempts to fulfil the Seven Corporal Acts of Mercy they were not to be decried. However, the scale of the social assistance should not be exaggerated: the aim was not to provide a primitive welfare state, except perhaps for some of their own members. The amount spent on candles almost invariably exceeded the sums paid in formal charity. Nevertheless, the wide range of connections and opportunities provided by fraternity membership could undermine the religious and spiritual element. For instance, those which were generous charitable institutions might easily be undermined by exploitative members. In 1492 the Scuola della Carità of Venice complained of the 'many men who enter this our Scuola neither from devotion nor to serve our Holy Lady Mary: they wish to live off the property of our Scuola . . . contrary to charity'.[20] The loyalties, identity, and spiritual independence which fraternities encouraged also affected reactions to them. Uncertainty, even distrust, appears in the reaction of Nicholas of Cusa during his legatine visitation of Germany in 1451, with his assertion that such associations 'do not contribute to Christian unity and do not produce the fruits which have been promised of them'.[21]

Domestic regularity

While much of religious life was conducted in the semi-public spheres of church and fraternity, the individual household itself could provide a forum for religious action. Here the evidence and its interpretation become more uncertain: there is a lot for some households, in certain social classes; but not much, or none at all, for most people. How far can what is known be extended to those unknown? Are particular households known precisely because they were extraordinary, and are invalid bases for generalisation? This, of course, depends on the type of evidence. That ranges from account books like those of the Willoughby family of Sutton Coldfield, which survive from the early sixteenth century, to correspondence like the thousands of letters left by Francesco Datini of Prato (d. 1410). Some evidence is impersonal, other material more subjective and questionable (the latter perhaps including material in funeral sermons, where individual achievements are likely to be overstated and the negative overlooked).

Consideration of the household rarely focuses on the nuclear family (if

---

[20] B. R. Pullan, *Rich and poor in Renaissance Venice: the social institutions of a catholic state* (Oxford, 1971), p. 78.
[21] D. Sullivan, 'Nicholas of Cusa as reformer: the papal legation to the Germanies, 1451–1452', *Mediaeval studies*, 36 (1974), p. 399.

that was a potent force), but on the upper levels of society with their servants and domestic organisations. The household thus becomes a rather large unit, one which might well need a private chapel to accommodate all its members. Some institutions, such as hospitals, were themselves little more than households under another name, and with more precise rules. The late medieval household is best seen as a private assembly comprising a core family and its dependents – especially the living-in servants. Size could vary greatly, contrasting the arrangements of an earl of Northumberland with the small-scale organisation revealed by occasional family rules.

The relationship between the family or household and the ecclesiastical establishment is occasionally problematic. One suggested trend in late medieval England is the increasing alienation of the upper levels of society from parish life, suggesting that the church was not ministering to such people at an appropriate intellectual level. However, this is debatable. Much of the evidence – including the proliferation of private chapels, and personal possession of books of devotion – is not specifically late-medieval: private chapels were widely distributed in England by the mid fourteenth century. Moreover, the claim that the gentry were retreating from parish life must face the fact that this supposed withdrawal coincides with two trends asserting gentry territorial domination of the parish church: the creation of the family pew, and the proliferation of massive tomb sculptures and other marks of 'ownership' in ecclesiastical decoration (stained glass windows, coats of arms on sculptures, heraldry on vestments, for instance). Rather than withdrawing from the parishes, the gentry were asserting control and domination, a domination shared with those lower down the social ladder who claimed authority as churchwardens, and in turn occupied space with pews, brasses, and other monuments. Similar processes of appropriation operated elsewhere, often reflecting social changes as much as spiritual or religious concerns. The proliferation of family chapels in the churches of Florence – where Santo Spirito was rebuilt after 1471 with no fewer than thirty-eight chapels, whose sale largely covered the rebuilding costs – appears as a somewhat localised phenomenon connected with the more open social and political opportunities available in the city. In other north Italian towns the provision of such chapels was more sparing, although the plastering of churches with coats of arms and other memorials was a commonplace in the late fourteenth and fifteenth centuries. In patrician Venice there was no equivalent burgeoning of chapels; while in Ferrara the demand proved insufficient for the numbers of chapels which were actually constructed.

The claim that private chapels reflect withdrawal from the parish church may misrepresent the actuality. The fragmentation of the parochial structure evident in several places across Europe may not indicate gentry withdrawal from the parish, but that they were taking the lead in asserting a local identity below the parish level – the individual township in England, or the subunits of the Italian *pieve*.[22] The family oratory could provide a focus for such identification, which might lead to the erection of a full-scale local chapel. When William Sewardeby, of Sewerby in Yorkshire, sought in the late 1300s to construct a private chapel outside his house (he already had arrangements for private ceremonies inside the mansion), he was opposed on the grounds that it would become the focus for the creation of an independent parish, with the diversion of revenues and devotions from Bridlington church. In Sewardby's defence, it was said that the local people already attended services in his existing chapel when access to Bridlington was impeded by bad weather. To some extent, the erection of such chapels and the hostility which some of them encountered re-enacted the rows which had erupted between the parochial clergy and the mendicant orders when the latter arose in the thirteenth century.

The household was capable of its own religious organisation. Precise scale and organisation varied – much would depend on whether a priest, possibly a friar, was available within the *familia* to offer private guidance, confession, and masses, something probably unlikely below the level of the gentry. The household's unitary nature gave ample opportunities for the development of a routine of prayer and instruction and the enforcement of a moral code, although there is a danger of extrapolating too much from a few known instances. There can have been few households which matched the demands of Elzéar de Sabran's code, with its insistence that married women be excluded and that everyone within the *familia* should live a life of chastity. Other codes also established rules for individual behaviour within a domestic setting. The *Decor puellarum* of John the Carthusian of Venice (d. 1483), for instance, offers a daily routine for a young girl, encouraging a regime of meditation whilst engaged on domestic tasks. Particularly during meals, this regime has affinities with one of the most explicit of such rules, presumed to be for a member of a gentry family in early-fifteenth-century England. This demands regular attendance at services, family-based discussion of sermons, reading during meals, and extensive private devotion. There is a constant exhortation to introspection; to 'Look back, like blessed Anselm, and see how your whole life has been barren and wicked'. Each day is to be lived for itself, and for the future, so that 'When you are in bed, go back to the beginning of the day, and look diligently in your heart: if you

---

[22] See below, pp. 244–6, 248.

have done any evil, and there be sorry; if any good, and there give thanks to God, always in fear and trembling, and do not think it certain that you will survive till the morrow'.[23] The regime established in these regulations seems to apply to a fairly small household, and cannot typify the arrangements in larger establishments, with their numerous personnel and private chapels, which might even include a choir.

Even if imperfectly revealed, the household's potential as a religious body and focus for devotional instruction must be acknowledged. If there was a private chapel there would be private masses, which the whole household would be expected to attend. Reading, and listening to reading, would be important; raising the possibility of doctrinal discussion and comparisons. This may be the milieu in which problematic texts like the Lollard Bibles and sermons circulated. However, while a normal household might cater for some aspects of spiritual development, it could not of itself provide much opportunity for a directly ordered life *qua* household: in the battle between Mary and Martha, between the contemplative and the active lives, within the household Martha would generally win, except in occasional individual cases.

The household might not be organised to create a deeply religious life for everyone, but it could permit individual members to find some personal spiritual fulfilment, to provide – in the contrast between active and contemplative lives – that ideal of the *via media*, Walter Hilton's mixed life. Individuals, tied to the world by their various responsibilities, might thus create private worlds for their religious devotions, which could impinge on the outer world but would not dominate or be dominated by it. Such an arrangement was perhaps best revealed in England in the case of Lady Margaret Beaufort (d. 1509), mother to King Henry VII; although her elevated status precludes the possibility of her being typical. She maintained a rigorous domestic round of devotional activities while vowed to a life of perpetual chastity (a vow taken while still married). As mother to a king, possessor of extensive estates, and closely involved in the patronage and political webs of her day, Margaret Beaufort could not hope to withdraw from the world – the world would not have allowed it, and anyway, she may not have desired it. Yet she successfully maintained a devotional life amidst the pressures of society, her round of masses and meditations, her patronage of printing and education, apparently encountering no major tensions (at least, no irreconcilable tensions) between the varied demands made of her. Margaret Beaufort expertly

---

[23] W. A. Pantin, 'Instructions for a devout and literate layman', in *Medieval learning and literature: essays presented to Richard William Hunt*, ed. J. J. G. Alexander and M. T. Gibson (Oxford, 1976), p. 400.

managed the prime balancing act of the mixed life: not to take the devotion too far and denigrate her rank. Her widow's garb might seem to match ill with ermine robes, but she wore the ermine because it went with her status. In contrast, when Louis IX of France piously failed to dress in a sufficiently kingly manner, his courtiers complained. Louis' later iconographic image paradoxically showed him in majesty, in stark contrast to his customary clothing in life. Even if he was a saint, a king had to look like a king.

Personal regularity: widows, hermits, and anchorites

The maintenance of individual commitment within a lay life was an important aspect of late medieval religion, affecting all levels which leave evidence, and doubtless others for which the evidence is elusive. It also opened up the possibility of some form of retreat, of formal separation from the world in a state of semi-monasticism. This might occur within a household, or could entail retreat into a private world without the supposedly complete break with the world imposed by the formal adoption of conventual vows. It is this type of private self-regulation which seems to be envisaged in *The abbey of the Holy Ghost*, a work translated from French into English in the later fourteenth century. The tract is explicitly addressed to those who, for whatever reason, cannot satisfy a vocation for the monastic life. Instead it suggests the construction of an interiorised monasticism based on moral precepts (presumably, as the Abbey is a nunnery, the addressee is a woman). Here virtues like Humility and Discretion acquire human identities as sisters and obedientiaries of the house, guided by the Holy Spirit as Visitor to offer protection against the forces of Evil.

The personal commitment required for obedience to such precepts could receive more public affirmation. Perhaps the most straightforward was by taking a vow of perpetual chastity; more demanding would be the life of a hermit, almost exclusively restricted to males; and most demanding of all the life of a recluse, an anchorite or anchoress.

Submission to a vow of chastity fell under Hostiensis' wide definition of a religious life, alongside submission to other vows of poverty and obedience. This was essentially a private matter, requiring no formal ecclesiastical involvement beyond reception of the oath. Even so, there were attempts at ecclesiastical oversight. In late medieval England such vows were almost routinely recorded in episcopal registers, with a formal subscription by the vowee. This may show that the church saw taking a vow of chastity – at least, one of perpetual chastity – as akin to admission to a formal order; but the evidence is inconclusive. It is quite likely that many oaths were proferred to ecclesiastics lower down the hierarchy than bishops, as Hostiensis envisaged. There are occasional signs of some testing of the vocation, but this is again inconclusive.

The English records suggest that vows of perpetual chastity were mainly taken by women, especially widows. The granting of a veil and ring which accompanied the vow clearly distinguished the recipients from the rest of society, but without actually making them nuns. The coincidence of the vow with widowhood of course raises other issues – including whether the vow was seen as a way to retain personal control of both body and wealth by rejecting the norm whereby widows and their fortunes wealth were rapidly snapped up in the marriage market. However, female vows of chastity were not restricted to widows; married women also took them, the best known instances being the two extremes of Margery Kempe and Margaret Beaufort. In the first case, Margery bullied her husband into compliance with her demand for a commitment to chastity as part of her own religious aspirations. Lady Margaret's action seems to have been chiefly an assertion of economic independence, although a religious element cannot and should not be excluded. Commitment to chastity was most obviously asserted by women duly considered for sainthood; which may be what Margery Kempe had in mind. Rejection of marriage was almost a topos of female hagiography, as with Catherine of Siena's stolid refusal of a husband. But not all women acclaimed as saints were unmarried. Delphine of Sabran (d. 1360) had originally rejected marriage, then reluctantly concurred in 1299. She persuaded her husband not to consummate the marriage, both of them eventually taking vows of chastity in 1317. Heroic as this instance of conjugal virginity was, it was not without some troubling aspects. Delphine was a candidate for canonisation in the 1360s, but the non-consummation of the marriage seemed to be an overt challenge to the church's teaching. Her associations with the Spiritual Franciscans also aroused suspicions: possibly those contacts had provided an impetus for her insistence on chastity.

While many presumably took oaths of chastity voluntarily, some women may have submitted under duress. This cannot be properly tested, although as women sometimes complained of being forced to become nuns, is not wholly unlikely. Certainly, some women's vows did release their husbands to achieve their own spiritual ends, as an anchorite, hermit, or priest: the twelfth-century Heloise was probably not alone in her self-sacrifice to liberate a husband seeking his own salvation.

A vow of chastity did not bind the vowee to any specific form of religious life; and there could hardly be a greater contrast than Margery Kempe and Margaret Beaufort. Nevertheless, it was reasonably assumed that those so bound would lead a life in which devotion was an important element. It is quite possible that many perpetual widows in fact retired to nunneries as pensioners or corrodians – taking on the spirituality without the responsibilities of the communal life. Perhaps, also, they were active in maintaining and servicing the hospitals of the period, whose personnel are often obscure.

While women are most often recorded as taking vows of chastity, this was not an exclusively female phenomenon: Hostiensis' discussion is in fact formulated in terms of men taking the required vows. Margery Kempe did persuade her husband to take a vow, with some reluctance. Charles of Blois (d. 1364), a claimant to the Breton succession who fell in battle and was popularly acclaimed as a saint, also took a vow after ensuring that he had heirs; while Elzéar de Sabran – Delphine's husband – remained chaste throughout his marriage. There is no evidence of any of the ceremonial which accompanied female vows of chastity, and little sign of the devotional routines adopted in consequence of the vows. With John Kempe, the commitment is in any case questionable.

Despite uncertainties about what obligations vows of chastity imposed, beyond the obvious, it is clear that many people took them as a devotional act. They presumably lived accordingly, although not without some temptations, as admitted by a woman of Apt who had taken her vow in the immediate aftermath of the Black Death. The possibility of making a short-term vow, as the beguines did, might limit the required commitment; but for those intending to remain chaste for the rest of their lives, these vows could be considered demanding.

While women provide most instances of vows of chastity, men appear as hermits. This may reflect social modelling: women desiring a formal religious life had to choose another option, usually involving complete retreat from the world and enclosure in a nunnery – where, admittedly, the retreat might not be total – or an anchorage. Men, however, could be allowed greater worldly contact. In some ways, a hermit's vows were analogous to those of perpetual widowhood; but only in some ways. Life as a hermit did entail greater commitment, at least in theory, to a devotional regime; even if not to one of explicit and detailed regulation.

The medieval hermit remains a somewhat obscure phenomenon. Historically, hermits were most influential between 1050 and 1150, the period which saw the decay of the Benedictine monopoly of monasticism and the gradual emergence of new and more ascetic forms of religious life. The hermits of Italy, of the Breton wastes, and of central France, were catalysts in the emergence of many of the new religious orders of the twelfth century. After about 1150, however, less is heard of them – although St Francis wanted to be one, and what became the Austin friars after 1256 began as an amalgamation of groups of hermitages in central Italy. Many hermits in western Europe between 1100 and 1250 were associated with religious houses and orders – the classic instance is the relationship between St Godric of Finchale (d. 1179) and Durham; but the existence of hermits associated with Cluny, sometimes actually monks, is also to the point. The Latin expansion in the Levant may offer a partial reason for the apparent scarcity of hermits in the thirteenth century: the deserts of the east were again open to colonisation, and were accordingly colonised.

While their history is often uncertain, it is clear that many men were labelled as hermits; a category which merged into – perhaps included – the southern French beguins and the German beghards. In England, they seem never to have acquired a sectarian name (unless it was that of 'Lollard', in the later fourteenth century). The *romiti* of fifteenth-century Italy also fit under the generic umbrella.

Modern connotations of the word 'hermit' conspire to produce a stereotype: a recluse, cut off by deliberate choice from contact with the world, confined to a specific restricted location, and somehow eking out an existence by uncertain means. The word conveys the image of a tramp, but a static tramp. Medieval hermits did fit that picture in part; but not wholly. The concept of 'hermit' was by no means narrow: while some had defined hermitages, others were more peripatetic. For many hermits their life was one of wandering, sustained by payment for undertaking vicarious pilgrimages and by begging. The English poet William Langland railed against such people in *Piers Plowman*, but they were clearly part of the normality. Italian *romiti* were characteristically wanderers: unkempt, uncontrolled, preaching a call to penance and issuing dire warnings of impending divine wrath.

Even when hermits were static, they were not cut off from the world. While some did retreat – as Richard Rolle of Hampole (d. 1349) did at first – many retained close links with normal existence. Rolle did later become more mobile, and maintained contacts with the world by acting as spiritual director to a nearby anchorite and group of nuns. His career, however, cannot be taken as typical: his theological awareness exceeded that of most known hermits, and his writings as a guide to consciences place him in a very distinct category.

The hermit's religious life was not particularly demanding, being based on meditation and a cycle of prayer. As most hermits were laymen, a close acquaintance with the liturgy was not needed: their spiritual obligations were primarily based on recitations of the psalter, creed, *Ave*, and Our Father. They were generally expected to live from physical labour as well as begging. Many maintained roads and bridges: indulgences for their upkeep may often have been intended to provide financial support for the hermit. So might the bequests for road building which appear frequently in late medieval wills. The relationship was, as is usual with such cases, reciprocal: the hermit received the money, in return labouring for the society which provided his upkeep and saying prayers for his benefactors. Donations for roads and bridges which were imposed as penances may also have been channelled through hermits.

The trouble with the hermit life was that it was essentially unregulated – perhaps justifying their being likened to 'medieval hippies'.[24] Hermits lacked formal integration into the church's structure, so appear only occasionally in official records. The decision to adopt the life was almost entirely individualistic, one over which the ecclesiastical authorities had little control. Richard Rolle, for instance, acted quite spontaneously, cutting up some of his sister's clothes to make the required habit. It is unclear that he ever gained formal approbation for his new status, even if it was tacitly accepted. Individuals became hermits by their own choice, and for their own purposes: the Italian *romiti* seem in several cases to have been reacting against an earlier life of sin, undertaking a very public penance. Some clearly did respond to a vocation, and received direction (as in the Carthusian Richard Methley's *Epistle to Hew heremyte*); but it might be a life recklessly adopted. Some decided that it was too tough and gave up. The role might be assumed for the wrong reasons (according to Langland, to live without working and to seduce women); here the lack of control was significant. Some even drifted into heresy. Several in England indulged in preaching, and known incidents of heresy there between 1200 and the outbreak of 'Lollardy' in the 1380s were often associated with hermits. Indeed, the first 'Lollard trial', of William Swinderby in 1382, seems to have been the trial of a hermit whose association with Wycliffism is purely fortuitous, if not entirely due to the imagination of his detractors. This experience parallels that of the German beghards, also called Lollards, whose begging and uncontrolled preaching stirred up hostility in the fourteenth century. Some of them proclaimed ideas which were given coherence by the authorities as the 'heresy of the Free Spirit'.

With misguided individuals wandering around, laying claim to a life of apostolic poverty, preaching, and possibly leading others into error, the church had to try to impose some form of discipline. Restrictions on preaching obviously played a part, and the attacks on lay preaching in England in the 1380s and after may have been directed as much against wandering hermits as against 'Lollardy'. England also reveals an attempt at

24 B. Hamilton, *Religion in the medieval west* (London, 1986), p. 186.

greater regulation of the hermit life, with the imposition of 'The Rule of St Paul the First Hermit' at a proper investiture. Here the would-be hermit made a formal profession to the bishop, received the appropriate habit, and perhaps was allocated to a specific place, tantamount to institution to a benefice. These changes may have helped to stabilise the hermits of the fifteenth century, at least in England. But there were still wanderers, ready to undertake vicarious pilgrimages. The lack of records makes it impossible to quantify the appeal of the hermit life, whether stable or peripatetic, over the later middle ages; as with female vows of chastity, the numbers were probably not insignificant. If a chance reference in a will of 1387 can be trusted, there may then have been about 500 in the vicinity of Siena: if that is correct and typical, the overall numbers were truly great.

Hermits, perpetual widows and perpetual widowers rather fall through the cracks in the extant evidence on late medieval religion. Equally obscure, except in rare cases, and relatively unstudied, is the third type of semi-regular life which needs consideration, the life of an anchorite. This was the most demanding form of religious life of the time, one of total reclusion. The status was somewhat ambivalent, being open to members of the regular orders as well as those not bound by conventual obligations. Such total retreat might indeed be the height of monastic perfection, moving beyond the need for communal existence. Yet, by moving beyond it, it also challenged conventual structures, offering a status which was in some ways extra-regular. For those not bound by such conventions, the anchoritic life posed different challenges, and raised different contradictions.

Anchorites carried the contemplative life to the extreme, with a strict regime of meditation and preparation for death. They were in theory entirely separated from the world – so fully that the ceremony for their seclusion (at least, as recorded in northern Europe) was effectively a funeral rite. But not all anchorites achieved such absolute withdrawal. True, they were often restricted to a small enclosure – sometimes a single room built on to a church – and their contact with the outside was officially only through an intermediary servant, or through a curtain. But they were not denied all contact with the world. An anchorite required support and many did secure their livelihoods before retreating, effectively living off private incomes in their seclusion. Some were provided for by endowments – rather like the funds provided for individual houses in beguinages – and might earn more by their own labours. Others lived by begging, which in fifteenth-century Germany led to their inclusion among those to be condemned as sturdy beggars.

Some retention of worldly involvements was unavoidable. Financial necessity meant that those outside the regular orders tended to be found in towns. This urban environment and the reputation for holiness which several recluses acquired meant that they often acted as spiritual advisors. Insofar as anchorites served a spiritual function, it was primarily as people obliged to pray for the world, and to offer spiritual counsel. This might be seen in a quasi-contractual light: the sustenance which the recluse received from the world was reciprocated by the prayers and spiritual advice offered in return. In England Margery Kempe visited Julian of Norwich (whose own book, the *Revelations of divine love*, is an attempt to influence the world outside her anchorage by public statement), while the monk-anchorites of Westminster were consulted by successive kings at the turn of the fourteenth and fifteenth centuries. In France, Jeanne-Marie de Maille (d. 1414), a recluse with the Franciscans at Tours, acquired a wide reputation as a prophetess and visionary.

The available evidence on English (let alone continental) anchorites is incomplete, often incidental and miscellaneous. It ranges from royal accounts which record donations to individual recluses, to episcopal registers and wills. Women predominate among those whose professions and seclusions are recorded: notices of male anchorites are surprisingly few. Despite this prevalence of women, the anchoritic life was not exclusively female. It might be a life entered in relatively advanced years as the culmination of a spiritual quest; indeed, the commitment and self-discipline demanded to live it successfully virtually precluded adoption in youth.

The available prescriptions for an anchorite's life may give a skewed picture of what was undertaken. The two main English sources are fairly early: the instructions prepared by Ailred of Rievaulx for his sister in the mid twelfth century, and twice translated into English in the fifteenth, and the tract called *Ancrene Wisse*, which in its first recensions dates from the early thirteenth century. Both were aimed at women, as were the contemplative works for anchorites compiled by Richard Rolle and the Cistercian adviser, William of Rymyngton. There is little directed explicitly to men, although the instructions could be fulfilled as well by them as by women, ignoring the address. The anchoritic life may have been considered more suitable for women: one author complained that men lacked the stamina to stick to it, whereas women were more steadfast.

For the anchorites from religious orders, the rule of their order would continue to apply, with appropriate modifications. Lay anchorites needed a different regime. It is this which is described by Ailred and the other writers, usually defining a routine based on the divine office, as in any regular life, and recitation of the traditional prayers. There was also provision for a good deal of contemplation, reading, and meditation, mainly on the Passion, in the search for some sort of transcendental union with God. The contemplation of the Passion particularly sought the abnegation of self through immersion in the details and import of Christ's self-sacrifice. The exhortations to contemplation stressed participation in His suffering, an affective and emotional participation which superficially appears unduly preoccupied with the gory. Yet the emotional sympathetic and empathetic response which was to be elicited – a real com-Passion – was what counted.

Overall numbers of anchorites cannot be assessed. Their commitment is equally untestable. Some took on the life for the wrong reasons and grouched under the yoke. Occasionally this generated scandal when the individuals concerned broke out of their retreats. Some must have been disappointed, did not achieve the desired mystical experiences, and were stuck with a life of tedious dissatisfaction; although in southern France cases are recorded where women were allowed to abandon their obligations without recrimination. Yet because they are often unrecorded, because they fell outside the normality of the ecclesiastical structure, these recluses rarely impinge on the foreground. Although there were failures, the continued relative popularity of the life and the degree of holiness commonly ascribed to its practitioners suggests that it was considered a truly religious life, which cannot simply be marginalised. When Henry VIII's commissioners dissolved the English anchorages, several of the recluses had to be forcibly ejected rather than rejoicing at their release. That there were so many who accepted the commitment, even if uncountable, is striking testimony to the strength of religious convictions throughout these centuries.

The varieties of religious experience offered within the broad confines of medieval catholicism meant that, although strands can be differentiated, the distinctions should not be too rigid. There is considerable inter-mingling. Between the poles of the active and contemplative lives, the mixed life allowed for various gradations of a *via media*, permitting individual development and changed priorities. Beguines might well leave their establishments to marry and engage on a more 'active' life; conversely, English judges might retire to the Franciscan order as William Shareshull did in the mid fourteenth century; or London merchants become anchorites as William Cheney did in the 1430s. Equally, tracts prepared for one type of religious experience could be applied to others: that Richard Rolle's works for the anchorite Margaret Kirkby found a wider audience shows this; as does the use of monastic and other regular observances outside the cloister.

Equally important, people might concurrently participate in several forms of religious life. The recluse of Farne in the mid fourteenth century was a type of anchorite, but was still a monk. Religious life was a personal experience, possibly increasingly personal in the later middle ages; but it was also a communal experience, which to be validated in a religion based on *caritas* had to be shared. The household had therefore to operate as a joint experience; guild members had to sink their separateness in fraternity. Individuals submerged themselves in the shared spiritualities of parish, fraternity, and even confraternity. To tease out the strands in the varieties of the religious life must not go to the extreme of unravelling the complex thread which tied most of them together. Any individual's opportunities for religious life were multiform, allowing several combinations which retained their specific features. Fraternity's ritualism could be expressed through the parish, through the town, or through a greater or lesser unit – even as large as a whole diocese in Pentecostal processions.

It is equally important not to exaggerate the spirituality of much of religious life.[25] There was a strong element of convention – social convention perhaps more than spiritual – which made the non-participants stand out as asocial or anti-social beings, liable to constraints imposed by a combination of outraged community and church authorities. Moreover, opportunities for religious fulfillment were opportunities for other types of fulfillment, only some of which might be emotional, as with charitable activity to relieve the guilt of wealth. Guilds, parishes, and such like provided mechanisms for individuals to achieve and proclaim social status, to gain political power, to give and receive patronage, to make commercial contacts, to establish peace-making processes which might be more effective and less costly than recourse to the full rigours of the law. None of these can be ignored in assessing the apparently religious life of the period, although it is impossible to determine the importance which any should receive in an individual case. The integration of religion and society was so intricate that quite probably an individual would or could not differentiate between the various motivations which were operating.

This complex mixture of possibilities for a religious life provided a framework within which people could advance beyond mere awareness of the faith and involvement in social structures to an expression of their faith through devotional practices. The formalised lives offered by the structured organisations and vows were, to some extent, responses to Christianity's social and moral demands, to the imperative of *caritas*. As

25 Below, pp. 312, 327–9.

such they addressed the obligations of the second of the Great Commandments. Obeying the first of those Commandments had to be a more personal experience. The specifically spiritual search which could occur under the umbrella of Christianity had to be expressed through devotional practices. They are the concern of the next chapter.

5

DEVOTION

The external practices of medieval Christianity took many forms. Some were dictated by the annual round, the accretions of tradition. Typical were the distribution of candles to mark the Virgin's Purification (Candlemas, 2 February), or the annual feasts for the poor around Avignon. As well as the calendar of celebrations there were other public devotional acts to demonstrate piety and seek help from God. These were often partisan, like processions to secure good weather, alleviate the plague, or invoke divine mercy to heal a ruler or secure or celebrate victory in battle.

Such activities were routine but purposeful. They aimed to secure God's favour on earth and achieve communion with Him here and in the hereafter. Most people probably focused their attention on the hereafter: without denigrating the widespread concern to appreciate and comprehend the Christian mysteries, the search for terrestrial intimacy with God was largely confined to the mystics and their ilk. Anxiety to join God in the afterlife generated a this-worldly concern to guarantee *post mortem* security, and therewith salvation. Numerous devotional practices sought that end, aiming through good works and pious foundations to secure prayers and other rewards to benefit the soul after death.

So bald a summary of the main concerns of medieval devotion provides insufficient indication of their nature. Any assessment of the spiritual attitudes inherent in the period's devotional activities confronts a major obstacle: the uncertainties about predestination and freewill as they affected the search for personal salvation. That dilemma raises questions about how much control any individual was perceived to exercise over his or her ultimate destination, and about the exact impulse behind the process of accumulating merit through works which were both outwardly charitable and spiritually self-centred. There is a tension between the duty of *caritas* and emotional response to suffering, and the self-interested desire to secure prayers and speedy transit through Purgatory. Purgatory is a critical element in any discussion of late medieval piety, for it impinges on virtually every aspect of religious activity. It even seems at times to overwhelm the dictates of *caritas* in the emphasis on procuring prayers and masses for souls, and on indulgences.

Purgatory explains only one facet of medieval Christianity; its rationale must be sought in the context of the full Christian pilgrimage which will be a concern of the next chapter. For the present the 'non-Purgatorial' aspects of devotion provide the focus for discussion, primarily in terms of earthly contact with the sacred. To begin with, further consideration must be given to attitudes to the mass. Thereafter, the intercessors between humans and God demand some thought: the relationship with Christ and his Mother, the proliferation of saints, and discussion of miracles, relics, and pilgrimage. The third main concern is with the intenser devotion of mysticism and the search for direct and individual contact with God. Finally comes the issue of attitudes which seem, to some modern commentators at least, incompatible with true piety, turning to the more superstitious aspects of devotion and the exploitation of the 'magical' nature of the divine power.

THE MASS

Celebration of the mass was undeniably the central point in catholic devotion.[1] Acceptance of transubstantiation made the mass the focal point at which to appreciate the corporeal humanity of an incarnate God. This found classic expression in the legend of the Mass of St Gregory, which told how a doubting onlooker was convinced of the truth of the Real Presence when a Host which Pope Gregory I had consecrated visibly changed; in some versions into a bloody chunk of flesh, in others into the crucified Christ. This tale and variants of it were extremely popular, re-appearing in prints, paintings, and on memorial brasses. Its appeal was doubtless enhanced by the addition of indulgences to some of the representations, as on the brass memorial to members of the Legh family in Macclesfield church. But the Mass of St Gregory was not the only occasion on which the Host became corporeal: in the 1520s a Lincolnshire man declared that when he looked at the elevated Host it seemed to

[1] See also above, pp. 98–102.

contain a child within a membrane of bread. His was a personal and private reaction, as were those of the many holy women whose *Lives* record their devotion to the Host in terms of an addicted demand for frequent communion.

A more public acknowledgement of the Host's power was the phenomenon of the Bleeding Host, several of which, like that at Augsburg, became foci for pilgrimages. These cults were primarily a continental phenomenon, with very few being noted in England. One host-miracle which might have generated a pilgrimage was publicised by Bishop Philip Repingdon of Lincoln in 1405, when the pyx containing the Host was virtually the only thing to be preserved when Yarborough church was destroyed by fire. That would almost certainly have generated a devotional centre in Germany, but seemingly not in Lincolnshire. A claim by the London Carthusians to a bleeding Host in 1515 seems to have been exposed as a fraud. One of the most important cults arose after 1383 around the Precious Blood of Wilsnack. Three Hosts recovered from a burnt church were alleged to have marks as though oozing blood. Although challenged by many leading churchmen – ranging from John Hus to Nicholas of Cusa – the devotion could not be constrained. Wilsnack became a pilgrimage centre of international importance, drawing visitors from all over Europe. Other Hosts discovered or recovered in peculiar circumstances attracted similar devotions. Some bleeding Hosts had their own particular messages. That preserved at Daroca in Spain had transformed at the mass held for outnumbered Christian forces facing a Moslem army in 1239, and was credited with having given the Christians the victory.

The mass – especially the elevated Host, and communion through the Host – did not just bring Christ down to earth. The celebration was more than an occasion or object for personal devotion; it was also a focus for a community in communion, even though priestly control over reception and rivalry over precedence in reception also imposed strains on that community. The effectiveness of the mass meant that it was needed often, with every priest being expected to recite it once daily. The series of masses ensured a continuity of celebration, almost perpetual worship, to guarantee the rite's salvific force: the mass was integral to the process whereby individuals sought and attained salvation. As consecration was a priestly prerogative, this also confirmed and enhanced sacerdotal authority by emphasising lay dependence on priests to procure the means to salvation (a point to be considered further at a later stage).[2]

The spiritual functions attached to the mass, its vital importance to the society as a whole and for its individual members, made it the pre-eminent feature of medieval religion. Endowment of a mass was a public benefaction. While some might conveniently be labelled 'private masses', personal or collective foundations for specific purposes, technically there were no private masses – not even those held in private chapels, which might be attended by household members and visitors. Every mass was for public benefit in some way, universally efficacious, for the good of the church in its widest definition. Certainly those who endowed masses claimed a pre-emptive share in their effects (a ghost from Purgatory was questioned about the maximum number of people who could be named in a mass and still receive a full share in its merits), but this could never exclude 'all the faithful departed' or some such inclusive phrase. Moreover, although the priest said the mass, an audience was often expected to witness the celebration and contribute to the rewards which its founder was seeking.

These lay participants, as audience and assembly of prayers, would have their own complex involvement with the liturgical event. Their presence and demands account for the evolution of one form of mass which, in terms of sacramental efficacy, was no mass. Alongside the mass as a means of providing access to the consecrated elements, there is the oddity of the holding of masses without any consecration. These 'dry masses' are one of the more shadowy elements of medieval devotion, ill-documented and little considered. According to canon law, all consecrations had to be completed before noon. An afternoon 'dry mass' was, however, permissible as a devotional exercise, as part of the ceremony of a wedding or funeral. The extent of such celebrations evades assessment: the very existence of the dry mass is rarely acknowledged. However, they may have taken place quite widely, and in a variety of circumstances. As there was no celebration, it is even possible that their celebration was not restricted to priests. They were held by post-Reformation nuns in Augsburg, so presumably could have been celebrated by them before-hand. Other laity may also have performed them. Reports of the 'masses' held by some 'Lollards' – including women – suggest that they omitted the words of consecration, perhaps then making them dry masses celebrated as devotional exercises. However, such reports may also imply that the dry mass was primarily a continental phenomenon, with the novelty of such celebrations in late-medieval England perhaps explaining why they were associated with heresy.

Overall, it is undeniable that a localised and personalised mass was what concentrated people's attention; the desire to trap and direct divine power through celebration for a specific purpose, or for named individuals. The missal of the Salisbury Use, for instance, contains masses for those setting out on a journey, to protect crops, for good weather or rain, to prevent death, for the souls of the dead, and many other purposes. People had masses celebrated for themselves while they lived – a form of health insurance – and for their souls after death in hope of a speedy release from Purgatory. Chantries established during a founder's lifetime served both purposes in succession.

The perception of the mass as a functional rite doubtless had unintended but unavoidable effects: it encouraged a mechanistic view which held God bound to reciprocate with the desired benefit when the appropriate mass was offered; it also generated a purely utilitarian and quantitative appreciation of masses, especially those for the dead, reflected in testamentary demands that large numbers be celebrated with almost indecent haste. Here, however, other issues may intrude. One analysis of the explosion of *post mortem* masses sees them as reflecting three different approaches.[3] First came the customary masses which were part of the death ritual: memorial celebrations linked to set periods within the first year after death. Around Avignon these occurred on the ninth day after death, and then at the year's end; in England they were the 'month's mind' and the 'year's mind'. These can be seen as forming part of the period of mourning. The second stage reflected a concern for perpetual memorial, the endowment of masses – daily, or as anniversaries and obits – intended to last in perpetuity and assist the soul through to the Last Judgement. The final stance resulted from the concern for the rapid celebration of great numbers of masses over a brief period: this may reflect greater awareness of Purgatory, and a desire to complete the transit speedily by using the merit of the masses as part of the process.

The differentiation is attractive, separating the strands in appreciations of the power and function of the celebrations: some essentially social, others self-centred. It may over-simplify, especially in distinguishing between 'perpetual' and 'cumulative' masses, if those produced by endowments of limited duration are counted among the latter rather than the former. Not everyone could afford a perpetual endowment, especially if it meant the alienation of real property (as it usually did). Most short-term chantries were based on cash payments, or the eking out of a sum of

---

[3] J. Chiffoleau, 'Sur l'usage obsessionel de la messe pour les morts à la fin du moyen-âge', in *Faire croire: modalités de la diffusion et de la réception des messages religieux du XIIe au XVe siècles. Table ronde organisée par l'École française de Rome, en collaboration avec l'Institut d'histoire médiévale de l'Université de Padoue (Rome, 22–23 juin 1979)*, Collection de l'École française de Rome, 51 (Rome, 1981), pp. 240–5; see also J. Chiffoleau, *La comptabilité de l'au-delà: les hommes, la mort et la religion dans la région d'Avignon à la fin du Moyen Age (vers 1320–vers 1480)*, Collection de l'École française de Rome, 47 (Rome, 1980), pp. 326–8, 339, 341–5, 352–3.

money for as long as possible: the aspiration would seem to be for a drawn-out commemoration, rather than the relatively swift blast.

Changing attitudes towards the celebration of the mass not only altered appreciations, they also amended its format. There was greater emphasis on Christ's presence in the host, which developed into the concept and feast of Corpus Christi, and also stressed the host's status as a relic. This led to its receiving more flamboyant veneration in its own right. The custom of elevation, with the coincident raising of lights and ringing of bells, was the clearest sign of this developing veneration. Linked to this was the practice of reservation of the consecrated Host, and the use of the monstrance as a sort of Host-reliquary. Outside the churches, veneration was demanded for the host *en route* to the dying in their homes. As it was escorted to its destination by candles and bells, bystanders had to offer due reverence. Failure to conform could lead to charges of irreligiosity, as alleged by Archbishop Arundel of Canterbury against some members of the Parliament held at Coventry in 1404. The ceremony without the substance could equally cause public scandal: in 1397 a Herefordshire priest was complained of for permitting bystanders to venerate an empty pyx which he was carrying through the streets. The concern for the host, and for the moment of elevation, also appears in some burial requests. People sought burial close to an altar, even at the spot where the priest stood at the consecration, as a statement of humility and perhaps in the hope of gaining some vicarious contact with the elements.

Other developments in the context of the mass – greater emphasis on the beauty of holiness, and the increasing use of music to raise the emotional response – also affected attitudes to, and appreciations of, what was occurring. However, and most crucially, the rite's climax, the consecration, was reserved for the priest. Lay reaction to such exclusion, and to being confined to the ranks of mere spectators, cannot be adequately tested. The general infrequency of communion meant that the laity shared in the proceedings not as actors but as onlookers, an audience who might be urged to offer prayers but were usually only witnesses. Even when the laity participated as communicants, they were still supplicants, whose claims to receive were individually assessed, and perhaps publicly rejected.

The available evidence for lay awareness of what occurred during the mass suggests an emphasis on the 'magical' and the meditative. In his *Instructions for parish priests*, John Mirk stressed the benefits which accrued from presence at a mass; for one thing, sight of the elevated host guaranteed preservation from sudden death for that day. The contemplative tradition seemingly found its emotional peak in the climax of consecration. That was when many went into ecstasy, or burst into uncontrolled weeping, the outcome of concentration on the sacrificial nature of the celebration as they mentally participated in an extremely detailed re-enactment of the Passion. These visionaries' attempts to make their visions concrete and share them with others often seem to have been influenced by church decoration, but it is the reaction, rather than the attempts to communicate it, which matters.

INTERCESSORS

Christ-centred devotions

The mass did more than restate Christ's self-sacrifice for mankind; it also repaid that sacrifice. Christ, having offered Himself, was now offered to Himself in recompense for Himself. However, most masses were also offered with a specific intention, integrating the celebration into a wider range of motivations. The sacrifice to Christ was addressed to Him as an intercessor, as one Person of the Trinity, to intercede with the Father to procure benefits for the performer and the commissioner of the mass.

The primacy of the mass and Christ in late medieval religion is well shown by the increasing number of feasts and devotions centred precisely on Christ and the Eucharist. Of these the most potent was Corpus Christi, a commemoration which also celebrated the unity of the church as Christ's body. Such a devotion was perhaps latent in any doctrine of a Real Presence; but its actual emergence was tied in with developments in spirituality linked to the beguines of the southern Netherlands. The first advocate of a specific devotion to the eucharist as Corpus Christi was Juliana of Cornillon (d. 1258), who secured its celebration in the diocese of Liège in 1246. The future Pope Urban IV was then an archdeacon in the diocese; following his elevation to the papacy the feast was proclaimed a universal celebration in 1264. However, it did not then gain widespread observance. In 1317 it was reaffirmed by John XXII. This time response was immediate, and it rapidly appeared on local calendars, being also supported by the burgeoning Corpus Christi fraternities. As it spread, it provided opportunities for the affirmation of faith through public devotion and the growth of the cycles of mystery plays which conveyed the history of the world and the full cycle of the redemption story.

Other Christocentric devotions also developed, concentrating attention on the Five Wounds, the Holy Name, the Sacred Heart, and so on. Many of these again sprang from localised beginnings which acquired wider acceptance. The devotion of the Sacred Heart began among the beguines, and has clear links with the ecstatic experiences of many of the female visionaries. The devotion of the Holy Name was principally associated with Bernardino of Siena (d. 1444), although it had earlier been encouraged by the German Dominican mystic Henry Suso (d. 1366), and votive masses (in a different tradition) existed in England by 1400. It too spread rapidly, especially among the mendicants. Such devotions stressed the intangible aspects of Christ, which demanded an emotional and spiritual response. They mark a new type of devotion, moving from the physical nature of the Passion towards a more mental, perhaps truly spiritual, appreciation of Christ. It would be dangerous, perhaps false, to make too much of this: these devotions could be gaudy, like the chantry chapel constructed in honour of the Holy Name at Bury St Edmunds church, with its glitter and colour; and the contemplative tradition never totally abandoned Christ's physical sufferings in meditations on the crucifixion. Yet the concentration on Christ alone, and on the Passion, may be a key feature in changes in spirituality in the fifteenth century, providing a context for the dependence on redemption through the Passion and through faith which became so important after 1515.

The emphasis on the Passion was matched by devotion to the Cross in reality (in the proliferation of fragments of the True Cross) and figuratively (in the role of crosses as pilgrimage points). Pilgrimage crosses might be simple roadside structures like that at Rippingale, Suffolk, which may have been established more to extract money from pilgrims than as a focus for valid devotion. Others were more elaborate. The Holy Rood of Bromholm was a mechanical contraption with rolling eyes, moving limbs, and foaming mouth, perhaps deservedly a tourist attraction but much derided by the sixteenth-century reformers; while the 'Beautiful Cross' of Troyes became so popular that the press of pilgrims was a public health hazard. Pilgrimage to crosses was a common aspect of late-medieval devotion, adding to the total of movements stimulated by a desire to visit holy places.

Of all intercessors, Christ was the most potent; but he was not the only one. The complete Trinity could be invoked, devotion being reflected in ubiquitous alabaster images, sometimes showing the concern for Purgatory with the Trinity receiving souls. The saints functioned chiefly as intercessors to gain the ear of the divinity for their adherents. There is something vassalic about the hierarchy of links created by this attitude, with the saints – the intercessors – acting almost as magnates who patronised their affinities, the humans who venerated them and in return sought benefits through their favour. The relationship with the saints was a major force in expressions of piety from the twelfth to the sixteenth centuries, serving a variety of functions and bringing in its train features which both enriched and (in some ways) cheapened contemporary spirituality.

Mary

Among the saints the Virgin Mary was unmatched. In the distinctions made between permitted degrees of veneration, she alone (according to Thomas Aquinas) could be accorded the intensity of *hyperdulia* which placed her above all other saints. Her status was not unproblematic – the question of her Immaculate Conception was hotly debated between Franciscans and Dominicans; the problem of its comprehension led one of her thirteenth-century biographers to postulate a whole genealogy of equally immaculate conceptions among her ancestors. Unlike other saints she had left no corporeal remains, an absence explained by and explaining the notion of her bodily Assumption, so that relics were so only by association. (The numerous phials which supposedly contained her milk were admittedly physical remains, but in a sense incorporeal.) The major Marian relics were therefore clothing and other objects: her veil at Chartres, the Holy House at Loreto (a cult born in the late thirteenth century), or the supposed reconstruction of the Holy House at Walsingham. What secured Mary's status among the intercessors was her relationship with God and his Son, which gained increasing attention during the period, and led to greater commemoration of her life and greater emphasis on her role in Heaven. Her designation as Queen of Heaven took hold from the twelfth century, with one of the most popular iconographic statements of her status being her Coronation by the Trinity. Images of her proliferated, to become foci of pilgrimages and devotion. Sometimes, as Thomas More complained, these images seemed to be in competition; their adherents arguing over their relative merits and effectiveness regardless of the fact that they commemorated the same person. In England, apart from the supreme shrine at Walsingham which, in 1535, appears to have been by far the wealthiest shrine in the country, there were major devotional centres at Doncaster, Woolpit, Worcester, Wakefield, and Ipswich; and innumerable minor shrines. In the Spanish realms, Mary was often the subject of visions. Again shrines proliferated, sometimes around images miraculously revealed after supposedly long burial. The legend of Our Lady of Guadalupe alleged that that image had been buried on the eve of the Moorish invasion, combining national and Christian recovery against the infidel to enhance the simple discovery of the statue. The major Spanish images had their own catchment areas, in which subsidiary images replicated the Virgin of Guadalupe, of Montserrat, and so on.

The cult of the Virgin was one of the most widespread and dynamic aspects of late medieval spirituality, with its own mystical connotations. The dedication of Saturday as her holy day almost placed her on a par with

Christ; and the calendar acquired several feasts, often with their own indulgences, which commemorated events in her life. Devotion to Mary stimulated devotion to her family, even if some of the personalities involved had to be invented. The feast of St Anne, her mother, was officially promulgated by Pope Urban VI in 1386; but her father, St Joachim, had to await the pontificate of Julius II for the formal establishment of his celebration. Marian feasts were distributed across the ecclesiastical calendar, the Purification (2 February), Annunciation (25 March), Visitation (2 July), Assumption (15 August), Nativity (8 September), and Immaculate Conception (8 December). She was the Mother of God, Queen of Heaven, and Empress of Hell, gaining other appellations as her various characteristics were stressed – Star of the Sea, Our Lady of Sorrows, and so on. Her role at the Crucifixion made her pre-eminently Our Lady of Pity, depicted in paint, sculpture, and (later) print in a form which became the Pietà, a highly potent image of the later middle ages. She was credited with being the sole repository of the faith in the days between the Crucifixion and the Resurrection. Her miracles were amassed in extensive collections. Her importance created its own prayers and praises, among them the *Ave*, and the *Salve Regina*. The former was one of the standard prayers which all Christians were required to know and recite regularly, with further clauses being added early in the sixteenth century. Recitations of the *Ave* accumulated into the Rosary, a devotion which originated in the thirteenth century and spread widely, bequests of appropriate beads for counting off the recitations being fairly commonly encountered in wills. Marian devotion is shown in church dedications (although many of these may date from the twelfth century, when some of the new reformed orders, especially the Cistercians, maintained a particular dedication to her), in guilds founded in her honour, in imagery and other church furnishings. Association with her could also become a political statement, demonstrated by the way in which the Teutonic Knights exploited their dedication to Mary to anathematise all opposition to their militaristic activities in Prussia.

Saints and their making

Although she was pre-eminent, Mary's cult did not swamp devotion to other saints. Medieval sainthood is a vast subject, so complex it defies complete analysis. Sainthood had varied functions, the saints themselves serving many purposes and being given individual responsibilities in terms of the favours sought from them. Old saints could legitimise new political orders, their cults being revitalised for specific political objectives. In England King Henry III thus named his two sons Edward and Edmund after the two major Anglo-Saxon royal saints; while the cults of Anglo-Saxon saints were boosted in the reign of Henry V (1413–22) to encourage English patriotism. When the Angevins claimed the throne of Hungary under King Charles Robert in 1309, much was made of his links to the saints of the French and Arpad dynasties, links which continued to be stressed during his reign. Saints could unite a country, bolstering its political order. In many of the north Italian communes, the commem-orations of the patron saint of the dominant city were augmented by the mandatory, and sometimes unwilling, participation of representatives of subject rural communities – subjection to the dominant city entailed subjection to its patron saint. The Capetian and Valois kings of France exploited their symbiotic links with the cult of St Denys to bolster their political status, but showed no qualms about defecting to St Michael as replacement patron when Denys proved too accommodating to the English in the Hundred Years War. Similarly, canonisations of kings and princes strengthened royal claims. The most notable case was the support given to the Capetians by the canonisation of Louis IX; while the first Tudors unsuccessfully sought confirmation of Henry VI's sanctity. (Royal sainthood could also be double-edged: Saint Louis IX was all very well until he was used after Philip IV's death in 1314 as the exemplar of the golden age against over-centralising royal authority.)

Beyond the political, saints had more mundane uses. They worked miracles, healing the sick, restoring the maimed, finding lost property, averting fires, and suchlike. Seen as protectors, as intercessors, their functions made them ubiquitous in medieval devotional life. Beyond the devotional, they provided opportunities for other activities: for pilgrimages which might be little more than jaunts, for the production of souvenirs and stimulation of trade at shrines, for moral instruction. Like the devotion itself, the concept of sanctity helped the integration of the ecclesiastical and religious into the norms of existence.

Expectations concerning saints in general may not have changed much over time; but the ability of individual saints to fulfil those expectations did. What people wanted of the saints may not have matched what 'the church' saw as their role. The accepted definition, the orthodoxy, about what made a saint could change over time, and did. The process was already well under way by 1200, with the papacy claiming that it alone could determine who should be canonised as meriting universal recog-nition as a saint. However, the popes did not claim to 'make' saints, merely to affirm their sanctity; they did not assert conclusively that the canonised really were saints in heaven, merely that the available earthly evidence suggested that they should be. It was accepted that the church might have been deluded; it was always more likely that real saints had somehow escaped recognition. Not much could be done about the former; but the omissions might eventually be rectified – there was no 'canonise by' date for sainthood. The papal monopoly on canonisation restricted additions to the calendar, although more processes were initiated than resulted in acceptance. This did not preclude the rise of local cults which might eventually gain formal recognition; they were in fact a necessary precondition for the process to occur. In theory canonisation merely confirmed a preceding recognition of sainthood which had no need of papal approbation. Lack of canonisation did not make a devotion illegitimate, unless the claims to sainthood were found to be totally ill-founded. There was a distinction between private devotion and public ceremony, which allowed presumed saints to be invoked as intercessors but denied any public veneration until after canonisation. It is a distinction explicitly spelled out in the case of Richard Rolle. A formal office was devised for him, for use

after he shall have been canonised by the church, for in the meantime it is not permitted to sing the canonical hours concerning him publicly in church, or solemnise his feast. However, anyone having evidence of his exceptional holiness and life may venerate him, and seek his suffrages in private prayers, and commend himself to his prayers.[4]

One consequence of the evolution of canonisation was that the processes to establish sainthood became more elaborate and judicial. Gone were the days when sanctity was recognised almost by acclamation – that someone was a saint because everyone agreed on it. While in some cases, like that of Francis of Assisi, canonisation was almost a formality, and the bureaucratic procedures were curtailed, after about 1200 a full investigation was normally required, which examined the life and works of the postulant saint, interrogated witnesses, and recorded and tested miracles. St Francis was canonised in 1229, only three years after his death; but usually things took longer. Thomas Aquinas, for instance, had to wait almost fifty years: he died in 1274 but canonisation was delayed until 1323. A wait of centuries was not uncommon. Leopold III of Austria, who died in 1136, gained recognition only in 1485; the Franciscan theologian Bonaventure (d. 1274) was canonised in 1482; while Franciscan missionaries martyred in Morocco in 1220 received the accolade only in 1481. Such delays mean that several who died between 1200 and 1500 and are now treated as saints only gained official recognition later. Ferdinand III of Castile died in 1252, but was canonised only in 1671, the

---

[4] R. M. Woolley, *The officium and miracula of Richard Rolle of Hampole* (London, 1919), p. 12.

same year as the Servite friar Philip Benizi (d. 1285). This has various implications, beyond that imposed by the hindsight that individuals were to become saints eventually. Canonisation processes reflect the definition of sanctity acceptable to those then in control, not necessarily when the candidate was alive. Successful processes may deflect attention from what contemporaries saw as the saint's most saintly features (as in the case of Elzéar de Sabran, whose virginity in marriage was played down). So, also, with processes which failed, possibly because the acceptable definition of sanctity had changed, or some other obstacle had intervened.

Canonisation processes demanded considerable investment in time, effort, and money from their promoters, unless lobbying was effective or political considerations made it advisable for the papacy to work quickly. The canonisation of Osmund, bishop of Salisbury, was achieved only in 1457; but he had died in 1099. The extant record of the successive, and lengthy, attempts to secure his formal elevation details the expenditure of over £700 in the fifteenth century. Investigations started in 1228 and continued intermittently over the next two centuries, with the repeated collection of details of miracles ascribed to him.

The bureaucratic evolution unavoidably affected the definition of sainthood, for the ecclesiastical authorities naturally imposed their own conceptions of the acceptable. Between 1215 and 1515 the well-born and those who had held high ecclesiastical office were obviously at an advantage, as the ranks of saints filled out with bishops, members of religious orders, the well-connected and the well-supported. Few, however, were popes. In fact, there was only one, Celestine V. He had been too holy to be effective, and abdicated after occupying the throne of St Peter for only a few months in 1294, dying a prisoner of his successor Boniface VIII. His canonisation in 1313 was in some respects a political act, revenge by the pro-French Clement V on Boniface VIII, a fierce antagonist of the French king Philip IV. (Other popes from these centuries have been canonised since 1515, notably Benedict XI and Urban V; but cannot count for present purposes.) Some royal dynasties almost claimed hereditary sainthood, with relatives of the Capetians and Angevins of Naples being regularly put forward as candidates, as were several of the Arpads of Hungary in the thirteenth century. Perhaps even more influential on the outcome of a cause was geographical proximity to the papacy: candidates supported from within the curia, or by the popes themselves, were more likely to succeed than postulants who had to be dealt with over long distances. The calendar therefore filled with Italians, inhabitants of southern France, and other western Mediterraneans. Germans, Netherlanders, and Britons were thin on the lists (although Scandinavians fared quite well), despite the many candidates. After 1200 only six English candidates gained success: Gilbert of Sempringham (1202), Edmund of Abingdon (1246), Richard of Chichester (1262), Thomas Cantilupe (1320), John of Bridlington (1401), and Osmund of Salisbury (1457). All were bishops apart from Gilbert and John; but they were both churchmen, Gilbert having established the only English-based regular order, the Gilbertines, and John being an Augustinian canon. Against this meagre total must be set the many potential English saints who did not make it. In at least two cases, it was close: Henry VI, and Thomas de la Hale, a monk of Dover killed in a French raid in 1291, whose claims were officially investigated in the 1380s. One other candidate's sanctity was tacitly accepted without formal approval: Robert of Knaresborough (d. 1218) gained inclusion in the calendar without opposition. Of other possibilities, many were bishops, for a variety of reasons. Some were perhaps saintly, like Edmund Lacy of Exeter, and Robert Grosseteste and John Dalderby of Lincoln. Others were supported mainly for political reasons: Robert Winchelsey of Canterbury for his defence of ecclesiastical liberties against Edward I; Richard Scrope as York's answer to Thomas Becket after his beheading on the orders of Henry IV in 1405 and as a martyr for Yorkist legitimism later in the century. Other candidates are more obscure, such as the abbot of Thorney whose cult was roundly denounced by Pope Boniface IX. Several of England's would-be saints were advanced for purely political reasons: Simon de Montfort, Thomas of Lancaster, and others as 'martyrs' in opposition to a rapacious crown; Henry VI as a victim of Yorkist ambitions and legitimiser of the Tudors. Some even suggested canonising Edward II, and Richard II. There were also various holy men, from John Schorne at one extreme, to Richard Rolle at the other. It may say something of contemporary notions of sainthood that Schorne's cult was seemingly more profitable than Rolle's. Many others gained some degree of devotion, often known only from a brief reference.

Influences other than geography and status affected papal reaction to requests for canonisation. Especially in moments of crisis, the response would be fairly immediate, but reflect external pressures. When the church was split, the official stance on canonisation could raise serious issues. During the Great Schism of 1378–1417, for instance, the separate lines of pontiffs created their own saints. Both successions sought support by offering the carrot of canonisations to their adherents: it may be no accident that these years coincide with considerable activity in England, with Richard II's advocacy of Edward II, the canonisation of John Thweng of Bridlington, and the near-miss of Thomas de la Mare (not to mention a revival of interest in Thomas of Lancaster, and the rebuffed cause of the abbot of Thorney). The rival pontiffs may have been trying to bolster their own claims by promoting canonisations of those who were considered particularly godly at the time, so enhancing their own legitimacy by association. Thus, the Avignon popes recognised Peter of Luxembourg, little more than a youth, but with a considerable reputation for holiness. On the Roman side, the principal canonisation was that of Bridget of Sweden. Nevertheless, it is notable that partisanship during the crises of the schism did not preclude recognition as a saint once it was over: Catherine of Siena, an adherent of Urban VI, was canonised in 1461 (admittedly by a fellow-Sienese, Pope Pius II), while Vincent Ferrer, an ardent supporter of the antipope Benedict XIII, secured recognition in 1455.

The bureaucracy of canonisation created no obvious chasm within the ranks of the intercessors between those accepted as saints by the authorities and those who were accorded sainthood by popular acclamation without formal papal approbation. Some 'unofficial' cults gained international status. The life of 'St' Zita, a Luccan serving-woman who died in 1272, exemplified the theme of *caritas* and contemplation in the world, providing a model of a pious servant which strongly contradicted contemporary prejudices about servants. Although not canonised, she attracted widespread devotion. Her very ordinariness and legitimisation of the domestic possibly gave her a following; so did the support for her cause from the powerful Faytinelli family in Lucca. In any event her cult spread across Europe, with commemorations in cathedrals and parish churches. While Zita's cult was tolerated, the church was wary of spontaneous 'canonisations', and sought to ensure that false saints did not slip into the calendar. To some extent, the naturally cyclical process of devotions served their purpose here. As determination was needed to complete the canonisation process, only those with stamina or friends in high places would stay the course. While local cults were constantly appearing, they usually died equally quickly. After a few years fashion would change or interest evaporate as miracles became rarer, and what might have produced a new saint in fact withered away. The process is well illustrated by the case of King Henry VI in England. After his death in 1471 interest in his claims to sanctity was widespread. Woodcuts, stained glass, statues, and alabaster figures all attest devotion to him; while the political support offered by Richard III and Henry VII, and the ambitions of the religious corporations which hoped to house his shrine (successively Chertsey abbey, St George's chapel, Windsor, and Westminster abbey) also helped. Despite extensive commemoration, with 174 miracles attested in the canonisation proceedings (which were begun, but not finished) and chapels and images erected in numerous churches, the devotion did not last. Support for his possible canonisation lingered into the reign of Henry VIII, and Windsor continued to attract pilgrims; but elsewhere the cult rapidly declined. At Great Yarmouth the record of offerings to his image shows that after an initial eruption of enthusiasm at the accession of Henry VII, devotion tapered off in the late 1490s and early 1500s. At Hereford evidence for offerings ends in 1512; while the only mention of an image at Ely comes so late that there were no offerings at all. As a national force the cult of Henry VI had effectively died out by around 1510.

Not all unofficial cults withered quite so dramatically. Indeed, that of John Schorne (d. 1314), a Buckinghamshire priest whose main claim to fame was to have conjured the devil into a boot, remained vital right through to the Reformation. So vital, in fact, that when St George's chapel at Windsor secured the appropriation of the church containing his remains, they were removed to Windsor with the full agreement of the ecclesiastical hierarchy – clear evidence that the distinction between official and unofficial sanctity should not be made too rigid.

Henry VI's murder and political utility assisted his claims to sainthood, but there is no evidence that he was considered a saint during his life. In contrast, many other prospective saints did gain a degree of recognition before their deaths. This was certainly the most difficult area for the authorities to control, for what the popular idea of saintly behaviour did not always coincide with the church's definition. Indeed, that many saints offered challenges to the church made them positively dangerous; the tensions being best demonstrated in cases where candidates were eventually condemned for their heresies.

In the thirteenth century, Franciscan spirituality in its more extreme forms produced strange results. The Guglielmites of Milan – a sect aiming to create a female-oriented church headed by a female incarnation of the Holy Spirit advised by a female college of cardinals – were one strand in that evolution. The sect's members shared the features of contemporary penitential piety which might be taken to indicate sanctity; small wonder, then, that at the foundress's death she was hailed as a saint, with the Cistercian monastery of Chiaravalle supporting her claims for canonisation. The resulting inquiries revealed her heresies, and the case collapsed. Such *post mortem* investigations often led to the suppression of popular cults, especially in Italy, unearthing unorthodoxies and in due course the unorthodox from the places of honour in which they had been buried. This is exemplified in the case of Armanno Pungilupo of Ferrara, honoured as a saint after his death in 1269, but exposed as a Cathar and eventually exhumed from his tomb in the cathedral and burnt in 1300.

Those recognised as saints whilst they lived were generally appreciated for their asceticism. Retreat, self-starvation, and extreme devotion seem

to have been the basic requirements. Many were credited with miracles
even before death; the ascetics often attracted groups of adherents who
collected relics shed before death – hair, nail-parings, even (according to
the devotees of Lidwina of Schiedam, who died in 1433) bits of intestines.
The relationship between such living saints and their societies was
complex and tense: that they were recognised meant that they were
perceived as providing something needed by their contemporaries. In a
real sense, sainthood was something to be orchestrated. It required the
active co-operation of the proposed saint and the audience, and a delicate
balance of control. In life, the relationships could easily be upset. Francis
of Assisi retained the upper hand, because his definition of sainthood was
a way of life. Lukardis of Oberweimar (d. 1309) ensured a balance with
her own community of nuns by becoming the focus of their own
mystical aspirations. Douceline of Digne (d. 1274) shows the balance
slipping: her sanctity was ecstatic, and easily manipulated and tested. Her
audiences would therefore trigger off her ecstacies and subject her to
fiendish physical testing in her trances, denying her the willing
complicity which the access to sainthood demanded. On the other hand,
the saint desired by the audience might reject the role: the friar Nicholas
of Montefeltro was credited with miracles during his life, but none
occurred after his death – supposedly because he had secured God's agreement not to perform any so that he could refuse the honours of sainthood.

Against complicity the demand for saints, the requirement that sanctity
be somehow public, made living saints highly vulnerable should they not
fit the bill precisely. The ascetic life was easily denigrated, as fraudulent,
as reflecting not devotion but a physical ailment. Attacks on the validity
of saintly experiences were as common as their upholding, and the saints
were to some extent on the defensive: in the triangular relationship
between themselves, God, and their contemporaries, they almost needed
the devotion of their fellows as self-validation. There was, therefore, some
degree of conformity to the stereotype imposed by society; although the
recognition as a saint also allowed the individual to change the stereotype.
This transformation is perhaps most apparent where the saint had an
amanuensis during life. The contact between saint and recorder was a
critical dialectic, the dialogues to clarify and check the meaning of
pronouncements acting as a form of control on the saint's doctrinal
exuberance. The role of the audience in the process could also be highly
ambivalent. Margery Kempe was condemned as demonically inspired,
even as a Lollard by some of her contemporaries who refused to accept
her self-promulgation. Even more dramatically ambivalent was the
reaction to Joan of Arc. For the French she was a voice from God, for
the English a witch inspired by demons – and burnt as such in 1431. The

verdict was quashed by a papal commission in 1456, but canonisation was delayed until 1920.

Because there was the preconception of saintly behaviour, it was possible to deceive, almost to market oneself as a saint. This self-perception and self-promulgation has been suggested for some of the English mystics, notably Margery Kempe and Richard Methley; but they do not seem to have been engaged on deliberate fraud. Others did, like the Holy Maid of Leominster in the reign of Henry VII who claimed to exist solely on daily eucharist, but was duly exposed. Fear of fraud did limit acceptance of living saints: even the revelations of Bridget of Sweden were doubted by some, including no less an authority than Jean Gerson.

Creation of a cult

The devotions associated with saints stressed their links with the divine, their role as powerful intercessors on behalf of their devotees. Death was the major turning point in attitudes to saints. Those who had saintly reputations during life could now work even more directly with God for their adherents; those who had not been recognised might now gain attention. There is no evidence for any ascription of sanctity to Richard Scrope during his life; but after his death in 1405 crowds flocked to his place of execution and tomb, the government eventually posting guards to keep pilgrims away for fear that their devotion was more political than spiritual. Peter of Luxembourg, on the other hand, was considered a saint during life. His death and burial in 1387 was the signal for a massive explosion of devotional activity, described by a correspondent of Francesco Datini then in Avignon:

Hardly had he been put in the ground, than the lower people began to place candles there, and certain one-armed people, the crippled and the lame, as well as various other sick people, had themselves carried to near the cardinal . . . and gathered around his burial place . . . since the very day of his interment up to today there are so many people that you would say it was a consecration. Certainly, a hundredweight of candles (and more) are carried there each day, and there are already so many wax images that they exceed a thousand, of one sort or another. This is the greatest happening and the greatest devotion that has ever been seen for a hundred years. The learned as well as the ignorant, the idiot, the poor, go there as though to a great indulgence, and that both morning, afternoon, and evening. Consider that every night 200 people sleep and keep watch out of devotion in that spot. Many sick people have gone there and, having completed their novena, have been completely cured. From outside, from the fortified villages of the region, have come the lame, the crippled, the one-armed and paralytics, who have been cured by the powers of God and this holy cardinal. Each day there are very great miracles, and it is a great wonder to see the wax images which are daily carried there.[5]

In this case the cult was supported by the local ecclesiastical authorities, including the papacy. The antipope Clement VII initiated the preliminaries for the canonisation in 1390. Peter of Luxembourg benefited because of his links with the Avignonese curia: encouragement of his cult in the context of the Great Schism would have obvious benefits, although in fact canonisation was delayed until 1527. But a death might expose the tensions between definitions of sainthood, and lead to disputes. A decade after Peter of Luxembourg's death, that of Marcolinus of Forli at Forli 1397 produced conflict between popular desire for a saint and the reluctance of his Dominican confreres to accept such popular acclamation. For the Dominicans Marcolinus did not match the preconceived pattern of sainthood. In the resulting battle of wills, the Dominicans were forced to back down. In contrast, the cult which developed around the tomb of Peter John Olivi at Narbonne was seen as threatening because of his links with the Spiritual Franciscans (the more radical wing among the Franciscans, who demanded strict adherence to Francis' ideal of apostolic poverty against the laxity and *de facto* possession of property which had come with the order's institutionalisation). The cult was forcibly quashed in 1317.

Many devotions erupted, but as quickly ebbed away. Much would depend on the effectiveness of the process of spreading news about the events. New cults could spread rapidly, but often this would be by accident, with obscure and new saints gaining adherents by chance, almost as a last resort in desperate cases. In 1382 a passing pilgrim suggested that those gathered round a child's corpse in Leicester should invoke Richard Rolle after all else had failed: it worked. This was over thirty years after Rolle's death, yet his devotion had clearly not spread much outside Yorkshire by then.

Once dead, saints became even more of a source of power than during life, a power available to be trapped and controlled. It was trapped by possession of relics which served as reminders of their human existences, and in the case of corporeal remains contained the essence of their force as intercessors. Control, rather more diffuse, could be gained by simple invocation, or by a visual representation. None of these was guaranteed effective: whether saints reacted was to some extent up to them. There was always a complex tension in attitudes here, for the saints needed the recognition offered by devotees as warranties of their status as much as their adherents wanted the favours conferred by the saints. Because most saints were dead, there was also a complex metamorphosis in perceptions of them. This obviously applies most to those who actually lived and died during the period under review. The reasons why they were saints could become relatively unimportant – it was what they could now do, rather than what they had been, which counted. It was the power they could exert as intercessors which became the decisive factor.

A saint's image also changed after death. The move from holy life, with all its discordances and contradictions, to holy death, produced major changes in the perception as saint. From being an individual, the saint became a type, available not simply for wonder but for instructive use. The transition is exemplified with Margery Kempe, even though she did not become a saint. Her autobiography of the 1430s, with its assertiveness, idiosyncrasy, disobedience, and individualism, contrasts strikingly with the submissive, quiet, pacific model of piety put forward in the printed abridgement of her book of *c.* 1501. After death, manipulation and containment changed the saint's identity, in response to the church's needs and the audiences' perceptions. Iconography best displayed the changes. Louis IX, the threadbare king, became St Louis, the majestic. Louis of Anjou, the ascetic bishop of Toulouse who sought a life of apostolic poverty with the Spiritual Franciscans and died *en route* to resign his see, became St Louis of Toulouse, portrayed in full pontificals. Even Jerome, the hermit-like translator of the Bible, became a cardinal.

Further manipulation might follow from changes in the contexts in which saints were located. Elizabeth of Spalbeek was a reclusive beguine of the late thirteenth century with a reputation as a prophetess, renowned as a visible stigmatic and for a devotion to the Passion which involved a one-person re-enactment at regular intervals. Her chapel remained the focus of her cult after her death, with its fresco decoration of *c.* 1350–1500 seeking deliberately – but implicitly rather than explicitly – to locate her within a wider context of healing and semi-regular piety which was primarily eucharistic and Passion-centred. This demonstrates an inter-dependence, almost circularity, in the relationships: Elizabeth's personal holiness attested the validity of such devotions; the recollection of the devotions revalidated her claims to sanctity.

If saints were to be useful in the long term, their memories could not be simply confined to oral tradition. Lives had to be written, to authenti-cate and authorise the experiences, and provide material from which commemorations could be constructed. But written saints' lives had other functions, and changed over time. Exactly what the appropriate response should be to medieval saints' lives is a matter of considerable debate, centring chiefly on uncertainties about how their intended audiences actually reacted to tales which are often quite incredible. To a great extent, the debate is as much about the perplexity which the *Lives* produce in modern scholars as about the medieval response to them. To judge such hagiography in purely historical terms may, however, be inappropriate: the historical reality of the saints was perhaps largely irrelevant to their spiritual and devotional utility. When Buddha could be Christianised in *Barlaam and Josophat*, and an unashamedly fictional ideal saint be portrayed in Llull's *Blanquerna* as an instructional device, it was clearly the message rather than the historical truth which counted. The uncertainties of modern reaction to the saints' lives may also derive from a failure to distinguish between different types of text. The nature of the written record does seem to have changed as a saint became chrono- logically more remote. This is particularly noticeable in the later middle ages, perhaps partly induced by the call for documentary proofs of sanctity associated with canonisation. A first life obviously had to justify the claims to sainthood, especially for those whose reputations were established while they lived. As the saints moved from being challenges to their contemporaries to being models for their posterities, so the format of the life would be revised. The initial record, with its assertions and dramatic claims, could be tempered for a new audience, one which accepted the sainthood as a fact and needed no further convincing. The changing utility of a saint's life may be most readily seen in the gradual evolution of the official biography of Francis of Assisi, although in this case the process was telescoped into only a couple of generations. The first official life was written by Thomas of Celano in 1228–31, at papal instigation, and for general consumption to demonstrate Francis's sanctity. The *Vita secunda*, composed by Celano in the 1240s, supplements the earlier version without replacing it effectively. However, it has a more obviously polemical intent, presenting Francis more forcefully as an advocate of poverty, presumably in reaction to the growing institutional- isation of the Order. The text's inconvenient reminders of how the Franciscan Order should have developed, and the problems of its incompleteness as a full *Life*, may explain why, in 1260, Bonaventure was commissioned to produce another, definitive, *vita*. Although heavily dependent on Celano's earlier work; by recasting and reordering Bonaventure offers a different picture of Francis. In the search to reconcile the developing divergent wings of the Order, 'to subdue disputation by removing the cause of offence',[6] he suppresses some of the

---

[6] R. Brooke, 'The lives of St Francis of Assisi', in *Latin biography*, ed. T. A. Dorey (London, 1967), p. 189.

Figure 3 Messages of sainthood. Simone Martini's panel showing St Louis of Toulouse with his younger brother, King Robert of Naples, painted after the former's canonisation in 1317. The majesty of the saint in episcopal regalia (although worn over his Franciscan habit) contrasts with the reality of his attempts to renounce his episcopal status and his declared sympathy for the Spiritual Franciscans. The whole image stresses the dynastic sanctity of the Angevin line: as the angels crown the saint, so he confers a terrestrial crown on his brother. There is also a political message: Louis had renounced his rights to the succession on becoming a Franciscan, so that the grant of a crown also legitimates Robert's succession.

more controversial details of preceding lives. This toning down of
Francis may make Bonaventure's text less useful as a historical document;
but it can be defended as offering a more spiritualised sanctity (a spirituality necessarily moulded by Bonaventure's own), and for developing the
parallel between the life of Francis and the life of Christ. This new *Life*
was intended to supersede the previous biographies, so totally that the
General Chapter of 1266 ordered all copies of them to be destroyed.

Transformation took other forms also. The history of the *Legenda aurea*
of James of Voragine, the standard compendium of saints' lives compiled
c. 1260, displays all the ramifications. Initially in Latin, and directed at an
Italian and clerical readership, it rapidly spread throughout catholic
Europe. The expanded readership imposed new demands, leading to
alterations and additions. New saints – both chronologically, and in
geographical coverage – were added to regional versions. Translations
into the vernacular created regionalised compendia with defined
circulations, some of them geographical, others among specific religious
orders. Translations for the laity also led to the excision of much of the
theological discussion; while re-editing for other purposes changed
the order, expanded some sections and reduced others, creating so many
different compilations that it would be stretching the point to give them
all the same title. Yet the lives produced an 'image' of the saint, which
would impact on the society in general and on individuals in particular: a
model, a paradigm, a warning.

Relics

In the search to control the power which saints could channel, relics had
an important role, and made a more general contribution to late medieval
devotional practices. Their chief function was as aids, to trap the power
of the saint and to assist the appeal for intercession; but that was not
all. Relics are usually thought of simply in terms of bodily remains –
skeletons, bits of hair, bones, and so on; they could be much more.
Objects only associated with saints, like clothing and other possessions,
also stimulated devotion: things like the shoe of St Thomas Becket much
derided by Erasmus when visiting Canterbury; or the comb said to have
belonged to St Edmund of Abingdon which was among the collection of
relics at Calne church. Articles associated with deaths were also important,
ranging from the bits of the grill of St Lawrence owned by Lichfield
cathedral, to the dagger which murdered Henry VI, kept at Caversham.

However, relics need not be so personal. Some were mere curiosities:
Durham's collection in 1383 contained two 'griffin's claws' and several
'griffin's eggs'; while in the 1490s a presumed bone of Livy was laid under

the altar of a chapel constructed by the humanist Giovanni Pontano at Naples. Relics also provided links with Biblical events, supposedly having been gathered at the scene: Lichfield cathedral's collection included bits of Golgotha and of the rock on which Jesus had sweated blood; while other English churches had objects associated with Daniel and Moses.

The curios, and perhaps the souvenirs of the Holy Land, must have been appreciated in a very different manner from the relics proper. The latter had a more specific, functional purpose: as reminders of individual saints, as a way of trapping their power, as aids to devotion. Their distribution was widespread. Major collections were built up by churches, prelates, and princes; fragments of the True Cross were innumerable, often being owned by lay people. (To account for the number of fragments, and avoid the need to challenge their validity, the theory developed that the Cross was self-replicating, like the loaves and fishes at the Feeding of the Five Thousand.) Churches naturally had the largest accumulations, of relics of both official and unofficial saints. Cathedral and monastic collections were huge; but even relatively humble parish churches would own some. The search for appropriate relics is shown in the fifteenth century with the building of a church in honour of the Northumbrian martyr-king, St Oswald, at Zug (Switzerland). An envoy was sent to Peterborough in England to collect a fragment from his arm which reposed there.

The acquisition of relics in this way was not unusual; and the transfer between laity of particularly holy heirlooms can be traced in wills and other records. They were, indeed, marketable: King Richard II of England acquired the presumed body of one of the Innocents murdered by Herod from a German merchant. The price was remission of customs duties for two years. Wars, with their opportunities for looting, provided plenty of opportunity for further redistribution. The tradition of acquiring relics by theft seems to have died out by the start of the thirteenth century; subsequent robberies were thefts of the reliquaries and their wealth rather than of their contents. However, relics were considered legitimate plunder. Alfonso V of Aragon acquired the bones of St Louis of Toulouse among the booty from a raid on Marseilles in 1423, and transferred them to Valencia. The interest in relics appears at its most profound in Louis IX's creation of the Sainte Chapelle in Paris, built as an appropriate setting for the relics of the Passion (including the Crown of Thorns) which he had acquired from the impoverished Latin emperor of Constantinople, Baldwin II. Even though the 'original' Crown of Thorns was already at Paris, having lain among the treasures of St Denis for centuries, the new relics were accepted and displayed without any qualms. Indeed, the multiplication of relics is remarkable, despite attempts by the Fourth Lateran Council to insist on verification before acceptance. Few had been as complaisant as the Irish St Abbanianus, or the Welsh St Teilo, both from the sixth century. The former settled a dispute over his remains by miraculously producing a second body; St Teilo went one better and left three. None the less, Europe contained several heads of John the Baptist, while both Monte Cassino and Fleury claimed – and claim – to be the true resting place of St Benedict of Nursia. The hunger for relics sometimes became quite gruesome. At Florence in 1246 the barely cold body of Umiliana de' Cerchi was torn to pieces by the crowd accompanying it to burial at Santa Croce. The relic industry is shown at its worst by Chaucer, in his portrait of the Pardoner in the *Canterbury Tales*, showing off false relics to dupe the guileless (as some undoubtedly did).

The ghoulishness of the relic hunting, the gullibility of the audiences, the confusion about identification, and the multiplication of bodies or fragments of them, makes the whole concern with relics seem slightly – or more than slightly – ridiculous. But to concentrate on the practicalities is to overlook the spiritualities: the veracity of the relics was largely irrelevant to devotion. As with the legends about the saints, it only matters that relics were accepted as genuine, and as such had a real devotional function. The duplications and historical discrepancies thus worry modern commentators more than they did contemporaries. People like Lorenzo Valla did inveigh against the fabulous aspects of saints' lives, which were sometimes edited out in humanist rewritings; but often the inconsistencies would not have been known or, more importantly, they may not have mattered. If relics and pilgrimages worked to direct and channel devotion, rather than specifically as the objects of devotion, then questions of veracity simply need not arise, or could be circumvented by treating all the instances with the same degree of devotion. In commenting to pilgrims to the church of St John Lateran who wished to go through a doorway supposedly used by Christ in a post-Resurrection appearance, the fifteenth-century English writer and Augustinian friar John Capgrave remarks that 'because no-one can truly say by which door Christ went out, for there are three doors, therefore pilgrims go through all three doorways'. Equally, noting inconsistency between chronicles on the fate of the bodies of Peter and Paul, he dismisses them as relatively unimportant 'because it does not concern the articles of our faith'.[7]

While most relics were linked with saints, those associated with Christ

[7] C. A. Mills, ed., *Ye solace of pilgrimes: a description of Rome, circa AD 1450, by John Capgrave, an Austin friar of King's Lynn* (London, New York, Toronto, and Melbourne, 1911), pp. 74, 71.

were more problematic, sometimes raising serious theological problems. If Christ had been resurrected, why were there relics like his foreskin (especially problematic as several places claimed to possess it)? Phials of Christ's Blood, as at Bruges and Hailes (Gloucestershire) were only slightly less worrying. But such issues only really perturbed the theologians: the fact of the relic's existence was probably sufficient for most, enough to justify a pilgrimage and the search for a miracle. Yet that there were physical relics of Christ perhaps reinforced the belief that the consecrated elements were also relics, with powers which could be exploited and used. The devotion to the Host thus evolves alongside, possibly overtaking, the devotion to the saints and their relics.

Images

The devotion to the saints shown in the proliferation of relics is also attested in the abundant images, whether sculpted, painted, or in glass. Saints' lives provided edification for the laity; depictions helped to concentrate devotion. Churches and chapels abounded with lights and images dedicated to particular saints, and sometimes maintained by specific fraternities. Their windows might show single figures, or a whole saint's story; painting on walls and other furniture was equally significant.

Such representations pose various questions, not confined to that of the validity of the image *per se*. Images could be a significant way of catering for non-liturgical devotion, even extra-ecclesial religion. Statues, like some of the Pietàs of the Netherlands, might be as well displayed in a public street as in a church, permitting a response which was unconstrained by a liturgical or ecclesial context. The devotion to images, and the proliferation of representations, was open to question. Notable among the challenges were those raised by English Lollards in the fifteenth century, who castigated such near-idolatry. Yet there was clearly a considerable investment of effort and money in these decorations; and the references in wills, in particular the grants to specific images or the requests for burial near a particular saint's altar, do suggest real devotion.

The problem is one of relationships: of the message, and its reception. Traditionally, all representations functioned as 'books for the unlearned'; they possessed no inherent power, but served to stir up and reflect devotion. Yet there was clearly room for ambiguity. A processional banner, like those produced in Umbrian towns depicting Mary protectively sheltering the town and its people under her mantle as Our Lady of Mercy, was clearly not static. The banner was for display, and to head a procession of intercession, probably usually against plague, given the regular depiction of St Sebastian with her. Even more complex are the

Schreinmadonna images of north-east Germany and Sweden. Here a Virgin and Child image opens out to become a protective Madonna, sheltering supplicants (often Teutonic Knights and royalty), and enclosing a smaller image of the Trinity. It, too, was a statement, often of protective political connections; but like the Umbrian banners the *Schreinmadonna* was also a channel for intercession. The possible theological implications of images of the Virgin enclosing the Trinity are staggering; but in the version known as the *Vierge ouvrante* it is well-attested throughout Europe.

The static quality of the depictions suggests something about the nature of these images. They were not meant to be realistic representations; they functioned primarily as aids to memory, mnemonics, and in a chrono-logical sense re-presentations of the whole story encapsulated in the depiction. This may account for some of the content of instructional literature: what is to be recalled when looking at a crucifix, for instance. It doubtless also explains how particular images stimulated the visionaries. A similar connection appears in some reports of visions experienced by those with no particular claims to sanctity. Several fifteenth-century Marian visions in Spain relate the appearance of a diminutive Virgin, who often seems to be modelled on contemporary images at important pilgrimage centres. This mnemonic quality may also account for the nature of some of the written saints' lives, providing material for recollection when the image was experienced. Nevertheless, images and depictions could only work if they were addressed to those already familiar with the story. The illuminations of the majority of the extant copies of Jean de Vignay's French translation of the *Legenda aurea* operate on this basis: they use traditional attributes to identify the saints, even though the episodes associated with those attributes often do not appear in the text.

Miracles

Devotion to a saint was no one-way arrangement. Saints had to earn veneration, had to demonstrate their power and justify their invocation. The wax offerings which rapidly accumulated around the tomb of Peter of Luxembourg can be matched by similar votives at other shrines. This was part of a process of gift-exchange, an offering in return for a benefit, and all part of the economy of salvation. The reciprocity was bluntly acknowledged by the Florentine government in 1419 in relation to the image of Our Lady of Impruneta, recording that the more she demonstrated her beneficence to the city, the more the citizens should honour her with gifts and alms when brought into the city. This bilateral relationship meant that saints who did not produce the desired response might be scolded, threatened with violence, or ritually humiliated. This seems to apply particularly to saints connected with weather or agrarian activities. In Germany, if St Urban did not provide decent weather on his day for the vine harvest, his image would be dumped in the mud; during storms the fishermen of Heist (Flanders) dunked the statue of Our Lady of Aardenburg in the sea in order to calm the waves. The demand for reciprocity made saints subject to market forces: dissatisfied supplicants would take their invocations elsewhere. This competition was particularly intense in moments of crisis, as when English pilgrims returning from Santiago in 1385 were imprisoned in Spain, being saved from execution by St Edmund the martyr (St James presumably having abandoned them); or when a London child was choking on a badge commemorating Thomas Becket (which any self-respecting saint would not have permitted) and was saved when pleas to King Henry VI caused it to be coughed up.

Once dead, saints could only reveal their power through miracles. This marked a major shift of emphasis in devotion. The justification for the saintly reputation – virginity, martyrdom, or whatever – became relatively unimportant for the supplicants. What counted was that the fact of sainthood gave access to power; and it was the exercise of the power which was sought.

In the gift-exchange relationship which saints' cults manifested, miracles were the archetypal proof of sanctity and the saint's power with God. All saints could perform miracles after death; many effected them during their lives as part of their *pre mortem* identification. Any prospective saint who failed to deliver after death would soon lose adherents; the decline in miracle working may explain the failure of some canonisation proceedings. After canonisation and recognition, miracles were perhaps less necessary; but they had to continue for a saint to retain popularity. Miracles proved that a saint had God's favour (it was, technically, He who performed the miracle, not the saint), and as an intercessor with the divinity could so benefit devotees. Such distinctions may, however, have been ignored in popular attitudes towards the powers and functions of saints.

'Miracles' were not uncommon. Although preachers claimed that they were rarer than in the past, the extant miracle collections of only eleven Bavarian shrines record around 12,000 for the years between 1346 and 1522. As the definition of the miraculous was extremely capacious, the number is not particularly surprising. The invocation of a saint, followed by the desired result, was regarded as a miracle simply on the basis of *post hoc ergo propter hoc*. Most recorded miracles deal with healing and the rectification of physical or mental abnormalities or deformities; although much else might fall within the scope of the miraculous. Records of *miracula* were maintained at shrines, like those in the northern Netherlands and Bavaria, or at Canterbury and Durham; such was the importance of the miracles to devotional practice that books listing them were printed from the late fifteenth century. Collections were also prepared for canonisation proceedings, as in the cases of Thomas Cantilupe and Henry VI. Miracles were not effected only by the intercession of saints: Christ and God could operate independently; shrines like that of the Holy Blood at Hailes also produced them, as did the Precious Blood at Wilsnack. The multiple shrines of the Virgin, the supreme intercessor, were also major foci of miracles. (Even the Devil could work miracles; but that inconvenient possibility can be ignored for present purposes.)

Many miracles would now be explained in physiological terms; others might tempt sociological analysis. But modern approaches cannot and should not replace the significance ascribed to such events by contemporaries. If they actually occurred at the shrine there would almost certainly be immediate celebration. Otherwise, they would be incorporated into the format of experience: they were wonders, but by no means inexplicable, for the simplest explanation was that they demonstrated God's illimitable power working within his Creation. As miracles were expected, their occurrence would be no surprise; if they did not happen there would be disappointment and the need for an explanation, usually found in the supplicant's own deficiencies.

While miracles were relatively common, they require careful treatment. Not only were what would now be explicable events considered miraculous; but what counted as a miracle was also relative. A 'cure' might well ignore the fact of a relapse (with, perhaps, the search for another miracle); the illness had remitted temporarily, and that was enough. Miraculous preservation might also be brief, especially with children. A foundling child, apparently dead, might have an obstruction to its breathing dislodged when moved and placed on an altar, and revive sufficiently to be baptised before dying – that it had recovered to receive baptism and the accompanying salvation was sufficient. Some places specialised in such miraculous resuscitations, and gained wide renown. Such 'sanctuaires de répit' were especially noted in France, spreading in the fifteenth century. That at Vienne recorded twenty miracles between 1450 and 1480.

Equally significant from the viewpoint of the authorities, miracles had to be checked, particularly if performed through the agency of those not yet officially recognised as saints. Because the devil and his minions could work miracles, and magicians and others claimed similar powers, such events might delude the faithful as well as reinforce their faith. Miracles linked with the unorthodox had therefore to be discountenanced. Fraud also had to be countered. Given the perception that miracles had become scarcer, the challenge presented by that decline also had to be addressed. Two courses were open, depending on how the miracles were to be exploited. It could be claimed that the early Church had greater need of confirmation of the truth of Christianity, but now that the battle against rival faiths had been won miracles were less necessary. Alternatively, miracles reflected the faithfulness of the people, and a decline in their occurrence was the saints' reaction to increased earthly sinfulness.

Pilgrimage

Most of the disparate aspects of devotion to the saints were unified in the practice of pilgrimages. Surprisingly, although it was extremely popular, pilgrimage is remarkably ill recorded. Narratives do exist, some of which, like the record of Margery Kempe's wanderings, are valid accounts. Pilgrim guide books survive, like those listing the glories of Rome, detailing the shrines and the indulgences gained by visiting them. There are literary creations, notably the *Canterbury Tales*, for which the setting is a pilgrimage; while something like *Mandeville's Travels* falls into a similar category, although being more a fictionalised description of the countries visited en route. Despite such material, it is virtually impossible to quantify the pilgrims visiting any particular shrine at any particular time. There is frequent, and intermittent, evidence of people moving about – certificates of completed pilgrimages for those who had them imposed as penances; lists of miracles which name their reporters at the shrine; chance references in official documents to people being en route, or receiving licences to travel for such purposes. Shrine accounts give an impressionistic indication of the flow, especially when they survive for major centres like Canterbury – there the periodic jubilees of Thomas Becket leave their mark in a record of increased offerings. Chroniclers and others offer impressions of movement and of the scale of activity. Particularly vivid is Italian comment on the flood of visitors to Rome during Jubilee years, especially that of 1300, the first, when over two million reportedly went, and the clerks of S. Paolo fuori le Mura are described as literally raking in the coins left by the visitors. Sometimes the movements seem to be by particular groups: Mont St Michel in France was apparently especially attractive to children, and there are scattered reports throughout the fourteenth and fifteenth centuries of virtual exoduses of children towards the shrine, from places as far apart as southern France and south-east Germany. The survival of pilgrim badges also contributes to perceptions of the scale and distance of pilgrimages, even if there is little concrete evidence relating to their sale. The scale of the traffic is sometimes revealed by figures. At Munich, 60,000 pilgrims were recorded in one week in 1392; Aachen supposedly received 142,000 in a single day in 1496. Over 50,000 pilgrim badges were sold at Regensburg between 1519 and 1522, while at Einsiedeln 130,000 were reputedly sold in a fortnight in 1466. Such movement gives some credibility to the claims made by the inhabitants of Mont St Michel in 1394 that they subsisted solely on the income from such sales. The scale of the business also explains the long-running contests to control sales which appear at shrines like Le Puy and Rocamadour, between the ecclesiastical shrine-keepers and the local souvenir producers. Usually, however, the evidence is fragmentary and impressionistic: there are few detailed and complete records.

Some shrines clearly were immensely important, and had international significance. In this class would come places like Compostela, Canterbury (at least for about a century after Becket's death), Wilsnack (following the discovery of the Precious Blood), and of course the myriad sites of Rome. In England the shrine of Our Lady of Walsingham was apparently receiving the most offerings when church wealth was surveyed in 1535; but there were many other pilgrimage centres, some of which were popular throughout the period. For most the lack of evidence precludes any assessment of the scale of the traffic. At Worcester, for instance, the paltry receipts at the shrines of Oswald and Wulfstan – rarely over 10s. a year throughout the 1400s – suggest that the cathedral received few pilgrims. However, around £40 p.a. was concurrently being donated to the Marian image within the same church. Receipts at Great Yarmouth shot up after the installation of an image of Henry VI, to decline slightly less rapidly in succeeding years. Similar fluctuations occurred elsewhere, for example at King's Lynn. Some devotions leave only a chance reference – when the church at Harlow was valued in 1398, offerings to St Petronilla were assessed at over £5 p.a.; but that seems to be the sole mention of them. Likewise, offerings to St Urith at Chittlehampton seem to leave no pre-Reformation evidence; but later testimony asserted that the shrine produced around £50 a year, a remarkable sum for so obscure a saint. Of course, the obscurity is only relative: St Urith was not insignificant to her adherents.

Pilgrimage was intimately connected with the cult of saints, with the search for miracles and the veneration of relics. Many pilgrimages originated in a vow, often to offer a candle to be burnt at the shrine if a desired benefit was received. A common practice was to measure a sick person's length in wick, which would be taken to the shrine to be made into a candle in the hope of, or thanks for, the miracle. Even without being taken to a shrine, such candles were a common devotional practice, the measuring occasionally not being confined to individuals. In 1482, to ward off pestilence, the authorities at Barcelona had their city walls measured, the resulting candle being burnt in five-foot lengths; at Nieuport in Flanders, under siege seven years later, a candle the length of the town's fortified defences was vowed to the Virgin.

As the popularity of individual saints fluctuated, the pilgrimage traffic to their shrines naturally ebbed and flowed. Relative popularity can rarely be tested – there were so many places which could be visited, even within a small radius, that it probably changed annually. English evidence suggests, impressionistically, that donation patterns shifted over the centuries. Several of the old great shrines were perhaps less popular after 1400: possibly their saints were losing ground to the Virgin, so that the change was merely in emphasis, rather than a real drop in the overall sum of donations.

The ultimate goal for pilgrimage would almost certainly be the Holy Land, and the opportunity to stand at the Biblical sites and recollect the events of Jesus' life. While the Crusader states existed – until 1291 – the opportunities to achieve that object were at their greatest; after all, the crusade was originally conceived as an 'armed pilgrimage', and it retained that character for some throughout the period. The decline and fall of the crusader states, especially the loss of Jerusalem in 1187 (although it was again in Christian hands between 1228 and 1240), inevitably reduced the catholic presence in the Holy Land; but it was not extinguished. Catholic religious continued to tend the shrines, and links were maintained with Christian outposts like the monastery of St Catherine at Sinai. Nevertheless, the resident Latin Christian population fell to few more than the Italian traders. Contacts were limited to those maintained by the Venetian fleets, which made annual trading expeditions and in due course established something akin to a timetable for a Holy Land package tour. Their sailings offered the only realistic means for pilgrims to visit the area after 1291, with several thousands being accommodated on the annual convoys. Many more declared the intention of going than actually went; not everyone who went returned.

Pilgrimage was an obvious demonstration of devotion; but many other elements could be integrated. Some pilgrimages were imposed as penances (some crusaders may have taken their vows for this purpose); possibly as a period during which tempers could cool if local relationships were becoming tense. Some might be taken to justify what was little more than a holiday (although all pilgrimages would have a holiday element, simply because of the opportunity they offered for sight-seeing and absence from normal routine). Pilgrimages could even be performed by proxy, matching the way in which crusaders might pay substitutes to fulfil their vows for them. Testators left bequests for pilgrimages to be performed on their behalf, perhaps by a hermit. Some may even have hoped to complete a pilgrimage after death in effigy. One Pisan testator in 1286 bequeathed a hefty sum to make a wax image of himself which was to be deposited in a church near Marseilles. Vicarious pilgrimages also occurred during life: the account book of Elizabeth of York, wife to Henry VII, notes donations made for her by pilgrims who did the round of sites in southern England, up the Thames valley to Gloucester and back, and down to Dover. The shrines listed were not just those of canonised saints: they included John Schorne, and at Tewkesbury Prince Edward, the son of King Henry VI who was killed there after his defeat in battle in 1471. This development of effortless pilgrimage could give a particular function to some of the pilgrimage guide books. Despite their recording of natural wonders and secular historical monuments alongside the religious sights and sites, they also offered the possibility of purely spiritual pilgrimage – 'armchair pilgrimage'. Felix Fabri's *Evagatorium in terrae sanctae* of 1494, drawn up for some Swabian nuns, was intended precisely for that purpose.

Personal devotion: names and naming

The possibility of a quantitative measurement of some aspects of devotional practices offers the chance to trace the evolution of particular cults and centres. Other tempting possibilities open less secure routes. At first glance, the tracing of patterns in the naming of children would seem to be an ideal way of assessing the scale of allegiance to a particular saint. In actuality, it is among the most problematic, although not without some utility.

While Thomas Aquinas placed devotional naming among his list of choices, and Antoninus of Florence tried to insist on it, people acted differently, following local customs and practices. In England, most children seemingly owed their names to the godparents, and were usually named after one of them. Some parents broke with the norms by deliberately choosing a specific saint's name: in the 1320s the naming of one Yorkshire girl provoked comment until the parents explained it by their devotion to St Catherine. As such children in turn became godparents, so a new chain of naming might be established, owing little to the original devotional inspiration. This may explain some of the apparent peculiarities in naming practices. While England evinces considerable devotion to St James, with Santiago de Compostela a popular pilgrimage destination, the saint's name appears infrequently, seemingly in restricted geographical and social groups. This old naming system was apparently cracking in the fifteenth century, with the list of acceptable names increasing greatly. More saints' names appeared more widely – including Christopher and George for boys, Ursula and Bridget for girls. Members of the regular orders also began to adopt 'names in religion' on admission, or assumed a supplementary name in honour of a saint.

Elsewhere practices differed, especially in the control over naming; but a general trend was the greater use of 'devotional' names across the centuries. This had local refinements, like the fifteenth century Florentine practice of giving a family name first, followed by a second (and sometimes third) name which had devotional origins. The integration of devotional names had a pervasive impact on all Tuscan names from the thirteenth century onwards, but motives for choosing particular names were complex. In 1443 Francesco di Tommaso Giovanni of Florence recorded that his son was named Piero

in honor of Saint Peter the Martyr, to whom [the mother] had made a vow to give this name at the birth of . . . [an elder brother]. The second name that I have had given to him, Giovanni, is in honor of Saint John the Evangelist: the devotion I bear him had made me intend to baptize [one of my children] with his name; but it is also to remake (*rifare*) Giovanni, our brother.[8]

Local cults clearly affected some naming practices. In south-eastern France 'Elzéar' gained in popularity in the fifteenth century, presumably because of the cult of Elzéar of Sabran. Female names also changed, with Catherine in particular becoming more common. Changes in Burgundy also reflected local devotions and evolutions. The influences remain obscure: Mary remained a rare female name; people do not seem to have been named for the patron saint of their village. Yet names associated with saints did become more common, as with the rise of Philibert around Châlons in the thirteenth century, or Claude at Dijon in the fifteenth. Names also disappeared, possibly reflecting a drop in some devotions. Constantine and Maurice appear among the stock of names at Dijon in 1357, but not in 1466.

Change also occurred in Germany, as the old Teutonic names generally gave way to non-Germanic saints' names. This shift seemingly began among the bourgeoisie and percolated down through society; the nobility retained the old names for longest. The transformation was

---

[8] C. Klapisch-Zuber, 'The name "remade": the transmission of given names in Florence in the fourteenth and fifteenth centuries', in C. Klapisch-Zuber, *Women, family, and ritual in Renaissance Italy* (Chicago and London, 1985), p. 290.

apparently quickest with girls' names, but 'Mary' was as elsewhere rare before the sixteenth century. If the Bavarian evidence is generally valid, by 1500 Germanic names survived mainly as those of German saints, like Wolfgang or Cunigunde.

In contrast to naming to reflect devotion, devotion may often have followed from naming. In Italy, in fact, the connection between names and devotional choices may actually have occurred at death rather than birth. In a country where surnames developed late, and most people retained patronymics for self-identity, the link with saints seems to have been stressed more in the construction of memorial chapels after (or possibly before) death. In the fourteenth century, many such foundations were dedicated for namesake saints, possibly as the only means of assuring remembrance of the name of the person to be commemorated. Such associations could produce a tension between allegiance and memory, strikingly demonstrated by the insistence of Francis son of Maso de Alferris of Florence in 1363 that his burial chapel be dedicated in honour of St Francis, even though it was to be built in the Dominican church of Santa Maria Novella. Sometimes the dedications reflected filial piety: in 1362 the Pisan Simon son of Benedict recorded that he had arranged the construction of a chapel in the church of San Michele in Borgo, dedicated to his father's name-saint.

Collective cults and guardian angels

Although there are clearly trends for personal association with particular intercessors, there are also signs that what mattered was quantity as much as quality. Multiple dedications and invocations accompany the specific, in a search for what might be labelled 'collective intercession'. The rise in south-east Germany of the devotion to the 'Fourteen Holy Helpers' suggests this search; but the quantitative urge seems more explicit in devotions to the 10,000 Martyrs (of whom there were two sets), or to the 11,000 Virgins who accompanied St Ursula to martyrdom – a cult which spread widely in the fifteenth century.

In the search for numbers, and for human intercessors, even those who were not yet saints may have been enrolled. If the souls in Purgatory used the prayers of the living to secure their own release, might not they – with their guarantee of heaven – have merits which were transferable to their orators? This may at least be the reasoning behind the regionalised devotion to the souls of Purgatory which developed around Avignon from the mid fourteenth century, with its whole panoply of confraternities and alms-collecting.

Even with such additions, there were not enough saints to meet all needs: even patron saints would have to be shared. In the search for intercessors, the concern to identify a personal mediator with God led elsewhere, towards the possibility of a non-human intercessor and the idea of the guardian angel.

Angels were an integral part of the Creation, whose existence was clearly demonstrated in the Bible, unavoidably in the narrative of the Annunciation. Their ranks had been well-defined by pseudo-Dionysius the Areopagite, the unidentified fourth-century author whose works were accepted in later centuries as having been written by St Paul's immediate Athenian disciple, and which exerted a major influence on medieval mystical thought. In consequence, it was accepted that there were nine Orders, of Cherubim, Seraphim, Thrones, Dominations, Powers, Virtues, Principalities, Archangels, and Angels. 'Angelology' was a serious aspect of theology. One of the major saints, the weigher of souls St Michael, long associated with cemeteries and the dead, was an archangel. If the saints were too few to provide the assistance humans sought, what more reasonable than to seek it from the angels?

The idea of the guardian angel seems to have developed as an aspect of ordinary piety mainly in the fourteenth century, although their existence was accepted by theologians from at least the early thirteenth century. The Parisian theologian Jean Gerson happily incorporated them into his instructional treatises for children in the late fourteenth century; and votive masses addressed to guardian angels appeared in missals of the early 1400s. Private prayers were also offered to them, like those recorded in a book belonging to a nun of Chester. The idea of a personal protector, specially deputed by God to deflect evil (perhaps specifically to counter the influence of a personal demon), was clearly highly satisfactory, and gained acceptance throughout Europe. It seemingly met with approval among the hierarchy as well: it seems impossible to divorce the notion from the spread of the devotion to St Raphael, an archangel, during the fifteenth century. Edmund Lacy, bishop of Exeter (d. 1455), was a major English proponent of that cult, instituting the feast in his own diocese in 1443 and encouraging its adoption elsewhere.

If individuals could have a personal angel (who according to one fifteenth-century visionary also accompanied the soul through Purgatory), why not institutions? The idea of a guardian angel for a city, even for a whole realm, seems to have found particular favour within the lands of the Crown of Aragon, where it was widely diffused in the fifteenth century. A missal of 1403 records a mass 'For the feast of the holy guardian angel of the realm and city of Valencia', with a collect imploring that the angel will 'protect and defend [the city] and the whole realm from the present perils of body and soul and future adversities'.[9] Several other cities and regions, including Majorca, Barcelona, and Zaragoza, had chapels dedicated to their guardian angels. Such cults were particularly associated with urban governments, some of which, as at Valencia, had the angel painted in their council chambers. The origins are unclear – the devotion at Barcelona was later said to have been instituted after Vincent Ferrer received an angelic vision during a visit in 1398. The angel's identification varied, Michael or Raphael being the most frequent; but the iconography of a sword to protect from danger (and to chastise), and holding out the possibility of a crown, was unambiguous about the purpose.

In the search for intercessors, the reverence offered to saints fitted into worship which was essentially public. After all, saints existed for the edification of all; relics were publicly displayed; miracles required public affirmation and recognition; shrines were public meeting places, as were images and altars in parish churches. Devotion to a saint had to be demonstrated. Although devotions could be performed in private, and personal dedication to saints was important, the public display mattered. Even so, in the full range of the Christian religion, intercessors were only accessories: a relationship with a saint or angel was not the same as contact with God. It was that contact, with God or his Son, which was the acme of religious and spiritual experience.

MAN AND GOD

Options

Christianity's ritualistic round may have been satisfying enough for most people. Reverential genuflections, recitations of Creeds and Our Fathers when appropriate, attendance at elevations during mass, the rites of passage which the church offered as a communal experience from cradle to grave, and annual submission to the process of confession and communion, would be commitment enough. The church may often have been unable to offer more. Much would depend on providing clergy of the desired quality to maintain a fully spiritual life, particularly in remote rural areas: St Yves Hélory (d. 1303), the only parish priest to secure canonisation in the period (in 1347), was renowned mainly for his pastoral

---

[9] G. Llompart, 'El angel custodio en la Corona de Aragón en la Baja Edad Media (fiesta, teatro, iconografía)', in *Fiestas y liturgia: actas del coloquio celebrado en la Casa de Velázquez/Fêtes et liturgie: actes du colloque tenu à la Casa de Velázquez, 12/14-XII-1985* (Madrid, 1988), p. 251.

achievements. The number consciously dissatisfied by the available level of spiritual care was probably small, if visitation evidence is any guide. People may complain about an absence of services, failure to provide chaplains and the desired round of sacraments, but that is not quite the same thing: a mechanical rather than emotional absence.

Not everyone would be so easily content; some demanded greater spiritual satisfaction. There are intermittent signs of spiritual hunger among the literate, the leisured, and in urban populations, among those with the opportunities to consider such matters. The desire for closer contact with God, to create a more private religion and an individual relationship with the divinity, was significant throughout the period. Access to books, the spread of private chapels and oratories, the creation of voluntary associations which employed clerics and had a spiritual function and were beyond the disciplinary control of the ecclesiastical authorities, all contributed to a greater fragmentation and availability of religious opportunities after 1200. Whether that religion then became more private and personal is debatable: even in a public gathering, people were meant to be maintaining a personal as well as communal relationship with God. The logistics of privatisation can also be doubted; but the possibility, and with it the likelihood of greater questioning of the status and activities of the clergy, did exist. Some of these strands also reflected general social transformations. The changes may even have had some official support. Artistic developments in the late fourteenth and fifteenth centuries which placed events like the Annunciation and the Last Supper in a domestic setting, particularly in Flemish and German painting, can be seen as encouraging the domestication of spirituality, with the complex and erudite iconography stressing the presence among the everyday of valid foci for spiritual contemplation.[10]

Perhaps more significant than retreat from the ecclesial structure into a world of private prayer and reflection was the increase in opportunities for people to choose the type of religion they wanted. The liturgical calendar's set round imposed some limitations; but there was considerable choice beyond them, which was exercised. Particularly in chantries and gilds, the laity gained a say in the construction and timing of services by writing prayers, choosing collects, and decreeing which of the liturgical

---

[10] C. F. O'Meara, 'Eucharistic theology and the house of God in late medieval and early Renaissance painting', in *Classica et mediaevalia: studies in honor of Joseph Szövérffy*, ed. I. Vaslef and H. Buschhausen, Medieval classics: texts and studies, 20 (Washington and Leyden, 1986), pp. 125–37. The complexity of the iconography may often have been a bar to effective understanding beyond the overtly domestic background. The implications of a 'house-church' were perhaps not foreseen.

Uses should be employed in the services. Benefactors could specify the type of mass they wanted, and when it should be said. Demonstrated in some chantry foundation deeds of the fourteenth and fifteenth centuries, in the timetables established for colleges of priests, and in the complex routines laid down for the inmates of alms-houses, such control primarily dictated the outward show of devotion, possibly without reflecting deep changes in the intrinsically spiritual life. However, the choices which were being made – perhaps especially in the prayers to saints, and the type of mass – may reveal some changes in that inner spirituality.

More coherent signs of such changes occur spasmodically from the thirteenth century, each adding to the complexities of the total picture. The efflorescence of emotional and devotional spirituality during the thirteenth century, even if it must be acknowledged as a continuation of developments of the twelfth, was part of the general penitential movement also attested by the beguines and beghards of the Low Countries. The thirteenth century also saw a surge in mysticism, associated pre-eminently with the Dominican Meister Eckhart in Germany. This was fairly widespread, and the involvement of women – notably that of the nuns of Helfta – entailed a significant overlap with other Rhenish spiritual developments. The general advance of the penitential life, even for laity, and the stress on *caritas* in a world whose ethics were increasingly challenged by the evolution of a money economy, created new spiritual currents which swept through the church.[11]

Later centuries built on these foundations. The personal search for contact with God was the keystone, generating varied responses. The Rhineland produced the *Devotio moderna*, Bohemia the reform movement centred on Prague, while the English strand is reflected in the activities of the English mystics (chiefly Richard Rolle and Walter Hilton) and the Lollards. Italy, France, and Iberia were also affected, although here the threads are less obvious. In northern France at least, under the leadership of a small group of theologians of the University of Paris, among whom Jean Gerson and Jean de Montreuil were the most prominent, theological approaches developed which might be considered a type of Christian humanism. A Spanish emphasis on the penitential life appears in the sermons of Vincent Ferrer. Italian developments are rather more complex, largely because of cultural evolutions within the peninsula. Some were channelled through the religious orders as they developed their 'Observant' tendencies, which sought to revitalise the regular life by reinstating the original Rules, although sometimes making constitutional

[11] See pp. 11–12, 14–15, 104–5, 108–9, 113, 210, 282.

changes which established greater institutional cohesion. The movement was a characteristic of the late fourteenth and fifteenth centuries, affecting both monastic and mendicant communities, and in the sixteenth century generating a rash of new orders. There was an increased penitential and caritative awareness, sometimes initiated by major preaching missions such as that of St Bernardino of Siena, shown in the creation of new charitable funds and in the occasional outbursts of violent asceticism like the Florentine support for Savonarola in the 1490s.

Humanism

In addition to these developments, from the mid-fourteenth century (if not earlier) the impact of humanism also has to be accommodated, especially in Italy. Precisely what 'humanism' was in the late middle ages is a matter of contention. The label has itself been bluntly labelled as 'pernicious'; but with the acknowledgement that it remains 'too convenient a piece of academic obfuscation to renounce altogether'.[12] The search for exactitude has produced a range of possible definitions, among which 'a middle-of-the-road definition . . . neither too wide nor too narrow to be useful' identifies humanism as 'the movement to recover, interpret and assimilate the language, literature, learning and values of ancient Greece and Rome'.[13] Assimilation may be the key here, emphasising the need to see humanism as a medieval phenomenon. Certainly, Christianity was a significant influence on Italian humanism, contributing to spiritual concerns which could be articulated even alongside apparent semi-paganism and the concern for the classics. As with 'humanism' itself, however, the idea of 'Christian humanism' remains a vague concept, perhaps best summarised as 'an amalgam of the values of classical antiquity, biblical, particularly New Testament, ethics, and patristic theology'.[14] This is more specific, and perhaps more satisfactory, than a wider definition which would make 'Christian humanism' an aspect of developments since the twelfth century, being humanist 'since it assigns to man as a created being an autonomous value and accepts that his earthly experience has its natural end in earthly happiness. It is Christian, because it acknowledges that man's supernatural end is

---

[12] D. Hay, *The Italian Renaissance in its historical background* (2nd edn, Cambridge, 1977), p. 9 and n2.

[13] P. Burke, 'The spread of Italian humanism', in *The impact of humanism on western Europe*, ed. A. Goodman and A. MacKay (London, 1990), p. 2.

[14] J. K. Cameron, 'Humanism in the Low Countries', in *The impact of humanism on western Europe*, ed. A. Goodman and A. MacKay (London, 1990), p. 163.

God.'[15] While there is room for overlap in the definitions, the precise amalgam of sources certainly seems to delimit the Italian version.

In that version, a key element was the approach to the past, particularly the synthetic treatment of the classics which sought fundamental Christian values in pagan thought and expression. This search, with its emphasis on human potential, involved individuals ranging from the Florentine chancellor Coluccio Salutati to the German cardinal Nicholas of Cusa – whose curial career justifies placing him here among the Italians. Many of the humanists, as a new brand of lay theologian, accordingly debated the relative value of the active and contemplative lives; while the concern to rediscover and re-evaluate the past led to several of them producing anti-Judaic writings in defence of Christianity. However, stress on the secularism and 'paganism' of the Renaissance may be misplaced: unavoidably, all the humanists were Christians, although not all Christians were humanists. While some humanists might seem to challenge the accepted religion, as in Lorenzo Valla's demolition of the Donation of Constantine and rejection of pious traditions about the origins of the Apostles' Creed (which led to accusations of heresy), this was no rejection of Christianity. Valla overtly accepted Christianity's spiritual demands, producing a commentary on the Lord's Prayer and asserting that philosophy and reason were insufficient tools for dealing with theology. Later Neapolitan humanists, while apparently concerned with classicism and fortune, also integrated Christianity's demands into their discussions. 'Fortune' might be synonymous with the will of God; while the insecurity of the human condition on earth could be contrasted with the security, stability, and perfection of the afterlife. Indeed, one current in the spiritual writings of the humanists is of the potential for the virtual deification of humanity, largely as a result of the Incarnation. This potential was most bluntly expounded by Marsilio Ficino in his *De religione Christiana* of *c.* 1476, urging 'let men cease now to doubt their own divinity, on account of which doubt they drown themselves in mortal things. They should revere themselves as though divine beings, and hope that they can ascend to God, since in a certain way it was worthy enough for divine majesty to descend to them'.[16] Such deification of Man was not, however, a claim to divinity. While the power of the human will was emphasised, that will was to be used with care, for good

---

[15] J. Chydenius, *The friendship of God and the two ends of man: a study in Christian humanism, 1100–1321*, Societas scientiarum fennica: commentationes humanarum litterarum, 68 (Helsinki, 1981), p. 52.

[16] C. Trinkaus, *'In our image and likeness': humanity and divinity in Italian humanist thought* (2 vols., London, 1970), II, p. 741.

rather than evil, creatively rather than destructively, charitably and virtuously rather than sinfully. Humanity, achieving its potential through will, thus became a co-creator with God in a re-ordering of the world, and in order to attain salvation after death.

Italian 'Christian humanism' blends in with that concurrently developing in northern Europe, which reached its apogee in the early sixteenth century in Erasmus. His career, with those of several of his contemporaries in northern Europe (in England Thomas More, John Colet, and John Fisher spring immediately to mind), clearly demonstrates that Christian humanism was by no means an Italian-centred phenomenon. However, the northern variety seems different from that found in Italy, according more with the wider definition of the phenomenon than with the specific classical features of the Italian type. While Italian humanism was often optimistic in its stress on human potential and latent dignity, the northern type, possibly due to greater continuity with the spiritual and mystical traditions of the preceding centuries, appears imbued with a more pessimistic view of sinful and powerless humanity. This was perhaps fundamentally irreconcilable with the Italian view. Moreover, the northern writers seemingly rejected the syncretic approach adopted by many of their southern counterparts concerning the relationship between ancient philosophy and Christianity, a reaction which had its own implications for theological developments in later centuries.

Mysticism

While humanism was an important aspect of intellectual developments, more important overall in the history of medieval spirituality was mysticism. This provides a constant and complex theme across the centuries. Uncertainty about how precisely to define mysticism may explain some of the wariness about when specific individuals actually count as mystics. At its simplest, mysticism could be a generic search for union with the divine; but beyond the simplicity of the statement there is the complexity of attainment. There were different strands or levels of mystical experience, although often perceived as stages towards the ultimate achievement. In her *Istruzioni salutifere* Angela of Foligno (d. 1309) postulated a threefold progression, in which

the soul is transformed in the will of God, sometimes with God, and sometimes within God and God within it. The first transformation is when the soul uses all its endeavor to imitate the life of Christ crucified, for herein is made manifest the will of God himself. The second is when the soul is united to God and loves God; not only because it so wills but because it has great knowledge and joy of

God, the which, however, it is able to explain and set forth in words. The third is when the soul is so entirely made one with God and God with it, that it knows and enjoys with God the most high things, which cannot possibly be set forth in words nor imagined except by him who feels them.[17]

The key feature of mystical activity was the search for access to God by contemplation, sometimes through strict enforcement of a regime both ascetic and contemplative. The heights of mysticism were considered attainable within the world, and there were clearly many who hoped (probably unsuccessfully) to attain them; while even the lowest levels of the regime could be made available through the instructional and devotional writings of the masters, and their sermons. There is a certain timelessness about this mysticism, so that some aspects of fifteenth-century spirituality seem to make sense only as a re-affirmation of theological stances first proposed in the twelfth.

Although there is a consensus that mysticism was important in late medieval Europe, there is no universal agreement when it comes to identification of the mystics. Most listings concentrate on Germany (Meister Eckhart and his successors, the nuns of Helfta, and the beguines) and England (Richard Rolle, Julian of Norwich, and others). Catherine of Siena, Bridget of Sweden, and some of the Italian ecstatics are also frequently included. France seems ill-represented, although Peter of Luxembourg and some of the female visionaries might be included; while from the Iberian peninsula only Ramon Llull (d. 1315/16) gets close to serious consideration. This may reflect more on the historians of mysticism than on the mystics, who have to be identified by their literary remains or the impact they made. Just as it was possible to leave mystical writings without being a mystic (as might be argued for Nicholas of Cusa and his *Vision of God*), so the reverse was equally – perhaps more – possible.

There seems to be a significant distinction in late medieval mysticism, between what might be labelled its 'affective' and 'intellective' strands. The first was an essentially emotional tradition, perhaps most open to those not seeking a highly intellectualised spirituality. Rooted in the search for identity with Christ by concentrating on the Passion and Christocentric devotions, often in language which is more than faintly erotic, it emphasised love and ecstatic achievement. The alternative was the older approach derived from the writings of pseudo-Dionysius the Areopagite, requiring self-negation and an appreciation of the ineffability

---

[17] V. M. Lagorio, 'The medieval continental women mystics: an introduction', in *An introduction to the medieval mystics of Europe*, ed. P. E. Szarmach (Albany, NY, 1984), p. 179.

of the divinity, of the immeasurable and indefinable nature of God, the individual becoming lost in contemplation of the vastness and fullness of the divine. However, while these clearly were different approaches to mysticism, this fundamental differentiation may be flawed. The eroticism and apparent excesses of the affective tradition could be integrated with the intellective. The language may jar on current sensibilities, but it has clear affinities with the traditional Christian allegorisation of the *Song of Songs*, with the mystic's relationship with God paralleling that of the soul to Christ, of the Bride to the Groom.

Both approaches were accepted and encouraged as valid ways of seeking contact with God, but the Dionysian was considered the more difficult, and in some respects the more dangerous. One possible outcome of such contemplation, of an appreciation of the way in which the divine affected and encompassed everything, was a mistaken assumption of an identity with God, which liberated the individual from all moral and other constraints because the assumption of divinity removed the stain of sin from any action. Even if the individual mystic did not actually reach those conclusions, attempts to put the experiences into words might lead to misunderstanding and interpretation in those terms. This was a problem encountered by Meister Eckhart, with propositions extracted from his works being condemned in 1326.

The emphasis on individualism and private contact with the divinity in mystical routes to God carried another danger. The direct link created by personal effort clearly by-passed sacerdotal mediation. Individuals might then seek to evade the church's discipline, putting personal revelation above ecclesiastical authority. This danger was shown in the reaction of the Spiritual Franciscans to St Francis and Peter John Olivi, claiming that their revelations had a gospel quality which superseded the controls exercised by the church.[18] Such threats had to be quashed: it remained necessary for salvation to submit to the church's sacramental regime, chiefly through confession and communion. Many mystics did willingly submit: they also wanted communion, often as a route to ecstacy and spiritual contact with God. Margery Kempe, for one, must have been an extremely tiresome individual, and her insistence on defending and obeying the instructions which she claimed to receive directly from Christ clearly contravened contemporary social and ecclesiastical mores. Yet although some accused her of heresy, and it was obviously hard to keep her under control, her own wish not to break with the church and her incessant desire to hear sermons and receive communion (even after her marriage with the Godhead), meant that she never posed the threat

---

[18] Above, p. 114.

offered by the heretics of the Free Spirit, who claimed that their own immersion in the divine freed them from all earthly forms of earthly authority.

The role of these mystics, particularly those not excluded from the world by confinement in a monastic cell or anchorage, was latently ambivalent. Being reputed holy, they could provide support for the church and strengthen its hold. As individuals who might reject the limits imposed by the ecclesiastical order and sometimes the social constraints imposed by the lay community as well, they were potentially disruptive and dangerous. Their self-perception varied. Some were highly individualistic; but many saw themselves as especially privileged because they had attained the desired communion with God, and sought to communicate the spiritual message of their experiences; although what they tried to share was essentially incommunicable. The problem is that there is a very real difference between mysticism and its recording. Almost by definition, mystical achievement cannot be adequately conveyed in words; the recording of the experiences, especially if at second hand, is bound to be insufficient. Nevertheless, the experience has to be set down: the mystic's function was not one of retreat into total contemplation, but of communication. Many therefore took on a didactic role, aiming through their writings and sermons to share their experiences, even if imperfectly; to encourage others to seek similar attainment and spiritual satisfaction. The polarisation of the models of active and contemplative lives is here eroded by the obligation of the successful contemplative to help others towards a similar achievement by communicating and offering instruction. The active involvement of many of the leading mystics is certainly remarkable, even making allowances for constrained circumstances. Eckhart was deeply involved in the business of his Order (the Dominicans), and engaged in extensive preaching. Catherine of Siena became embroiled in the politics of the Great Schism; the nuns of Helfta instructed their neighbours and influenced their behaviour. Communication was clearly considered a major aspect of the role mystics assumed, whether by preaching (Eckhart), writing (Richard Rolle, Julian of Norwich), or even acting (Elizabeth of Spalbeek).

The affective was apparently the more widely adopted of the two mystical routes to God; the steps to union being mainly extensions of sensory perceptions. Richard Rolle, for instance, stressed the importance of heat, taste, and smell – that the presence of the divinity could be known by experiencing a series of such sensations – and this provided an important guide for his followers, possibly including Margery Kempe. The highly physical nature of devotional experience was also conveyed in the instructions for contemplatives, with the emphasis on sharing in

Christ's sufferings in an almost physical manner. For some it did become physical. The Flagellant movement demonstrated the desire to share in Christ's pains; some of the more extreme Imitations of Christ fall into the same category. Recent analyses of female devotions also stresses their physical aspect, the way in which bodily deprivation was seen as a means of access to Christ.[19]

Modern sensibilities tend to find these visionary and sensory elements of devotion rather disturbing. That people were instructed to meditate on the blood dripping from Christ's wounds, for instance, seems highly artificial and at times repulsive. It is important that such descriptions were highly traditional: the fifteenth-century *Book of the craft of dying* instructed the dying penitent to seek solace in the love which Christ had manifested in the crucifixion, quoting St Bernard's exhortation to 'Take note and see his head bowed to greet you, his mouth to kiss you, his arms spread to clasp you, his hands trembling to hold you, his side open to love you, his body stretched taut to give himself wholly to you.'[20] Such instructions were taken seriously precisely because people did want to experience the contemplation, were seeking ways to lose themselves in God.

The impact of mystics and visionaries on the church authorities is one thing; their impact on their fellows is another. However, the intensity of their experiences could be somewhat counter-productive; and in Margery Kempe's case it is significant that her presentation in print *c.* 1501 expunged the prickly aspects of her relationship with the church to emphasise her orthodoxy and piety. Many remained in relative obscurity: the meditations of the Monk of Farne were lost to sight for centuries, while Julian of Norwich's writings had minimal circulation. In other cases, obvious holiness secured considerable popular support, even if the lives were rather unorthodox. Support perhaps increased if the people concerned were somehow wondrous. Levitating beguines were a feature of the thirteenth century; while the supreme wonder, and the one most worrisome to church authorities, was acquisition of the marks of Christ's Passion, the stigmata. St Francis provided the archetype (but possibly not the prototype) for such experience, the reality of his reception of the wounds being endorsed by the church. Others, often women, also claimed to carry the marks, spiritually if not visibly. Some gained popular acclaim and their abodes, like that of Elizabeth of Spalbeek, became the foci for pilgrimages.

While mystics existed as real individuals, mysticism as a process was

[19] This is a key feature of the works of C. W. Bynum.
[20] R. N. Swanson, *Catholic England: faith, religion and observance before the Reformation* (Manchester, 1993), p. 130.

cumulative: the mystics' instructional writings, devotional exercises and guides, and written lives, all outlived them. Immediate impact and reaction might vary; but continued accessibility was critical. Particularly noteworthy here is the major revival in the fifteenth century of interest in twelfth-century spiritual writers, especially St Bernard; while Nicholas of Cusa's theories on Man's links with God derive from Thierry of Chartres and other twelfth-century writers. This cumulative contribution allowed mystical language and experience to become part of the currency of late medieval spirituality. When summarising the route to God in 1506, Jacques Lefevre d'Étaples unself-consciously placed Nicholas of Cusa alongside Dionysius; while his publication programme seems deliberately to have included a wide corpus of post-Patristic mystical writers, ranging from the twelfth-century Victorines to Ramon Llull, from St Bernard to the Flemish hermit Jan van Ruysbroeck (d. 1381). Indeed, printing and translation gave many of these older spiritual writers a new lease of life and new audiences: almost 300 editions of Bernard's works were printed before 1500 (often including material wrongly attributed to him), while one volume produced by Lefevre in 1513 contained works dating from the third century (but wrongly ascribed to a contemporary of St Paul) through to the thirteenth, including contributions from major female writers like Hildegard of Bingen (d. 1179) and Elizabeth of Schönau (d. 1264).

Magic and sacramentals

The sublimity of the mystics and the high-mindedness of the humanists and others searching for spiritual regeneration offer a stark contrast with other manifestations of devotion which appeared over the years. These, although still centred on the divinity, seem more utilitarian, self-centred, and functional. The concern was apparently to harness God, to make the master the servant. Such devotions stress the more 'magical' aspects of the relationship between God and man (as did some features of the cult of the saints), exploiting religious practices and traditions to secure benefits and control the elements.

Such activities include the use of the Host for its amuletic qualities: through its power, crops blessed with it would produce good yields, the weather could be controlled, even fires abated. The Host itself could be used as an insect repellent when crumbled on growing vegetables, or for other purposes not approved by the church. Concern for the practical did not contradict a more spiritual devotion to the Host; rather, they were complementary. Nevertheless, such actions clearly reflect a different awareness of the importance of the holy. A similar exploitation is evident with relics: while they were devotional stimuli, reminders of the saint, they also possessed magical force. Various other devotional activities reflect analogous appreciations, like the use of a holy girdle to ease the pains of childbirth. Charms and incantations used Christian words and signs for what might appear unChristian purposes, although that makes the term 'Christian' more specific than contemporaries would have accepted. Religion was power; power which was both magical and physical – hence the fear of excommunication. In 1309 a Latin grammatical rule recited by vested priests at a group of Irishmen made them flee in panic, believing that they were being cursed; while in the sixteenth century the inhabitants of Northwood (Middlesex) had their excommunication transferred to a field of brambles. When this was done, the brambles withered.

Obviously, not everyone subscribed to (or, at least, admitted) such beliefs; and it would be wrong to exaggerate them. The clergy were forever complaining that people ignored excommunication; but the fear instilled by the curse perhaps varied over a lifetime – to be excommunicate on one's deathbed was much more dangerous than to be excommunicate and healthy. The 'superstitious' element in medieval religion cannot be quantified: much was close to the limits, whatever they actually were, but did not quite cross the boundary. Votive masses are a case in point; as are the notions attached to certain saints, like the belief that sight of St Christopher was a preservative against death that day. Similarly, invocation of patron saints and guardian angels – perhaps especially the latter – sought to control the power of the supernatural, and use it against both the natural and the unnatural.

The most significant 'magical' contribution to medieval Christianity was provided by the 'sacramentals', a wide range of practices which developed alongside the clerically controlled religion. Alongside and in association with it, for many of them utilised priestly power in their initial stages.

Sacramentals can be divided into three main species. First come what the church itself categorised as sacramentals: blessed objects which were widely distributed for use by the recipients. These ranged from objects associated with specific dates in the liturgical year – the candles of Candlemas and the palms of Palm Sunday, for instance – to the water ritually blessed each Sunday. The priest's role in conferring the blessing clearly established some ecclesiastical control over their existence, but the distribution then released them for wider use. The objects themselves were ascribed a protective character, and also served devotional purposes.

Candles might be lit at a death-bed, or in association with celebration of
All Souls; they would also be lit for protection during thunderstorms. This
fitted them into a pattern of ritual use of other holy objects, like the
ringing of church-bells to calm storms: the inscription on a bell at St
Martin's, Cambrai, made in 1395, asserted that God heard its ringing, and
that it offered protection against storms as far afield as its sound carried.

The second category was similarly under some clerical oversight, in the
minor rites and benedictions performed by priests to ensure a beneficent
natural order and so in some ways akin to the votive masses for good
weather or a safe journey. Many were linked with agrarian practices: the
need to protect crops from pests, to ensure good weather, and to preserve
humans and animals. Often this entailed the use of other objects.
Considered most powerful was the consecrated Host, but the sprinkling
of blessed salt and water on seed-corn, or giving water blessed on St
Blaise's day to horses, is part of the same pattern.

The final type of sacramental – although here the word is perhaps
employed for lack of anything better – is the use of prayers and
incantations to gain protection or other benefits. Many such prayers
circulated in purely oral form; but others penetrated official religion, like
the 'prayer of Charlemagne' which appears in many Books of Hours.
Here the invocation of sacred power needed no clerical intervention; the
conjuration was not restricted by time or space.

The integration of these sacramentals into life's normality clearly
emphasises appreciations of the 'magical' aspect of religion: these rites
deliberately sought to control the physical world. However, whether that
makes them magical in a truly superstitious sense is debatable: to assert
that supposes a distinction between magic and Christianity which may not
have been apparent. As God, Christ, and the saints are participants in the
proceedings, the differentiation becomes even more questionable.

Élite and popular religion

The use of the sacramentals perhaps confirmed the validity of a laicised
religion which operated alongside – but not in contradistinction or
opposition to – the clericalised religion located in church and sacraments.
While in theory the rites and the objects were not sacramental *per se*, but
gained their efficacy from the disposition of the user; in practice an
extension which made the rite or the object the effective agent would be
hard to prevent. Something similar may have applied to the incantations
and prayers – the power lay in the words themselves, not in the speaker.
Maybe sacramentals, ill-documented though they are, do offer access to
a 'popular religion'; but perhaps not one which merits the somewhat

disparaging overtones that label sometimes carries. On the contrary, their use may conceal 'a kind of popular Catholic version of the priesthood of all believers, for they are seen to work virtually *ex opere operato*'.[21]

Nor can this be seen as activity which the clerical élite disdained. While printed French Books of Hours do seemingly include fewer of the incantational prayers than similar English Books, possibly thereby indicating greater concern to censor their use (although they were used, being copied into the books by hand); the French church still invoked its powers against natural disasters when needed. Animals and insects which threatened crops might thus be excommunicated and anathematised, as happened in the dioceses of Mâcon and Autun in 1487–8. In one Autun case, it was the bishop's vicar-general who instructed the parish clergy to command the insects to cease their depredations. Should the pests not stop, they were to be proclaimed accursed by the authority of the vicar-general, God, and the church, the priests being ordered to publish the anathema against them. The official stance on many of the sacramentals was clearly ambivalent, as German evidence reveals. In the rash of synodal legislation and ritual texts produced following Nicholas of Cusa's legatine mission of the 1450s, there is notable inconsistency in the treatment of sacramentals. One diocese might accept a practice, a neighbour denounce it. The blessing of holy water for St Blaise and St Stephen was prohibited as superstitious and idolatrous in Passau from 1470, but quite clearly considered legitimate in nearby Salzburg.

Such contradictions raise a massive question about the devotional practices of medieval Christianity: just how devout were they? Essentially, that is an unanswerable question – maybe a false one in its presuppositions that there is a universal and atemporal standard against which devoutness can be measured, and on which present-day commentators are qualified to pass judgement. There certainly is extensive evidence for practices and beliefs which seem irreconcilable with what would now be defined as 'Christianity'. That evidence provides the basis for attempts to cleave devotional and spiritual practices into different levels, making a distinction between 'élite' and 'popular' religion. The problem is expressed in its most concrete form in the case of St Guinefort, the 'Holy Greyhound'.

That cult had ancient origins, reflecting a tale common in folklore of a faithful hound which in its master's absence protects the family heir by killing a serpent. The blood spattered during the fight to the death is misunderstood by the returning master, who assumes that the child has

---

[21] R. W. Scribner, 'Cosmic order and daily life: sacred and secular in pre-industrial German society', in his *Popular culture and popular movements in Reformation Germany* (London and Ronceverte, 1987), p. 12.

been killed by the bloodied hound, which he immediately slays. Only thereafter is the child found safe, with the dead serpent. The martyred protector is then buried, and honoured after death.

The Guinefort version had taken root in the Dombes region of France before 1200, with the local peasantry treating the dead hound as a saint, making pilgrimages and offering votives at the grave, and going through other rituals in the hope of procuring cures for sickly children. Stephen de Bourbon came across the proceedings around 1250, condemned the credulity of the devotees, and had the site destroyed. However, the cult was not eradicated: traces persisted into the nineteenth century.

Ostensibly, the Guinefort case provides perfect evidence for the lack of Christianisation in late medieval Europe. But it may not be that straightforward. We know what Stephen of Bourbon reported, but how many of Guinefort's adherents knew the legend? There were human saints called Guinefort, honoured at Bourges, Pavia, and Sens. Devotion to them often involved ritual actions to determine whether a sick child would live or die. How many of the Dombes devotees were praying to a Christian saint, how many to a popularly canonised dog? How many, indeed, conflated both manifestations yet achieved what they considered a satisfactory reconciliation of the obvious contradictions, assuming that they were perceived as obvious? The holy wells and other healing sites scattered across Europe pose similar questions: were such places holy by themselves, because of their curative powers, or from their association with a particular saint whose powers alone were responsible for the curative effects? If individual healers are integrated into the picture further questions arise. With the apparently hereditary miracle-working power of the kings of England and France to heal scrofula, for instance, which was holy: the office of king, or the blood of the dynasty? This was a valid question in late medieval France, where the growth of the 'royal religion' all-but divinised the blood of the heirs to Clovis.

What seems to emerge from the prevalence of 'folklorised ritual', 'magical ritual', and the simply magical, is a delicate balance between a theologised religion and physical aids to survival in this world and the next. Historians for years have debated the division between 'élite' and 'popular' religion, between a spirituality advocated by the educated who knew their theology, and a more generally accepted religion (although Langmuir's 'religiosity' may be the more appropriate term) which worked more on ritualistic, mechanistic, and magical or superstitious levels.

The difficulties with the differentiation, most forcefully advanced by Jean Delumeau, lie in its presuppositions. These include the assumption of a concrete definition of Christianity as a constant, rather than something which is constantly changing and evolving. What Delumeau defines as 'The "folklorization" of Christianity' cannot be challenged as a construct. Few would dispute that in medieval Europe 'The mental structures and the sluggishness of a still-archaic civilization encouraged the folklorization not only of ceremonies and feastdays but also of beliefs'; but whether the assumed immediate corollary, that this 'thereby brought about a species of relapse into paganism' actually follows is less certain.[22]

The crux lies in the concern to fragment and dissect. 'Folklorization' exists historically, but can only be identified with hindsight, and perhaps with a deliberate rejection of the rationale for the actions. Contemporaries just lived their lives, with their beliefs as an incoherent whole. Fairies, ghosts, and suchlike were accepted; as was the devil. Masses, prayers, invocations of saints and incantations gave the desired results, so they worked. The extraordinary prayers in the Books of Hours; the custom of measuring candles to saints in the hope of relief from threats; the ringing of bells to turn away thunderstorms; the blessings of fields; all operated not as independent entities, but part of a totality. Yet to call this a relapse into paganism does distort: it imposes the historian's definition of Christianity onto what Christianity actually was. As Eamon Duffy has recently succinctly summarised the pre-Reformation amalgam of 'folklore' practices: 'This is not paganism, but lay Christianity'.[23]

The division between 'élite' and 'popular' is also a type of distortion, creating divisions which do not exist. Indeed, there is a good deal of evidence for the élite as participants in the 'folklorized' religion: it was they, after all, who paid for the chantries with their innumerable masses; it was they whose literacy often communicated the required prayers. Indeed, it was often their prayer books which contained the prayers: the manuscript Book of Hours of Margaret Beaufort contains many of the major incantations of the time, and being a manuscript must reflect a deliberate commissioning for their inclusion, rather than being part of the job lot which came with a printed text.

Even whether the distinction can adequately be between 'lay' and 'clerical' cultures is questionable. Many of the rituals required clerical participation – especially in the blessings of fields, and the distribution of sacramentals. As most of the lower clergy had to survive within, and derived from, a peasant culture, they would have been imbued with its beliefs and rituals long before they acquired those which went with clerical status. In the attempt to divide between 'élite' and 'popular', or

---

[22] J. Delumeau, *Catholicism between Luther and Voltaire: a new view of the Counter-Reformation* (London and Philadelphia, 1977), pp. 166–7.

[23] E. Duffy, *The stripping of the altars: traditional religion in England, 1400–1580* (New Haven and London, 1992), p. 283.

between 'clerical' and 'lay', it is usually overlooked that the 'élite' and the 'clerical' had to be consciously acquired, and were often a veneer over the 'lay' and 'popular', not a total replacement. Some perhaps did consciously reject a previous belief system, but before the Reformation there is little sign of it. Maybe there are hints as the fifteenth century ends, with the emergence of the reform movements; but even then the attacks often seem half-hearted, and certainly inconsistent.

Cosmology

Part of the problem of 'superstition' may derive from a failure to appreciate the totality of the medieval cosmology. The world which Christians inhabited was the playground of powerful forces. Evil constantly threatened the unwary, the Devil and his minions were realities to be taken seriously, necessitating defensive measures. This is the context in which an actor in a play at Avignon in 1470, inverting Faust, made a notarial pact to preclude the devil laying claim to him, protesting that 'by the invocations and anathemas of the demons which he makes in the play . . . he does not intend to speak from the heart but only in the manner of the play, and that on that account the enemy of human kind, the devil, should not have any claim on his soul.'[24] The world was also populated by other less malevolent forces: fairies, such as those known to Joan of Arc in her childhood, which had to be placated; ghosts which returned from the dead to threaten and terrify the living. The powers of nature might also be hostile; and if astrologers were right the stars also affected lives. All these challenges, these potential and actual threats, had to be faced and if possible controlled.

The search to control these forces often brought conflict with the ecclesiastical authorities. Fate controlled by the stars clearly contradicted doctrine; yet the science of astrology attracted many intellectuals, even if as many wrote against it. The difficulties about reconciling the acceptance of astrology with the demands of Christianity are, however, primarily a product of modern presuppositions and attitudes. In medieval cosmology astral forces were treated as part of nature, so not all aspects of what would now be considered fortune-telling or astrology were equally reprehensible. The planets might be accorded influence over purely physical natural events; but to grant them the power to affect acts carried out by human free will was illicit. The fifteenth-century French preacher Simon Cupersi thus allowed the calculation for auspicious days for events

[24] Chiffoleau, *La comptabilité de l'au-delà*, p. 389 n92.

which depend on a natural cause, for instance on the influence of the planets or the course of the stars, as in the taking of a medicinal potion, the sowing of fields, the planting of trees, and such like. That is not a matter of idolatry, but of sagacity and prudence: there is nothing sinful in this.

By contrast, if similar calculations were made 'in other actions which depend solely on a person's free will, like commerce, marriage, the gathering of medicinal herbs, and such like, that is a matter of mortal sin'.[25] The critical point was to leave room for the operation of human free will, to liberate humanity from the status of an automaton whose fate was determined by the stars and planets and was accordingly predictable. The church could not, however, deny that the future might be foretold: that was, after all, the function of prophecy.

The treatment of magic was slightly different from the treatment of astrology: it was not a matter of discovering, but controlling malevolent forces for private ends. Here, again, there was dualism: even the devil worked miracles. The claims made for saints, sacraments, and sacramentals were the mirror-image of those made for magic; it was often the status of the practitioners which determined whether the actions were licit or not. Whether they were felt to work might also be a consideration: commissioners might not complain, victims or those who believed themselves victims would.

The integration of magic into the world-view need not lead to worries about witchcraft, although it did towards the end of the fifteenth-century. However, acceptance of magic did affect overall perceptions, and Christianity might be used to the same effect. After all, if saints could be controlled and exploited, why not the power inherent in other aspects of Christianity – in prayers and symbols? Hence the development of the sacramentals and their use for purposes which were practical rather than devotional.

The process of 'folklorization' which has been read into many late medieval devotional practices, the reinterpretation of rituals and events for purposes which were not explicitly devotional and not necessarily 'unChristian', clearly carried the risks of 'superstition' and, more seriously, of letting people think that they could manipulate and control their lives. In some ways, this is a terrestrial equivalent to the 'Pelagian' approach to Purgatory. Yet to distinguish between such activities and 'Christianity' would be false: there are many similarities, and the two strands merge

---

[25] H. Martin, *Le métier de prédicateur en France septentrionale à la fin du moyen âge (1350–1520)* (Paris, 1988), p. 365.

together. Sacraments too had a salvific effect; prayers released souls; absolution removed sins. Was there all that much difference in practical terms? The willing involvement of clerics in many of the sacramental practices clearly indicates the integration of the two strands, alongside the attempts to curtail the wilder excesses.

While it may be posed, the question of the reality of devotion may be improper. Devotion might be a facade; but devotion was often a social as well as religious ritual. As such it could merge into the folkloric, as with the charitable feasts celebrated in the Avignon area which both reflected the demands of Christian *caritas* and reaffirmed community on the basis of more ancient models. But to differentiate between 'folkloric' and 'Christian' makes anachronistic distinctions. In many French towns, dragons were part of the Rogationtide processions, and as such may reflect old folkloric practices and also act as symbols of urban unity. Yet they also often appeared in towns where the patron saint's legend included tales of dragon taming – St Clement at Metz, St Quiriatus at Provins, and most notably St Martha at Tarascon.

In medieval Europe, there was no real alternative to catholicism, except on the frontiers, and that required a formal act of rejection. Sometimes heresy did offer a choice, of another conformity – Catharism, Hussitism, and other deviations imposed their own regimentations. Some frontier alternatives were merely different brands of Christianity; Greek orthodoxy rather than Latin catholicism. Most people had no choice. Insofar as society was professedly Christian, and Christianity provided both the justification and means of continuation of that society even as it changed, devotion could not be other than real. It might not be what the twentieth century would call 'true Christianity', or especially 'spiritual'; it may appear ritualistic, repetitive, and somewhat shallow; but for contemporaries it seemed to work. It had a reality on its own terms, and it is those terms which have to be accepted.

6

THE PILGRIMAGE OF
LIFE AND DEATH

•

Vital to perceptions of how medieval Christianity operated was the belief
that earthly life was only part of existence, a preliminary to the afterlife
which, after the cleansing of Purgatory, promised Heaven. But Purgatory
and salvation were not guaranteed; and even if Purgatory was attained,
what was desired was a swift passage through. Hell was another, and more
ghastly, possibility. Earthly life was a phase of the journey, the *peregrinatio*,
the pilgrimage, in which individual Christians sought to merit, even earn,
the reward of Heaven; to make a bargain, perhaps a contract, with God
to secure eternal felicity. Contractual obligations could, obviously, be
fulfilled without the spiritual element being very strong; but the contract
would be considered real (at least by the human party), and therefore the
tasks to fulfil it taken seriously. The process of securing a successful end to
the earthly pilgrimage went beyond the spirituality of devotion, to the
practicality of the demands of *caritas*, as that virtue marked out the various
steps on the road to salvation.

Devotional practice in the years between 1215 and 1515 offers a
kaleidoscope of responses to the demands of faith, yet the whole period
seems to be overshadowed by four words used as a poetic refrain by the
English monk John Lydgate (d. 1449/50) and the Scot William Dunbar
(d. *c.* 1520): *Timor mortis conturbat me* – the fear of death sets me in
turmoil.[1] Taken from the Office for the Dead, they might stand as a motto

---

[1] H. N. McCracken, ed., *The minor poems of John Lydgate*, II, Early English text society,
original series, 192 (1934), pp. 828–32; J. Kingsley, ed., *The poems of William Dunbar*
(Oxford, 1979), pp. 178–81.

for late medieval catholicism, which appears to be dominated (especially after the Black Death of 1347–50) by an obsession with death and its consequences, and by a somewhat panic-stricken desire to limit the effects of divine retribution. The interpretation which saw death as a shadow over everything found its most evocative expression in the writings of Johan Huizinga, for whom it was a major aspect of 'the waning of the Middle Ages'.[2]

Huizinga's analysis has been much criticised; but the fact remains that death was inescapable, and inescapably significant, for all Christians. It marked the second of the pivotal points in life; the first being baptism. It ended the period in which whatever freewill humans possessed could be deployed: thereafter, they depended on the mercy of God, and the consciences of their posterities. Death decided the ultimate destination of Heaven or Hell, even if access to the former was mediated by the uncertain duration of Purgatory. Relics of this awareness of death as a fulcrum, and of its aftermath, offer the most prominent personal statements from the period: the concern for founding chantries and securing prayers; the wills with their urgent distributions of charity and restitution of ill-gotten gains; the painted and carved dooms on chancel arches and church doorways; the cadaver tombs with their gruesome depictions of emaciated corpses left to the appetites of snakes, worms, toads, and insects. Over all hovers the persistent injunction: 'Pray for me!' – although the precise tone of that injunction, commanding or imploring, is rarely discernible.

This prevalent concern for death may be misleading. Death was only a stage en route to that Final Judgement awesomely portrayed in the sonorities of the *Dies irae*, composed in the thirteenth century. Judgement, and its implications, did overshadow everything; but the final outcome could be influenced (if Man had freewill) during the earthly existence. The search to ensure that death remained hopeful was therefore critical. Life had to be lived subject to Christianity's dictates, but always as part of a journey which would return the Created back the Creator. That over-all pilgrimage obviously needs attention, both in terms of the terrestrial journey and in appreciations of what happened at death. The search for a successful earthly pilgrimage in fulfillment of the prime demands of charity in human relationships also enters here. Finally, as the search expanded to control the second stage of the journey by drawing on the demands of *caritas* over posterities, it is necessary to look beyond death and at attitudes towards Purgatory. This requires a consideration of provisions

---

[2] J. Huizinga, *The waning of the Middle Ages* (London, 1965), esp. chapter 11.

made for souls stimulated by that belief, and the interdependence thereby formalised between the living and the dead.

The idea of pilgrimage and the battle against sin

The human journey towards the certainty of death and the uncertainty which followed it was a dangerous trek. Man alone, sinful, wilful, impotent, the plaything of uncontrolled forces unleashed by fellow humans, by the devil, or by God Himself, desperately needed assistance to follow the route effectively, and take the correct turning at the crux of existence which was death. There were only three certainties: sin, death, and judgement. Each affected perceptions, and individuals.

During life, the fact of the fall from grace in Eden and the resulting congenital stain on the human character greatly weakened any individual's ability to return to God unaided. For the catholic, assistance was available in the organisation and regulation of the Christian life. The sacraments were vital – the purificatory rituals of baptism and extreme unction at either end, and penance in between – and offered the hope of grace to supplement and overcome human inadequacy. Christianity as faith provided a model, which could be set out and aspired towards. According to the moralists, faith and hope together offered the two most potent supports for the Christian pilgrim, to sustain even in the darkest moments. They so operate in one of the most influential texts dealing with life as an allegorical pilgrimage, Guillaume de Deguileville's *Le pèlerinage de la vie humaine*, the first version of which was written in 1330–1. However, even faith and hope required support, and at critical points direct assistance might be needed. In Deguileville's work *Grace Dieu* intervenes to extract the pilgrim from the direst predicaments, and the need for grace to perfect aspirations was an unchallenged constituent of the progress.

Deguileville's work found a ready audience, being translated into English, Dutch, Spanish, and German, and being repeatedly printed. Other texts also used the theme of life as a pilgrimage: entertainments like Chaucer's *Canterbury Tales* outline a similar progression, the Parson's final contribution suggesting that the pilgrims' ultimate goal was not Canterbury but the celestial Jerusalem. His *Tale* responds to the failings revealed in his fellows' narratives by urging repentance and reformation. The pilgrimage theme may well be implicit in other texts. Morality dramas, like the late-fourteenth-century *The Castle of Perseverance*, also fit into the pattern. Here Mankind is torn between sin and repentance, is the object of the battle between the Vices and the Virtues, suffers death, and the fate of his soul is debated between Mercy and Justice. Echoes also appear in instructional and devotional material, for example, in *The abbey of the Holy Ghost*.

A feature of all this material is the emphasis on the battle against sin. Sin was one of the dominant concerns of late medieval Christianity, for potentially it obstructed access to heaven. The need to identify and reject sin and its attractions is therefore a prime concern in much of the instructional and devotional literature of the period, with major tracts detailing the battle between the opposing poles of the human character. In many respects the instructional and devotional works functioned as guides to the pilgrimage, to assist the progression from sin to devotion. There is a dialogue inherent in the material: it was not written for its own sake, but to provoke a response in action and personal reformation. The principal means of achieving this was through emphasis on charity in its widest sense, although this may be implicit rather than explicit. In *Le miroir de vie et de mort*, composed by Robert de l'Omme *c.* 1266, the main concern is with the seven deadly sins. However, the discussion of them is sandwiched between appeals to the audience to engage in good works – the second being especially striking. It appears in the final dialogue between Life and Death, as Life tries to stave off Death because she is unprepared through her association with sin. Death will have none of that, citing the Gospel injunction to 'Watch, therefore, for you know neither the day nor the hour'.[3] Death interprets this as 'To watch is to do good works such that are pleasing to God'.[4]

Sin was a major distraction (or attraction) of life. Humans had to steer the path between the advice of their guardian angels and personal tempters. The battle was an internal one, the set-piece *Psychomachia* between the vices and the virtues, between the body and the soul, earth and heaven. The Church's function was to aid each individual to victory by offering advice and the practical weapons of confession and penance which would allow the reception of grace. The concern to remedy sin is displayed in the numerous manuals and other works produced for confessors. These, with their minute analyses of the possibilities of sin, cast something of a pall over perceptions of late medieval religion. Sin is everywhere, categorised, analysed, condemned. However, these works must be set in a proper perspective. There is a difference between the lengthy catalogues, in a succession which descends from Raymond of

---

[3] Matthew, 25: 13.
[4] A. Långfors, '*Le miroir de vie et de mort* par Robert de l'Omme (1266): modèle d'un moralité wallonne du XVe siècle', *Romania*, 47 (1921), p. 529.

Figure 4 The way of perfection. The route to heaven, as illustrated in the 1483
Strasbourg edition of the *Scale Coeli* (*Ladder of Heaven*) by Johannes Gobi jr.
(d. 1350). The transition to print attests the continuing influence of this
fourteenth-century text. The illustration shows the means by which humans rise
towards God. For those embarking on the process (*proficientes*) the initial stages
are confession, satisfaction, and destation of vices. The elevation beyond that to
perfection (*perfecti*) requires, progressively, the practice of virtues, firm resistance
to temptation, purity of heart, love of God. The supreme achievement is
contemplation. At all stages angels and devils compete to encourage or distract
from the right way.

Peñaforte's *Summa de penitentia* of 1220–40, which were largely written by and to some extent for lawyers; and the more pastoral works concerned with the practicalities of achieving a good confession. Emphasis has to be placed on the latter, rather than on the cataloguing: that often serves more to expose the uncertainties and contradictions of the compilers about the identity, nature and effect of specific sins. All these tracts had a pastoral imperative, to assist in the successful completion of the terrestrial pilgrimage. While they may seem to pile guilt on guilt, the hypotheses of the canonists (for many of them are hypotheses, covering eventualities which might never arise) sought to ensure that individuals did not deviate too much from the prescribed path and to help those administering the confession to give the correct advice. The intrusive questioning envisaged in the manuals for the parish clergy (and, often, for the laity as well) was not there to give a vicarious frisson of excitement, but to ensure that the confession was complete, that all had been disclosed and the magnitude of the offences properly appreciated. Even though the texts can easily be read as deeply pessimistic, the intention was positive: to incite contrition and a willing acceptance of the penance which would eliminate the stain of sin, providing restitution to God and Man as part of the process of reconciliation.

If confession had been the burden it is sometimes made out to be, it would justifiably have been unpopular. There is little evidence of that. Rather, the signs suggest a ready acceptance of the need for confession. This may be because the evidence is biased, in favour of compulsive confessors like Margery Kempe and other ecstatics, and the well-to-do who could employ a private confessor, or join Italian flagellant confraternities with their own confessional regimes. Signs of wider acceptance emerge from the struggles between the secular clergy and the friars. These suggest that what most people disliked was not the confession itself, but the penance and its public nature. The seculars objected that the mendicants gave penances which were too light; but rarely complained that people did not confess. Paradoxically, as Purgatory became more important,[5] so the call for full penance on earth became less insistent: the stress could be placed on moral regeneration, on contrition and reception of grace to allow access to Purgatory and thence to Heaven, rather than a full clearing of the slate on earth. That also stimulated insistence on good confession – even though that itself attracted increasing legalistic analysis – and the concern to assist rather than condemn.

While sin was against God, its main victims were human relationships. The human pilgrim had to acknowledge such relationships, and accept

---

[5] Above, pp. 36–8.

individual responsibility for a communal fate. Langland's *Piers Plowman*, in the search for grace and the best way of living, emphasises the need for effective and charitable human relationships in recounting Piers' quest – a quest unsatisfied at the poem's end, perhaps indicating that purely human relationships were insufficient to complete the journey. Christianity emphasised the human, the injunctions of mutuality which had spiritual as well as physical aspects.

Although it was clearly valid, the idea of human experience as a pilgrimage is somewhat unsatisfactory. For while the ultimate goal lay in the afterlife, the pilgrimage's practical function on earth is not always clear. Was the aim actually to create a better society? Or was the intention merely to go through the prescribed rituals, to match the stereotypes, and have done with it? Was the aim to achieve an earthly Utopia; or just to pass all the tests to attain the *post mortem* Utopia?

Individuals, and groups, offered varied responses; but there is no overall sense of direction. The formulations demanded a response from individuals, their overall aims lack precision. The vagueness of the intended outcome leaves many questions unsettled – but they may not have been asked at the time anyway. Sometimes the church sought to define and restrict roles within an overall pattern of relationships: sermons in early-fifteenth-century England were still asserting the tripartite social divisions of 'those who pray, those who fight, and those who work', defining roles within the church as well as society at large, so outlining social as well as charitable relationships. Some preachers did demand a complete social transformation: in 1233 the north Italian movement of the 'Alleluia' sought to replace communal warfare by peace, with the activities of the Dominican John of Vicenza at Bologna including the settlement of disputes and a drive against usury. In 1494–7 Savonarola sought a similar transformation in Florence, his period of domination being again marked by the denunciation of exploitation and the enforced destruction of 'vanities'. Even more radical desire for change appeared among the Taborites of fifteenth-century Bohemia. However, the call for social reform need not be revolutionary: conservative calls for the restoration of an ordered society of mutual responsibilities were just as positive in intention.

In some cases Utopianism clearly breaks through, linking in with strands of Christianity which anticipated the end of the world. Outbreaks of Chiliasm – 'The expectation of imminent, supernaturally-inspired, radical betterment on earth before the Last Judgement'[6] – were almost

---

[6] R. E. Lerner, 'The Black Death and western European eschatological mentalities', *American historical review*, 86 (1981), p. 537.

unavoidable offshoots of mainstream devotion. The neo-communism of the English Peasants' Revolt (1381) may be based on one reading of the Christian message and the recreation of an earthly Eden. The Flagellant movement of 1349 seems to have had similar motivations initially; while the radicals' aspirations in fifteenth-century Bohemia reveal the impact of hopes for a changed society. There the regimes of common chests established in Taborite strongholds, with goods being redistributed according to need, temporarily supplanted the established social order. The Taborites, however, took things further. Adopting an ideology of violence, for a brief period in the early 1420s they waged total war on surrounding social, moral, and ecclesiastical structures. In expectation of the Second Coming, they assumed the role of avenging angels, seeking not just the transformation but the termination, the culmination, of Christian experience.

If any general strand has to be found, it may be one which might now seem rather negative. The idea of this existence as a staging post, imperfect and distracting from the reality of Christ which could only be attained after death, had long encouraged within the Christian tradition a literary genre not merely of renunciation, but active rejection of the world – the theme of *contemptus mundi*. Mankind, frail, filthy, the antithesis of divinity, was trapped in an environment where, pitiably and pitifully, sin attracted more than its opposite. Contemptible, and condemned to decay, Man nevertheless had to survive the world, acknowledging vileness and preparing for death.

One of the most forceful expressions of this contempt for the world was produced by none other than Lothar of Segni, the future Pope Innocent III. Written *c.* 1196, the tract, *On the misery of the human condition*, clearly touched a chord: it survives in over 400 medieval manuscripts and numerous editions printed before 1500. Frequently translated, into several languages, it influenced many writers. Chaucer may have produced an English version in 1390–4; Eustache Deschamps versified a condensed text in 1383. There were several independent productions in the genre over the centuries, on the general theme of renunciation and the ghastliness of the human condition.

Such works, with their insistence on bodily decay after death, lie behind some of the more macabre attitudes towards the body and death in later medieval Europe. Contempt for the body appears notably in wills of the late fourteenth and fifteenth centuries, with demands for burial in demeaning locations. In England these wills, with their references to 'stinking carrion', have been associated with Lollardy; but similar sentiments in continental wills suggest that it was more of a topos.

The final inevitability of the earthly pilgrimage was death itself. Here there were perhaps changes in perceptions over time, and an awareness of a changed proximity of death in the later middle ages. Death had always been part of life: medieval life expectancies made acceptance of its inevitability and imminence unavoidable. Before 1350 the circumstances in which death might be anticipated were fairly predictable, and reasonably specific – chiefly war, childbirth, famine, and industrial injury. After 1350 a more indiscriminate element was added by new forms of communicable and epidemic diseases, especially plague. Death's impact became ever more arbitrary, perhaps more sudden as well. The period's general chaos may also have made death appear more present than before, certainly in the regular recurrence of urban epidemics. The idea that 'in the midst of life we are in death' was unavoidable, in some producing the response of 'eat, drink, and be merry'. Others indulged in a morbid fascination with death or stressed their contempt for the world, as did the Brethren of the Common Life. Death's proximity, and the consequent urgent need to prepare for reconciliation with God, was a constant theme for preachers – whose sermons often incorporate cautionary tales of people given the opportunity to repent by witnessing the deaths of their friends and receiving a due warning, or being visited in dreams which similarly offered the advice to repent to secure salvation. The arbitrary impact of death made such preparations even more essential, accounting for the mushrooming of pre-mortem foundations, the concern to collect indulgences, and the popularity of the fraternities.

Death

Death, the unavoidable, became increasingly prominent in spirituality after 1300. There is seemingly, perhaps actually, a connection here with the transformations in Europe after the ravages of the Black Death in 1347–50; but it cannot be positively asserted. The elaboration of death rituals may pre-date the plague, but could still be linked with the economic downturn of the early fourteenth century; yet the plague does seem to have accentuated the urgency of the need to get through Purgatory.

The concern for death is most obvious in the iconography of the period. The 'dance of death', with skeletons leading the various ranks of humanity in a grotesque cotillion, became almost a commonplace, its portrayal on the cloisters of the cemetery of the Innocents at Paris a tourist attraction copied for the Pardon churchyard at St Paul's in London. The *danse macabre* (whatever its origins) spread throughout Europe, attaching itself to other artistic and literary *topoi* which told of encounters between the living and the dead. Artistic confrontations, with their implicit or explicit dialogue warning the living to prepare for the encounter, were widely distributed, from the Campo Santo in Siena to the engravings of Dürer. Portrayals and interpretations varied – the *danse macabre* might be a dance of 'the dead' or the dance of 'Death'; encounters might be between one person and death, or groups (traditionally, the Three Living and the Three Dead). The group encounters were probably meant to be read individually: Guyot Marchant's Parisian edition of the *danse macabre*, produced in 1486, was described on its title page as a 'mirror' for its readers, suggesting that it required a personal response.

One of the more gruesome manifestations of the stress on death is the so-called *transi* tombs, constructed in the late 1300s and for some centuries after. The decaying body is depicted in all its nakedness and vulnerability, prey to worms, snakes, toads, and other agents of decomposition, emphasising the dust-to-dust nature of human existence. Sometimes, as in some of the tombs in St Denis in Paris, the emaciated dead appear alongside statues taken from life – possibly a statement of the hope of the eventual resurrection of the body.

Such tombs were not common: their cost precluded that. Some of them are certainly magnificent structures; until its destruction in the French Revolution that of cardinal La Grange at Avignon was perhaps the most impressive. Certainly they convey a message, sometimes spelt out in inscriptions reminding the passer-by that this is his or her own destiny. But how much impression they did make is again uncertain; equally unclear is how far they reflect the feelings of their subjects about death. There are suggestions that some merely responded to fashion; but even if this was so (although their occurrence alongside wills decrying the vileness of the human condition is noteworthy) the fashion for such a concern with decay still reflects contemporary perceptions.

While the concern with death appears across Europe, signs of regionalism in some of the treatments hint at slightly differing reactions to the fact of death. The *transi* tomb is relatively rare in Italy and Spain; Bohemia has no pre-Reformation tradition of the *danse macabre*; while depictions of death in triumph, based on Roman imperial models, are restricted to fifteenth-century Italy. While a general concern with death is undeniable, and the mélange of images has considerable similarities, it would be wrong to make the reactions too homogeneous. Given the varied origins which have been suggested for the Dance of Death, the late medieval developments may have homogenised and generalised a range of local derivations from 'folkloric' religion.

How these widespread portrayals of death were actually integrated into perceptions of Christianity is hard to determine. With the cadaver tombs, several possible interpretations can be advanced. Some straight-forward sculptures of decaying corpses may have been commissioned in humility, and to serve didactic purposes as a warning that the dead body must necessarily decay – and that just as the corpse is consumed by vermin, so the living are consumed by sins. Some, with their double portrayals of the decayed and revived, clearly do proclaim hope in the resurrection – and, by implication, the expectation of a very precisely physical reconstitution of a specific body from its specific remains. Others served slightly different purposes. Cardinal La Grange's tomb was not just a warning to the living, but a proclamation of devotion to the Virgin, its sculptures incorporating depictions of five of her feasts.

To concentrate on the physical depictions of death may actually miss some of the point. While death was a universal concern, and panic a not unlikely response to its approach, the inevitability of death as the threshold to a new form of life was ambiguous. Much of the iconography is emphatically aimed at the living, and contributes to the didactic 'texts' against sin. At a slightly different level, the depictions also comment on social inequalities: for labourers and the poor, death offers release, even reward; for the rich and powerful, death brings retribution. The Triumph of Death has as its subtext the parable of Dives and Lazarus, of the rich man condemned for eternity because he did not assist the outcast at his gate.

Death might be generalised in the *danse macabre*, and possibly in readings of the cadaver tombs, but it was necessarily an intensely personal experience. It was to be expected during life, and prepared for accordingly. But as the pivot for the totality of existence, death was the threshold of something unknown and unknowable save by individual experience, unless ghosts and dreams gave clues. The only certainty about death was that it preceded the final judgement so graphically depicted in many churches, that decision whether individuals went ultimately with the angels, or with the horrific red-faced demons through the gaping jaws of Hellmouth into eternal despair and torment. Death was, therefore, something to be feared; but in a paradoxical way also something to be welcomed, for it opened the way to completion, to the final ascent to God. The fear of death – like the fear of God – could be the beginning of wisdom, an appreciation of the totality of human existence. In the *ars moriendi* ('the art of dying'), a theme in European literature which was widespread throughout the period after the Black Death, authors giving instruction on how good Christians should greet death made it something positive: at second-hand, the *Book of the craft of dying* proclaimed death

a release from prison, and the ending of exile, the discharging of a heavy burden
(that is, the body), the termination of all infirmities, escape from all perils,
destruction of all evil things, breaking of all bonds, payment of the debt of
natural duty, return to the homeland, and entrance into bliss and joy.[7]

Until around 1300, and outside chivalric conceits, the possibility of 'a
good death', an edifying death, was largely restricted to the obviously
holy, effectively the saints alone. The art of dying was something to be
perfected mainly by members of the religious orders. This changed in the
early fourteenth century; as sainthood became available to laity without
the pains of martyrdom, so the possibilities of a good death were also
'democratised'. The deathbed of Elzéar of Sabran (d. 1323) posited an
ideal for the laity: his patient suffering, devout reception of the
sacraments, contrition and penitence, battle against assailing demons, and
final commendation of his soul to divine judgement, could offer a model
for others. Certainly this is the deathbed which appears elsewhere, for
instance in the *Revelations* of Julian of Norwich. The development of the
ars moriendi ensured that even if many people did not live like saints, they
could be instructed in how to die like them. The stipulations of wills
which require the reading of devout works and prayers around the
deathbed, and commendations of the soul to God and a veritable litany of
saints, reflect the penetration of the art of dying throughout Europe. The
dying individual might be catechised by a priest, faith be tested and
affirmed in response to questions about acceptance of the statements of the
Creeds. Death became a textbook exercise, on an international scale.
What became the chief text seems to have been cobbled together from
earlier material (including work by Jean Gerson) around Constance in
the early 1400s, its dissemination channelled through members of the
Council of Constance as they returned home from that assembly, and
through the Dominican network. Over 230 manuscripts survive, only
about half in Latin, the rest in vernaculars. About 100 incunable editions
are recorded, together with block-book versions and detached sheets
which seem to have been meant for use as posters. Other instructional
texts for the dying also appeared in the vernacular, throughout the period
and beyond. These works all aimed to counter a fear of death, and
encourage hope: death was not the end, but a new beginning.

Yet what did it begin? Precisely because what happened at death could
not be experienced by the living the afterlife could be debated. This is
the context for Pope John XXII's declarations on the Beatific Vision.[8]

---

[7] R. N. Swanson, *Catholic England: faith, religion, and observance before the Reformation*
(Manchester, 1993), p. 126. The source of the quotation is not identified.

[8] Above, p. 44.

Certainly the evolution of Purgatory can only have complicated the problem of *post mortem* experience, for admission to Purgatory presupposed admission to Heaven, and therefore some immediate judgement at death about the ultimate destination. Awareness of those problems may be reflected in literary debates between the soul and the body at death, possibly also in the incorporation of the Four Daughters of God – the prime merits – into debates about the weighing of souls after death. Yet formal doctrines developed only slowly: Benedict XII's affirmation in 1336 that the just did enjoy the Beatific Vision at death settled one issue, but it was only a decree of the Council of Florence which formally declared that there was an immediate personal judgement at death which would precede the Final Judgement.

Prophecy and apocalypse

The anticipation of a Final Judgement had to be built into perceptions, of the pilgrimage of the individual, and the pilgrimage of humanity. Christianity's whole teleology demanded it: time, inevitably, would end. To that extent the future was already known, but the details remained to be worked out.

For some people the knowledge of judgement, and their own uncertainty of their fate, were a heavy burden. The confessional works took the problem of the over-scrupulous conscience which simply refused to accept the possibility of salvation very seriously. Despair – the loss of hope – was also addressed in the *ars moriendi*: again the concern was to assist and fortify, to make it clear just how little was actually demanded to secure the promises of Purgatory.

For humanity as a whole, expectation of Christ's Second Coming was a given of human history. Unsurprisingly, therefore, millenarian expectations were aroused intermittently. There was, necessarily, an assumption that the end would come; the problem was to know when. Here the legitimacy of prophecy within Christianity, as an inheritance from the Judaic past, gave life to varied prognostications which mingled with astrology and other arcane knowledge. Accumulations from the past, and new prophets, all had their say. Sibylline oracles, Merlin, the prophecies of Hildegard of Bingen (d. 1179), and from later centuries Arnau de Vilanova (d. 1311) and Jean de Roquetaillade (d. 1362), added to the versions of the future which influenced the present. Such prophets were particularly prominent in crises like the Great Schism, when the rival parties each sought to identify their opponents with the foretold evil popes. However, prophecy was not confined to crises. The production, reproduction, and recycling of prophecies was continuous between the

thirteenth and sixteenth centuries. While many were deliberate falsifi-
cations, reflecting deep anxieties and hopes about the present and future,
their generally unchallenged reception is a telling comment on
contemporary appreciations.

The most important contributor to such developments was Joachim of
Fiore (d. 1202). To replace the traditional six ages of the world, where the
period between the Incarnation and the Second Coming was the last, he
developed a Trinitarian structure, locating himself within the Age of the
Son, but with an Age of the Spirit imminent. His complex numerological
analyses suggested that the Third Age would be heralded by a new
religious order, an argument which became ecclesiastical dynamite when
the Franciscans were identified as that order in 1253/4 by Gerard of Borgo
San Donnino in his *Liber introductorius* to a compilation of Joachite works
which were proclaimed as a new Eternal Gospel to replace the Old and
New Testaments. Like all good prophecies, Joachim's were imprecise:
analysts who expected the new age to dawn in 1260 were disappointed;
but that merely invalidated their calculations, not Joachim. His writings
remained a powerful force throughout the Middle Ages.

Joachim's complex calculations reinforced an eschatology which found
occasional expression in popular outbursts. Some of the 'people's
crusades', like that of the Children in 1212, fitted in here. So did the
Flagellant outbreak in 1260. The Bohemian Taborites of the fifteenth-
century – among the most extreme of Hussites – also expected an
imminent end of the world, and accordingly fled to the hills and established their own social structures in expectation of the Second Coming.
It is even possible that Christopher Columbus was responding to
millenarian expectations when he embarked on his voyages. Certainly
late-fifteenth-century Spain was affected by such expectations – particularly among the Jews and *conversos* – and if he did confidently expect that
he would find a terrestrial Paradise, it would seem that he had imbibed
similar ideas.

The expectation of the Last Days included acceptance of the idea of
an Antichrist who would terrorise and delude the world; but whose
destruction would herald an indeterminate era of peace to end with the
Second Coming. The incorporation of Antichrist into Christian
perspectives is widely reflected, in sermons, chronicles, plays and pictures.
Most importantly, Antichrist was constantly expected: hardly a decade
passed without his arrival being suggested somewhere in Europe, often in
association with Joachite prophecies or major afflictions like the Black
Death. The Turkish advance in the fifteenth-century was similarly
interpreted. Against the view of the Franciscans as heralds of the Joachite
Third Age because of their purity, their opponents saw them as the

pseudo-prophets who were the precursors of Antichrist – an identification repeated even in the fifteenth century by one dean of St Patrick's cathedral in Dublin. Whether such identifications were more than polemical is sometimes open to question: when thirteenth-century popes railed against the Emperor Frederick II as Antichrist, it was perhaps political rhetoric rather than a reflection of their actual beliefs.

The influence of prophecy was also felt in political terms. A major theme throughout these centuries was that of 'the last emperor'. At some stage, an earthly ruler would recover Jerusalem for the Christians, and there receive his crown. He would then go on to conquer the world, thus giving the signal for the Second Coming. The idea seems to have attracted many. Frederick II was cast in the role in the thirteenth century; his death produced a revision to make him a sleeping king who would one day return. In the fourteenth century the French Valois seemingly promoted themselves for the task; while in the fifteenth the emperor Sigismund at times seemed a likely candidate – especially in the context of the Council of Constance and the reunification of the western church. How widespread the sentiments were cannot be assessed – necessarily these ideas appear most as a literary conceit; but that they existed is the important point, within the framework of Christian teleological expectations. Slightly less significant generally – although with a clear importance within specifically ecclesiastical circles – was the expectation of an 'angelic pope': those who believed that he had come at the election of Celestine V in 1294 were to be bitterly disappointed.

The penitential regimes and apocalyptic expectations are often hard to disentangle. This especially applies in periods of what appeared particularly dramatic divine chastisement – most notably the years of the Black Death. The view of Man as a sinner who merited punishment could not lie far below the surface of reactions to crises. A God who had sent the Flood, and even after that destroyed Sodom and Gomorrah, might yet intervene on earth to punish sins and demand satisfaction. Small wonder, then, that extreme penitential sentiments sometimes found outlets in broadly based movements demanding an end to sin and disorder. Typical were the Alleluia of 1233, and the Bianchi of 1399, both of which occurred in Italy; and the more widespread Flagellants of 1260 which began there but reached as far as Poland. Savonarola's rule in Florence in 1494–7 was based on similar feelings, the invasion of Italy by Charles VIII of France in 1494 having conveniently verified his predictions of the destruction to be rained on Italy.

While there were millenarian tendencies in many of these movements, equally striking is their insistence that they sought to assuage divine wrath, actually trying to avert the destruction they proclaimed. This attitude certainly seems to apply to the Flagellants of 1349, at least initially. Here, however, internal developments suggest more complex and subtle links. In Germany it seems that the Flagellant groups which reached places before the plague acted as averting forces, demanding purification and reformation – a situation which encouraged 'anticlerical' radical sentiments on the grounds that priestly deviations had incurred the divine displeasure. However, where the Flagellants arrived after the plague had struck, their routines were more penitential and submissive. France was equally susceptible to such emotions, as shown in the mass pilgrimage of children from Avignon to Mont Saint Michel in 1393, and the various Shepherds' and Children's Crusades.

CARITAS

The role of charity

Sin's effect threatened human existence; its negation offered security. The concern to act in preparation for death generated a regime of good works which were both physical and spiritual – but the works had to be undertaken in the right spirit. Here the driving force was *caritas* – 'charity' or 'love', although neither translation conveys the word's full meaning. *Caritas* underlay the two Great Commandments and the Decalogue, uniting the Old and New Laws. St Paul's comments on its pre-eminence were important for practical behaviour, with good works attesting faith – a view reiterated in the Epistle of James, perhaps the most succinct statement of the Christian social code.[9] Besides the Commandments, there were the requirements of the Corporal Acts of Mercy, which paralleled treatment of fellow humans to the relationship with Christ; while the Beatitudes set out ideals of human behaviour which offered hope of reward.[10]

The all-embracing and fundamental significance of *caritas* is clear in the wide definition advanced by Thomas Aquinas in his *Summa theologica*:

Charity is said to be the form [i.e., the perfection and animating principle] of the other virtues, not as exemplar or in essence, but rather as efficient, in as much as it impresses its form on all of them . . . Charity is likened to a foundation or root because it sustains and nourishes all the other virtues . . . Charity is called the end of the other virtues, because it directs all the other virtues to its own end. And . . . charity is called the mother of the other virtues, because from desire of the ultimate end it initiates the action of the other virtues by charging them with life.[11]

---

[9] I Cor., 13; Jas. 2: 14–26.   [10] For the Beatitudes, Matthew, 5: 3–16.
[11] Thomas Aquinas, *Summa theologica, vol. 34: charity (2ᵃ2ᵃᵉ, 23–33)* (London and New York, 1975), pp. 32–3.

Guillaume de Deguileville's *Le pèlerinage de la vie humaine* showed Charity as an efficient force. At the beginning of the pilgrimage, Charity offered peace as a preliminary to Penance and the receipt of communion. But some avoided Charity and the peace which she offered from Christ, ignored penance, yet still took communion, coming away more stained than they had been before. Charity's active role in Deguileville's text seems fairly minor: as many of the tracts dealing with the human pilgrimage focused on the battle against sin, charity is rarely prominent. Yet it was implicitly significant. In *Le voyage de paradis*, by the French poet Rutebeuf (fl. 1245–85), Pity is the guide towards the purifying house of Confession, warning against being inveigled into the houses of the individual sins. But Pity is married to Charity. Essentially charity was not an act, but an impulse to act. Its greatest impact on human existence had come with the Incarnation: for Deguileville, it was Charity which drove Christ to suffer Incarnation. Charity was thus an appropriate recompense to Christ as well: the Biblical setting of the Corporal Acts of Mercy made that perfectly plain – 'insofar as you have done it to one of the least of these my brethren, you have done it to me'.[12] However, to be obvious, charity had to be enacted. This requirement brought in its train a flurry of activities and relationships, some highly personal, others institutional. They also reflected regional or social preferences and priorities. Donations for the relief of prisoners were made across Europe; but offerings to assist in ransoming Christians captured by the Moors were primarily a Spanish phenomenon, regularly encountered as bequests. Given the variety of manifestations, a brief survey of charitable activity is necessarily inadequate; nevertheless, it is worth considering some aspects of it.

Charity and social imperatives

As a state of mind, charity was not easily achieved. While its pecuniary aspects are most visible, *caritas* as an imperative was not a matter of salving consciences, but of changing them. Its function was somewhat Utopian: the establishment of a state of reconciliation between individuals, to ensure an integrated social body which fulfilled the second of the Great Commandments.

The importance of reconciliation is dramatically revealed in tensions surrounding the reception of communion. To receive was a declaration of charity with the community; communion could therefore be refused or interrupted if disputes were unresolved. Reconciliation had to be real, not dissembled. One sermon *exemplum* warned of the dangers by recalling

---

[12] Matthew, 25: 40.

how a proud woman who feigned reconciliation had been seized by
the devil after having offered forgiveness in order to receive communion,
but later declaring that it had been done only verbally, and not in her
heart.

The integration of *caritas* into processes of social re-formation also
appears in the 'spiritual' penalties imposed by various bodies on errant
members. In late medieval England, the fines imposed for infractions of
rural communal customs were sometimes divided between the lord of the
manor and the parish church or (as at Alrewas in Staffordshire) between
the lord and the chantry within the church which the community itself
funded. The payment to the lord was a penalty for breach of jurisdiction,
but that to the church or chantry can be seen as reconciliation with the
community. The fines demanded by craft guilds and other fraternities are
similar, cash payments to the jurisdictional authorities being matched by
spiritual forfeits of wax to light the image of the fraternity's patron saint.

The use of spiritual penalties to achieve reconciliation could take other
forms. In the Low Countries and northern France, expiatory pilgrimages
were often imposed in such processes, for breach of trade regulations, and
in some cases of violence or slander. They had an obvious penitential role,
often involving long journeys – homicides in fourteenth century Lille
might be sent to the Holy Land; at Ypres the destinations most frequently
stipulated included Our Lady of Rocamadour, Compostela, and St
Andrews in Scotland. Of course, there was a practical social aspect:
imposed pilgrimage was temporary banishment, especially if the duration
was also specified, allowing passions to cool; but this fitted into the
process of social reconciliation. The duality of penance and reconciliation
even appears at the highest level of peace treaties: that between King
Philip V of France and the count of Flanders in 1316 required the latter's
second son to make pilgrimages to Le Puy, Saint-Gilles, Vauvert,
Compostela, and Rocamadour; while in 1326 the compact to end a
rebellion by the Flemish towns against their count required Bruges and
Courtrai to expiate their offence by sending 100 inhabitants to each of
Compostela, Saint-Gilles and Vauvert, and Rocamadour (although this
was not actually done).

The same category might also include some of the donations to Italian
Monti di pietà, the charitable pawn-shops established by communal
authorities in the fifteenth century. Some loans to the *Monte* founded in
Florence in 1496 were actually compensation payments imposed by the
courts to be invested in it in trust, often to provide a future dowry but in
the meantime to serve the purposes of *caritas*.

Charity's penitential and restorative force also appears in some of the
restitution clauses in wills. 'Restitution' here has to be given its widest

sense, as the settlement of all business uncompleted at the point of death. Compensation was thus provided for forgotten tithes, for debts yet unpaid, for promises not kept (including pilgrimage vows). But restitution was also specific, for extortions and other sharp practices. Sometimes the testamentary stipulations regarding these were very precise. The London goldsmith, Sir Edmund Shaa (d. 1488), had a troubled conscience about his role in the unjust distraint of two oxen some forty years before making his will, and requested that recompense be made either directly, or in expenditure for the good of his soul. In 1481 the Genoese merchant Bendinelli Sauli ordered that his books be checked after his death to see whether he had engaged in illicit contracts, and if so to arrange restitution. The general pattern of the demand for restitution is shown in the will of Francesc de Granollacs of Barcelona, made in 1420, which required that

Firstly, and before all else, I wish and order that all the debts that I owe on the day of my death be paid, and that all those injuries to which it appears that I am bound to give restitution on the said day of my death should be restored and amended by my . . . executors swiftly, straightforwardly, summarily, and in full . . . [13]

The importance of restitution in intention even if not effect was shown in compositions made for ill-gotten gains: if the offended party could not be found or identified, the money was diverted to other good works, generally towards the relief of the poor. Sauli, for instance, had profited from speculation in the Genoese public debt. In the eventual settlement of 1484, his heirs were to pay 15,000 *lire* for charitable causes, including investments in the Genoese dowry fund.

Where usurers and other exploiters failed to make appropriate restitution before death, they ran the risk of being denied Christian burial. This happened to the usurer Jan Pulsere in Bruges in the fourteenth century, who was denied burial until those with claims against him had had the opportunity to seek restitution.

Rich and poor

Practical and visible charity focused on the Corporal Acts of Mercy, which made 'the poor' the chief objects of charitable activity. However, the definition of those 'poor', and general attitudes towards them, greatly complicated the picture. The poor may be always with us, but poverty is

---

[13] C. Batlle, 'Els Granollacs, metges de Barcelona (segle XV). De la cort del rei a la beneficència parroquial', in *La pobreza y la asistencia a los pobres en la Cataluña medieval; volumen miscelaneo de estudios y documentos*, ed. M. Riu, Anuario de estudios medievales, 9, 11 (2 vols., Barcelona, 1980–2), II, p. 409.

relative, in its hardships and in the sympathy it elicits. Some are born poor, some achieve poverty, and some have poverty thrust upon them; reactions to these different types of poverty varied. Many were born poor; their unavoidable lot one of suffering and want. Some attained poverty, through will, or wilfulness. These included the wastrels, those whose laziness and irresponsibility incurred poverty, and who would not act to improve their state. These were the professional beggars, the petty criminals, and those who, given relief, drank or gambled it away with their cronies. Such scroungers were perhaps mainly an urban phenomenon – possibly a feature of large towns rather than small settlements. People who chose poverty were at the opposite extreme of the spectrum: those who adopted Holy Poverty. From around 1150, as poverty and the possessionless following of the possessionless Christ became the ideal of the *Imitatio Christi*, those who renounced all to follow Christ were given a special status among the poor. For many these new apostles, begging for a living as Christ-substitutes, were worthy recipients of charity; the scale of donations suggests that this was a common perception. Others, however, condemned the mendicants as much as the scrounging poor: if the friars and their ilk had the strength to work, they should do so. As 'sturdy beggars' they were depriving the deserving poor of their due deserts, were acting contrary to their Christian obligations. This stance became more vocal after 1350, when attitudes towards the poor generally hardened, with Wyclif being among the most vociferous in his condemnations.

The last category of the poor included some (primarily widows, orphans, and prisoners) whose poverty was fictitious, in that their lack of power placed them among the *miserabiles* who legally counted as *pauperes* regardless of wealth. Others had suffered real misfortune, by accident or natural forces. The constant threat of fire, the dangers of warfare, the mishaps of normal life, might suddenly destroy a person's livelihood and possessions. For such victims, charity was the only recourse: they clearly had a justified call on their fellow-Christians. Their plight often gained a favourable response; although there were distinctions, and different ways of distributing the charity. The right – the expectation – of charitable relief had a social element: perhaps those at the bottom of the social scale were left to fend for themselves, whereas those whose status was really threatened by such mishaps were treated more generously. The status-consciousness of late-medieval society identified those who could no longer maintain their appropriate social standing as as much afflicted by 'poverty' as the pauperised – and possibly even more entitled to assistance to alleviate their shame. Many mechanisms for the relief of 'the poor' were directed at these people rather than the truly indigent. In England such discrimination meant that personal licences to unfortunates to collect relief went mainly to members of the better-off classes. In Italy many of the new charitable institutions focused on the relief of these afflicted citizens, the 'shame-faced poor'. Fraternities had arranged charitable distributions to them in the fourteenth century, but only in 1442 were the Buonomini di San Martino established in Florence precisely to assist such people, setting a precedent soon followed in other Italian towns. The other Italian novelty of this period, the charitable pawnshops of the *Monti di pietà*, were similarly concerned more with the shame-faced than the truly poor: it was, after all, necessary to have something to pawn in the first place. Other *monti*, such as those which offered dowries, similarly directed their energies at maintaining social distinctions rather than proper 'poor-relief'. The treatment of the 'shame-faced poor' shows the usual problems of identification and analysis. As a category they seem to be completely missing from the English evidence (at least, under readily identifiable labels); in Sienese wills they are mentioned only extremely rarely before 1500 despite evidence of awareness of their existence elsewhere in Italy; whereas they are a regular feature in charitable distributions and arrangements of late medieval Catalonia.

The relationship envisaged between rich and poor was symbiotic. Each side had responsibilities, and rights. For the Franciscans, alms were the hereditary right of the poor; but it was not a one-way traffic. Donor and recipient were both to gain. The poor might already be undergoing a form of Purgatory, which would reduce their pains in the afterlife; but the rich needed the poor to ensure that their own experience of Purgatory would be less horrific. As Giordano da Pisa stated the relationship in 1304:

God has ordered that there be rich and poor so that the rich may be served by the poor and the poor may be taken care of by the rich . . . Why are the poor given their station in life? So that the rich might earn eternal life through them.[14]

This sense of mutuality and reciprocity is clear in the extensive concern with the tale of Dives and Lazarus, and in the vehement attacks on those of the rich who ignored their responsibility to ensure the equitable but decidedly not egalitarian distribution of their wealth. Fifteenth century testators sometimes proclaim awareness of this obligation among the rich by refering to their goods as having been lent to them by God – with clear implications of the duties of stewardship. Few matched Richard Caistor, vicar of St Stephen's Norwich, whose will in 1420 declared that 'the

---

[14] D. R. Lesnick, 'Dominican preaching and the creation of capitalist ideology in late medieval Florence', *Memorie Domenicane*, n.s. 8–9 (1979–80), p. 237.

goods of the church . . . are the goods of the poor', and left most of his possessions to them.[15]

Mutuality and reciprocity were hard ideals to maintain. Even if charity was a Christian obligation, the attitude in which it was offered varied. As claimants, the holy poor were generally given priority. As they had to possess in order to renounce, such people came mainly from the better off and more elevated levels of society – the charitable here again caring for their own. Slightly less deserving, but with a real claim, were those not responsible for their state, having either been born poor or fallen into poverty, and who accepted that fate without complaint – as a trial, or an earthly Purgatory, and with Christian meekness. Charity to them was again obligatory; but doubtless offered with attitudes ranging from Lady or Lord Bountiful through Do-gooder to true *caritas*. The concept of the 'shame-faced' gave a clear social element to such charity; equal concern to ensure social order may be read into distributions which eased tensions. Last came those whose poverty was their own fault, or who having been born or thrust into poverty grouched against their condition, blaming God and others for their ills. Although having a claim to assistance, they were not particularly deserving; some indeed said that they had no right to charity at all. Hostility to them grew in the late middle ages, as donors became more careful with their money and clerics like Francesc Eiximenis (d. 1409) in Catalonia urged more systematic and discriminating charity rather than blanket support to beggars. Such scroungers should provide their own remedies. The danger was that the label of scrounger was easily applied, so reducing the personal responsibility to offer assistance.

Giving: death and life

Most charitable actions which leave real evidence were made at death, via wills and other *post mortem* donations. Statistical analyses of such activity have usually focused on wills; whether in Avignon, Siena, or late medieval England. The documents supply information which can be quantified in the search for access to medieval mentalities. Sums are distributed to the religious orders, with offerings to the mendicants perhaps being especially notable; donations made for the upkeep of bridges, roads, and churches; gifts given to hospitals (which were more sheltered accommodation for the poor and elderly than places for treating the sick) and for the support

---

[15] N. P. Tanner, *The church in late medieval Norwich, 1370–1532*, Pontifical institute of mediaeval studies: Studies and texts, 66 (Toronto, 1984), p. 232.

of almshouses; prisoners receive alms; dowries are set aside for poor girls. All this – and more – besides personal bequests and arrangements for *post mortem* liturgical commemorations.

But wills are often misleading documents: their functions may vary, their completeness is often questionable. What a will omits may be more significant than what it actually says; but the gap usually cannot be filled. Wills needed executors; much of what they had to do might be taken as read and left unspecified. Changes in testamentary practices may reflect altered assumptions of what the executors would do, rather than an evolution of charitable customs. Being made under the shadow of death, and other unknown influences, the voluntary nature of the dispositions is also doubtful. Bequests could be 'suggested' by bystanders or by the scribe of the will, who might also add to its religious sentiments, so perhaps falsifying the testator's spirituality. Regional will-making arrangements would here be important. Local priests probably wrote many English wills, allowing considerable clerical influence. Mediterranean wills, in contrast, were drawn up by notaries, and the clerical impact would be less; although as the Aragonese kings repeatedly sought to restrict the use of priests as notaries, rural wills there were presumably cleric-influenced. The local fiscal regime must also be taken into account: Florentine wills were made under the threats of testamentary taxation and total confiscation of the estate in the face of a posthumous accusation of usury. English wills technically covered only movable goods, lands being dealt with by other means (the testament) – a division with serious implications for assessments of the commitments made at death. In fact, often the distributions foreseen in wills proved impracticable, and they must be seen as records of aspirations rather than of actuality, sometimes happily disposing of wealth which simply did not exist. Moreover, they depended on others for their implementation: that, as visitation and sermon complaints amply record, could not be assumed. Even when implemented, the distributions might be less generous than the wording implies: in Italy the wide definition of 'poverty' was exploited to ensure that resources theoretically alienated in many bequests 'for the poor' in fact stayed within the family.

While death and its prospect of judgement clearly stimulated extensive charitable bequests (regardless of real sentiments and motivations), for the true Christian charity preceded the death-bed preoccupation. Indeed, for *caritas* to involve true care and a reduction in the donor's resources which would actually be felt as a real redistribution of resources, it had to occur during life. Thus, according to the theorists, the relative spiritual value of charitable acts declined as death approached, making gifts given whilst in health of much greater import. As a French preacher evaluated things,

Whoever gives a penny to the poor for God whilst in good health, it will be worth a florin after death. And to give a penny in sickness is worth a gros tournois. And to give after death, that is a leaden penny, because there is no great value in giving what one cannot hold on to.[16]

Unfortunately, although it occurred, lifetime charity is incalculable. Despite the commentators' insistence that it was better to give pennies in life than pounds at death, it is the pounds which are recorded and can be counted. This raises a major problem: how can the evidence on charitable activity during life be assessed? Is lack of evidence for charity evidence of a lack of charity? While the quantifiable rightly commands attention, what of other aspects – the time spent helping in hospitals or assisting the elderly and infirm; the distribution of food and reduction of rents; the offers of hospitality to travellers? This, usually, is lost to record, although there are some hints. An English domestic account book of 1509 records a few small donations: 4d. for a pardoner of Burton Lazars; 4d. to a friar; 2d. towards mending a bridge; with further offerings in similar books of the 1520s. The assumption that charity would be offered is made in the petty indulgences to aid those in misfortune and a plethora of minor good causes; but the evidence is usually scanty and unsatisfactory.

Additional interpretative problems arise with the 'public benefactions', gifts which went beyond the kin, affinity, and friends to affect the wider society through road-building, gifts to hospitals, and such-like. What motivated these grants? Were they altruistic expressions of concern for fellow-humans, and a restoration to society of the wealth which one individual had abstracted from it? Or should they be viewed cynically – even when funding masses – as an attempt to establish a reputation, buy popular favour, proclaim wealth, and gain public recognition of the status which wealth and its disbursement could bring? With such polarities it is also necessary to consider how individuals might see their donations as essentially contractual, the donor obliging the beneficiaries to offer a counter-gift of prayers for his or her health and soul. The supposed concern for educational expansion in some university college foundations of fifteenth-century England may mask several motivations. At Lincoln College, Oxford, in 1427, the foundation was meant to provide a bulwark of theological training against the threat of heresy; but the enterprise also gained its founder a reputation as a benefactor, fulfilled the social obligations of wealth-display and status-declaration, provided a new nexus of patronage ties (in some colleges especially formalised by the system of 'founder's kin', giving his family a prior claim on the endowment), and

---

[16] H. Martin, *Le métier de prédicateur en France septentrionale à la fin du moyen âge (1350–1520)* (Paris, 1988), p. 506.

secured prayers for his soul after death – prayers which were often to take precedence over the educational concern should the money run out. A similar multiplicity of motivations could underlie any donation. Links between individuals would be equally multi-faceted: the bequest of dowries for poor girls, for instance, was an act of charity in itself, possibly a restitution of ill-gotten gains, a proclamation of Christian concern, a means to purchase prayers, and more. Supplying funds for a named scholar was a gift to the church (as scholars often followed clerical careers), an act of family or affinity loyalty, an act of patronage, and a way to secure *post mortem* prayers. A comment in Edmund Dudley's *Tree of commonwealth* (1509) is here particularly apposite: he urged his compatriots to provide maintenance for university students, for 'a better chantry shall you never find'.[17]

As in other cases, regional practices varied; practices also changed over time. The Black Death seems to mark a major transition, from the indiscriminate spreading of gifts to secure prayers to a more targeted distribution, maybe hoping to ensure a more effective reciprocity of gift exchange. Even the saintly Richard Caistor requested that the distributions to the poor made under his will be concentrated on his own parishioners. The insistence on targeting is perhaps most obvious in the shifts in Siena, where by 1363 the number of charitable gifts mentioned in wills had fallen markedly, even though their value increased. There the stress was on funding dowries. Changes in distributions could also reflect changes in the charitable structures – the increasing civic control over hospitals, evident in Barcelona and the Netherlands as much as in the Italian towns; and the establishment of intentionally charitable funds in the Italian *monti*. Indeed, in some instances charitable bequests were virtually or actually compulsory. In Venice, for instance, notaries were required under threat of penalty to 'remind' testators of the Lazzaretto hospital, a device adopted also in the 1470s to secure funds for the state-supported hospital established as Gesù Cristo di Sant'Antonio.

Structured charity: fraternities

Among the significant channels for charitable distributions, and for caritative concern in the wider sense, fraternity membership had a special place. Whatever the functions which congealed around such bodies,[18] and thereby concealed their original stimulus, a prime purpose was to offer a form of mutual insurance for their members. While they had a public face,

[17] Edmund Dudley (ed. D. M. Brodie), *The tree of commonwealth* (Cambridge, 1948), p. 63.
[18] Above, pp. 120–1.

the fraternities were usually introspective: the principle on which they operated was of self-help more than a social conscience. Schools, charity, and masses were provided mainly for their own members: it was the poverty-stricken fellow-member who had first claim on the fraternity's charity. As friendly societies, their expenses could not realistically exceed income or reserves – if they did, the perceived value of the investment would fall, new members would not be recruited, and the fraternity would wither, possibly completely.

Amid their many functions, most fraternities prepared for deaths. When a member died, the guild arranged the funeral, the rules often requiring every member to attend on pain of a fine. Most brotherhoods also offered *post mortem* benefits, by at least the maintenance of a collective obit for their deceased members. Wealthy guilds which could afford to maintain a priest throughout the year might go further and arrange daily masses for their members, living and dead, or act as trustees for chantries. Such benefits were not to be ignored. At some point this merges with the second main aspect of the accumulation of lifetime benefits, the acquisition of indulgences; but not quite yet.

The guilds and fraternities were not restricted to displays at death. They also manifested Christianity in life, and could become quite disciplinarian institutions, as they tried to assist their members through the pilgrimage of life. Some widened their responsibilities, by assuming greater social roles. Fraternity regulations often reinforced the demands of *caritas* and Christian morality on their members, by rules against sexual mis-behaviour, against swearing, or other anti-social activity. The success of these rules, and indeed their distribution, is not absolutely clear; nor are they unambiguous. Which would be the more potent restriction of such misbehaviour: dread of the Last Judgement for breach of Christian regulations, or the immediate social loss incurred by public expulsion from the group with its consequent loss of status, especially if it was the local élite? Similarly, were the guaranteed social position shown in a decent funeral, and the contacts enjoyed through guild membership, more important than the fear of an eventual judgement which might, after all, be in the individual's favour regardless of membership of any particular association?

A striking feature of fraternity membership – at least in England – is the prevalence of multiple membership, mainly of the larger institutions. In part this was only nominal: individual guilds saw some people as good catches, and would actively seek them out as members. There was clearly some cachet to being in the same fraternity as the local bishop or earl, even more if the monarch was a member. But others who joined several guilds were making a choice, which reflected personal preferences. Some fraternities might be joined solely for their promised *post mortem* benefits: when a London testator linked his fraternity memberships with the membership of wider groups whose main common feature was the offering of an indulgence, such aspirations surely come into play.

Similar considerations might apply to continental guild membership; possibly even more complex ones. It is clear that the function of fraternities, and their activities, changed in time. Whereas England appears to lack fraternities created to oppose heresy, or to assume city-wide charitable obligations, they do appear in Italy.

Indulgences

If self-interest and self-preservation were major impulses to charitable activity, as was arguably the case, the extent of those imperatives becomes most blatant in the links between charity and indulgences. Indulgences were perhaps the easiest way to build up credit for the afterlife, and might well be seen as the most secure, as they required no action by others after a death. They sometimes overlap with fraternity concerns and show some of their ambiguities. They were dispensed by a wide variety of institutions, many called fraternities or guilds – although often more akin to the confraternity which was established with religious orders and individual houses. Indeed, several major indulgences of late medieval England were dispensed precisely on behalf of religious institutions, the purchasers participating in the full spiritual benefits of the institution. There is extensive evidence of distributions on behalf of the London hospitals of St Anthony, St Mary at Bethlehem and St Mary of Roncesvalles (among others), in the north for the Trinitarian house of St Robert of Knaresborough, or in the Midlands for the hospital of Burton Lazars. Elsewhere, the Cambridgeshire chapel of St Mary in the Sea (established in the early 1400s at Newton) and the Trinitarians of Hounslow were also large-scale vendors. Purchases might be equated with fraternity membership, confounding attempts at precision when considering lay reactions to either type of institution.

At first sight, the theory of indulgences seems straightforward – the idea of the Treasury of Merits, an eternal sinking fund against which penances to be satisfied in Purgatory could to offset – but their practical operation is less comprehensible: how could allocations of time operate in a non-chronological Purgatory? Theologians were uncertain – not even Aquinas managed to explain the system rationally, and fell back on arguing that the church would not offer them if they did not work. How were 'years' of indulgences to be treated? The confessional writers appreciated the problem, evolving the idea that the remission operated as though the stated period of penance had been completed on earth. The base tariff clearly remained that of the old *Penitentials*, which during their period of operation before the end of the twelfth century had defined the penance formally due for each particular sin. Even if penitential and confessional practice had developed to make priestly-imposed penances more tolerable, the old tariff was still held to reflect the due penance. That indulgences might actually be cashed in against terrestrially-imposed penances – which is the logical application of the practice to the tariffs of the *Penitentials* – was certainly accepted by some late-medieval canonists; indeed, in fifteenth-century England there may have been a regionalised doctrine of indulgences which sought to preclude their application to Purgatorial penance. Continental canonists such as Angelo Carletti of Chivasso (d. 1495) also accepted the idea of terrestrial application; but he advised that the earthly penances be performed even if harsh, and the indulgences saved for Purgatory on the assumption that the earthly penance would not actually cover the full amount due by the nature of the sin.

This double standard, of a penance which could be tolerated on earth and that actually due to God, may have been widely accepted, possibly lying behind the great concern to accumulate indulgences. Certainly the staggering totals of years which were amassed make sense only on the basis of a heavy weight of sin and penance such as that defined by the *Penitentials*. Yet popular conceptions of what indulgences did remain unclear: many believed that the indulgence operated of itself, failing to integrate it into the full penitential system which required confession and contrition as the igniting forces to give it effect. If sold, as many were, by the unscrupulous; if inflated out of all proportion, as they were after 1350; and if acquired by the credulous; they might wrongly be seen as securing total release from the effects of sin.

The scale of the demand for indulgences is certainly impressive. In 1498 a Barcelona printer contracted to provide 18,000 copies for the abbey of Montserrat; while the London hospital of St Anthony sold over 30,000 a year around 1500 (assuming a general rate of 4d. per letter). Lesser institutions had more limited appeal, and with very local collections the number of recipients would be small: the Trinitarians of Thelsford leased out a questorship for only 10s. a year. Even so, the total of indulgences distributed solely in England must have been staggering; with western Europe added in, it would approach stupefying levels. As with other aspects of religion, however, regional variations may have to be built into the analysis. On the evidence of printed indulgences, it seems that Italy provided much less of a market than Germany.

Letters of indulgence testify to the urge to accumulate, with the collection made by Henry and Katherine Langley perhaps not atypical. This included indulgences for the war against the Turks (1476), for the relief of Rhodes (1484), in support of Saintes cathedral (1487), for the chapel of St Mary at Newton, and the Boston guild, plus confraternity with the Dominicans and Trinitarians. The Willoughby account books of the early sixteenth century mention frequent purchases, the same indulgences being bought repeatedly over the years, even within the same year.

Such wide dissemination of indulgences was assured by the appointment of touring questors to collect contributions: the pardoners who often earned a bad reputation, especially those who trafficked in forged grants. The machinery went back a long way: monks and canons soliciting building funds toured Europe with their relics in the twelfth century, and questors for religious orders (the Carthusians in particular) are mentioned in thirteenth century synodal statutes. Its extension to indulgences meant that some secured national and international distribution. In post-plague England the four major national institutions were the London hospitals of St Thomas of Acon, St Mary of Bethlehem, St Anthony, and St Mary Roncesvalles. The last two began as dependencies of continental institutions, centred respectively on Vienne in the Dauphiné and Roncesvalles in the Pyrenees; but the links had been effectively severed by 1400. Evidence of collecting for all four appears in almost every English diocese. Of the decidedly international concerns, crusades were supported during the thirteenth century and into the fourteenth. Papal efforts to defend Constantinople against the Turks also gained support; while under the first Tudors indulgences were being touted in England for the support of the monastery of St Catherine at Sinai. The papacy supported many projects, sometimes for its own ends, and controversially. The indulgence offered by Pope John XXIII to those supporting him against King Ladislas of Naples was bitterly attacked by John Hus; while a century later the papal grants to those assisting the rebuilding of St Peter's at Rome incurred the ire of Martin Luther.

The irrepressible demand for indulgences and the questionable activities of pardoners were a constant worry to the church. Buyers and sellers invested massively in indulgences; and as the sellers were marketing what was effectively a commodity, they sometimes over-sold their wares. The criticism of indulgence-mongering which finally stimulated Luther's outcries was not unique; but while the sellers are easily condemned, the buyers cannot be ignored. They were quite happy with what was being offered, were if anything desperate to accumulate these little slips of parchment. The outlay involved must be put in perspective. The general level of 4d. per pardon in early-sixteenth-century England was still substantial for a craftsmen; so perhaps the purchasers were mainly from the wealthier layers of society, with artisans and people below them content with the indulgences which required effort but not money, like repetitions of prayers or visits to churches. However, not all indulgences were so cheap. Those for crusades, and for the Roman jubilees which were sold outside Rome, supposedly required commutation of the costs of personal participation. For the Jubilee of 1500 the collector in England, Jasper Ponce, set a sliding scale of charges varying with landed income or the value of movable goods. For the landed, the cost ranged from £3 6s. 8d. for incomes over £2000 down to 1s. 4d. for the £20–40 category; for the others from £2 for those with goods over £1,000 down to 1s. for those in the £20–200 group. People falling below £20 paid what they felt able to contribute out of devotion.

Although the speedy attainment of Heaven was a constant aspiration associated with indulgences, perceptions of them unavoidably changed over time. When first granted, from the late eleventh century in association with crusades, indulgences were ill-defined. Plenary indulgences offering total remission of sins were exclusively linked to crusade or activity against heretics. They became more widespread from about 1300, especially in association with the years of Jubilee proclaimed by the popes. The theory evolved as the institution became more entrenched, but slowly. While popes may have known what they were granting, they were rarely specific, and sometimes contradictory. A magisterial definition of indulgences was issued only under Pope Clement VI (1346–53), but still unrevealing about how they were implemented. The complexities which theologians developed to differentiate between the *culpa* (the guilt of sin, which a priest could remit) and the *pena* (the penalty due to God) were doubtless too subtle for most. Moreover, during the years of the Black Death, a major change seems to have occurred in connection with indulgences: their increasing proliferation and extension, which needs consideration.

Initially indulgences were granted only for short periods. Popes rarely granted more than seven years' remission, usually in combinations of years and 'Lents', periods of forty days; cardinals could grant a hundred days; archbishops and bishops forty. The small scale of grants suggests that, until the 1350s, non-plenary indulgences were not all that significant in medieval religion; although the number of grants was considerable. There may have been problems about linking the idea with the practice: the scale and formulation of the early grants is certainly more appropriate to a penitential system based on externals, on real periods of time in this world, which would emphasise a connection with the *Penitentials* and the practicality of 'cashing in' the accumulated days against the impositions under their regulations. As the system of the *Penitentials* fell into abeyance, with a greater stress on contrition and interiorisation of penance, so increased emphasis on Purgatory and the purgatorial process – and its guarantee of ultimate bliss – meant that the uncertainty of the function of indulgences could be switched to the afterlife, to apply to the journey through Purgatory.

After 1348–50 the multiplication of indulgences, and the excessive periods gained, must have changed attitudes towards them. Extraordinary totals of pardon were now offered. Visits to Rome could earn phenomenal amounts, according to the guidebooks; in the fifteenth century, the recital of five Creeds and as many *Aves* and Our Fathers before a Pietà, even a printed one, brought remission of up to 33,000 years for each repetition of the package. A direct inspiration might be claimed for some of these large-scale indulgences. The testimony of the recipient of a vision of the Virgin at Cubas in Spain in 1449 gave assurances that those who fasted on the Virgin's feast days earned 80,000 years of indulgence. Forged pardons had circulated before the Black Death, but presumably not on a scale to bring the whole system into disrepute. Unavoidably, forgery continued after the plague, but the forgeries were clearly treated as valid, as were the great totals ascribed to minor acts. It seems that for most people it was the repetition of the exercises, the desire for the pardon to be valid, which actually gave the validation. Although the authorities condemned this abuse of indulgences, it was also legitimised by them; and it was the legitimisation which secured popular credibility. Depictions of the Pietà, of the Mass of St Gregory, or the *Arma Christi* (the instruments of the Passion) gained in popularity as much for their associated indulgences as for the emotions they inspired.

While there were attempts by the authorities to limit the escalation and misinterpretation of indulgence, the chasm between theologians' understanding and their popular appreciation was not a simple division between 'clerical' and 'lay' perceptions. The clergy who disseminated indulgences – from bishops downwards – often shared the attitudes of the lay hoarders. Cardinal Albert of Brandenburg gave one of the few totals of remission in the late fifteenth century, calculating that he had acquired 39,245,120 years off Purgatory. Indulgences were generally treated and advertised as cumulative, even though grants were meant to be valid only for the life of a granting bishop and perhaps only for that bishop's own spiritual subjects. Thus, those receiving the indulgences offered to members of the fraternity of St Chad in Lichfield cathedral were said to enjoy benefits dating back to the episcopate of St Chad – an historical impossibility; but such minor inconveniences could be overlooked. Papal indulgences were similarly said to be cumulative.

Although indulgences became more prolific after 1350, their earlier importance should not be undervalued. Most evidence for the reaction to them post-dates the Black Death, which skews interpretations. Indulgences had been offered regularly before then, which would not have happened if the proposed recipients considered them valueless. Equally clearly, the pardoners who distributed indulgences were active well before the plague years, with their collecting areas and licences. That most evidence used for the distribution of indulgences before 1348 concerns crusades and crusaders or would be crusaders may be an artificial twist in the sources or a measure of historians' failure to notice the material.

Crusade and the relief of the Holy Land took priority over all other grants, most notably with the indulgence for those going forth to fight under the sign of the Cross. To include crusade among acts of charity may seem bizarre, given that the purpose – to remove the infidel – could most effectively be achieved by killing. However, for its proponents crusading could be seen as an act of love: towards Christ and other Christians, even towards the infidel by ending the opportunities for sin. The terms in which the message was conveyed, let alone received, were ambiguous. The proposed relationship to Christ might be more one of vassalic fealty and duty than *caritas*; although with a strong appeal to reciprocal responsibility towards a God who had so suffered to offer redemption. These sentiments may have declined after about 1250, as the format of crusading altered; although the chivalric element remained strong. Later crusade indulgences, granted most prolifically to those contributing cash, were probably seen as much like other grants. Nevertheless, the fact remains that even after the extinction of the Crusader states, crusades and their indulgences continued in the west; while assistance to the defence of the Hospitaller outposts off the coast of Asia Minor continued to attract offerings in return for indulgences.

As the theory of indulgences developed, with the opportunities for marketing, so their link with charitable actions in the widest sense became more pronounced: not unreasonably, it required an act of merit to be entitled to draw on the Treasury of Merits. The schemes so encouraged ranged from attending the sermons of named preachers to aiding the construction of a church, from the redemption of prisoners to the building of bridges. The generalised charitable indulgences remained a strong element throughout the middle ages: the papacy regularly made grants for the maintenance of churches, which usually required the recipient to visit the building on specified dates within the year. Most other projects, like bridge building, benefited from grants of episcopal indulgences: among other things, Bishop Robert Hallum of Salisbury

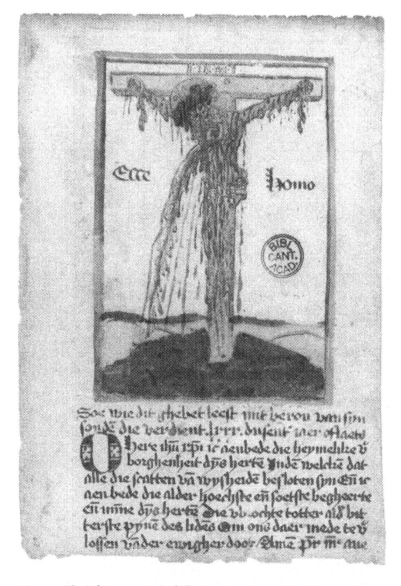

Figure 5 The inflationary spiral of affective piety. A woodblock image of a
blood-drenched Christ on the cross, to serve as a devotional stimulus and focus.
Produced in Flanders c. 1450, the image carries a promise of 80,000 years of
indulgence, a large amount even for a work such as this. Widespread
distribution would be encouraged by that offer, and by the technology of
reproduction. The vernacular prayer is clearly addressed to a relatively literate
audience, but one geographically restricted by dialect. The Latin inscription on
the image emphasises the focus on Christ's sufferings as a human being; the tag
and the demand for a *Paternoster* and *Ave* after the Flemish prayer presume an
acquaintance with liturgical language.

(1407–17) offered grants for the support of the hospitals of St Catherine at Lusty by Bruton and of St John the Baptist at Malmesbury; for visitors to the shrine of King Edward the Martyr at Shaftesbury; to those participating in prayers for the good of the realm; for those assisting selected individuals who had fallen into adversity, or had insufficient funds to allow them to go on pilgrimage; and for the rebuilding of Laverstock church, recently destroyed by fire.

Perhaps the most problematic aspect of indulgences, until the late fifteenth century, was whether they could be acquired for the dead. The question engaged some of the best theological minds of the period, reflecting disputes between Dominicans and Franciscans, papalists and anti-papalists, lawyers and theologians. Market forces operated – indulgences which could be bought for the dead would certainly sell better; but the fundamental issue was whether the papacy had jurisdiction over the dead or not. Here opinions were fiercely divided. The need to limit over-enthusiastic preaching of indulgences appears regularly in the sources: the Council of Vienne condemned those questors who claimed that their indulgences benefited those who were already dead. In the thirteenth century, crusade indulgences were offered as applicable to the dead, and there was clearly a belief that the living could divert their acquired indulgences to benefit the dead. This had appeared with the early crusaders, who might take the cross for the benefit of a relative's soul; while a fourteenth-century dialogue between a friar and a ghost (supposedly based on a real interview which occurred in southern France in 1324), ended with the former transferring his indulgences accumulated over the preceding year to the benefit of the deceased soul.

The first formal grant of an indulgence for the dead seems to date from 1343, made by an Italian Dominican bishop. The final stage in the evolution occurred under Pope Sixtus IV, who in 1476 officially extended the benefit of indulgences to the souls of the dead; although his declaration provoked even more controversy and uncertainty, needing repeated clarification. If indulgences had earlier been post-dated cheques on the Treasury of Merits, the cheques could now be issued retrospectively. Indulgences bought for the dead became a relatively common phenomenon; their availability perhaps eased the pressures on the living, possibly even eased their consciences, in the same way that enrolment of the dead in fraternities may have been stimulated by the prospect of their enjoying the benefits of the indulgences as well as the prayers offered by the association.

Regardless of cost, whether fiscal or physical, indulgences were a major feature of the economics of salvation in medieval Europe. With each acquisition the prospective pains of Purgatory would be partially offset, and Heaven be that much nearer.

PRAY FOR ME . . .

Caritas worked in this world to affect the next. A positive response to Christianity's demands in the first stage of the human pilgrimage, it prepared for the second, Purgatory. That Purgatory was a continuation rather than a new start was clearly reflected in the writings of the theologians. Albert the Great (d. 1280) insisted that those in Purgatory were still travelling towards their ultimate goal; however, having now left the world they were incapable of further sin, although they still had to make reparation for their earlier faults. The sense of continuity also appears in the literary works. Guillaume de Deguileville produced a sequel to his tract on the earthly pilgrimage in 1355–8, a *Pelèrinage de l'âme* which traced the soul's journey through Hell, Purgatory, and Heaven – a theological parallel to Dante's *Divine Comedy*.

The formalisation of new caritative relationships was a prime strategy in preparation for the experience of Purgatory, to establish mechanisms to ensure a speedy transit. Indeed, death's role as a crux in such charitable links is exemplified in an Avignonese couple's request that the letters of indulgence which they had acquired during their lives should be displayed at their funerals: now was the time for the promissory notes to be exchanged. That the available evidence for charitable activity coincides with the imminence of death is significant. Despite the positive tone and somewhat hortatory stance of many texts of the *ars moriendi*, it is reasonable to suppose that most people dreaded death. Indeed, the temptations against which the dying are warned in the *Book of the craft of dying* clearly attest such fear. Preachers' emphases on sin and judgement, and the terrors of the afterlife, would more than counter any suggestions that all was well.

Several works purported to recount visions of Purgatory and the horrors to be endured there in order to expiate sins. Even more dramatically, just as there was meant to be a terrestrial paradise awaiting discovery, so Purgatory reputedly had outlets on earth. Mount Etna was one among them; but the most famous was St Patrick's Purgatory, a subterranean cave on an island in Lough Derg, Ireland. Given continental renown by diffusion of the record of a visit by the knight Owen in *c.* 1146/7, knowledge of St Patrick's Purgatory spread via sermon *exempla*, thereby also expanding general awareness of Purgatory (not without uncertainties, as the original text was constructed before the theologians had completed their identification of Purgatory as a definite location).

Despite its remoteness St Patrick's Purgatory received a steady trickle of British and continental visitors across the centuries. Some of them, like the Aragonese Ramon de Perelhos in 1393, produced their own statements of their experiences. In 1497 Pope Alexander VI ordered that the cave be closed; but Pius III allowed it to reopen in 1503.

A major concern in response to the threat of Purgatory would be to mitigate its terrors, through good deeds and pious works, seeking to eliminate the debit balance of sin. The concern to control the future has led to charges that late-medieval religion was at least semi-Pelagian, if not completely so. This desire to tie God to a bargain (with other humans) was expressed not only during life, but also in attempts to control events *post mortem* by securing commemorations and arranging other beneficial acts. This raises the question of motivations: how much were people acting out of fear, how much out of devotion? Do such worries indicate vital spirituality, or are they mere conventions, the fulfilment of expectations which cloak and obscure individuality? Full answers cannot be provided: too many strands need analysis, in combination, which it would be invalid and improper to disentangle, always assuming that it could be done.

Strategies for remembrance: post mortem commemorations

As the nodal point of human existence, death had to be approached strategically. As death came and passed, the individual lost control of his or her redemption, exchanging some dgree of control for total dependence on the generosity of God and the consciences of heirs. Except for a few ghosts, death marked the point of no return; it was the individual's last chance to influence his or her own destination. Most assessments of *post mortem* arrangements to exert that influence derive from wills, simply because normally only they provide the information. As with other charitable undertakings, however, wills reflect events incompletely, especially as they generally ignore arrangements made in life.[19] This may be important in regional assessments. The lack of charitable donations in wills from Barcelona and Cordova could be explained by arrangements being made during life rather than by an absence of piety. Not only do wills freeze one point in existence, which may present a false picture; they are also incomplete snapshots – many acts to purchase prayers are baldly summarised in general requests for the residue to be distributed 'for the good of my soul'. Failure to act in life also made a testator dependent on the charity of his executors to

[19] Above, pp. 212–13.

implement his bequests, which was by no means guaranteed. Nevertheless, wills offered the last opportunity to express such concerns: the final plea for assistance from the saints, the last attempt to bind those left behind to act for the good of one's soul, to offer recompense and restitution for ills committed, and to meet the obligations of *caritas*.

Apart from charitable distributions to secure prayers (including recitations of psalters by nuns and other religious women) in return for largesse, bequests for *post mortem* spiritual benefits usually sought to secure masses which would invoke the name of the deceased, sometimes in association with others, to identify them to God as especially deserving of speedy release from Purgatory. The organisation of such provision was a complex business, rarely under the testator's complete control. The complexities may be historical as well as administrative: it is here that Chiffoleau's proposed tripartite scheme for the dealing with masses for the dead comes into operation.[20] Certainly wills rarely express concern for *post mortem* masses in the thirteenth century, the first noted from around Siena appears only in 1269.

The simplest way to secure masses was to buy them (or, avoiding the imputation of simony, to pay a priest for their celebration). But the taste of simony was unavoidable; there was apparently an accepted rate per masses, which were paid for pro rata. In late medieval England, the charge was generally 4d. each if celebrated by a secular priest, although the stingy might hope to secure them for as little as 1d.

The number of masses purchased, and the stipulations about their celebration, are indicative of attitudes towards both the mass and the fact of death. The quantity could be staggeringly high – 1,000 is not all that uncommon, although the number of people who could afford so many was limited. Even fewer were those who might purchase 10,000 masses, sought by Archbishop William Courtenay of Canterbury in 1388, or the 25,000 demanded by Bernard d'Escoussans, seigneur of Langoiran, in 1338. The overall record seems to be held by Jean de Grailly, *capital* of Buch, who in 1369 requested 50,000. As in other spheres, regional and class influences may operate here: such large quantities are unknown in the Sienese material, or in Catalonia. The appeal for masses is almost obsessive, reflecting an urgent desire to get through the Purgatorial experience as quickly as possible. Some testators bluntly demanded that masses be said as swiftly as possible, or within an almost impossibly brief period after death: one English testator asked for 1,000 masses within three days of his death, which would have provided employment for at least 334 priests at extremely short notice. Beyond the numbers, there were also

[20] Above, p. 140.

dedications: as votive masses became more common, so the form of the mass could be specified. Some testators (like Archbishop Courtenay of Canterbury) were not content with an ordinary mass, presumably of *requiem*, but demanded masses of the Virgin, the Holy Ghost, and other votives, suggesting personal devotion as well as the general concern with death.

Often, beyond the bulk purchases, arrangements were made to provide a series of masses by employing a priest for a specific period. This was not the establishment of a formal chantry, but came close. It probably reflected the testator's economic standing more than desire for *post mortem* commemoration: while the wealthy could hire a priest for several years, their poorer fellows would make do with shorter periods. What mattered above all was that the soul benefited, and the period in Purgatory was reduced. The priest would celebrate daily, and the deceased would reap the reward.

Such benefactions were not established simply to secure mention of the deceased's name. A mass also had an audience: although the priest was being hired, he was employed as a professional to lead the amateurs among the congregation, who would be enjoined to pray for the benefactor. As the endowment of any mass was a public benefaction, beneficial to the living, it was fitting that they should reciprocate for the founder even if still alive by offering prayers on his or her behalf.

For those seeking long-term commemoration without excessive cost, other arrangements could be made. The anniversary or 'obit' amounted to a funeral without a corpse, celebrated with a mass at least once a year, usually on the anniversary of the death, and often accompanied by a charitable dole. As they did not entail the full-time employment of a priest, anniversaries were often undertaken by the parochial clergy. In some French parishes such endowed masses could provide a major part of a cleric's income. In 1496 one Auvergne parish had no fewer than 180 endowed masses, although the foundations were at their peak in the fourteenth century. Obits and anniversaries could be conveniently sited in colleges and religious houses – and as one of their functions was an annual display to reinforce memory, high attendance from the members of those institutions was to be encouraged.

Other devotions arose to cater for the desire for *post mortem* memorialisation. Sometimes it was a matter of buying a package of masses. Catalonia developed a regional cycle of thirty-three masses, known as the mass of Sant Amador. More usual in England and France was the trental, a series of thirty (in Siena trentals do not seem to have been standardised until after the Council of Trent). Whereas the Sant Amador masses could be distributed among the celebrating institutions, the trental was arranged as a block. They appear frequently in wills, often being purchased from mendicant houses, with the request that they be said soon after death.

One form of trental gained a special following in England, although it also appears on the continent, the so-called Trental of St Gregory. This more elaborate series of masses was held on thirty specified feast days over a year – supposedly because masses then were more effective than on other days. As it took a whole year it was more costly than a normal trental, especially if hiring a secular priest. The expense limited the market; but also opened up the range of celebrants. It seems probable that it was mainly celebrated by regulars: as their livelihood was already secured, they could perhaps undercut seculars in pricing.

A perpetual chantry provided the most elaborate *post mortem* spiritual security. Duration depended on the founder's finances and the strength of the local economy; regional and other considerations which affected the format of local spirituality were also influential. Perhaps chantries were less popular in some areas than others; their dearth has been noted in the wills of late medieval Catalonia, but such absences might merely reflect vagaries of the sources. Here will evidence is perhaps especially untrustworthy, as chantries were probably often arranged in their founder's lifetime to ensure their existence. The nature of the chantry affects its visibility in the records. In England, chantry endowment to create a formal ecclesiastical benefice with real property required a royal licence to alienate in mortmain from the late fourteenth century, the foundations being suggested by the inclusion of the licences on the Patent Rolls. As these were for benefices, the local bishops retained administrative oversight, and institutions were entered in their registers. Many founders evaded this process by alienating the endowment to 'feoffees to uses', effectively in trust. They became the legal owners of the property, paying the priest's salary from the income. The chantry was based on a legal fiction and its priest lacked real ownership of the property, having neither freehold right, nor ecclesiastical benefice. Other chantries were endowed not with land, but with cash – this often occurred in dealings with friars, especially if one of their number was to say the masses. Other religious houses also had such arrangements, but were probably more reluctant to assume perpetual obligations for short-term gain: the chronicler of Meaux abbey complained about one arrangement when the monks had to provide the services even though the cash endowment had long been spent. Such cash-funded chantries might be unnoticed by state and ecclesiastical authorities.

Chantries, especially if established as full benefices, required considerable investment by their founders. They also reflect the founders' concern for the salvation of their souls, and for the form of the services to be said on their behalf. A founder often detailed the services to be held – identifying the collects, the amount of singing, the Use to be adopted if there was a choice, and so on. Equally evident is concern about the quality of the priest to be employed, and for the continuity of the services. Foundation charters frequently lay down conditions for the priest, setting out precisely how he should and should not spend his life; stating the time allowed for holidays; asserting the duty to ensure the maintenance of the services if incapacitated; and more. The continuity of the services was a prime concern, often producing intricate arrangements to ensure that any vacancy was brief, relying on the competitive urge to act as patron by establishing a succession of reversionary rights if there was no nomination within a specified short period.

The prayers and daily masses secured by chantries operated principally for the souls named by the founder in his ordinances. The choice of those to be prayed for obviously reflects varied imperatives – the founder and immediate relatives would naturally be named, but diplomatic and other considerations could extend the list. In England, for instance, the need for a mortmain licence encouraged the naming of members of the royal family as beneficiaries. Most foundations also extended the prayers to the founder's kin and benefactors, while 'all the faithful departed' were tacked on as an unavoidable afterthought. For those too poor to make their own arrangements, this might be their only 'chantry' commemoration.

Many chantry founders sought to maximise returns by extending the impact of their benefactions. The simplest expansion was perhaps implicit: a chantry would augment parochial worship, its priest becoming part of the local ecclesiastical system. Chantry priests certainly did assist the parish incumbent to provide the round of masses and other services sought by the parishioners. In rural areas of England, the link between chantry and parochial pastoral care might be formalised by making the chantry into a chapel of ease, its priest becoming a subsidiary curate. In the dioceses of central and eastern France the priestly complement was similarly augmented by groups of *prêtres-filleuls*, identified with specific parishes. These were very localised: membership was restricted to priests born and baptised within the parish, who formed semi-collegiate bodies and lived chiefly from the income provided by endowments for *post mortem* masses.

Specific social benefits were also provided, ranging in scale from small doles for the poor to the foundation of almshouses and large-scale educational provision. Most medieval social provision was emphatically based on ideas of reciprocity: the benefactor gave in charity, but expected acknowledgement through the prayers of the beneficiaries. Almshouses, hospitals, schools, and university colleges all fitted into this mutual structure, often carefully linked to chantry functions. Indeed, many foundations would be virtually inconceivable without the chantry element. The founders of schools often explicitly demanded prayers from their scholars for themselves and their nominees. Hospitals and almshouses equally demanded the inmates' prayers for their founders, alongside a rigid regime of religious observance.

Local circumstances produced variants on the general pattern. A common foundation in Germany was the *Seelhaus* ('Soul-house'), inhabited by women whose prime function was to pray for souls. These were similar to almshouses, often being owned or patronised by individual families, possibly as a focus for active charitable work by the women of the family. Several may have been linked with beguines originally; but this had changed by the late fifteenth century. Beguines were formally banned from the houses at Nuremberg in 1478, when they were required to assume more hospital-like functions. In the Augsburg houses membership could be temporary, with the women leaving to marry or at will. While the houses were tied to particular families, their inhabitants had a wider role. Each house in Augsburg was linked to a specific church or religious house, and attended the anniversaries held there. Usually one woman would hold vigil over the grave, while the others attended for the anniversary mass, being individually paid for their presence.

The integration of the varied manifestations of a concern for souls into a strategy of remembrance is demonstrated in the arrangements for Hosyer's chantry in Ludlow, founded in 1486. The feoffees to uses received property for several purposes, which entangled the Ludlow Palmers' guild and the local priory in a system of mutual checks and balances to ensure that the scheme was completed and kept in operation. The endowment was firstly to cover the stipend of a secular priest to say daily masses for John and Alice Hosyer, the audience being required to join him in the remembrance. Secondly, some of the church choristers were daily to sing psalms at their burial place. Thirdly, there was to be an annual obit. The almshouse established by the Hosyers before their deaths was to be maintained. Every Sunday the Ludlow parish priest was to urge his parishioners to pray for their souls at the common bidding. All this is definitely a strategy for eternity, the list of benefactions being recalled twice daily in the call to pray for their souls addressed to the inhabitants of the almshouse.

Besides providing the impetus for the formal endowment of *post mortem* prayers, death stimulated other kinds of commemoration, usually linking benefaction and the reciprocity of prayers. From the thirteenth century onwards, most church furnishings functioned as memorials. Some were bluntly intrusive: massive tombs bearing effigies of the dead and inscriptions for them, which could clutter up the building. Not all tombs were intrusive: some also served as altars, or provided the base for an Easter sepulchre. Other donations were less oppressive, donors' names being inscribed or embroidered on plate or vestments, or incorporated into windows and floortiles. These certainly contributed to the beauty of holiness while proclaiming the benefactor, and made a real contribution to the worship and transmission of the Christian message. Explicit in such benefactions was the desire to be remembered, and a request for prayers – often demanded in inscriptions, notably on windows. Here again the urgent desire to be remembered could be bluntly intrusive. When Alice Chester gave a hearse cloth to the parish of All Saints, Bristol, in the mid-1400s, a simple gift was not enough. The cloth carried an inscription requesting prayers for herself and her husband, a demand which silently but insistently usurped some of the suffrages each time it was used.

The giving of windows, vestments, and furnishings clearly served the church's needs as well as securing remembrance. Chantry endowment provided not just the priests but the material needs of the services – and sometimes extra income – which would reduce the financial demands made on other parishioners and so earn their further gratitude and prayers. But self-centredness was always there, perhaps most blatantly with tombs. Testators often requested burial and a tomb at a stated spot in the church: the available space would be remodelled as the long dead were shunted around to meet the wishes of the most recently deceased – Archbishop Courtenay of Canterbury demanded burial in Exeter cathedral, and that three deans be moved to accommodate him. Tombs, however, perhaps demonstrate better than other memorials the spirituality of their intended occupants. This is sometimes seen in the basic decoration, certainly in the demand for prayers which almost invariably appears on the inscriptions. Decor which included depictions of the Sacred Heart, or the Passion of Christ, also conveyed a spiritual message.

The dead and the living

Although the benefactions made to secure *post mortem* remembrance may reflect spirituality, many of them raise other questions, and had other purposes. The doubly contractual aspect of the prayers – between the living and the dead in the reciprocal economy of intercession, and between the dead and God to gain early release from Purgatory as reward for increasing divine worship – hints at a mercenary approach to the whole business of death, and an appreciation of the possibilities of salvation which was at least semi-Pelagian. Beyond that the scale and ostentation (or lack of it) of the benefactions make statements about both the individual and contemporary society. The investment in some of these arrangements was enormous, probably increasingly so as time passed. In the fifteenth century whole inheritances were affected. In England, it could take decades for feoffees to uses to accumulate the capital necessary for an endowment. After the death in 1439 of Richard Beauchamp, earl of Warwick, the inheritance was kept from the main heirs for several years as over £3,000 was gathered to build the Beauchamp chapel in St Mary's church, Warwick. Even national politics could be affected: in France the executors of Philip IV (d. 1314) were forced to ignore his extravagant testamentary provisions, because they threatened government finances; England's Richard II similarly set aside the will of his grandfather, Edward III (d. 1377). In Lancastrian England, the crown's financial independence was hampered after 1422 as the feoffees to perform Henry V's will and establish his chantry at Westminster collected the required funds from the alienated resources of the Duchy of Lancaster. Such lavish endowments adversely affected the greatest in the land; lesser alienations would proportionately diminish the expectations of lowlier individuals – hence the universal concern about executors who did not meet their obligations. This depletion of inheritances perhaps distorted the relationship between the living and the dead. The living might increasingly resent the impositions on them, especially as they increased over the generations, while still being concerned to impose demands on their own heirs.

The decoration of the chantry chapels, the proclamations of social status in memorial displays, and the colonisation of ecclesiastical space by the enclosures of chantries and the intrusion of table tombs, used the fact of death to overawe those left behind. In a real sense, the dead burdened the living for their own ends, seeking from the grave to retain control – over their heirs, and over the priests and recipients of charity whose prayers would, they hoped, ensure their own deliverance from Purgatory. Yet the precise motivation behind the panoply of prayers and foundations is still elusive: did they merely reflect social convention, possibly no more than the tides of fashion? Did the insatiable demand for prayers for souls attest a fear of death and its aftermath, an unseemly anxiety to hasten through Purgatory? Or, putting things more optimistically, was all this activity a proclamation of hope, of steadfast trust that with the contract fulfilled on all sides, and in the true spirit of reciprocal *caritas*, Heaven would assuredly be attained?

The role of this ubiquitous and inevitable death in late medieval catholicism raises necessary questions about a religion which appears so death-centred. Answering them is not easy. Late medieval Christianity may be excessively morbid, with an unhealthy insistence on individual responsibility for securing salvation in which, literally, the devil took the hindmost. But the quantitative and qualitative inaccessibility of much medieval religious activity means that any assessment of the reaction is only impressionistic. Any reaction also slants evidence which is undeniably ambiguous. In the pilgrimage of life, death might actually be welcomed, as an opportunity rather than an obstacle. The available evidence for the relationship between the living and the dead almost precludes any appreciation other than in terms of mutual exploitation, with the dead (over-)burdening their successors. But was this actually resented? A wider relationship between the living and the dead might not require this economy of reciprocity, of prayers in return for charity. Hints of this appear in 'non-Christian' manifestations, in the awareness of ghosts, and the use of necromancy to maintain contact with the dead. 'Cultural relationships' were also maintained, in communal events integrating the dead with the living on All Souls' Day; while regional German practices associated with the idea of *Armenseel*, in which the dead in Purgatory returned to dance in churchyards (one proposed origin for the *danse macabre*), show a similar awareness of continuity after death. But such traditions, 'folkloric' rather than 'spiritual', are precisely the sort to fall through the gaps in the evidence.

Whatever is made of death, it was critical to the Christian journey, the unavoidable crux of the pilgrimage. Whilst living and breathing, an individual catholic could assume some responsibility to meet the Christian obligations, and so satisfy the demands of *caritas* among his or her fellow humans, as well as honouring God in religious practices at church, in private devotions, and in personal spirituality. At death, that control lapsed: the soul became a dependant, on God, and on those left behind. *Caritas* required the Church Militant to aid the deceased through the pains of Purgatory and into the eternal joys of Heaven. Only then would the pilgrimage be over.

7

PRIESTS, PEOPLE
AND POWER

·

Medieval catholicism sought to establish an individual and collective unity with God, through personal and joint fulfilment of Christianity's moral and disciplinary dictates. While the resulting programme required personal action, lay people did not fully control their destinies. Christianity's stress on the sacramental, especially the role of penance and communion (with extreme unction considered here as a form of penance), equally emphasised those who provided access to the sacraments, the priests. Sacerdotal participation was not needed for all sacraments. Lay people could baptise, but were meant to do so only *in extremis*; the hierarchy struggled to ensure that marriages were solemnised in church rather than entered into in the uncontrolled manner accepted by the canon law. However, the sacraments validated only through priestly mediation effectively defined the religious obligations of the institutionalised late medieval church: essentially penance and the Eucharist. Their mediation *through* the priest is important, for it was not actually he who implemented them, but Christ. The mental leaps required to appreciate the distinction, and the consequent problems for definitions and appreciations of priestly power and status, had significant repercussions on late medieval catholicism.

Such issues raise many questions, for the relations between priests and people – essentially power relations – were complex, and always unstable. Two essential issues must be tackled. What was the perceived status of the priest, as it changed over the centuries? Just what did the laity want from him? This second point immediately directs attention to how the laity expressed their opinions, in writing and through their influence on clerical careers. It is also important to address the clergy's role in controlling developments in lay religion. As devotional practices were always 'demand-led' when they were securely planted, how the church authorities reacted to the more extreme or dubious displays needs some examination.

The priests and their roles

Although the question has not been investigated in great detail, perceptions of priesthood in catholic Europe in 1215 were probably very different from those held in 1515. It could be argued, indeed, that in 1215 priesthood as a reality was a relatively recent creation, largely due to the impact of the 'Gregorian reform' of the late eleventh century. This had sought to make priesthood, even clerkhood, a human condition quite distinct from laity. The emphases since *c.* 1050 had been on liberating the priest from worldly concerns, freeing him to serve God and his flock. This meant divorce from family, from the demands of kinship, from obligations to anyone outside the ecclesiastical structure. The demand that clerics be freeborn rather than serfs; be economically independent (reflected in their title for ordination); be celibate and chaste; with their benefices likewise liberated by replacing proprietary rights over churches by a system of mere patronage; all combined in the twelfth century to revolutionise priesthood.

The entrenchment of the parochial system also affected the status of the incumbent priest. The insistence in 1215 that everyone should confess at least annually to his or her 'own priest' (*proprius sacerdos*) and receive communion at Easter formalised ties both jurisdictional and geographical. For Robert of Flamborough, writing only a few years later, confession to a priest other than one's own was a form of spiritual adultery; although the stance was soon outdated by the rise of the friars as confessors. The ties between a parochial incumbent or his authorised deputy and his flock were very real: 'The priest might be considered as the spiritual lord of that part of the diocese committed to his governance. He owns "his parishioners" in the same sense that the feudal lord owns "his men".'[1] That 'feudalised' relationship was clearly expressed in the payment of the mortuary fee: the formulae in some English manor custumals make it

[1] J. Avril, 'A propos du "proprius sacerdos": quelques réflexions sur les pouvoirs du prêtre de paroisse', in *Proceedings of the fifth international congress of medieval canon law: Salamanca, 21–25 September, 1976*, ed. S. Kuttner and K. Pennington, Monumenta iuris canonici, series C: subsidia, 6 (Vatican City, 1980), p. 471.

quite evident that the mortuary was a recognition of spiritual lordship paralleling the heriot due to the lord on the death of a tenant. Another parallel is suggested by the Poitevin custom whereby the priest collected an *ultimum vale* when a parishioner moved away: it compensated for the lost mortuary, but it recalls the fee paid by a serf to a lord for permission to quit the manor. To be confessed or take communion outside one's own parish without permission from the parish priest was also an offence.

Whatever the reforming popes and their supporters desired in the eleventh and twelfth centuries, priests were human, and worldly pressures remained: patronal influence, concubinage and fornication, over-involvement in worldly affairs through attempts to maintain a decent standard of living which made priests seem parasitic by demanding tithes and fees for services rendered, and family pressures which kept benefices under dynastic control or secured safe clerical careers for relatives. Hereditary parochial benefices had not been completely eliminated by 1215, and other local practices which contemporary reformers wished to eliminate as vices proved equally resilient. John of Abbeville's legatine tour of Iberia in the 1220s discovered over 1,700 bastard clerics in the archdiocese of Braga: they were dispensed en masse, lest the whole pastoral edifice collapse. In some regions the battle to transform the priestly caste proved unwinnable. In Iceland, clerics were almost immune to outside influences; in fifteenth-century Ireland the popes had in reality abandoned the struggle in the Gaelic areas – benefices, even bishoprics, were all but hereditary; and concubinage was the norm even if regularly condemned. Moreover, loopholes allowed old influences to return: patronage did not eliminate family benefices, it merely changed the system of succession. In ministerial terms, the ideal of priesthood developed by 1215 also demanded almost superhuman clerics. If the priest represented Christ, and exercised some of His powers on earth, did that not make him virtually Christ on earth? Was ordination itself a sort of transubstantiation, a form of divinisation of the priest? Orthodoxy insisted that it did not, although writers in the hierocratic tradition immediately compromised that qualification by their insistence on the pre-eminent status of the clerical caste, placing the least priest above kings, even if below angels. The awesome nature of priesthood which followed from this was well recognised among the Brethren of the Common Life in the Netherlands. Precisely because of the virtual impossibility for a mere human to live up to the demands which this view of priesthood dictated, many of the Brethren refused to put themselves forward for priestly ordination, resting content with the diaconate or lesser orders. Neverthe-less, the priest was merely human; Christ operating through him actually effected the sacraments. The validity of the sacraments owed nothing to the quality of their visible operator – it derived *ex opere operato* not *ex opere operantis*.[2] The insistence on humanity and the call for perfection were often irreconcilable. One hostage to fortune left by the reformers legitimised the refusal of money to or sacraments from a priest judged unfit for his duties. Such injunctions became part of canon law, with the potential of a two-edged sword. While the regulations offered a weapon for prelates to discipline the diocesan clergy, as when a bishop of Geneva in the early fifteenth century instructed the people of Musinens to refuse payments to the appropriator of their parish until he provided a priest, there were other implications. If the laity were bound to withdraw from an impure priest – and not to pay money for his support – did that not legitimise lay control and judgement over the qualities of a true priest? Alternatively, it could suggest that the sacraments of an impure priest, one lacking the Christ-like perfection commensurate with his status, were *ipso facto* invalid? The laity thus had two weapons against the clergy – control of the purse, and judgement of actions – and could claim power for themselves. Clerics fought hard against these pincers: the latter had been condemned by St Augustine as the heresy of the Donatists, and needed little reinforcement but frequent reiteration; against the former the canon law requirement that tithes and fees should be paid sometimes had to be restated, as against Lollards in fifteenth-century England. Yet the demand for control through the power of the purse might come from quite orthodox quarters. The author of *Dives and pauper* cited canon law, including Gregory VII, on precisely this point; while around 1405 the inhabitants of Saltash threatened to withhold tithes from the appropriators of their church if they did not remove a particularly unsatisfactory and disreputable vicar.

The priest's vital role in controlling remission of sins and access to the Body and Blood of Christ – and as lieutenant of St Peter by conferring extreme unction – gave him a focal role in the church's disciplinary structure. The extensive priestly interference and control over lay actions can be interpreted as a search for social control; perhaps primarily in the use of the confessional. The stress on the social aspects of Christianity could take extraordinary turns: in 1387 Simon de Cramaud, bishop of Poitiers, ordered that burial be denied to excommunicates, arsonists, those who had died drunk or were guilty of violating churches or striking clerics. The concern to maintain and defend priestly status evident here encouraged priests to stress the church's disciplinary

---

[2] Above, p. 33.

aspect. However, tensions also arose from the ambiguities of the church's own stances. This is most obvious in changing attitudes to marriage, and the increasing insistence by 1500 on a clerical solemnisation. The canonical theory of marriage had evolved in the twelfth century on the basis that the consent of the parties created the sacramental bond and validated the union. Clergy present served only as witnesses, a weakness which the authorities could not circumvent. Nevertheless, they pressed for solemnisation, to ensure public awareness of the union, and to impart a spiritual rather than carnal element to the proceedings.

The priests stressed the sacramental quality of certain ceremonies. But priestly duties were more than ceremonial: priests were the guardians of doctrine, and transmitters of truth. Their educational function, as pastors to preserve and strengthen the faith of their flocks, was also important - particularly in the thirteenth century with missionary activity within Europe to standardise the faith, and the evolution of catechitical material for both priests and laity. Teaching also necessarily extends into preaching. But the preaching function was not necessarily confined to priests: the laity might be allowed to bear some sort of witness; to preach, which might be synonymous with instruct, by example. Yet priests did have a duty to preach (or instruct) on doctrinal matters. They alone had the authority to discuss theology in its truest sense, to expound the deeper recesses of the faith. The distinction between discussion of doctrine as a priestly task and mere witness as something open to the laity had produced the clash between Pope Alexander III and the Waldensians in 1179; the tension was unresolved. Lay preaching remained a questionable activity in later centuries, although it is not clear how much there was, or how lay its practitioners actually were. Opposition to it appears in several of the heresy trials of these centuries, especially those involving beghards and hermits, many of whom were laymen. It was presumably they who most engaged in 'lay preaching', alongside the pardoners stirring devotion or fear to sell their indulgences. Lay preaching was not confined to such lowly levels: King Robert of Naples (d. 1343) was notorious for his sermons. Possibly because of the problems lay preaching aroused, in England perhaps mainly after the rise of Wyclifism, disciplinary procedures were invoked to ensure that doctrinal preaching was strictly reserved to the clergy. Even those advocates of preaching and the spread of the Biblical message who condemned Archbishop Thomas Arundel of Canterbury for his constitutions of 1409 which severely limited the scope and personnel of preaching nevertheless defined preaching as a strictly priestly activity. The author of a set of sermons which has actually been labelled 'Lollard' asserts precisely that the first condition to be met by a legitimate preacher is that he be 'duly ordained or ordered by a prelate'.[3]

Even if lay people did not preach, they might still encourage preaching. Towards the end of the period, town councils were organising local sermons, and wills sometimes established preacherships or provided funds for students to become preachers. Some were long term and static, like those set up in German towns in the fifteenth century, which remained under the patronage of the endowing family or the urban government. Others, like the grant for one year provided in the will of the London merchant Philip Malpas (d. 1469), were for travelling preachers. Possibly the paymasters sought some say over the content of the sermons; they did try to ensure the quality of the preachers. The anxiety to secure top quality preachers is shown in the competition to attract the services of Geiser von Kaysersberg in 1478. He had already negotiated employment at Würzburg, but the *Ammeister* of Strasbourg made a more persuasive offer, personally funding the endowment for the new preachership.

The priests' disciplinary, doctrinal control, extensive oversight of lay morality and judgement of worthiness to receive the sacraments, gave them considerable latent power. But power is only real if used – and if used may cause resentment. Such resentment was expressed in the late middle ages. Moreover, even if powerful the clergy were also dependants: they might have some control, but their ability to use it was tightly constrained by the very nature of medieval catholicism. The status accorded to priesthood, lay acceptance of priestly claims to authority, the demands made of priests by their supposed subjects, were all variables within a system of belief and observance which was always evolving. This fluidity meant that the priest's position was always threatened with instability: by its nature sacerdotal power required recognition and willing acceptance by the laity. The impotence of a parish priest in the face of a determinedly recalcitrant excommunicate showed the true weakness of the construct: people had to believe in and obey the authority claimed by priests, otherwise it was irrelevant. Such mutuality demanded a willingness of the priests – indeed, the whole ecclesiastical institution – to be responsive to popular demand; to alter the way powers were exercised to accommodate changing tastes and desires. As devotions altered, and lay religion was affected by changing spiritual currents, so the status and power of the priesthood would itself be affected.

---

[3] G. Cigman, ed., *Lollard sermons*, Early English text society, original series, 294 (1989), p. 4.

Here several strands converge. After 1215 two opposing currents both reinforced and undermined priestly status. The growing stress on communion and the rise of a eucharistic cult, together with the demand for masses for the repose of souls which each demanded a consecration, produced increasing awareness and acceptance of a priest's power to effect the transubstantiation. More frequent communion also entailed more frequent confession, with greater emphasis on a priest's power to remit sins; as did the full procedure to secure indulgences. That trend would clearly strengthen the priesthood. Against this must be set the search for a more intimate and personal contact with God, exemplified in mysticism. Such direct access to the divinity worked against the priests: it challenged the need for their mediation, sometimes even denying priestly sacramental authority.

Challenges to priestly mediation might well expose the extremely fragile bases of some clerical claims, as to the monopoly of sacramental authority in the mass. Against the insistence on consecration solely by a priest, the doctrine that the sacraments were effective *ex opere operato* paradoxically posed a radical threat to that monopoly. The insistence that the words of consecration of themselves caused the transubstantiation (possibly only if said in Latin, thereby permitting their translation in explications of the mass) meant that, technically, any repetition of them by anyone would produce the same result. This was acknowledged in a fifteenth-century French *exemplum*, according to which some shepherds by reciting the words over a piece of bread had caused it to convert into a lump of flesh. Their temerity incurred divine wrath:

immediately, by the will of God, fire descended upon them from heaven, and they were all burnt and consumed. And therefore the wise Fathers ordained that these words should be said in a low voice; and also that no-one should say them who is not a priest.[4]

Although worded as protecting the laity from their own audacity, there is clearly a recognition here of the threat to priestly power, and a concern to protect it.

Lay expectations

Most relationships between laity and clergy were bilateral. The laity demanded of their priests just as the priests demanded of their subjects. Moreover, as the laity paid the clergy for their services, they felt able to

[4] V. Reinburg, 'Liturgy and the laity in late medieval and Reformation France', *The sixteenth-century journal*, 23 (1992–3), p. 533 n16.

dictate to some extent; although such dictation often caused conflict and discontent.

Summarising lay expectations of the priesthood is not too difficult. On the one hand, they were defined by actions: the priests provided the power and protection of the sacraments and sacramentals. This might be purely spiritual, by granting absolution, the cleansing of extreme unction, and the fact of transubstantiation. It might be more utilitarian – the benefits of the blessing of crops; prayers and masses for good weather or a safe journey, or the many other purposes covered by votive masses; and protection for humans and animals by providing blessed candles, bread, and water.[5] Beyond that, the laity simply wanted a clerical presence: clergy to provide spiritual services in celebration, instruction, and a good example. Here they clearly matched the ideals demanded by the church hierarchs, as constantly reiterated in synodal decrees. The exemplary and instructional duties of the priest are frequently recited in other works as well. That they were taken seriously appears from the attack made *c.* 1405 by the parishioners of Saltash on their vicar, condemning his failure to instruct, his failure to provide spiritual relief, and his disruption of the community. These complaints are in marked contrast to the approval of their rector voiced by the parishioners of Saint-Pierre-des-Champs in the diocese of Narbonne in 1404, that he 'was and is an honest and knowledgeable man, and has and does serve the church well, instructs the people, ministers the ecclesiastical sacraments, and maintains due hospitality'.[6] The laity wanted clergy who would be well-behaved, as forces for peace within the community, capable of living up to the exalted status of their order. But, primarily, they wanted priests who would do what they wanted, quickly and efficiently.

The reality of these lay aspirations regarding their priests becomes clear where the laity could make their views explicit. Lay disappointments are shown in complaints and attempts to invoke the church's disciplinary machinery against clerics who failed to match expectations. Church court records, perhaps most comprehensively the surviving evidence of parochial visitations, show the laity's concern about clerical actions. Often this was straightforward misbehaviour; at times almost exclusively sexual misbehaviour, although the worries about that fluctuated, and may actually reflect the concerns of the hierarchs more than the parishioners. Although some of the material is highly salacious, there is no reason to suppose that the laity, the rural laity especially, considered unchaste priests

---

[5] Above, pp. 139–40, 182–4.
[6] V. Chomel, 'Droit de patronage et pratique religieuse dans l'archevêché de Narbonne au début du XVᶜ siècle', *Bibliothèque de l'école des chartes*, 115 (1957), p. 93 n6.

particularly repellent: if anything their attitude was pragmatic – rather the priest had his own wife than a neighbour's. Urban reactions may have been more hostile: contacts between clerics and women roused disquiet in places like Augsburg, although this was perhaps more a male fear of the threat to familial control than hostility to priests as priests. Attitudes might, however, change under the influence of charismatic preachers. Fifteenth-century France may have witnessed a virtual campaign by preachers against concubinary priests, with the laity being encouraged not to attend their masses and services. According to unsubstantiated reports of such boycotts in Burgundy, Brittany, and Normandy, the procedures had the desired effect. If these campaigns did occur, it must have been with the encouragement and at the promotion of the ecclesiastical authorities, possibly irrespective of actual local opinion on the issue.

More important than the sexual material are complaints against clerics who did not maintain services, left infants unbaptised and the dying unshriven, or who totally neglected to provide masses. Such are the most commonly encountered complaints about spiritual provision: failure to preach was a less frequent worry (it need not imply that preaching was regular, just that it was not missed), while reports of a lack of hospitality or failure to instruct are relatively rare. The key concern was that a priest should be available when needed, to supply the required ministrations. Here problems of late-medieval ecclesiastical 'abuses', like pluralism and non-residence, would affect the picture; but it is likely that complaints were made only if the parish totally lacked a priest: most parochial ministrations rested on the shoulders of curates, who might be in post for a long time and so ensure continuity in the services. This may mean that the clergy were providing the religion that the laity wanted – although possibly only a very simplistic religion, in which instruction and example made few demands.

The influence of lay aspirations also became apparent in the thirteenth century with the rise of the friars, possibly in reaction against the strictures or deficiencies of parochial priestly rule. The mendicants' definition of their apostolate matched contemporary spiritual aspirations, with the emphasis on preaching and the call to repentance. As papal privileges gave them virtually all the spiritual powers of the parish clergy, so the friars' popularity increased. Whether justified or not they gained a reputation for a willingness to absolve easily, to grant light penances more readily than the seculars. Easy and quick absolution, from a friar who was unlikely to spread the details of the confession around the neighbourhood, could tap a ready market; and the signs, albeit offered by often hostile sources, are that it did. As the friars' appeal grew, as they attracted penitents and disrupted the disciplinary control of the parochial clergy, so hostility rose between the two branches of the clergy which persisted through to the Reformation. This hostility must not be exaggerated – there is ample evidence that seculars and mendicants could and did work together – but the opposition to mendicant interference in the spiritual care of parishioners by their rectors and vicars cannot be ignored. While the conflict undeniably had economic motives, as the friars diverted money from parochial receipts (a problem which the papal bull *Super cathedram* of 1300 tried to resolve), the disciplinary element was important, and remained so. To some extent the disputes demonstrate that the laity did not trust their priests – either to keep the secrets of the confessional, or to impose tolerable penances, or (resulting from that control over absolution) to allow them access to communion.

The second main strand of mendicant activity, preaching, may also have affected relationships between clergy and laity. The mendicants' prime function from about 1250 was to take over much of the church's preaching mission; this perhaps made them more receptive to and aware of lay aspirations. In particular, they may have been more in tune with lay theological developments. Looking at their position cynically, given that they depended on lay alms for survival, they may have tuned their sermons to stimulate offerings. Sometimes this did happen, as in London in the 1460s when the Carmelites proclaimed their purer apostolic poverty against the worldliness of the seculars to divert offerings to themselves. Assertions that tithes were free alms and distributable at will, as made by the Franciscan William Russell in London in 1425, clearly correspond to contemporary 'Lollard' statements about the disposal of tithes. Perhaps some friars hoped that by contrasting their own holier lives with the decadence of the seculars, some of these disposable tithes would go to them. It may be no coincidence that another Franciscan, Thomas Richmond, was hauled before the York Convocation in 1426 for publicly asserting in a chapel controlled by the city's government that a sinful priest was not a true priest. Friars did claim to be more obviously 'holy' than the seculars – at least in the early thirteenth century, and later in some places, mainly under the purifying influences of the Observant movements. They were not as overtly enmeshed as the seculars or some monks and canons in the local church's proprietorial and disciplinary structures. Nor were they totally detached: they were eventually embroiled in the benefice system, and the anti-mendicant tracts stress the sham of their claims to poverty.

The laity in control?

The desire to have ready access to a priest found clear expression in the growth of localised communities which sought ecclesiastical autonomy.

The evolution of parishes itself encouraged communal feelings and a sense of cohesion, although this varied with the size and nature of the parish structure. Cohesion was especially fostered when the laity took responsibility for the fabric and church property, as evidenced in the rise of the churchwardens in England, and their equivalents elsewhere (*fabriques* in France, *opere* in Italy, *vitrici* in Poland, and so on). That could work against the clergy, making them almost interlopers in a community who had to enforce their own ideas of how local religion should be organised against the traditions evolved by the parishioners. The contracts made between parishioners and clergy throughout fifteenth-century France, and in England arrangements like that of 1432 whereby the rector of Ludlow temporarily became little more than a pensionary of his parishioners, show the situations which could develop.

The rise of sub-parochial communities complicated the issues. Domestic chapels privatised access to the sacraments; but more important were the communal fragments represented in chapelries. They too sought ecclesiastical autonomy and a resident priest, challenging the idea of parish as unity and community. Everywhere chapelries struggled to break away from their mother-churches. Italian rural *pieve* split into smaller units; in France daughter-churches (*filiales*) sought independence; English chapels petitioned the pope to be granted full parochial status, or took their rectors to court for failing to provide adequate local services. The new churches were often funded by the local populace, as happened in many of the German *Gemeinde*. In 1440–1, the bishop of Geneva authorised the erection of a new church at Longirod, its endowment provided by the parishioners acting as a confraternity of the Holy Spirit. Their contract with the future priest allowed them to seek a replacement if he proved negligent, retaining the patronage for themselves. The claims to autonomy might be thwarted, meeting resistance from incumbents who saw their income threatened, not to mention the parishioners of the mother churches who would become burdened with a greater share of the maintenance costs if the attempt to break away succeeded. The search for autonomy could be a lengthy process. The German village of Balgach first secured a weekly mass in its newly built chapel in 1424; only in 1521 did it gain formal parochial separation from Marbach.

These processes of fragmentation had to be legitimised by the local authorities, sometimes with the parish priest giving permits for parishioners to attend other churches; but it does appear that the old rigidities were being extensively undermined by 1400 at the latest, and people were acquiring considerable freedom to choose their place of worship. Clashes on this tended to be as much between rival lay communities as between clergy and laity – for any reduction in the numbers contributing to the upkeep of the mother church necessarily increased the burden on those who could not avoid the responsibility.

Lay people also sought satisfaction of their aspirations by other means. Their involvement in the appointment of clerics, especially where fraternities appointed to chantries, gave them an important outlet to express and implement their views. The laity had a significant influence on parochial benefices, even if not in the proprietorial sense which affected or afflicted such churches until the thirteenth century. In the twelfth century, the replacement of lay ownership of churches by rights of mere patronage (presenting the prospective incumbent to the authorities for appointment rather than simply granting the church) reduced the lay impact on parochial incumbents' careers. Even so, and despite regional variations, many benefices were in the gift of lay families, the patrons responsible for presenting suitably-qualified candidates. Yet, given the significance of such rights in the whole gamut of the patrons' concerns, primarily to demonstrate local power and provide jobs for their dependants, the pastoral or ministerial abilities of their protégés must often have been of secondary importance. The same would apply to benefices in monastic patronage, although many other influences could affect the situation. That a religious house held the patronage did not mean that it actually used it: alienations were common in late medieval England, and presumably elsewhere. External influences might covertly affect things, while benefice farmers (who leased the collection of revenues and responsibility for the financial obligations in exchange for a fixed regular payment to the incumbent or appropriator of the parish) could sometimes acquire the nomination, putting in priests who were cheap but ineffective. The parish priest was more directly accountable to the parishioners in those regions of Europe where the community had retained rights of election. This applied in parts of Italy, although it was being undermined in the fifteenth century as bishops sought greater authority over the *pieve* and magnate families asserted claims to patronage which displaced community nominations. Nevertheless, in 1390 the parishioners of S. Piero Buonconsiglio in Florence elected their own priest, and when a cardinal tried to over-ride their claims and act as patron, took their case to the Florentine government and won. Beyond Italy, the right to elect the priest lingered in marginal or remote areas like the Austrian Alps or the Pyrennean valleys.

Parishioners might complain about patronal exploitation; they also acted positively to extend their use of patronage. The establishment of chantries to offer masses for the souls of their founders was one route. In some ways the chantries represent a revival of the old proprietorial concerns, a proprietorship which could be reflected in the disciplinary control claimed by the founders, even from the grave. Many chantry foundation documents incorporate stipulations regarding the quality and behaviour of the clergy. Those in England especially rail against gaming and tavern-haunting, and sometimes impose the ultimate sanction of deprivation for failure to maintain the stated levels of conduct. Even if the chantry was only a short-term benefaction, the testator's demands (such creations usually being indicated only through wills) may reveal something of the definition of an acceptable priest – although possibly only in the vague and unsatisfactory demand that the hireling simply be a 'good' priest.

The foundation of rural guilds and chantries was also important in expanding pastoral provision. One outcome might be an increased sense of local cohesion, and of proprietorship over the local church. That seems to be reflected in the English manorial practice of dividing fines between the lord and the church: the church here represented the community and its self-identity.

The creation of alternative employment structures obviously affected clerical control over the laity. This may have been especially important in towns, where the nature of parochial life is sometimes obscure and the scale of commitment to parochial structures uncertain. In Bristol it has been argued that the weakness of familial links actually increased lay concern to make a presence felt within the urban church by extravagant donations at death; whereas in southern French towns the parish ties seem to have been weaker. In Italy urban fraternities may have replaced the parish as the main religious body; the weakness of parish attraction in Catalonia has also been noted – although for Italy and southern Europe 'very little is known about the late-medieval parish to ascertain whether confraternities really were syphoning off the adherence of the local inhabitants'.[7]

These alternative ecclesiastical structures gave the laity some control over the clergy. Some English urban councils created what amounted to a visitatorial jurisdiction over the chantries they supervised; in individual parishes the same may have applied to chantries overseen by the churchwardens. With clerics being appointed effectively 'during pleasure', the need for them to be accommodating also increased. The pressures on the priests – and lay attitudes towards 'outside interference', even from the church authorities, were demonstrated at Lichfield in 1470. The dean and chapter tried to inhibit masses in the town church until

[7] J. Henderson, 'Confraternities and the church in late medieval Florence', *Studies in church history*, 23 (1986), p. 69.

those in the cathedral were completed. The priest who received the inhibition passed it to one of the guild which paid the chaplains. He violently ejected the chapter's messenger, threatened to make him eat the inhibition, and asserted that he would have 'his' mass, regardless of instructions from the cathedral.

Similar pressures appear on the continent, often reflecting developments in lay spirituality and demands that clerics provide an ever-increasing round of sacramentals. The clergy resented demands for more work without increased payment. In 1509 the bishop of Strasbourg ordered a halt to the spiralling demand for clerical action. It was not that simple. When church authorities in Germany sought to restrict the use of the consecrated host in blessing crops, and other sacramental practices, the lay response was to withhold tithes from priests who obeyed the rulings, threatening some with violence unless they maintained the old ways.

This clearly shows a shift in the balance of forces; but usually that shift is obscured by lack of evidence. That much of late medieval devotional activity occurred outside the church's administrative confines and evaded the tentacles of the canon law means that it leaves few explicit records. The comment that in Germany 'the communal church finds its niche in gaps in ecclesiastical law, where believers are no longer the subjects . . . but the partners of the priest'[8] might be applied elsewhere in Europe – with the idea of partnership often being replaced by lay dominance. The relationship was always a delicate balance: the priest retained his Christ-derived and Christ-like authority, to which the laity often willingly deferred. The sinful laity's need for sacerdotal ministry was more urgent than the priests' need for lay support and maintenance. The power of the keys was the priests' main source of power, and the spiritual dependence born of the general perception and acceptance of the significance of actions which only priests could perform.

The acceptance of sacerdotal authority meant that priests could exploit their powers for their own ends: their concern for their souls made the laity dependent on the clergy at critical moments. The rejection of candidates for communion who had not paid their tithes was often criticised – although it is unclear how much it happened. Priests also exploited their power of excommunication to enforce subjection.

Such abuse of the power of the keys doubtless generated antagonism. As priests were seen to be using the church in their own interests, so they

---

[8] P. Blickle, 'Communal Reformation and peasant piety: the peasant Reformation and its late medieval origins', *Central European history*, 20 (1987), p. 225.

were criticised. If priests used their disciplinary powers, especially excommunication, to enforce their own rights and status, so their powers would be resented. Here, however, some difficulty occurs. Sometimes excommunication was imposed by the clergy but reflected more popular feelings; the disciplinary procedures of the church courts functioned to impose not merely priestly standards of behaviour and morality but those of 'the community'. Indeed, more individual standards might be imposed, if personal conflicts led to excommunication. Yet it would be the priest who fulminated the sentence, who would be responsible for its enforcement, and who might therefore become a focus for the hostility of the excommunicate.

The problem of 'anticlericalism'

The existence of conflicts between priests and their flocks leads on to what is possibly the most difficult issue in assessing relations between clergy and laity at this time: the extent, even existence, of anticlericalism. The word is imprecise, allowing definitions ranging from simple antipathy to individual clerics, through generalised hostility to the clerical class, to active opposition to sacerdotalism. The first can be seen in the individual complaints at parochial visitations, or actions in the church courts. The second appears in some of the more popular movements of the period, for example some of the Flagellants of 1349, or among Lollards in England after 1380. Genuine anti-sacerdotalism comes through, by definition, only in the heresies; perhaps most explicitly with Taborite extremists in fifteenth-century Bohemia. However, vocal anti-sacerdotalism was rare: possibly the only group to advocate it in a positive and coherent manner were the Cathars of southern France and Italy. They, however, were trying to establish a rival hierarchy, which effectively had its own form of priesthood in the *perfecti*, and so cannot really be counted.

The crux of the problem lies in the interpretation of the complaints made against the clergy which appear regularly over the period, and actions taken against them. One strand must immediately be discounted: the essentially political struggle to control the church waged by secular governments against papal claims. The progressive 'nationalisation' of Europe's churches after 1215 is itself a saga, but governmental restrictions of the church's administrative, jurisdictional, and fiscal independence and immunity are largely alien to the issues of religion or spirituality being considered here. Dramatic as they might be – and the catalogue of conflicts which erupted in German cities over fiscal immunities is certainly that – they had little real bearing on questions of religion and devotion. Nor are the changes in political thought of much immediate concern.[9] The focus must be on the rather different relationship between the clerics and their flocks – although among the smaller political entities, especially in Germany and Italy, the distinction is sometimes rather hard to make.

There were strong objections to some clerical activities: their sinfulness, their embroilment in secular enterprises, their pride, absenteeism, sexual faults, and claims to privileged status when dragged before secular justice. Every century, and every region, could offer evidence of such complaints and resultant conflicts. Almost every major writer of the period, especially those using the vernacular and presumably addressing a primarily lay audience, at some point complained about the state of the church and its ministers. More significantly, ecclesiastical writers joined in the chorus: Robert Grosseteste, John Colet, John Wyclife, Jean Gerson, Nicholas de Clamanges, Nicholas of Cusa . . . the list could be endless. Yet what does this actually reflect? At one level it becomes little more than the search for a scapegoat; with the failings of the clergy being used to account for outbreaks of divine retribution. At another level, such complaint may be considered as acting as a safety valve to ensure equilibrium in a society where interaction between clergy and laity, between the ecclesiastical and the secular, was unavoidable. This may particularly apply to the secular literary outpourings. Comments on specifically Italian literary anti-clericalism may here have wider application, so that it is seen

not . . . as the expression of a real need for change, nor as a sign of crisis, but rather as an almost instinctive reaction to intimate familiarity with the clergy . . . a healthy blowing off of steam which served to reinforce the system which it claimed to challenge. In order to survive, the . . . system of total osmosis between Church and civil society needed a certain dose of anticlericalism, a control mechanism that drew attention to excesses and ensured that collective ethical sensibilities were not seriously violated.[10]

In a slightly different formulation, the existence of defective clerics and the ability to criticise them also helped to lessen the pressures on the laity themselves, who may have felt a real spiritual and moral inferiority to those clergy who did live up to the clerical ideal. For the pious laity (here, perhaps, primarily men),

[9] For the later stages of the battle, see J. A. F. Thomson, *Popes and princes, 1417–1519* (London, 1980). Developments in England are analysed in P. Heath, *Church and realm, 1272–1461* (London, 1989). For political thought, see A. Black, *Political thought, 1250–1450* (Cambridge, 1992).

[10] S. Seidel Menchi, 'Characteristics of Italian anticlericalism', in *Anticlericalism in late medieval and early modern Europe*, ed. P. A. Dykema and H. A. Oberman, Studies in Medieval and Reformation Thought, 51 (Leiden, New York, and Cologne, 1993), p. 274.

the holiest nuns and the most austere priests threatened their own ideals more deeply than did dissolute nuns and whoring priests, for the success of a celibate way of life relativized and therefore devalued . . . their own ideal of the harmonious and hierarchical household . . . [T]he very existence of wayward clergy eased the moral pressure placed on their own ideal way of life by the existence of another, stricter, harder way to salvation. This sensibility – relief at the clergy's imperfections – lies behind much of the anticlerical humour of the pre-reformation age. A wayward clergyman might arouse anger, but not spiritual intimidation.[11]

It it did serve these functions, then criticism of the clergy could also become a commonplace: the clergy – and the church as a whole – were always in need of reform, because they could always be said to be in decay. The clergy were human, and subject to human failings. Just as the visitation records of monastic houses can make depressing reading, but must be recognised as highlighting the failings of individuals rather than a system inherently flawed, so allegations about individual clerics must be put in the correct context. Good clerics rarely caused comment, unless they could be made into saints; but there were, admittedly, few such. The records, being usually records of failings, highlight the wrongs and ignore the rights. But if put in perspective it is quite probable that most people were receiving the spiritual care and ministration which they felt appropriate or not bad enough to justify complaint. There is rarely any overt denial of the general validity of priestly ministerial or sacramental functions, although there were objections to priests who claimed their tithes in the wrong manner, neglected their instructional responsibilities, or caused discord. The amalgamation of particular instances could create a stereotypical 'bad priest'. Stereotypes were constructed – and perhaps seen as such. They are only valid as generalisations, which must be tested against individual experience, even if they sometimes mislead. Stereotypes also exist as warnings; and it is in this warning mode that the stereotyping in such harangues as John Colet's sermon to the Canterbury Convocation of 1512 have to be taken. There, Colet advances a wholesale condemnation of ecclesiastical abuses, but it is a singularly unsubstantiated tirade. By scattering his shot widely, he would hit several marks; but how many of his audience (or, later, readers) actually felt that his comments applied specifically to them, and how many of the catalogue in each case, is unknown and unknowable – just as no quantitative assessment of the validity of his accusations is possible.

[11] T. A. Brady, jr., ' "You hate us priests": anticlericalism, communalism, and the control of women at Strasbourg in the age of the Reformation', in *Anticlericalism in late medieval and early modern Europe*, ed. P. A. Dykema and H. A. Oberman (Leiden, New York, and Cologne, 1993), p. 206.

For all their ubiquity, complaints about the clergy therefore defy full interpretation. Crucial to the problems they present is their ambiguity, which sometimes generates the false stance that all complaint must be considered anti-clerical. More often than not, this ignores the purpose of the charges. That was rarely negative, almost invariably positive: complaints about abuses sought a re-ordering of the structures, not their demolition. As it has recently been put, '"Anticlericalism" usually had little to do with religion itself: most "anticlericals" wanted churchmen to behave just as churchmen, rather than officious, interfering, lordly bureaucrats.'[12] There is indeed a paradox in some of this vocal resentment of clerical privileges, especially those with jurisdictional and fiscal implications. The impact of many depended on the scale of local land-holding by ecclesiastical bodies; yet the main agents for the increase of such holdings in mortmain were the laity themselves, with their constant giving to secure *post mortem* commemoration through the establishment of chantries and other memorials. Lay people were willing to grant lands and privileges to secure their own souls; but resented the exercise of those privileges when they touched their bodies.

Even in the individual accusations made before the church courts or during visitation proceedings, the hope was that a remedy would be provided, the recalcitrant cleric be reprimanded and forced to amend his ways. Amendment is the key; to ensure that the clergy lived up to the demands of their status, maintaining the behavioural standards and detachment from the world which were meant to be the hallmarks of the true priest. In that sense, most apparently 'anti'-clericalism is nothing of the sort: it is rather a contribution to the disciplinary process, seeking to chastise the errant to enforce true clericalism. Far from denying clerical status, if anything it elevates the clergy's role as mediators between God and Man, separate from the sinful world of the laity, meant to provide examples of godly and good living and give moral leadership to their flocks. This is, at root, a new form of hierocracy, even if sometimes couched in old language like William Melton's pronouncement of *c.* 1510 that the clergy were higher in status than angels. It is not a rejection of priesthood.

Who controls piety?

Despite its complexities, the relationship between clergy and people had to be worked out jointly. Over time the priests' functions had mutated to meet lay demands; the evolution of the parish system with its pastoral

---

12 E. Cameron, *The European Reformation* (Oxford, 1991), p. 61.

obligations, particularly after 1215, had been a major sign of such change. Later, the new emphasis on preaching had met local desires; while the massive explosion in the demand for masses had similarly forced a realignment of the role of the priest by increasing the number of auxiliary and stipendiary clergy, who were to a great extent divorced in career terms from the obligations and requirements of pastoral parochial ministry, so that many priests became mere officiants.

The basic driving force in the development of medieval catholicism and its practices was always one of supply and demand. Many of the changes in practice were the outcome of lay pressures; and like Corpus Christi, the rise of chantries, and the demand for indulgences, the result of lay invention. The clergy had an authoritative position which allowed them to direct some of the signs of change, and legitimise or condemn particular strands; but their control was limited. Even more limited was the control of the ecclesiastical hierarchy if lay practices caught on among the lower clergy, no matter how derided by the higher authorities. Thus, especially in regard to local saints, it was a combination of clerical and lay concern and enterprise which spawned and encouraged a multitude of small cults, even though prelates might try to curb such devotions. In Exeter diocese in the early fourteenth century, the local clergy were seemingly more sympathetic to local pilgrimages and potential saints than the bishop. Elsewhere, as in the advocacy of the shrine of Santa Maria a Cigoli in Tuscany in 1399, clerics orchestrated the emergence of a new devotion. Indeed, the complicity of the clergy in the development of new devotional practices is a striking feature of transformations in lay religion which challenged the sacrament- and church-centred religion of the authorities. This conflict of interest among the lower clergy, torn between people and prelates, might be ascribed to their hopes to profit from the celebrations. Although not without some truth, this is probably a misleading analysis of the position. These clerics' religion probably did not differ greatly from that of their parishioners, especially if, as with the groups of *prêtres-filleuls* in France, priests from the community stayed within it as clerics; and they would presumably only sponsor practices which accorded with their beliefs. A willingness to tolerate perhaps also affected higher levels: when the 'miraculous' properties of a healing spring were being investigated at Plaigne in southern France in 1443, some wished to allow its 'pilgrimage' to continue simply because the waters might really have curative powers, albeit not miraculous; arguing that to ban access would show lack of charity. (The inquisitor of Toulouse countered that such arguments ignored the sacrilege and superstition in the treatment of the spring, which lacked any saintly connection and so had to be quashed.) The difficulty for the authorities was that they could only dictate the compulsory aspects of Christianity; essentially those which were explicitly credal and sacramental. But beyond them was a whole apparatus of voluntary and supplementary religion which might be labelled 'traditional',[13] of fraternities, pilgrimages, indulgences, private devotions, and sacramentals (some of which merged into the sacraments, but were not compulsory). Clerical oversight of such practices was much less sure-footed. To invalidate might undermine their own status: here, while concerned, the authorities could rarely intervene, unless the expressions were explicitly anti-Christian; they could only harangue and verbally condemn.

Part of the justification for the hierarchy's concern to test and evaluate was clearly to prevent fraud – as with the validation of relics demanded by the Fourth Lateran Council. Part also reflected awareness of the church's duty to keep its tradition as pure as possible, and not allow uncontrolled and uninformed opinion to mislead. As the Toulouse inquisitor picturesquely put it in the Plaigne case, that the Incarnation had been revealed to shepherds did not mean that everything reported by those guarding animals was divinely inspired. Finally, and most important in the overall context of medieval Christianity, there was the responsibility for the preservation of souls. This meant that misapplications of Christianity had to be quashed. The facts of diabolical deceit and an imminent Antichrist required that revelations be checked for veracity, especially when novelty could deflect towards sin. Again in the Plaigne case, the bishop of St-Papoul insisted on the church's right of final judgement; his condemnation referred specifically to the activities of Antichrist and the presence of diabolical legions in the nearby Pyrenees.

The clergy might originate a cult; perhaps more frequently they had to respond to – and capitulate before – lay demands for revisions in the nature of their ministrations. The increasing numbers of votive masses; the numerous benedictions of crops and animals; the expanding range of 'sacramentals'; were mainly the result of lay acceptance or rejection. Yet, while conceding some lay demands, the clergy retained their authoritarian attitudes. They, or perhaps more precisely the higher authorities in the church, continually sought to control excesses and frauds, to limit and eliminate those elements of piety which appeared to contradict the requirements of 'official' religion, especially in pilgrimage and the 'ritualised folklore' of the sacramentals. The church, therefore, still asserted its right to validate, to have the final say. To cite the bishop of

---

[13] E. Duffy, *The stripping of the altars: traditional religion in England, 1400–1580* (New York and London, 1992), pp. 3–4.

St-Papoul in 1443 again, the people were to be instructed, not followed: the prelates were emphatically the leaders.

The Plaigne proceedings nevertheless hint that the spring could have been legitimated in slightly different circumstances. In comparison with the Spanish apparitions which generated shrines, all that was needed was a statue awaiting disinterment. A ruined chapel did exist nearby; but not quite close enough to allow an immediate connection between it and the spring. The chapel held a tomb which was conveniently identified as that of its dedicatee, St Julian; but no one knew which St Julian it was, and anyway there was nothing to connect any saint's legend with that place. As the healing powers were ascribed precisely to the spring rather than to a saint operating through it, visits to the chapel being secondary aspects of the process, the veneration could not be legitimised.

However, while the authorities might condemn, whether they could actually halt practices which they disapproved of is another matter. The autonomy of many late medieval religious practices precluded such control. Even with pilgrimage sites, disapproval might be ineffective. Despite Stephen de Bourbon's claim to have destroyed the cult of St Guinefort, it seems to have lingered in the penumbra of popular practices until the nineteenth century. Attempts by Bishop Grandisson of Exeter in 1351 to quash a new-born pilgrimage at Frithelstock which was sponsored by a local house of canons may have faced passive resistance, with the visits continuing – although unrecorded – for some time after. In 1386 Bishop Buckingham of Lincoln banned veneration of a recently erected cross at Rippingale, but was simply ignored: in 1392 its supporters reacted with a petition for papal ratification of the devotion, pushing its origins back over a century while doing so.

Objection to novelty was not confined to the clerical hierarchy. Lay people could also disapprove. Here the reactions to Margery Kempe in England are illuminating: perhaps most intriguingly, the main opposition to her apparently came from other lay people, while she gained the approval (or, at least, tolerance) of the bishops and other prelates with whom she made contact. Her career shows how the church lacked control. She was very much creating her own religion; although Langmuir's 'religiosity' might be the more appropriate term. Her reliance on the church is undeniable; but she was also modelling her life on ideas which did not need ecclesiastical mediation. Her illiteracy prevented a complete severance; but the increase in lay literacy in the later middle ages undeniably weakened the church's hold over lay ideas, and increased the spiritual autonomy of those with access to books. Admittedly clerics still originated most of the texts; but that monopoly was fragile. What was at issue was not the construction of an individual theology; but maybe an individual ecclesiology, and a redefined relationship with the church. This should not be seen as rejection and withdrawal from the church, but rather as a new stage in the evolution of lay relationships with it. Admittedly, again, the numbers affected would not be great; but as the chances increased of lay people having better access to and awareness of theological issues than their intended teachers, so the church's authority would be adversely affected. This might apply especially to towns; might also differ between regions.

The development of individual forms of piety has to be added to the expression of other claims to religious autonomy. Pilgrimages always threatened to get out of control; possibly by 1500 they had. Fraternities were primarily lay creations, often treated with circumspection if not hostility by prelates in the thirteenth century. Lay people could construct their own acceptable Christianity, hence the proliferation of indulgences and reliance on the sacramentals, while staying accountable to the priests for their souls but insisting on reciprocal priestly accountability for the quality of the ministrations. Overall, the balance of forces was uncertain; the relations between clergy and laity ambivalent and ambiguous. There were tensions, but they were rarely overt. To let them become so would probably have been more threatening: doubtless it was often safer to leave the issues undefined and unresolved, than provoke a battle for dominance by one side or the other. Intermittent skirmishes, over particular cults or practices, or individual priests and their behaviour, offered no significant threat to the equilibrium. Yet maintaining a balance so that the clergy were not marginalised in the lay religion, or the laity totally subjected to priestly authority, was a hard task. That makes the relative absence of complaint and anticlerical actions the more striking aspect of the situation. Most complaints were *ad hominem*, not about the clergy in general; most clerical reactions were to specific crises rather than attempts to secure total dominance over the laity. This suggests that the rules of the game were accepted, that the concern was actually to maintain the balance. That this was done, on the whole, was in fact a considerable achievement.

8

INCLUSION AND EXCLUSION

———— • ————

From its own perspective the Latin church was destined to be truly catholic, not merely Roman Catholic. Its spiritual message to the 'Gentiles' imposed a missionary obligation; its very definition as catholic required that it seek to encompass the whole world. Achieving that ambition was not easy. For the church, the struggle necessitated the disciplining of its own disobedient members, constant vigilance against challenges within its own geographical area, and active expansion beyond. Internally the church wrestled to reconcile the many tensions inherent in the demands and dictates of its social message and spiritual quest. That process occasionally obliged it to chasten by exclusion, using its powers of excommunication and interdict. Sometimes serious questions were raised about the status of people who were otherwise undeniably catholic – notably serfs and slaves (discussion of whom also raised questions of relationships with other religions), lepers, and most importantly women. For an expansionist catholicism the relations with non-catholic spiritualities were also problematic, both in areas under catholic rule, and the non-catholic realms beyond. The problem of heresy was important here; but attitudes to Judaism and Islam had to be addressed in some areas, and treatment of Greeks, Armenians, and other 'denominations'. Catholicism faced issues of self-defence against such threats, of self-identification as the true religion, and (with regard to the non-Latin churches) the question of whether to be 'catholic' actually required acceptance of the Latin definition of Christianity. Several of the threats could be amalgamated as attempts at diabolical subversion; but it was only towards the end of the period that fears of actual diabolism were widely voiced, focussing on concern about witchcraft.

What must be investigated is how the desire to include within a church outside which there was no salvation impacted on catholicism over the centuries, when affected by anxieties to exclude those who threatened subversion and to defeat opponents. Those anxieties, at times paranoia, are a vivid comment on the religion. However, the reactions also vary geographically and temporally. Moreover, the processes of inclusion and exclusion provide an area where any distinctions required between élite and popular perceptions of Christianity are immediately apparent; but whether that is the right framework for the analysis is debatable. Certainly, the battleground between Christianity and other religions was defined by the intellectuals, and it was they who incited others to action. Equally, the tasks of converting could only be assumed by those properly trained for the work, again primarily intellectuals. In the social considerations, also, the formulation was primarily by the 'élite', with the broader mass of Christians developing their own responses.

Much here depended on the immediacy of the contact with those affected by the proposals. Abstractions could be shared; the realities were immediate, personal, and localised. The real conflicts, of interest, of warfare, of ideologies, could only occur when rival parties physically confronted each other. What must be examined is the emergence of what for convenience – and at present no more than that – might be called the 'élite programme', and the degree of broader participation in its implementation, how its ideas were shared or rejected among the Christians who made up 'the church'. Reordering the issues listed earlier, three main strands can be distinguished. First, there is the explicitly expansionist tendency of Latin Christianity: the conscious effort at mission beyond the areas subject to catholic rule, and the military attempts to expand that area by crusade. In time, this crusading stance also becomes defensive, as the attempt to bring infidels into the church transforms into a desperate anxiety to keep them out of Europe. The second main strand is more inward-looking, the attitudes towards religious minorities and what might be called 'the enemy within'. The scale of this concern varied greatly; but it requires some assessment of the response to alternative forms of Christianity, especially to heresy, and particularly of the approach to non-Christian religions, notably Judaism and Islam. This is also the place to consider the early stages of the hostility to witchcraft as a manifestation of concern about that other internal enemy, Satan. The final strand must turn to more generalised and social approaches: how catholicism tackled issues of inclusion and exclusion among catholics. Some of this was merely disciplinary; but it is also necessary to look at the moral issues of slavery and serfdom, particular types of outcasts, and the recent burgeoning of interest in women's response to medieval Christianity.

A side-effect of the clarification of what was unacceptable, and of the concern to eliminate its perceived threat, was the creation of an intolerant society. To use the word 'intolerant' is to adopt a loaded vocabulary, for much was tolerated within the medieval church – features which Protestant (and some catholic) reformers of the sixteenth century wanted to eliminate. There is, however, a difference between the tolerance which in the medieval church was often a product of necessity and the balance of forces between clerics and laity in a demand-led religion, and the determined intolerance displayed towards outsiders, those who rejected or perceptibly threatened the norms of catholicism. The 'persecuting society' of the middle ages had its own antipathies: to Jews, to heretics, and to others who threatened to infect or subvert the normal order.

The ramifications of all these strands affected catholic spirituality in complex ways, sometimes purely personal, at others affecting whole regions, if not the whole church. They add to the other tensions which constantly forced examination of what Christianity was, and what it entailed. At the same time, however, the processes of inclusion and exclusion reflected social developments which did not necessarily accord with religious or spiritual imperatives. That oppression occurred in the name of a religion does not necessarily make that religion itself oppressive:

> If religious structures are used to justify oppression by people who regularly disregard precepts of equal gravity from the same moral code, or if prohibitions which restrain a disliked minority are upheld in their most literal sense as absolutely inviolable while comparable precepts affecting the majority are relaxed or reinterpreted, one must suspect something other than religious belief as the motivating cause of the oppression.[1]

BRING THEM IN . . .

The search for universal Roman hegemony – as dictated by the self-identification of catholicism, and the Gospel injunction to bring all to Christ – required expansion. This was marked by a forceful extension of the frontiers of Latin Christendom through the use of crusade in the thirteenth century, and by a conscious policy of mission which aimed at conversion.

---

[1] J. Boswell, *Christianity, social tolerance, and homosexuality: gay people in western Europe from the beginning of the Christian era to the fourteenth century* (Chicago and London, 1980), p. 7.

From the Latin perspective, the position in the early thirteenth century was by no means gloomy. The conquest of Constantinople, the progress of the Reconquista, expansion in the north-east of Europe, the defeat of Catharism, were all positive movements, despite weaknesses in the Levant (which were not seen as irredeemable). Only after 1250 did the tide visibly turn, and retreat begin. By 1500 the position was very different: crusades which originally sought to bring the infidel in now more anxiously tried to keep them out; missionary efforts in Asia had largely petered out; heresy had struck hard in central Europe; converts from the non-Christian minorities within Europe were feared as a fifth-column undermining the purity of the faith; Antichrist was at the gates and Satan's minions within them.

Problems of conversion

The development of a catholic missionary spirit primarily reflected a search for an intellectual means of defeating rival faiths. It had to address both those within the fluctuating area under the political control of catholic Christians, and the peoples beyond the frontiers. As an intellectual effort it could only develop as a consequence of the philosophical and theological revitalisations of the twelfth century. The assurance of faith and the logic of scholasticism combined as weapons in the process of conversion: in R.I. Burns' forceful phrase, 'the non-Christian was to be inexorably syllogized into the Church';[2] so too were non-catholic Christians and, where possible, heretics. The principal addressees of this effort were the Jews and the Moslems. Pagans were also encountered among the Baltic tribes, in Lithuania, and in contacts with the Mongols. The missionary effort in the Mongol-ruled territories was often impressive, and met with some degree of short-term success, although subjected to frequent rebuffs.

As Judaism and Islam were intimately related to Christianity in Christianity's claims to have superseded the former and Islam's assertion that it in turn replaced Christianity, the prime task of any intellectual missionary endeavour had to be to persuade the Jews that Christ was actually their promised Messiah, and the Moslems that Mohammed was a fraud. This required that the argument be taken into their own territory and languages. Judaeo-Christian contacts were not too difficult to

---

[2] R. I. Burns, 'Social riots on the Christian-Moslem frontier (thirteenth-century Valencia)', *American historical review*, 66 (1961), p. 399, reprinted (same pagination) in his *Moors and crusaders in Mediterranean Spain* (London, 1978).

establish: in the twelfth century, Jews were widely distributed around western Europe, the flowering of Biblical studies then and in the following century among western theologians drawing extensively on contacts between the two peoples. For Jews to survive in western societies, they had to be bilingual, and so more easily open to efforts at conversion. Except in Spain, contact with Islam was more difficult; but the thirteenth century saw the establishment, largely under Dominican auspices, of a network of language schools to train missionaries to take the gospel overseas. These were primarily located in Spain and along the north African coast – notably at Tunis, whose ruler was constantly rumoured as about to convert. The most ambitious project among these missionary dreams was proclaimed at the Council of Vienne, which ordained instruction at selected universities in Hebrew, Greek, Arabic, and 'Chaldaean'. After initial signs of interest, the project sank.

The effectiveness of this missionary effort seems fairly paltry, forcing the Christians to confront the question of how to deal with non-Christians in territories under their control.[3] What conversions there were usually occurred in circumstances of at least implicit coercion. The number of converts could be impressive among the Moslems; but this cannot be ascribed to successful mission: in some cases they were simply mass baptisms regardless of desire. It is perhaps too easy, also, to overstate the significance of the conversions. Speculation concerning the Levant that 'If the Crusading Kingdom [of Acre] had continued to exist, the number of converts might steadily have mounted and the Muslim population constantly dwindled'[4] appears unwarranted, given the realm's frontier status. Moslem populations were usually strongly resilient to persuasion: after all, their religion claimed a status in relation to Christianity similar to that claimed by Christians with regard to Judaism. Disputations between catholics and Moslems are virtually unknown, especially in the areas where they might be most expected. The rivalries of Holy Wars were doubtless a critical feature, for the Moslems did have a tradition of debates with Oriental Christians which continued during the Crusader occupation of the Levant. However, as the Moslems also considered their own religion undebatable, and pro-Christian proselytism incurred the death penalty, major obstacles obstructed any serious exchange aimed at conversion to Christianity. As some missionaries

---

[3] See below, pp. 268–9, 278–81, 284–91.
[4] B. Z. Kedar, *Crusade and mission: European approaches toward the Muslims* (Princeton, NJ, 1984), p. 154.

recognised, the only way to convert Moslems was by utterly undermining the validity of Islam, which seemed much more demanding than convincing the Jews that Christ was the fulfillment of their expectations. The closest parallel to Acre was probably Valencia where, in more propitious circumstances for the Christians, Moslems still comprised a third of the population over two centuries after the conquest. It was perhaps a recognition of the futility of seeking converts from Islam which accounts for the seeming lack of vitality of missionary effort in Islamic states. In the Middle East in the thirteenth century, missionary activity seems to have ground to a halt once the Mongol rulers determined on Islam, although competition to secure defections from other eastern Christianities seems to have remained lively.

The search for conversions had little room for popular participation. There are some cases of lay involvement, with informal debates between traders perhaps offering the main opportunity for such participation. In the missionary territories beyond the rule of catholic powers, merchants formed the nuclei of expatriate communities which by providing interpreters certainly would assist the catholic efforts; but the scale of their active involvement in mission is uncertain. In the west, the clearest instance of lay action is provided by the Genoese merchant Ingheto Contardo, who disputed with the Jews of Majorca in 1286. However, lay participation could be counter-productive: the sermons delivered to captive audiences of Moslems and Jews before a crowd of Christians inflamed the latter even if they had little impact on the former, causing riots and other disturbances. The dangers were acknowledged in the later thirteenth century, with the insistence that ordinary people be excluded from the sermons to remove the dangers.

Unfortunately for those seeking to spread the gospel, conversion was not a one-way traffic. The aim was to convert others to Christianity, specifically catholicism, but catholics might themselves defect. This was most likely to occur in non-catholic realms, especially among the victims of military defeat or piracy whose presence was thenceforth likely to be permanent. An important consideration here would be continued access to catholic services. When the Genoese hold on Kaffa in the Crimea was ended by Turkish conquest in 1475, the catholic colony secured liturgical continuity by purchasing catholic priests in the slave markets of Constantinople. Where catholic continuity was interrupted, the switch might be not from Christianity to Islam, but from catholicism to another type of Christianity. Italians in Egypt are occasionally noted as adopting Coptic practices in the absence of catholic priests.

Christian conversion to Islam raises different issues. It probably occurred most in the Crusader states, perhaps under threat of death following military defeat and capture, as Joinville records of Louis IX's crusade to Damietta. Converts were also encountered in later centuries in Egypt: the guide provided in Cairo for Lionardo Frescobaldi during his extensive pilgrimage in the east in 1384–5 was a converted Venetian, with a Florentine wife. Possibly his conversion was not entirely one of conviction; he does seem to have maintained contact with his family in Venice. The degree of actual choice reflected by such conversions is probably questionable: normally linguistic differences and the inaccessibility of the Koran would make the transition from Christianity to Islam difficult for those lacking cultural immersion in Islamic life.

Movement from Christianity to Islam also seems to have occurred fairly often in the Spanish lands (perhaps primarily in Valencia and along the Granadan frontier); although it is likely that many of these 'apostates' were actually reverting to a former religion unwillingly and incompletely abandoned. Apostate Christians were a substantial minority in Granada, so large that when the kingdom fell in 1492 the ex-Christians (*elches*) were formally guaranteed freedom of their new religion; despite the fact that apostasy normally incurred social death, with physical death as the legal penalty. Despite the legal position, Christians and former Christians often worked together in north Africa, where intermingling was common. There most of the converts to Islam were captives who had abandoned hope of redemption. How many were intellectually convinced into the new religion, rather than drawn simply by cultural evolution, simple pragmatism, or baser motivations, cannot be assessed. There are signs of individual confusion, with some who had voluntarily converted later switching back; while especially along the Castilian-Granada border there were striking overlaps in Moslem and Christian customs, even to the extent of sharing shrines. Islam did have a potential for intellectual attractiveness, dramatically revealed in the 1380s when Anselm Turmeda, a Franciscan friar, converted after having apparently concluded that Mohammed was the personification of the Spirit in a Joachimite interpretation of history.

Evidence of Christians converting to Judaism is much rarer, but it did happen, usually drawing attention because those who apostasised suffered the death penalty. As well as the fear of anti-Jewish violence, one reason for the exclusion of ordinary Christians from the Christian-Jewish conferences may have been fear of the seductiveness of the Jewish responses, which might undermine catholicism (as Joinville again noted for the reign of Louis IX of France). Such undermining appears in the case of Jean Langlois at Paris in 1493: his faith having been eroded by contacts with the Jews of Avignon, he had desecrated the Host at Notre Dame and denied the Trinity, and was accordingly burnt.

Crusades

Ideally, Christianity was to expand as a voluntary movement: forcible conversions were in theory banned. They did sometimes occur, and the resulting baptisms were upheld by theologians, making any who reverted to their former religion liable to the penalties of apostasy. However, the ideal was that Christianity should be willingly embraced rather than half-heartedly imposed. This attitude caused some difficulties, especially with the non-Christian groups living in realms ruled by catholics. The outcome has been described as a 'theological and canon law vice that explicitly guaranteed the right of the Infidel to live unconverted under Christian rule, but used every method short of forced conversion to draw him into the Christian faith'.[5]

A programme of conversion perhaps presupposed some degree of territorial expansion. Indeed, for much of the later middle ages expansion of Christianity was a matter of territory as well as – possibly more than – minds. This allowed greater popular participation than in the specifically intellectual missionary endeavours, involvement which became an important aspect of medieval devotional practices as it was formalised into the crusades.

Crusading was the most dramatic and enduring of the mass movements which affected the Latin church during the period under review. Stimulated in 1095 by Pope Urban II's desire to recover Jerusalem for Christianity, it continued in various guises through to the Reformation and beyond. Despite the loss of Jerusalem in 1187 and the later weakness of the crusader states in the Levant, crusades retained a potent appeal – especially voyages to the east – throughout the thirteenth century. Although the Levantine cause thereafter withered, with the loss of the last Palestinian foothold in 1291, the aspiration for an eastern crusade did not disappear entirely. In the 1460s Pope Pius II hoped to send a large army to confront the advancing Turks; while proclamations of a desire to engage on crusade were intermittently issued by western princes even later. Realistic concern with recovery in the Near and Middle East had declined after 1291, although the last 'crusader state' – Cilician Armenia – lingered until 1375, and the Hospitallers kept Rhodes and some coastal castles for even longer, losing Rhodes only in 1522. Crusading endeavours after 1300 were frequently directed elsewhere, to Spain, and the north-eastern ranges of Europe along the Baltic; not to mention the use of crusading indulgences for political purposes to support papal

---

[5] D. S. H. Abulafia, 'The end of Muslim Sicily', in *Muslims under Latin rule, 1100–1300*, ed. J. M. Powell (Princeton, NJ, 1990), p. 130.

military and political aspirations in Italy and elsewhere. The numbers actively engaged in the fighting were obviously limited; the reasons for their participation varied. With the Italian crusades, which were essentially concerned with papal political aims, most of the fighting was seemingly done by mercenaries, paid in both cash and indulgences. Other expeditions, including those to Spain and Prussia, and perhaps most ostentatiously the disastrous crusade of Nicopolis of 1395, had features of chivalric excursions, almost the medieval equivalent of the Grand Tour.

The response to the crusading call varied greatly. For northern Europeans, visits to Spain might well be jaunts; for the Spaniards the Holy War was a reality, meshing in with the sense of national identity and the political structures of the kingdoms, especially Castile. There the crusade's strong religious aspects were maintained. Christianity had, after all, advanced with the frontier, leaving its own devotional contours in a succession of shrines: in Castile 'The late medieval frontier was a Mariological one'.[6] Political crises might also stress the demands of Crusade; as happened in 1465. Hopes for a more complete Islamic submission were reinforced by dramatic representations like that at Jaen in 1463, in which the 'King of Morocco' acknowledged military and spiritual defeat and accepted baptism. For many, the elimination of religious outsiders by the conquest of Granada and the expulsion of the Jews in 1492 was but a prelude to greater things. As early as 1486 Ferdinand of Aragon had been hailed as the future conqueror of Africa and liberator of Jerusalem, destined for universal monarchy.

Elsewhere, the more mundane approach to crusade as a grand tour is perhaps personified in Chaucer's Knight, who had seen active service across Europe from Granada to Prussia, and had participated in the attack on Alexandria in 1365. However, the superficiality of crusade in the later middle ages is perhaps best shown by developments in the north-east of Europe.

The expansion of Christianity among the pagan tribes of the Baltic and Slav lands had been led by the Teutonic Knights, a military order which had switched its centre of operations from the Holy Land in the early thirteenth century. Its role in the Baltic lands had been legitimated by successive thirteenth-century popes. This crusade needed a new justification. Normally a crusade was legitimised on the grounds that the area where it was to occur had at some earlier time belonged to Christians, who were therefore merely recovering their own. This could

---

[6] A. MacKay, 'Religion, culture, and ideology on the late medieval Castilian-Granadan frontier', in *Medieval frontier societies*, ed. R. Bartlett and A. MacKay (Oxford, 1989), p. 230.

not apply to the Baltic: here the demand for an initial conversion was the sole justification. However, changes in the canonistic attitude to non-Christians which derived from an analysis of the relationship by Pope Innocent IV somewhat undermined the claims of the Teutonic Knights. The new theory upheld the property rights of non-Christians, although it justified Christian military intervention in their lands if they obstructed missions. As the territories of the Teutonic Knights became increasingly a state, and as the surrounding territories themselves became Christian realms, so the rationale for the Knights' activities diminished. They were accused of being more concerned with conquest and dominion than with conversion and mission – indeed, they were said actively to obstruct the conversion of their subjects to justify continued warfare. As Poland and Lithuania expanded as catholic states, so territorial disputes occurred more frequently, climaxing dramatically at the Knights' defeat at Tannenberg in 1410. In the aftermath of that, there was a major debate about the status of the Knights and the rights of the Poles and Lithuanians (pagan and catholic) at the Council of Constance. There Paulus Vladimiri, for the Poles, vigorously challenged the Knights' claims, advancing ideas which, by emphasising the hypocritical nature of their Baltic activities, made their defence of their actions tantamount to heresy because they were essentially justifying war for its own sake rather than to benefit the church. The impact of his criticisms is hard to evaluate: certainly there was a fall in the later Europe-wide appeal of the Baltic crusade; but that may have been primarily because the area was now seen as merely another political cockpit, rather than a region where the faith was seriously threatened.

Lawyers and theologians might debate the continued validity of crusade; but its continuation depended on active military participation. The number who could be fighters was necessarily limited; but the scope for popular involvement through offerings, bequests, prayers, and purchase of indulgences, knew no bounds. Crusading appeals, extending over the whole of western Christendom, could be highly effective, and served to make the donors feel part of a more than local church. A papally sponsored indulgence for the relief of Constantinople from the Turks in 1399–1401 may have secured over £2,000 in donations in England alone.

While the practical support for such military ventures in western Europe can be vaguely assessed, the emotional and devotional reaction to them remains elusive. Was there a real concern for the Holy Land, for the defence of Constantinople, for the future of the Order of St John; or was the response to the appeals part of the more mercenary traffic in the purchase of salvation? This again requires a return to individual values, insofar as they can be considered. In the fifteenth-century collection of indulgences made by Henry and Katherine Langley, the defence of

Rhodes against the Turks is on a par with support for the building fund of Saintes cathedral, and participation in the spiritual benefits of confraternity with the mendicant orders. There is no indication of priorities, or of the nature of the spirituality behind the purchases. Some individuals might make the personal commitment of a crusading vow even in the early sixteenth century; but for most the only involvement with 'crusade' was probably in response to a brief exhortation among a list of good causes in a bidding prayer at mass, like that from the English diocese of Lichfield in the fifteenth century which enjoined the congregation to pray 'for the holy cross which Christ suffered his passion upon, which is in heathen men's hands, that God for his mercy bring it out of their hands into Christian men's keeping'.[7]

THE ENEMY WITHIN

A threatened church

Assured, but not completely convinced, of its status as the ultimate revelation, medieval Latin Christianity was in many respects an insecure religion. Surrounded by enemies, threatened by demonic forces, anxious about an end ever imminent but always delayed, catholicism was constantly embattled: even if there were no real enemies, they could be imagined. While challenges which were geographically external were immediately recognisable, and could be fought, more insidious were challenges which were geographically internal, offered by religious minorities whose existence was a constant reproach and was perceived as an equally constant threat. Awareness of the double challenge was shown at the start of the period of conscious catholic expansionism, with the massacres of Jews in the Rhineland in 1096 during the First Crusade: if that expedition was to clear Christ's enemies from lands which should rightly be Christian, should not the spiritual cleansing start in the west?

The simple fact was that, despite the church's universalist and all-encompassing aspirations to include all humanity, outsiders always existed. Some refused to be included; others adopted definitions of the Christian life such that for its own safety the church felt obliged to exclude them. Those who refused inclusion generally belonged to other religions. In some places, catholicism overlapped with other Christian identities, notably in the Crusader states of the Levant and the Aegean, and for a while in Constantinople itself, and on Europe's eastern frontier as the

---

[7] E. Calvert, 'Extracts from a fifteenth century MS', *Transactions of the Shropshire archaeological and natural history society*, 2nd ser., 6 (1894), p. 104.

Latin and Russian churches spread to smother the intervening paganism. Other outsiders, rejecting the current church whilst being excluded by it, comprised the heretical sects of the period; groups which, if the catholic definitions were accepted, could be large, and in their own ways challenged Romanist hegemony. It is therefore necessary to consider, if briefly, the relationships with the varied sects which appeared within western Europe, and the issue of 'denominations'. Perhaps the main medieval context in which that word's modern connotations apply is in the eastern Mediterranean – certainly in terms of territories ruled by catholics but with substantial non-catholic populations. Greek Orthodoxy was the most significant of the kaleidoscope of Christianities encountered elsewhere by the Latins, which also included the Armenians in Asia Minor, and Maronites, Jacobites, and others in the Levant. As catholic missionaries expanded contacts in Asia, Nestorians were found among the Mongols, and eventually even Thomasists in India.

While heresy and other 'denominations' offered challenges to catholicism from within Christianity, Judaism and Islam were explicit non-Christian challenges. Their continued presence in Christian-ruled lands raised questions of co-existence which had to be addressed, especially given their resistance to attempts at conversion.[8]

The attitude towards Jews was ambivalent. They were a problem simply because they adhered to the religion which Christianity claimed to replace. The stance towards them therefore differed qualitatively from that taken towards Moslems. Jews had failed to recognise Christ as the Messiah when He appeared; Moslems had consciously rejected the Christian message and had chosen to be deluded by the false message of Mohammed (according to some legends Islam originated in apostasy from Christianity). Moreover, Jews were integral to the Christian cosmology: the idea inherited from the Fathers was that their continued misguidedness served to confirm the validity of Christianity, while in traditional Christian eschatology their final conversion would indicate that the Second Coming was near.

The treatment of Judaism and Islam had its oddities. Often the two were conflated, especially in discussions of their legal status. The *consilia* of Oldradus de Ponte (d. ?1337) bring some of the peculiarities to the fore. Most of his comments on Moslems are exegesis of canons concerning Jews, or pagans. In considering conversion of a Jew to Islam, he remarks that 'If each is in a state of damnation, it does not matter to what sect he belongs', yet argues (perhaps perversely, because of the circumstances) that 'the Saracen sect is not as bad as that of the Jews'. He urges peaceful

---

[8] Above, pp. 260–3.

conversion and co-existence, arguing that 'we ought not to despoil peaceful Jews, pagans, and Saracens . . . Jews and Saracens are not idolaters, although otherwise infidels; nor are they the public enemies of ruling Christian princes; therefore they ought not to be expelled'.[9]

Not only did the doctrinal approaches towards Jews and Moslem differ; there was also a difference in awareness of them. By 1200 Jews were distributed throughout Europe, and maintained a presence in many countries for much of the following three centuries. Their presence in the Bible meant that they had to be integrated into Christian awareness even if there was no personal contact. Consequently, even in countries with no Jewish population (like England after 1290) anti-Jewishness could still be expressed, simply because of the Jews' place in the Biblical record of the life of Christ. Moslems, however, were decided rarities outside Mediterranean areas, so that the reaction to them was necessarily regional and localised. As Islam had no role in the Biblical story, or the overall scheme of salvation, and was believed to be inevitably destined to be converted out of existence, it perhaps posed less of a spiritual threat, even when it became a major territorial challenge. Considered simply wrong, it could be ignored.

For purely historical reasons the Iberian peninsula offered the main laboratory for the evolution of practical Christian reactions to both rival religions. (It also provided a laboratory for the evolution of relations between Moslems and Jews, which necessarily occurred within the context of subjection to the Christian majority. The patterns of alliances which drew on antipathies and similarities reveal complexities which clearly transcended purely religious considerations.) What is striking in Spain is the use of eucharistic tales in the weaponry of Christians against both Jews and Moslems, with the Host being an indefatigable source of power and support for Christians and their religion against opposition. More insidious was the continued use of such tales against the Christianised Jews (*conversos*) in the fifteenth century, to affirm that their conversion was somehow incomplete, and they remained the enemy within.

The persistent and unavoidable fear that catholicism might be undermined could reach hysterical proportions, perhaps best shown in the perceived combination of threats which provoked reaction in France in 1321. In that year rumours spread of a major conspiracy among lepers to poison the waters of the kingdom so that all orthodox Christians would be afflicted with the disease. The poisons were supposedly supplied by

---

[9] N. Zacour, *Jews and Saracens in the consilia of Oldradus de Ponte*, Pontifical Institute of Mediaeval Studies: studies and texts, 100 (Toronto, 1990), pp. 62, 63, 67.

Jews, acting as agents of the Moslem Sultan and the king of Granada, being given to the lepers at ceremonies which entailed a blasphemous rejection of Christianity obviously modelled on allegations levelled against the Templars a few years before. Despite the outlandishness of the accusations (and, as far as is known, the absence of any Christian deaths which might be ascribed to such poisoning), their acceptance led to a strong reaction which cost many lepers their lives, and may have contributed to a further expulsion of Jews from French royal lands.

A similar awareness of concerted threats may be posited for the fifteenth century, although not so well enmeshed. Yet the Turkish advance then (seen as the arrival of Antichrist), the manifest revival of heresy (notably in Bohemia), and the economic distress of the early fifteenth century perhaps all contributed to generate a concern for defence against the arch-fiend, Satan, reflected in the contemporary demonisation of magic and onset of the witchcraft trials. As this concern grew, as conspiracy theories spread and the search for scapegoats intensified, so the vocabulary and its attendant overtones became a tool for that process. The contagion of leprosy became an analogy for heresy; the 'judaising' of Spanish *conversos* was also a leprous heresy; the conquest of Granada from the Moors was an attack on leprosy.

Over-enthusiasm

The issue of doctrinal purity – or the removal of doctrinal confusion – was a major worry for the ecclesiastical authorities throughout the period. In spiritual matters, possibly the main threat to the church's inclusiveness was the polarisation of individual and collective responses: on one side Christianity defined as a collectivist religion, emphasising shared responsibilities and a spirituality embodied in a communion of the faithful; on the other the desire for individual awareness of and links with God, which sometimes (most extremely with anchorites and some mystics) meant an apparent rejection of the social, a losing of the self in the divine which superseded all other responsibilities and totally negated any idea of familiarity with other Christians. Even if not so extreme, the desire for a personal relationship with the divinity (or, if God was aiming too high, with specific saints) did mean that people might try to avoid participation in the collective and seek their own salvation. Social and other considerations also operate here, with further fragmentation as individuals, families, or other small groups, distanced themselves from the collectivity of the parish (without totally separating from it) by withdrawing into domestic chapels, or privatised space within public churches. Yet the private chapels, fraternities, and suchlike, were always supplementary to the established structure, capable of being incorporated within it (no matter how inharmoniously), and never total replacements for it. Equally, while an individualist contact with God through mysticism or claims to personal revelation might lead to heresy and rejection *of* the church, they were not always rejected *by* the church. Indeed, some forms of mysticism – like that encouraged by Richard Rolle in England – were integrated into a developing orthodox spirituality. It was not the actions of mystics, but their conclusions, which might be held suspect – as in the case of Meister Eckhart and his disciples in Germany. The church did not totally oppose private revelation: it condoned the revelations of Bridget of Sweden, and seems to have accepted those of Julian of Norwich. It was the self-proclaimed relationship between the recipients of the revelations and ecclesiastical authority which appears to have been crucial: Margery Kempe, while claiming revelation, did not reject the church's disciplinary or sacramental authority, despite her frequent contretemps with individual clerics.

Such developments were ambivalent, and enthusiasm was always close to the limits of the acceptable. At the start of the thirteenth century, it was touch and go whether Francis of Assisi's response to his understanding of Christianity's spiritual challenge would gain official sanction or not. It did; but the transformation of that spirituality as it was institutionalised only accentuated the tensions between it and more conventional forms of religious organisation, and did eventually push some versions of Franciscan spirituality into heresy. Indeed, the wider movement of spiritual ferment in north Italy in the thirteenth century, which can perhaps be generically classified as 'Franciscan spirituality', was highly ambiguous: it could generate pro-ecclesial movements like the anti-heretical fraternities of Milan and other major communes; it could also lead to the establishment – again in Milan – of movements like the Guglielmites, with their emphasis on the female, and their desire for a feminised church. Later novelties introduced by members of the religious hierarchy also sometimes encountered opposition from within the system. Bernardino of Siena's advocacy of the cult of the Holy Name, and particularly his distribution of its monogrammatic representation, stirred up accusations of idolatry (notably from the Dominicans, partly as a reflection of the continuing rivalry between the two major mendicant orders). Some even identified Bernardino as an apostle of Antichrist, with the monogram as a one of his signs.

Worries about uncontrolled enthusiasm extended to other areas. Julian of Norwich was clearly uncertain of the status of her personal experiences: she relates that she first considered her revelations as ravings, and had to be convinced of their validity by a priest. Her book reveals an insistent concern to proclaim her conformity with the church's beliefs, even when her formulations superficially appear to conflict with its formal teachings. The fear of being wrong, of being misled (and misleading) by personal revelation, resonates throughout her work; in stark contrast to the attitude of Margery Kempe, who evidently felt no such qualms. Yet Margery Kempe's behaviour was seen by some as a direct challenge to the church, more directly perhaps to lay expectations and definitions of behaviour within the church, with her white clothing and constant tears and sobbing. Concern, fear, that legitimate spirituality might become illegitimate spiritual arrogance also appears in some of the regulations for houses of Sisters of the Common Life in the Netherlands: the insistence that the inmates were not beguines in the sense condemned at the Council of Vienne, and the stipulation that anyone found upholding the beguine propositions condemned at Vienne or adhering to the mysticism of Eckhart should be expelled from the community.

Fears of an unwitting descent into heresy were frequently expressed by those with responsibility for the care of souls. There was often concern that people were being misled through their misapprehension of preachers' subtleties, or by the spread of heresy through access to books or even to the confessions of other heretics. Reactions to the demands of religion and devotion might stimulate greater conformity to the demands of the catholic faith in the efflorescence of pious works and charitable activities, and in a variety of devotional practices; but the search for a truly religious life in conformity with Christ could also stimulate real heresy.

Heresy

The sheer range of medieval heresies, and of the church's responses to them, preclude any detailed analysis here. Yet heresy cannot be completely ignored. It is clear that many people in late medieval Europe did exclude themselves from the church by their interpretations of Christianity's demands, and by their insistence on following those interpretations in preference to the church's dictates. Those affected ranged from the Cathars of the twelfth and thirteenth centuries, insofar as they could be called Christians, through to the Lollards and Hussites of the fifteenth; embracing a wide range of smaller groupings and individuals as well. Several of these heretical stances reflected reactions to the uncertainties of Christianity, or to the apparent incompatibility of the decreed tenets of the faith with the reality of the physical world. Much of the tension originated in definitions. Such was the case with Catharism, which as a response to the problem of the existence of evil in a world created by a God by definition good, resolved the issue by developing a doctrine of dualism – of the existence of twin and opposing powers of good and evil – which perhaps more accurately coincided with 'common-sense' appreciations of the world. Similarly, the denial of transubstantiation ascribed to the Lollards, while it may be connected to the intricacies of Wyclif's theories on the Real Presence, could with more justice be related to the sheer mental problem of accepting that bread is actually flesh when all sensory perceptions dictate otherwise. Sometimes heresy was chiefly a matter of discipline, as with the moderate Hussites' insistence on giving the chalice to the laity (although other branches of Hussitism incorporated purely doctrinal elements, like an insistence on predestinarianism). The frontier between heresy and orthodoxy was hard to define precisely, and clerics in particular seem to have been prone to transgression. The problem of the knife-edge was particularly acute in the early thirteenth century, when there were only the alternatives of orthodoxy and heresy: only as the century progressed was the possibility of a middle stance developed, of 'error' which was technically not as heterodox as formal heresy. The distinction between 'error' and 'heresy' was commonly made in later discussions of unorthodoxy among intellectuals; but whether lay appreciations attained such levels of refinement is less certain.

While all heresies obviously threatened the church and its orthodoxy, the scale of the threat varied from case to case. Catharism was the only major movement which was an alternative religion in the fullest sense. Its development of its own ministerial system, including a diocesan structure and hierarchy of bishops, made its challenge to the Roman church political and territorial as well as doctrinal and disciplinary, and may account for the vehemence of the eventual response to it. Most of the other sects offered no formal challenge to the status of the catholic church, at least initially, being more concerned with the interpretation of doctrine and with disciplinary matters. They were, in a real sense, all within the church, whose necessity they did not deny. The arguments generally focused on the direction which the church was to take *as a whole*: the heretics – who are, after all, only historically heretics because they lost the struggle – were as convinced as their opponents of their rightness in setting out a programme for the totality of Christendom. A prime reason for the weakness of Lollardy was precisely that it had no effective structural substitute for the extant ecclesiastical system in England. Similarly, with Hussitism, the moderates' conviction that catholicism had abandoned them, rather than *vice versa*, meant that their determination to maintain a legitimate hierarchical diocesan system considerably weakened their challenge to orthodoxy.

The problem of heresy was intermittent, and regional. The search for heretics went through phases, but the establishment of the Inquisition in the thirteenth century was not the foundation of a major repressive institution crushing all independent thought. Apart from its activities against Catharism in southern France, the papal inquisition, directed by members of the mendicant orders, was seemingly of limited impact, and rapidly became almost moribund. Not only was its distribution limited, with several governments denying it admission to their territories; even where it did exist its scope for independent activity was limited, as in Venice. Nevertheless, the fact of the Inquisition attested an acceptance that heresy existed as a real threat. The Inquisition may also have encouraged an approach which, if heresy did not actually exist, caused it to be invented. That certainly appears to be the case with the 'heresy of the Free Spirit' – although that anything like an organised sect of Free Spiriters actually existed is unlikely. Often the accusations may be no more than clerical horror stories, on a par with earlier assertions that all heretics by definition indulged in sexual excesses and the murder and cannibalisation of the resulting offspring in parodies of the mass.

What real heresy there was remained fairly localised – the Cathars in southern France and parts of Italy, Spiritual Franciscans in Provence and Italy (especially the south), Wycliffites and Lollards (if they can be differentiated) in England, Hussites in Bohemia. The Waldensians and their affiliates may have had greater geographical distribution, but they were also more obscure and less identifiably a sect, and so attracted less attention. The geographical concentration of the major heresies was matched by their chronological limitations. Catharism posed little real threat after 1280, although the famed heresy-hunt at Montaillou in 1318–25 shows its survival into the early fourteenth century in a much-debased form, and an awareness of the need to be vigilant against it.[10] The Spiritual Franciscans were a real problem only from about 1260 through to the 1330s, but there were lingering remnants in southern Italy in the later fourteenth century. In England Lollardy was always fragmented, so that while it persisted from the 1380s until the Reformation, its adherents were scattered and its beliefs lacked coherence. Hussitism, generated in the first years of the fifteenth century, ceased to be a radical force by the 1440s; a moderate form gained disciplinary

[10] The case of Montaillou is immortalised in E. Le Roy Ladurie, *Montaillou: Cathars and catholics in a French village, 1294–1324* (Harmondsworth, 1980). However, his treatment of the sources, and consequently his interpretation, is open to some challenges. See especially the comments in L. E. Boyle, 'Montaillou revisited: mentalité and methodology', in *Pathways to medieval peasants*, ed. J. A. Raftis, Pontifical Institute of Mediaeval Studies: Papers in mediaeval studies, 2 (Toronto, 1981), pp. 119–40.

toleration in 1436, lost its heretical label, and continued in Bohemia until the seventeenth century. Less significant heresies rose and fell, adding their names to the catalogue of the intolerable, but posing no continuous or particularly potent threat – as with the beguines and beghards, who constantly teetered on the borderline between orthodoxy and the unacceptable from their twelfth-century origins through to the Reformation.

Greeks and other 'denominations'

In comparison with heresy, the problem of relationships with other Christian 'denominations' was less insidious, but still occasionally significant. Following the Fourth Crusade of 1204 and the Latin conquest of Constantinople, a catholic veneer was laid over much of the former Byzantine empire, and the aspiration to end the Greek schism became more significant. The concern to reunify the church was essentially limited: few were highly aware of the distinctions between the demoninations, and to that extent the debates of the Council of Lyons in 1274, or which led to the reunification decree at the Council of Florence in 1439, were irrelevant to mainstream developments in religion. Nevertheless, contacts with the Greeks and other non-catholic Christians were unavoidable along the frontiers, or in areas ruled by Latins but populated by others, including the Aegean islands and the Morea, and the Genoese coastal holdings around the Black Sea. Occasional minorities existed further west. There were some Greek speakers, and some Greek monasteries, in southern Italy, whose numbers were reinforced with the flight from the Balkans as the Byzantine empire decayed. Groups of Armenians also fled to Italy in the fourteenth century, establishing a minor presence; while the Armenians also had a bishopric at Lvov in Poland.

Generally, such contacts provoked little concern, except among intellectuals. Exotic visitors, like the Indians and Ethiopians who are occasionally recorded as pilgrims in Italy, were scarcely more than temporary wonders. However, contacts with the non-catholic churches did raise the question of the degree of diversity which catholicism could accommodate, especially with regard to the Greeks. The hope at the fall of Constantinople in 1204 had been for a speedy reunion of the churches: Pope Innocent III and his successors expected that Latin dominance would evolve into a full reintegration of the two traditions. The legitimation of non-Latin rites at the Fourth Lateran Council reflected this hope of reconciliation, presumably in the expectation that the Greek church would be gradually but inexorably catholicised, its distinctive rituals and theological stances being eroded until the singularity of a Romanised Christendom was achieved. Unfortunately for this plan, the Greeks did not come round, and within decades the popes were condemning them as heretics and instigating crusades to bolster the collapsing Frankish empire of Romania.

Relationships between Roman and other Christian traditions evolved in two main spheres. In the aftermath of Lateran IV, and greatly stimulated by the arrival of the Mongols, there was the major effort to export catholicism to new lands. A great deal of missionary endeavour, hope, and wishful thinking was expended on these eastern missions, which featured major novelties like the celebration of the liturgy in Turkic and Armenian rather than Latin. If one of the Mongol rulers had converted, and if that conversion had led to the firm implantation of catholicism among his subjects, that would been a dramatic success. There were some princely conversions, but never enough, and never sufficiently permanent. While the Yuan and Ming rulers of China eventually turned Buddhist, the western competition between Christianity and Islam for Mongol souls ended with the victory of Islam: thereafter catholic missions in the new Islamic realms were generally little more than expatriate outposts, with restricted opportunities for proselytism.

While the Turkish and southern Mongol realms accepted Islam fairly rapidly, missionary effort lasted longer among pagans north of the Black Sea, and in the Caucasus. Here, particularly, acceptance of the validity of non-catholic rites complicated things, for the Latin approach to mission and denominational diversity was nothing if not ambivalent. While proclaiming the desire for reunification of all the churches under papal primacy, the missionaries were both in competition with the various local denominations to secure the adherence of non-Christians and seeking converts from those local churches. The competitive approach, which often insisted on the establishment of Latin hierarchies alongside those of the non-catholic churches and in the same towns, was not particularly endearing. Meanwhile, the repetitive search for union challenged the claims of the Latin rite to universal application. While leaders of many of the eastern churches were ready to accept papal primacy and union with catholicism, they often could not carry their flocks with them, thereby further fragmenting Christian unity in the east. Among the Maronites of Lebanon, for instance, there were rival pro- and anti-union groupings in the thirteenth century, even though union had been proclaimed in 1180 and was nominally unbroken thereafter. Repeated declarations of union with the Armenians similarly provoked backlashes and opposition. Nevertheless, the search continued: the Council of Florence in 1439 reasserted union with the Greeks, as part of a concerted papal drive for reunification which in subsequent years saw further declarations of union with the Copts, Armenians, Maronites, and others.

A major part of the problem lay in the understanding of 'union'. From the Roman standpoint, that was often considered equivalent to submission, with papal primacy of jurisdiction thereafter intended to be a reality. However, the arrangements between the denominations were if anything complicated by such proclamations: these were to be uniate churches, not part of a unified church. The validity of their rites and hierarchies, subject to some modification, was to be accepted alongside the Latin structures. This pluralism within what was meant to be a single structure had its drawbacks. Latin theologians claimed to determine the validity of the non-catholic practices and theology, as when early-fourteenth-century concern about Armenian practices generated a series of major tracts by such as Richard FitzRalph. Pluralism, moreover, was not to confer choice: in 1448 Pope Nicholas V fulminated against those who were switching from observance of catholic rituals to adoption of Greek rites, regardless of the union of Florence. Equally, the establishment of conformity with catholicism could be provocative. A policy of piecemeal but insistent change to this end, as adopted with the Lebanese Maronites, could be effective in the long term. But swift and radical Latinisation aroused opposition, especially if encouraged by the catholic authorities over the heads of the local hierarchs, and if it fundamentally challenged local traditions. This seemingly happened among some of the Armenians, where the establishment of a fiercely Latinising group centred on Qrnay (in Armenia proper) resulted in papal approbation in 1356 of a new Order of 'friars of Greater Armenia known as Unifiers'. The fundamental questioning of Armenian theological and ritual traditions by other Armenians – including insistence on rebaptism – provoked a reaction which gained ground from around 1380. Although the Unifiers and their flocks remained in existence, their numbers were considerably reduced by the early fifteenth century.

The area where practical relationships developed over the longest term covered the islands of the eastern Mediterranean, the petty states and colonial holdings bequeathed by the Fourth Crusade. There catholic minorities co-existed with and ruled over Orthodox majorities. In some places, notably the islands of the Venetian empire, the authorities insisted on a fairly rigid separation between the two traditions. Elsewhere the principle of erosion – or 'acculturation' – worked against rather than for the Roman church. In the early fourteenth century Pope John XXII railed against those who defected from the Latin to the Greek observance; but as the rulers became more integrated with the ruled, this was an unavoidable development. There is little sign of any effective Latin breaches in the Orthodox structures or missionising among the local populations, despite the planting of Latin regular orders, including the friars. By the fifteenth century assimilation had created a hybrid in many places, which eroded the aloofness of the Latins. Some churches used both rites, with a Latin chapel appended to a thoroughly Orthodox building; one observer stated that there were even priests who celebrated in both traditions. Throughout, the catholic rites were those of the rulers, the interlopers; small wonder that as the Turks advanced and the islands fell, the Latin tradition was expelled and the Orthodox revived.

Jews

With regard to the two major non-Christian faiths, interaction between catholics and Jews provoked the more debate and action. Christian attitudes towards the Jews had developed and changed considerably in the course of the twelfth century. Even around 1200 some still argued that their conversion should not be attempted, that it had to be left to God in fulfillment of divine providence. However, in the early thirteenth century the concern to convert did grow. Equally important, Christians began to claim the right to oversee Judaism, largely on the basis of their religion's origins. Christianity had to be the only possible development beyond Biblical Judaism: with the termination of the Old Dispensation at the Incarnation, Christian theologians asserted that Judaism had lost any right to further autonomous evolution. It had now to be preserved as at the time of Christ, a reminder of what was past, rather than a religion capable of further development. Hence, the violent thirteenth-century assault on the Talmud, condemned by Christians as a perversion of the reality of Judaism.

The shared past of Jews and Christians did weaken Christian intellectual resolve: the dependence of Biblical scholars on Jewish exegesis sometimes brought charges of Judaising. On the other hand, the development of intellectual anti-Judaism does appear to coincide with periods of active Christian concern to gain access to Hebrew scholarship, which increased the Christians' awareness of their shared past, and their conviction that Christianity was the necessary fulfillment of Judaism. This certainly seems to apply in the twelfth and thirteenth centuries; while a notable aspect of the humanist concern with Hebrew scholarship and retranslation of the Bible in fifteenth-century Italy is the parallel production of anti-Jewish tracts by those same humanists, as with Giannozzo Manetti's *Contra iudeos et gentes* of 1454, or Marsilio Ficino's *De religione Christiana* of *c.* 1476. In the early period, a growing awareness of the temptation of Judaism may have increased the concern to ensure conversions; the reaction of converted Jews against their former religion also made an important contribution. There is a striking number of deracinated Jews among the leading antagonists of Judaism in this period: Nicholas Donin, who led the attack on the Talmud in thirteenth-century France; Petrus Christiani in the Barcelona disputation of 1263; Jeronimo de Santa Fe at Tortosa in 1413–14; and the *conversos* who rose to high ecclesiastical office in fifteenth-century Spain.

Popular reactions to Jews seem to have been more emotional, possibly more spasmodic. Anti-Jewish action often appears as a response to the incitement of an emotive appeal. There is frequently a sense of orchestration, the violence being whipped up by such as Ferran Martinez, archdeacon of Ecija in Seville, whose preaching precipitated the Spanish pogroms in 1391. At lower levels, it is also possible that some of the action was led by former Jews reacting against their past. In 1302 the collector of Jewish taxes in Valencia claimed among his expenses a bribe to a former Jew who had tried to provoke an attack on his former co-religionists.

The anti-Jewish violence responded to a variety of triggers. Sometimes it was calendrical, tending to occur at major Christian feasts, notably Christmas, Easter, and Corpus Christi. Attacks on Jews almost became part of the liturgical round, as at Gerona in Spain. The sermons delivered to Jews, berating their obstinate refusal to accept Christ, stirred up their Christian auditories even more. Plays depicting Jewish involvement in the Crucifixion, or host desecrations, similarly produced a violent response. At Freiburg-im-Breisgau, anti-Jewish plays were banned in 1338; while in 1469 the town government set guards to protect Jewish houses when plays were put on. Actual or rumoured host desecrations, let alone charges of ritual murder, also triggered violence. This was partly because the myths of Judaism developed by Christians from the twelfth century demanded active as well as passive opposition to Christianity, to emphasise otherness and reinforce Christian perspectives. Having given Christianity its founding martyr by their responsibility for the death of Christ, so the Jews were falsely reputed to cause further martyrdoms by the ritual murder of Christian children. Such ritual murder charges began with the case of St William of Norwich in 1144; they later became a regular feature of anti-Jewish activity, as at Berne in 1294, Messina in 1347, and several Italian cases between 1478 and 1492 (that of Simon of Trent in 1475 being the most important). Although the charges were denounced by Frederick II in 1236, and by several thirteenth-century popes, and although local authorities may have joined with Jews to prevent accusations being voiced, as seemingly happened at Barcelona in 1301, the possibility of such charges – and Christian presumptions of their validity – necessarily soured links between the two religions. So did charges of host profanation, seen as a repetition of the Jews' deicide. These first appeared near Berlin in 1243, and were rapidly absorbed into the mythology. They were frequently associated with miracles, as at Paris in 1290. Some, like that at Brussels in 1370, generated pilgrimage sites which again served to reinforce Christian self-perceptions against the Jews, and to perpetuate the hostilities. The need for the Jews to be actively opponents of Christianity, and therefore hostile to Christians in general, also triggered violence against them as scapegoats for natural disasters, or as presumed conspirators against Christians. They were accordingly accused of spreading the Black Death as a means to overthrow Christianity; while a common charge, seen in the French scare of 1321 and elsewhere, was that they poisoned wells and water supplies used by Christians.

The most dramatic Christian response to Judaism was not attempted conversion, but expulsion. Why Jews were driven from specific places varied: Jewish-Christian relations were always a complex mix of social, political, religious, and economic inter-actions, and anti-Jewish activity sometimes has to be explained in terms of social, economic, and political scapegoating rather than deep religious convictions. Some places experienced no expulsions, so that in the sixteenth century the Spanish Habsburgs tolerated a Jewish presence in some of their domains, notably Milan and Naples, but not in others. Some expulsions reflected the power of governments and the ecclesiastical authorities. The expulsion from France was a piecemeal business, reflecting the personal whims of individual kings and the varying degree of royal control in the provinces. Nevertheless, France's Jewish population had all been converted or driven into exile by 1400. In Brussels in 1350, and Berlin in 1510, charges of host-desecration lay behind the expulsions, a pattern very similar to the relationship between the case of the Holy Child of La Guardia in 1491 and the Spanish expulsions of the following year. However, although the Spanish expulsions were the most dramatic, the reasons for them are still matters of controversy, made even more complex by the presence of an extensive *converso* community in the fifteenth century.

The Spanish *converso* community had arisen following a crescendo of anti-Jewish outbursts, beginning in 1348 and climaxing in 1391. Many Jews had converted then or later (notably in the aftermath of the preaching campaigns of Vincent Ferrer), usually under duress. The treatment of Spain's former Jews matched a pattern seen elsewhere, for the *conversos* were left very much to themselves. A major difficulty with Christian attempts to convert Jews was that the Christians usually had no idea of what they were actually demanding. 'Conversion' was an end, but not a practically thought-out policy. Judaism was not something which could simply be sloughed off; its social structures and mental habits were not washed away with the waters of baptism. When religious conformity was something lived rather than merely thought, the total change in *mores* demanded by conversion could not be achieved at the touch of holy water. Yet 'old' Christians had that expectation: this perhaps accounts for many of the fears expressed about those who did convert, whether in thirteenth-century England or fifteenth-century Spain, that they remained Jews at heart. Yet as little was done to integrate the converts into their newly adopted faith and social systems (in England the establishment of the under-funded *Domus conversorum* under Henry III may have provided a new social structure, but one which functioned almost as an alternative ghetto), they naturally retained many of their old links, habits, and customs. It has been rightly said that converted Jews were left with few resorts, 'frequently finding their only secure haven in the ranks of the Christian clergy, or hovering indecisively between two hostile religious communities'.[11] The Christians were reluctant to absorb them, the Jews anxious not to let them go. A surprisingly large number of converts did find a new religious rationale in the Christian priesthood, which may explain their vocal antipathy to their erstwhile religion; but many converts were distrusted, and the reality of their conversion doubted. Fears that the *conversos* were crypto-Jews became most vocal in Spain, as that population grew and social and fiscal tensions increased. The condemnation and distrust of 'renegades' was not a purely Spanish phenomenon and nor was it confined to converts from Judaism to Christianity. In 1310, Sicilian legislation ordered that converts from Islam should not be called 'renegade dogs', while Christians who defected to Islam seem to have been equally distrusted by Moslem authorities in the Middle East. The fear that converts from Judaism were incompletely Christians – were perhaps proselytising to subvert the true religion which they had only superficially adopted – was used to justify some expulsions of the Jews. This was in some ways an answer to the problem, for by removing the old social systems those who wished to be truly Christians would have no other structures in which to participate.

While attitudes born of theological conflict between Judaism and Christianity were undeniably important in determining some aspects of the relationship between the two peoples, for those with the power to organise the links Christian ideas of *caritas* may also have played a part in some cases. The stereotype of the Jew as usurer developed mainly in the

---

[11] J. Cohen, 'The mentality of the medieval Jewish apostate: Peter Alfonsi, Hermann of Cologne, and Pablo Christiani', in *Jewish apostasy in the modern world*, ed. T. M. Endelman (New York and London, 1987), p. 23.

twelfth and thirteenth centuries, as the demands of secular governments boxed Jews into having no other occupation (except in Spain and parts of eastern Europe, where they seem to have been more economically active). Much of the vocal antipathy to Jews was based on that stereotype. However, while the stereotype certainly served to 'identify' the Jew, possibly the prime objection was not that the usurers were Jews, but that they were simply usurers: usury seems to have been the chief sin in the early stages of the transition to the money economy, stimulating extensive polemic and numerous *exempla*. The hostility to usury continued in later centuries: usurers were dragged before the church courts; the doctrine of the restitution of ill-gotten gains was applied specifically to usurious profits. Admittedly, Jewishness compounded the hostility: Jews could not be brought before the church courts, and were often supported in their exactions by secular governments which usually took much of the profit in taxes and by exploiting the notion of the Jew as a state serf; while in Italy it is noteworthy that Jews could not charge rates of interest anything like those demanded by Christian money-lenders. Yet perhaps most tellingly, in the debates over funding the public debts of Italian communes, and especially over the establishment of the charitable pawn-shops of the *Monti di pietà* which were meant to remove the need for borrowing from Jews, several major canonists came down forcefully against either the payment of interest (for the debts) or its collection (for the *Monti*). Both were condemned as usurious.

The attack on usury was thus directed at both Christians and Jews. In the early French edicts, where there were signs of real principles being stated rather than a cover for exploitation, the attacks on money-lending and the demand for expulsion apply to Christians as much as Jews. However, the Jews posed special problems, precisely because they were exempt from the normative arrangements of the ecclesiastical courts which determined matters affecting *caritas*. Obviously the various anti-Jewish decrees were framed in ways to exculpate their originators and show them in a good light; but the association of Jews with exploitation of Christians as an affront to *caritas* may have been seen as a valid form of attack.

The removal of Jews from large areas of Europe long before 1515 raises the intriguing question of awareness of Judaism and its spiritual impact in those places without Jewish inhabitants. By definition, formal accusations of ritual murder and host desecration could be levelled only against specific Jews. While the charges might pass into the general mythology of Jewishness, and while some tales might be completely apocryphal, if there were no Jews present then such accusations and the devotional practices they spawned simply could not arise. England may have originated the ritual murder charge; but after the expulsion of 1290 there could be no further accusations there and St William of Norwich, Little St Hugh of Lincoln, and the others, became figures of the past, incapable of replication even if their cults survived.

How appreciations and the impact of stereotypes changed in the absence of Jews is hard to determine. England was probably the only realm to expel all its Jews early enough for the issues to arise and evolve; although France – or regions of France – might pose the same problem by the early sixteenth century. England had witnessed all forms of anti-Jewish action before 1290: the first ritual murder charge had created the devotion to St William of Norwich in 1144; in 1189 York was the scene of one of the most notorious Jewish massacres of the middle ages. But what happened to the appreciation of the Jew in a Jewless land? Most of the evidence is necessarily literary; although there may have been instances of pseudo-Jewish fortune-tellers, like a woman encountered in Durham in 1503, who exploited ignorance (and perhaps fear) of Judaism for their own profit. The ritual murder accusation reappears in Chaucer's *Prioress's Tale*; Jews could not be excluded from the play cycles, with Herod as a ranting tyrant who swears by Mohammed; host desecration charges are the basis of the Croxton *Play of the Sacrament*. All the old elements of anti-Jewish myths are there; but how people reacted to them is not revealed – in the absence of Jews they could not really be incited to acts of forthright anti-semitism. Nor was it worth stirring up anti-Jewish sentiments in sermons, perhaps precisely because it could not be enacted. Yet latent anti-Jewish violence possibly existed: in the Castilian civil war of 1366–9, the English forces supporting Peter I massacred the Jews of Villadiego and Aguilar de Campo (the French soldiers of Henry of Trastamara likewise joined in the massacre of the Jewish community at Briviesca). These may have been simply displays of soldierly brutality, and the victims only accidentally Jews; but the alternative possibility cannot be avoided. The continuity of anti-Jewish sentiments in a Jewless Flanders certainly appears in fifteenth-century Flemish ballads. Indeed, it may be that by the end of the period, Christianity actually needed Jewish subversiveness even when there were no Jews present. The case of Jean Langlois, burnt at Paris in 1493 for rejecting aspects of Christianity supposedly after contact with the Jews of Avignon, has provoked the comment that 'unable to condemn real Jews . . . the Church caused the appearance of neo-Jews over which she gained the victory'.[12]

Nevertheless, in the absence of Jews the stereotype might change its function. 'Jews' might become merely archetypes of the opponents of

---

[12] J. Delumeau, *La peur en occident, XIVe – XVIIIe siècles: une cité assiegée* (Paris, 1978), p. 289.

Christ, transferable by analogy to other and more immediately perceived threats. That would apply most obviously with plays centring on host desecrations, like that of Croxton (written after 1461), where the play's defence of the doctrine of transubstantiation could be turned mentally against other detractors of the true faith; in the context of late medieval England these would be the Lollards.

Where Jews remained, that would not happen. The concern would be with the realities, rather than a dramatic enactment. In Castile the affair of the Holy Child of La Guardia in 1491 was no entertainment. Even though this most publicised of ritual murder accusations failed to produce a child's corpse, it left several Jews and *conversos* dead in its wake. The case was a prelude to the decree of 1492, the culmination of a century of developing tensions caused by the mass conversions of 1391 and after. In Castile after around 1450 questioning of *converso* commitment to Christianity became more intense, as the *conversos* were increasingly subjected to social and political vilification which may have been linked with the rise of a sense of Castilian – possibly 'Spanish' – identity which had strong anti-semitic features. The introduction of the new Inquisition in 1478–80 was one attempt to resolve the uncertainties created by the *converso* presence; but it was not a complete solution. After some regional expulsions within Castile, in 1492 the Jews were finally given the choice of conversion or exile, a policy also extended to Aragon. This was one of several expulsions around the Mediterranean during the last decades of the fifteenth century. The motives for the decree of 1492 seem to have been principally religious: a perception that the only way to secure the *conversos* for Christianity was to expel the Jews who continued to influence them. The decree's immediate impact on the Jewish and *converso* populations is still debated. Uncertainties about the size of the Jewish population in 1492 are only part of the problem. At one extreme it is claimed that 'the scale of conversions was impressive . . . possibly a half Spain's Jews converted'; yet others assert that 'The entire Jewish population left Spain'.[13] The *converso* population which remained after the expulsion obviously had not completely broken with its Jewish past. Many perhaps hankered for their old religion, as suggested by the outbreak of strongly Judaic Messianic expectation in 1500. However, by then the Inquisition had undeniable

---

[13] Both comments appear in *Spain and the Jews: the Sephardi experience, 1492 and after*, ed. E. Kedourie (London, 1992): H. Kamen, 'The expulsion: purpose and consequence', p. 84; H. Beinart, 'The conversos and their fate', p. 114. Kamen's calculation includes converted returnees of later years; these may include those forcibly converted in Portugal in 1497, which might allow the two comments to be reconciled to some degree.

but not irresistible jurisdiction over the new Christians: their hopes were literally reduced to ashes.

Even after these expulsions, catholic Europe was not devoid of Jews. Many Italian states did not expel them; they still remained in parts of Germany and the empire; the largest population was in Poland. There was even a continued Jewish presence at the heart of catholic Europe, in Rome itself, which survived under papal protection although subject to periodic ritual humiliation.

Islam

The catholic reaction to Islam was rather different from the reaction to Judaism. Even though the Turks were advancing in the Balkans from the mid fourteenth century, and by 1500 had reached the Hungarian frontier, only the Iberian pensinsula had extensive and direct experience of a Moslem presence, and was certainly the only area which had had to tolerate a Moslem minority of any size. Moslems were also known to Italians through their overseas trading colonies; through a minor Moslem presence in the south which persisted into the thirteenth century; and through the presence of Moslem slaves, some of whom adopted Christianity in due course. But this Moslem presence in Italy was nothing like as deep-rooted or wide-spread, or threatening (until the temporary Ottoman seizure of Otranto in 1480–1) as the presence in Spain. Obviously, too, Islam had been the numerically dominant religion in the Kingdom of Acre; but that kingdom's elimination in 1291 removed the issue. (In the other crusader states, the principality of Antioch and the county of Tripoli, the majority of the population may have been non-catholic Christians rather than Moslems.) Moslems would still be encountered by travellers, especially by pilgrims to the Holy Land; but how much impact that experience actually made in other than pilgrimage terms cannot be assessed. Even in areas which were conquered, reaction to Islam was generally muted; making it easy to forget on the basis of western material that these were originally, and sometimes still actually, non-Christian territories. Where the religious divide was so fundamental that compromise was inconceivable, and the Latin Christians were in no position to impose their views, the only recourse was what has been labelled an 'ideology of silence'.[14]

---

[14] C. J. Halperin, 'The ideology of silence: prejudice and pragmatism on the medieval religious frontier', *Comparative studies in society and history*, 26 (1984), pp. 442–66. Halperin sees this as a common feature of what he calls 'religious conquest societies'. It may apply in specific instances, 'in which rulers and ruled practiced rival exclusivist religions'

Even in Spain, the distribution of Moslems (known as *mudejars*) was patchy. As the frontiers of Castile and Aragon moved southwards in the thirteenth century, so at first they corralled a relatively large Moslem population, to be integrated or not. Later revolts meant that some of those who had initially stayed were driven out or fled: by 1400 Castile's Islamic population was small and scattered, being only some 17–20,000 by 1500. These were clustered in the south-east of the country: Moslems were perhaps as rare in Asturias as they were in Scandinavia. In the realms of the crown of Aragon the presence was more substantial because of the nature of the thirteenth-century conquest, the biggest concentration being in Valencia. It has been estimated that, by the late fourteenth century, Moslems comprised a third of the population of Aragon proper, some 3 per cent in Catalonia, and two-thirds of the population in Valencia.[15] Even by 1500, Moslems constituted almost a third of Valencia's population, and Arabic was still spoken. The completion of the Christian Reconquest in the seizure of the kingdom of Granada in 1492 suddenly increased Castile's Moslem population by some 250–300,000, in a highly localised concentration which would need to be integrated and if possible converted to Christianity.

Outside Mediterranean areas, contact with and proper awareness of Islam was effectively non-existent. While there was doubtless awareness of the existence of another non-Christian faith, its content was virtually unknown. In the vocabulary of medieval England, a faith which was certainly not idolatrous could provide the words for a form of idolatry (mawmetry) and for the dolls and images (mommets) used by children and misused by pagans. Nevertheless, antipathy to Islam was ensured by the lingering concern for crusade: from 1300 Spain was a welcome alternative to the Holy Land for those anxious to fight for the faith, with a constant trickle of non-Spaniards to attack Granada. For them, perhaps, any Moslem was an enemy who had to be fought, threatening the *convivencia* which had been established beyond the frontiers in Spain. Certainly when a French force passed through Navarre in 1341 *en route* to support Alfonso XI at Algeciras, the *mudejar* quarter of Tudela had to be protected against them.

Reaction to the Jewish presence had burst into violence and forced conversions in the pogroms of 1391, but nothing similar is recorded for

---

(p. 442), but seems less applicable to the Latin expansion into the Baltic areas, or the Orthodox territories subjected to Latin rule.

[15] R. I. Burns, 'Muslims in the thirteenth-century realms of Aragon: interaction and reaction', in *Muslims under Christian rule, 1100–1300*, ed. J. M. Powell (Princeton, NJ, 1990), p. 94.

the Moors until the last decades of the period. While many *mudejars* were reduced to serfdom, if not slavery, there is little sign of any concern to ensure their conversion; indeed their religious autonomy was often guaranteed in the surrender documents of the Reconquest. The lack of interest in conversion may also have been due to the Moslems' servile status: conversion in Aragon would have deprived their lords of a valuable resource, and so was not tolerated. (Paradoxically, however, Christians seem to have protected Moslems who defected to Judaism.)

The scale of the Moslem presence in Aragon made them a force to be reckoned with. In 1311 the Council of Vienne decreed that muezzins should no longer be allowed to issue the call to Moslem prayers in Christian realms; but this was strongly resisted in Valencia, by the king as well as by the barons who wanted to retain the loyalty of their tenants. Even when the ban was reiterated by local clerics, at the synod of Tortosa in 1360, and in the *corts* of Valencia in 1371, the crown considered compliance impolitic. However, willingness to enforce a ban may have increased as the Moslem population declined: the Aragonese kings were enforcing it in the fifteenth century.

Undoubtedly there were some real conversions in the Iberian realms, at all levels of society from peasant farmers in northern Portugal to the former ruler of Valencia, and provision was made for the converts in the legal codes. But conversions do not seem to have been numerous. Nor did Islam make much general impact on Christian perceptions, except in the case of renegades. There was a *mudejar* religious literature in the fifteenth century, but there is no sign that Christians were affected by it, or even aware of its existence. The fall of Granada in 1492 dramatically changed perceptions. Geopolitical considerations in the peninsula were altered; the coincidental expulsion of those Jews who refused to convert to Christianity perhaps showed a way forward. Initially the Christian approach to Granada was one of relatively gentle mission: *mudejar* status had been guaranteed, but Christian institutions and ecclesiastical structures were extended to the newly conquered territory. The Christian authorities under Granada's first archbishop, Hernando de Talavera, do seem to have sought a proper programme of conversion, acknowledging the linguistic problems and trying to provide preaching and instruction in Arabic. In the long run, the insufficiency of the parish clergy doomed this scheme to failure. In the short run, within a decade of the conquest, the *modus vivendi* collapsed as the Christian attitude hardened and the surrender agreements were ignored. Crass intervention by Cardinal Cisneros in 1499 provoked a major Moslem rebellion. For the Christians that justified the abrogation of the surrender accords: in 1502 the Moslems were offered the choice granted to the Jews in 1492, to convert or leave.

The decree's wording preserved the religious justification, in that Moslems were being expelled to prevent subversion of the faith of the newly converted; but logistical restrictions on departure made conversion the only real option. The majority therefore 'converted', to adopt a conformist outward Christianity while retaining (perhaps more self-consciously than the Jewish *conversos*) the practices of their 'abandoned' religion. However, 'the conversion of 1501 only entailed a change in the juridical status of the Moslems, because the same problems which had arisen between the Mudejars and the Christians continued to exist, getting worse day by day.'[16] Wiping out the formal Moslem presence created the problem of the Moriscos.

Granada was primarily a Castilian problem; but Moslems existed in every Iberian realm. The catholic nationalism and concern for 'religious cleansing' which was coming to a head in late-fifteenth-century Castile could be exported elsewhere. In fact the first formal expulsion of *mudejars* was from Portugal in 1497, when under Castilian pressure the free Moslems were given the choice of conversion or exile – many left for Castile! In 1515, after Castile's annexation of southern Navarre, the small *mudejar* community there was given the same choice: they moved to Aragon. By 1515 Aragon was the only Spanish realm with an explicitly Moslem population, and that fairly large. Moreover, the Aragonese lords had made King Ferdinand promise not to impose conversion on this Islamic remnant. Perhaps it was the case that the further from the military frontier, the more pacific the relationships between the religions were. Certainly the generally peaceful contacts between Christians and Moslems within the crown of Aragon are notable, after the initial settling down from the conquest. However, despite the co-existence, the religious differences could not be totally elided. Islam could not be other than the enemy – especially when it was also politically an opponent, whether in Granada or the Turkish Mediterranean advance. The political ramifications of the religious divide were considerable. In the crisis of the reign of Henry IV of Castile in 1465, his pro-Moorish affectations were used against him; he was even accused of trying to persuade Christians to apostasise. Late-fifteenth-century Spaniards would have been aware of the Turkish advance in mainland Europe; fears of co-ordinated action by Granada, Turks, and *mudejars* naturally induced jitters. As long as the Moslem political presence in Granada and Spanish ambitions in North Africa could justify crusade, there would be anti-Islamic preaching, which might stir up Christians against the Moors within as well as those

---

[16] J. C. de Miguel Rodriguez, *Los mudéjares de la corona de Castilla*, Cuadernos de investigacion medieval, 8 (Madrid, 1988), p. 76.

without. Awareness of the dangers is evident in attempts by Aragonese rulers to limit the incendiary nature of such preaching, and punishment of those who went too far. Yet local Christians could probably differentiate between 'locals' and 'the enemy', if they wanted to. In Valencia in 1496–7, anti-Moorish violence seems to have been directed solely against North Africans, not Valencians. Nevertheless, there are signs of popular Christian antipathy to the *mudejars* in the 1520s. This was perhaps more economically and socially motivated than spiritual, with the anti-*mudejar* violence of the *Germanias* primarily seeking to undermine noble economic power. It seems, on the whole, that Christian-*mudejar* conflict was ancillary to wider social and economic problems, which over-strained society and in such circumstances made the religious distinction the identifying characteristic of the scapegoat and victim. In the *Germanias mudejars* were forcibly baptised by the rebels, sometimes as a preliminary to being massacred. The theologians insisted that the baptisms were valid; and Aragon thereby acquired its own Morisco population, although the final conversion edict was not promulgated until 1526, without the option of exile.

The problem of scapegoats

While the authorities were much exercised about the presence of heretics and members of other religions in catholic lands, hints suggest that ordinary catholics did not always share those anxieties. The *convivencia* in Spain was very real, with frequent legislation to try to curtail Christian patronage of Jewish or Moslem butchers, while the clothing regulations seem to have been treated very laxly. There was even some intellectual overlap, at least with the Jews. A Castilian version of Maimonides' *Guide for the perplexed* was available in the fifteenth century, while the spread of kabbalistic studies among humanists of Renaissance Italy secured a cross-fertilisation between the two cultures in their Messianic expectations. Elsewhere, the small size of many Jewish communities – there were only three 'households' in Trent at the time of the ritual-murder trial of 1475 – meant that they constantly mixed with their Christian neighbours. What is often notable is the lack of overt hostility: that usually had to be orchestrated in times of social and economic unrest which caused the religious 'other' to be penalised as the scapegoat. 'Popular' identifications of the heretical – or the Jewish – might differ from those advanced by the ecclesiastical and other authorities. To call someone a 'heretic' was a blanket accusation; often a sign of general opprobrium rather than a charge of formal doctrinal deviation. It might therefore be riposted by an action for defamation in the church courts, rather than embarking on the full procedures of a heresy trial. Similarly, with Jewishness, popular antipathy to the *conversos* in fifteenth-century Spain may have been mainly a political phenomenon, which exaggerated the extent to which the *conversos* had retained Jewish customs in order to legitimise social conflict; whereas the church hierarchs were prepared to be rather more tolerant. In Spain there are indications that Jews were integrated within the wider Christian society: attempts to segregate them constantly failed; and in some places Jewish rituals were accorded a status almost equivalent to Christian sacramentals, with the exposition of the Torah being treated as a rain-making ceremony to benefit everyone. In thirteenth-century England, Christian women who had been employed by Jews as servants and wetnurses refused to abandon their jobs even when placed under excommunication. The Jews of fifteenth-century Trent gambled with their neighbours and employed Christian midwives.

The anxiety about the erosion of Christianity because of over-close contacts with non-catholics certainly did tax the authorities. This fear of the subversion of Christianity was one of the prime directives in reactions to the internal minorities. The major drive to convert the Moslem settlement at Lucera in southern Italy, initiated in 1233, was perhaps stimulated by the fear that their use of Italian as their normal language might result in the undermining of local Christianity. While Christians can be condemned for failing to convert and integrate the minorities, the aim may have been precisely to ensure that they remained identifiable as minorities, excluded by their own customs, languages, and practices. That the maintenance of barriers preserved Christianity could have been considered more important than that those barriers prevented conversion.

The determination to maintain barriers also accounts for the legislation against Christians being slaves to Jews and Moslems, or even working for them as servants. Hence, also, the demand that non-catholics wear some distinguishing mark. The enemy within had to be visible, so that Christians could be on their guard against seduction. This, however, raises issues of identification and stereotyping. The insistence that Jews, Moslems, and heretics wear a special mark suggests that often that was their only identifying sign. Clearly this would be so with heretics, as full members of the same community; but the application to Jews and Moslems suggests wider issues, primarily that the distinctions were not being made on overtly racial grounds. How far that can be sustained is unclear: the intermarriage of converts and Old Christians was certainly a feature of Mediterranean societies, and the numerous offspring of slaves and Christian masters must also had blurred the racial barriers. Racial distinctions between Christians and Moslems in most reconquered areas of Spain must have been minimal. Perhaps that explains attempts to ensure that religious identity was not obscured in other, more subtle, ways. Thirteenth- and fourteenth-century Spanish legislation banned the use of 'Christian' names by Jews and Moslems: a name was to be a proclamation of religious identity, part of the process of ensuring the distinction between the included and the excluded. However, a sense of racial difference cannot be totally denied. The emergence in the fifteenth-century of the idea of *limpieza de sangre* (purity of blood), especially when directed against converts from Judaism, introduced a more blatantly racial element to anti-semitism; while it seems that in Castile and Aragon North Africans were always assumed to be Moslems, and were therefore more often victimised than 'native' Moslems.

The enemy could only be recognised if easily identified. Lax enforcement of the legislation imposing segregation and distinction must have weakened awareness of the differences. In any case, heretics could operate for years before being detected and flung out of the church – having built up their flocks. Those with authority, perhaps primarily as parish priests, could spread their ideas widely as orthodoxy, without their followers being aware of the faults until revealed by chance at a visitation. Possibly even more dangerous was the threat of subversion from those who were newly Christians, and who retained their old intellectual traditions after baptism. That may have been part of the problem of the *conversos*, retaining habits of Jewish exegesis and Messianic expectations which were incompatible with contemporary norms for the Old Christians (although they too had their Messianic expectations).

The devil and his disciples

Most of the enemies which Latin Christianity confronted on its own territory were self-identifying: they formally rejected the dictates of catholicism by espousing their own definitions of Christianity or a totally different religion. There was one other enemy who had to be faced, the perennial enemy of the human race but for whose agency the whole saga of redemption would have been unnecessary: Satan.

Although a few rash individuals dismissed the devil – along with Hell and Purgatory – as mere priestly fantasies confected to terrify ordinary Christians into obedience, there is little reason to doubt that belief in Satan was part of the normality of religion, or that the devil was seen as working actively to deprive people of their salvation. Indeed, demons were treated as part of the physical creation, as capable of being controlled and exploited by humans for their own purposes. The charge that he had a domesticated demon was one of the many accusations hurled against Pope Boniface VIII (1296–1303) by his enemies. In the purely spiritual sphere, encounters with the devil were usually personal, and confined to matters of temptation and the struggle for the soul on the deathbed. For theologians, however, Satan's presence was more ubiquitous, especially for inquisitors whose careers entailed frequent contact with those apparently under his sway. The first mention of a Satanic cult appears with the career of Conrad of Marburg as first inquisitor in Germany, in papal bulls of 1232–3. Later inquisitors' attempts to extend their powers over sorcery were resisted: their domain was heresy, they could act against sorcery only if it was associated with heresy. The developing science of demonology and awareness of sorcery was manifested in the attacks on the Templars after 1307; but only in 1326 was sorcery formally assimilated to heresy and brought under the inquisition's remit. The demonisation of magic which resulted both led to a greater insistence on Satanism in sorcery – as opposed to the purely practical magic which was not part of the theological tradition – and to the evolution of the idea of a demonic anti-church which had its own rituals and cult practices. The concern about Satan as a real actor in human affairs grew considerably from the later fourteenth century, in parallel with developing apocalyptic expectations, allowing fear of the diabolic to merge with other tensions which had horrific long-term consequences.

Magic was a given in Christian Europe, offering a means of controlling nature in parallel with Christian practices. After 1400, for reasons not fully clarified, uses of magic which previously had been denounced as ignorant and misguided began to attract attention as diabolic and Satanic. If there is a sphere in which an 'élite' culture created a specific spiritual concern, it is probably here, for the formulations used against witchcraft as Satanism originated among preachers and theologians. The late fourteenth and fifteenth centuries witnessed a flurry of texts on demons and devil-worship which contributed to the overall picture; texts such as the *Directorium inquisitorum* of Nicholas Eymerich (written in 1376), or the *Formicarius* of the Dominican Johannes Nider (written 1435–7). Bernardino of Siena instigated a hunt for witches in Siena in 1427; the classic witch-hunter's textbook, the *Malleus malificorum*, was produced by two Dominican inquisitors in 1486. The printing of these works secured a wide audience for them, spreading the stereotypes and the fears more effectively than would otherwise have happened. The stereotype of the witch, as broadcast in later centuries, owed much to the traditional bogey of the heretic, with the practices ascribed to them – cannibalism, child-murder, sexual orgies, and desecration of Christian symbols – repeating allegations made about heretical sects for centuries. That most of those eventually accused were women only adds to the range of tensions and anxieties which the accusations reflected.

The development of witchcraft accusations before 1515 again raises questions about popular appreciations, especially in the context of religious and spiritual practices. After all, some charges may well have been levelled by dissatisfied clients. In many late medieval trials the Satanistic charges seem to be added to the original accusations. Cases might start as mere sorcery, brought by a supposed victim or dissatisfied commissioner of ordinary magic; but in the hands of the inquisitors – and their torturers – the specific became generalised, the magic became Satanic, the wise woman became a witch. The devil became a necessary agent in sorcery because somehow magic had to be explained, and if God was not the co-operating force then Satan was the only theologically acceptable alternative.

CHRISTIAN SOCIETY

Tensions

Questions of inclusion and exclusion were not just matters of mission and reaction to challenges from religious outsiders. They also arose among catholics, often in ways which do not seem to be very closely allied to religious or devotional matters. Awareness of church membership stressed other forms of participation and unification, from the national downwards; and assisted the growth of divisions between the segments. The developing cults of national saints played a clear part in this, especially in the fifteenth century: patrons helped to identify their clients, and when the clients of St Michael were the kings of France and their subjects, and the clients of St George the kings of England and theirs, this only reinforced divisions within Europe. Any group identified itself partly through its religious and devotional practices, especially the communities of parish, chapelry, guild, and fraternity. Each, in its own way, identified a community – even if only a community of interest – and distinguished it from others which might be rivals. It is therefore unsurprising that many of the disputes between local communities in the later middle ages rested on questions of submission to ecclesiastical definition: chapelries which sought independence from a mother church, or mother-churches which tried to dominate lesser units. Beyond these contrasting communities (the rivalries of fraternities and guilds are also important), religious practices also operated inclusively in processions and collective devotions. A local procession asserted identity, possibly, as in some towns, transcending other jurisdictional boundaries; nationally, processions to avert plague, or secure the health of a monarch, stated inclusion within a larger entity. The arrangements for these processions made other proclamations, with the local hierarchy being restated by the ordering of the participants. Processions and public celebrations thus had a declaratory function, stating public (or the ruling group's) perceptions of organisation, or group-identity. This could also cause discord. Processions were public demonstrations of a fixed order; any challenge to that order by a parish seeking to change its place in a Pentecostal procession or a guild disputing its position in the urban ranking as manifested in a Corpus Christi procession threatened disorder. Events intended to demonstrate peaceful hierarchy, social organisation, communal unity and cohesion might, and often did, become occasions of unruly fracas and conflict.

The idea of a Christian society also generated other tensions. Christianity as a social imperative, demanding social action, had ideals which often contrasted with the realities of contemporary life. Those ideals, as things of the spirit, had to face the facts of the world. There Christians actually lived, there they played off the demands of survival in this world and survival in the next. As catholicism had to exist within the real world, and reach some accord with the realities found there, it came up against challenges to its appeal as the universal cement between humans. The compromises which had to be developed in the confrontation with worldly realities in turn generated tensions which questioned the church's ability and willingness to be fully inclusive. Some of these features have been built into the idea of the formation of a 'persecuting society' by 1250, in which Jews, lepers, and homosexuals (as well as heretics) were the prime victims.[17] However, the notion of a 'persecuting society' also brings into focus tensions which existed between the lip-service to religion and the reality of spiritual and social forces. A persecuting society need not reflect a persecuting religion, although separating the two can be difficult; especially if distinctions were formulated in primarily religious terms.[18] In their concern for self-preservation or self-justification, people sometimes openly contradicted their theoretical spiritual stances.

Further apparent contradictions between Christian precept and practice arose from other social issues. Historians have to respond to these; but contemporaries perhaps were relatively untroubled because they had argued round them sufficiently convincingly for their own needs. Difficulties about poverty would be high on the list; the elevation of 'God's poor' on the one hand contrasting with the increasingly harsh and discriminatory attitude to mendicants and vagabonds as social threats and economic exploiters which becomes more noticeable after 1350 but

---

[17] R. I. Moore, *The formation of a persecuting society* (Oxford, 1987).
[18] Above, p. 259.

may have existed, in some cases, long before. With lepers, as in other instances, the problem of the connection between spiritual motivations and social discrimination is very real. It can be extended to attitudes to slavery and serfdom, and most significantly for numbers and current historiographical concerns, to women.

An excluding church: excommunication and interdict

The testing of social and power relations in the evolution of the relationship between the church and the surrounding society has its more precisely ecclesiastical manifestation in the way in which the church authorities sought to maintain disciplinary control over their flocks through their own processes of exclusion, through excommunication and interdict. As punishment for sin and the refusal to acknowledge the church's authority, primarily as exercised through the ecclesiastical courts, excommunication was usually only a short-term weapon. However, the numerous breaches of canon law which brought automatic and possibly unwitting excommunication meant that many may have incurred it for some time without realising their predicament. Moreover, some would always remain obdurate, either because they thought the sentence unjust, or invalid; while over-use of the weapon would reduce its effectiveness. Excommunication gained its potency in two ways: personally, through an individual's fear of being deprived of the church's sacramental solace, perhaps mainly the exclusion from deathbed absolution; and socially, in the exclusion from society which followed from the legal and customary impediments to business activities and involvement in litigation which were imposed on the culprit. Excommunication rippled through a society: contact with an excommunicate incurred excommunication, the consequences spreading through a community until eventually all social links dissolved, in theory. In some cases, excommunication was taken to have more immediate and perceptible effects. Here regional responses perhaps varied, especially when excommunications were allied to other maledictions. In the diocese of Llandaff, the 'excommunication of St Teilo' was considered particularly effective: a record of its promulgation against those who infringed the rights of the cathedral church in 1410 noted that 'within a few days seven persons who had thus transgressed went wildly insane, and remained that way for the rest of their lives'.[19]

The reaction to such punishments is often hard to determine, because there are few appropriate records. Excommunication might be so easily

[19] L. K. Little, 'Spiritual sanctions in Wales', in *Images of sainthood in medieval Europe*, ed. R. Blumenfeld-Kosinski and T. Szell (Ithaca and London, 1991), p. 79.

incurred that it became ineffective. Those who felt unjustly punished might feel embittered; some would use the fact of their excommunication as a weapon. If an excommunicate was in church, the services had to halt: what better way to gain revenge than to insist on going to church, thereby preventing others from receiving the sacraments as well? Administrative inefficiency doubtless also undermined the effectiveness of the punishments. In the mid thirteenth century, Pope Innocent IV counselled against further excommunications in Toulouse as they were simply ignored; however, in southern France the formal excommunication of Cathar heretics who explicitly denied the church's jurisdictional authority was perhaps a rather futile action anyway. Where excommunication was imposed as a partisan act – as during the Great Schism – its validity would again be challenged or ignored.

An important aspect of excommunication was that it often operated more as a social than spiritual phenomenon. From 1245 canon law held that excommunication was soul-threatening only if it was ignored or resisted; that is, if nothing was done to have it rescinded by absolution. In some ways, the authorities here recognised a basic weakness in their stance. They could only declare excommunication as an earthly sentence; as with sainthood, they could not assume that their sentences exactly coincided with God's. The result was that the excommunicate was ostracised, but remained technically part of the overall Christian body. As such he or she perhaps posed greater theoretical problems than those of other religions, although legists could work their way around most of them. As a primarily legal state, excommunication became a legal weapon, which could be used by parties against each other with no regard for its spiritual implications. It may have been chiefly used to enforce contracts; certainly the threat backed up debts registered before the dean and chapter of York in the early fourteenth century; while dead excommunicate debtors might be denied burial until their executors had made fit satisfaction. Excommunication was also invoked against those who broke political compromises; while the appreciation of its status as a primarily legal and social sanction is most stunningly indicated by its being used even against Jews – clearly against them the spiritual punishment was ineffective, but the social ostracism was still a powerful constraint for the settlement of disputes.

Interdict, the church's other main disciplinary weapon, formally banned religious services in the affected area, including burials in consecrated ground and masses for souls. Its potency was mainly personal: to make people fear for the health of their souls because they were deprived of the sacraments. Like excommunication, interdict could provoke resentment, especially if seen as being exploited by clerics for their own purposes. The cyclical battles over clerical immunities in German cities often climaxed in an interdict, a weapon to which there was usually no effective lay response. The complete cessation of church services usually brought the laity to heel, although doubtless increasing the resentment in the process. The main threat to clerical solidarity usually came from venality, and from the institutional rivalry between the secular and mendicant clergy, with the latter sometimes continuing their services despite the decree.

On the other hand, collective obstinacy could be a potent weapon against such ecclesiastical censures. The diocese of Utrecht was under interdict for three years from 1428 and 1431; Italian communes often incurred the ban, for varied reasons (often linked to papal schemes to establish effective political control over the papal states). Yet the power of the keys was not usually easily ignored. Even if a bold face was maintained, the resulting disruption could be severe. Florence, for instance, was under interdict from 1376 to 1378, which proved a particularly trying experience, threatening the city's commercial standing and encouraging revolt among the subject towns of the contado.

What was striking about the Florentine interdict of 1376–8 was its impact on the city's spiritual life. While there was a party which wished to break the interdict by simply ignoring it (a tactic which occasionally worked elsewhere, sometimes even in Florence), that proved impossible: when the interdict was broken, it stirred up even more controversy and proved counter-productive from the government's standpoint. Most people were not prepared to threaten their souls by taking such extreme action (a caution which reappeared later: Savonarola's support dwindled on his excommunication because people feared the spiritual consequences of continued association with him). They seem to have compensated by an upsurge of more private, non-ecclesial devotions, notably penitential processions, including mass flagellation, and an increase in confraternity activity – activities which, by their avoidance of the need for priestly action, perhaps were even more threatening to the church's institutional standing. The interdict also affected testamentary practices: as parish churches could not supply masses for souls, alternative provision was made with houses of religious orders not subject to the ban. Yet interdict, like excommunication, had its drawbacks for the church. The cessation of much devotional activity was detrimental for many of the clergy, especially the unbeneficed. A lengthy interdict could lead to the withdrawal of clerics from the affected place, sometimes under orders from the hierarchs, with the result that the dearth of services would outlast the interdict. Moreover, the suspension of orthodox devotional activities might permit the incursion of heresy. This was certainly a problem in

Florence in 1376–8, where the withdrawal of official services allowed members of the *fraticelli* (the descendants of the Spiritual Franciscans) to spread their message. Similar problems had appeared in the early thirteenth century, when interdicts on other Italian towns, including Assisi, had allowed increased activity by the Cathars.

Lepers

The tensions produced by the ambiguity of inclusion and exclusion, by the problem of an avowedly Christian persecuting society, perhaps become most obvious in the treatment of lepers. They became the victims of a form of moral panic from the twelfth century onwards, their affliction becoming a key component of the vocabulary of rejection. Fear of contagion produced a policy of segregation, which in the circumstances acquired institutional formats which were almost unavoidably religious. Leprosy was seen as the fruit of sin, in some cases a divine punishment: Henry IV of England was said to have incurred the disease as punishment for his judicial murder of Archbishop Scrope of York in 1405. Whatever the illness actually was – many 'lepers' may not have suffered from what is now medically identified as leprosy – its victims were put through a rite of exclusion which was effectively a funeral service. In some forms this was held in an open grave, others incorporated a figurative burial by casting earth over the leper's feet. Lepers were then denied further immediate contact with almost everyone, presumably also with the sacraments unless they inhabited a leper hospital or were served by a leprous priest. The way of life enjoined on them thenceforth was manifestly penitential: those living individually had their closest parallel in anchorites; those living collectively in hospitals were given a strict rule of life and devotional exercises which matched those of other hospitals.

However, there is inconsistency and ambiguity in the treatment of lepers. It is debatable whether the exclusion was primarily a spiritual or a social act – and even whether it was the latter, as those who broke hospital regulations could be expelled back into the community which had theoretically rejected them. As in other cases, regional and chrono-logical developments affect the picture. The orders for the seclusion of lepers seem to cluster in northern France and England, and refer specifically to the seclusion of individuals in their own remote cells rather than to admission to a hospital. They also post-date the Black Death. Perhaps, then, they reflect the late medieval concern with death, and the changes necessitated in provision by the decline of leprosy as a wide-spread disease. On the other hand, the effectiveness of the seclusion process is questionable. In Normandy, several 'lepers' apparently remained living among the healthy despite repeated denunciations to the ecclesiastical authorities. Possibly lepers were also more tolerated in rural areas than in towns: there fears of contagion were presumably more violently expressed.

In another perspective, lepers took on characteristics of God's poor, suffering perhaps more than most a living Purgatory, each an incarnate *memento mori*, a reminder both of that Lazarus raised back to life by Jesus (but, according to tradition, without a full reversal of the decomposition he had suffered in death) and of the other Lazarus dependent on charity at the rich man's gate. Leprosy might even be justified as a sign of divine election. The seclusion liturgies provide hints of this, with the leper's receipt of the insignia of his affliction, the uniform, clapper, and bowl, being almost akin to a religious profession. In such a state, lepers also acquired a right to charity, which is also reflected in the liturgies when some of the French versions impose on the churchwardens an obligation to provide sustenance for the isolated leper as an act of charity. Indeed, for some people, service to lepers became a spiritual ambition; and association with them, following a model provided by St Francis, one of the marks of a putative saint.

Serfs and slaves

Some apparent contradictions between Christian precept and practice lay at the very heart of the medieval social system, especially when related to lordship and dominance. The evolution of 'feudal' society raised the issue of serfdom, in which individuals were legally bound to a particular territorial lordship, being deprived of legal rights and required to acknowledge subservience through a range of economic obligations, social restrictions, and limitations on their freedom of action. Serfdom evolved over time; but it always had the elements of seigneurial exploitation and legal incapacity (so that manumission, freedom, was the acquisition of legal identity as much as release from exploitation). The issue of serfdom's compatibility with Christianity became prominent when serfdom was most threatened, and perhaps when it was also on the rise, as in eastern Europe in the fifteenth century. It can be set alongside a slightly different problem, of the persistence of slavery in many Mediterranean areas.

Of the two, serfdom was less problematic, although it did raise ethical issues about domination which taxed some clerics and the serfs much more than the lords. Late medieval attacks on lordship often sought justification in Christian ethics, as in the Biblical undertones to the complaints in the German reform tract of *c.* 1438, the *Reformatio Sigismundi*. In heartfelt prose, this proclaimed that

It is an incredible outrage that there should be in Christendom today a state of affairs where one man may say to another, before God, 'You are my property!' as though we were pagans . . . God himself has removed all bonds from us, and no one should be so bold as to claim ownership of a fellow being . . . [W]hoever calls himself a Christian and holds other men in bondage, let him either emancipate them voluntarily, or else be stripped of his goods and chattels and made to do penance.[20]

Defenders of serfdom sometimes did justify it on specifically religious grounds. The servile status of the Jews was ascribed to their failure to acknowledge Christ. In the fifteenth century, Catalan serfdom was justified on the ground that the serfs descended from Christians whose pusillanimity when the Carolingians urged them to rise against their Moslem lords had validated the transfer of lordship to the new conquerors as punishment; the integration of status into a divinely ordained plan must have impacted on the serfs' relationship with God, although the lack of any statements from the serfs' side hides their feelings. The rise of serfdom in central and eastern Europe in the fifteenth century may also have affected matters – it might be expected to alter parochial organisations and communal religious practices – but so far the issues have not apparently been investigated.

Slavery posed more insistent questions. As the individual slave was merely a chattel, held in full ownership rather than merely being subjected to exploitation, slavery differed from serfdom and raised different issues. Slavery had died out in northern Europe before 1200, but remained a feature of Mediterranean societies, persisting in the Iberian realms, Italy, the eastern Mediterranean and around the Black Sea and, while they lasted, in the Crusader states. It was not a static phenomenon, major changes occuring particularly in the areas from which slaves were obtained. In the slave markets of Sicily, Saracens were the main group sold in the period 1280–1310, giving way to Greeks from 1310 to 1360, and thereafter to Tartars until black Africans became prominent from the 1440s. However, at the western end of the Mediterranean, north Africans probably predominated throughout; at the eastern end peoples from the Balkans and around the Black Sea. In some places, slavery perhaps became more common as time passed: it was re-established in Florence only in 1363, and swiftly spread throughout Tuscany; while the opening of West Africa increased slavery in Portugal, and paved the way for the Atlantic expansion.

Initially, slavery was incompatible with Christianity. Until around

---

[20] G. Strauss, ed., *Manifestations of discontent in Germany on the eve of the Reformation* (Bloomington and London, 1971), p. 24.

1230, it was assumed that a slave who became a Christian would be freed: Christian slaves were theoretically inconceivable, unless slavery was imposed as a punishment. (In practical terms, Christian slaves must have been common in earlier centuries, especially if western society remained primarily a slave society until the late tenth century.) The traditional equation of freedom and Christianity persisted in some areas, notably Catalonia. Elsewhere the situation was altered by a papal ruling of 1238 which allowed the baptism of slaves without changing their juridical status. This legitimisation of Christian slavery doubtless eased consciences in places like Italy where slave populations were fairly large, at least in towns, into the fifteenth century. In Genoa in 1381, for instance, some 15 per cent of the inhabitants may have been slaves. The proportion of slaves in the population was admittedly falling: in 1328 Majorca's slave population was 36 per cent, but in rural areas was down to 18 per cent a century later. The one major restriction was that Christian slaves should not be owned by Jews or Moslems, but this may have been surreptitiously circumvented at times. Possibly because it was part of the inherited social and economic pattern, slavery as such was relatively unchallenged throughout the period. However, signs of a changing attitude appeared at some levels as Christendom's expansion to the Americas and the rise of the Atlantic slave trade led to doubts about both developments. At Santo Domingo in Hispaniola in 1511 the Dominican Antonio Montesimos preached vehemently against the oppressions of slavery, to the indifference if not hostility of his slave-owning audience. This nevertheless sparked off a major debate on the rights of native peoples which taxed Spanish intellectuals throughout the sixteenth century.

Until the late fifteenth century, most slaves were Moslems, chiefly North Africans. There were regional variations, with Tartars being common in Italy. Some were Slavs, and therefore Orthodox in religion; while others were imported from the Caucasus region, and might similarly be non-catholic Christians. Criminal catholics might also be condemned to servitude. Questions about the compatibility of slavery and Christianity did cause some tensions. Florence's slavery laws at first banned trade in Christian slaves; but this soon changed. Slaves imported into Florentine territory were almost automatically baptised on arrival: race swiftly replaced religion in the definitions. Religious discrimination may well have applied at the ports of embarkation. At the Genoese colony of Kaffa in the Crimea (and presumably elsewhere) slaves were meant to be inspected by the local ecclesiastical authorities, who would claim all catholics and others who declared a willingness to convert. Their juridical status may not have been seriously affected: many do appear to have been resold, presumably to other catholics. Of the remainder, the key issue seems to have been to prevent Christians – presumably non-catholics – from falling into the hands of Jews or Moslems.

Setting aside the problem of slaves who were already Christians, the tensions surrounding slavery merge into the tensions between Christianity and Islam. In the early thirteenth century Jacques de Vitry complained that Christian lords in Palestine were oppressing their slaves and preventing their conversion to Christianity because that would entail automatic liberation. In Sicily in 1310, King Frederick III legislated that lords should allow their slaves to be baptised, but guaranteed that their legal status would be unaffected. Property rights had to be preserved, at the cost of spiritual principles. This could be an opportunity for other means of 'conversion': the same laws stipulated the baptism of the off-spring of Moslem slaves, a practice also adopted elsewhere. The contrast between property rights and religious principles was perhaps most bluntly revealed in Aragon, where conversion to Christianity of Moslems tied to the soil was much opposed by their owners, who sometimes sought compensation from the church for their losses. After the forced conversion of the Granadan Moslems, the Aragonese magnates sought assurances from King Ferdinand that a similar policy would not be adopted in his realms.

The complexities of attitudes towards slavery are well demonstrated in the Portuguese treatment of slaves imported from West Africa. The trade's expansion in the fifteenth century had initially been justified as a 'crusade', to legitimise enslavement of the vanquished; but from 1455 a major theoretical support for the trade, buttressed by a papal bull, was that the slaves were open to Christianisation. Despite the ideal there is little sign of a real attempt to convert all these African slaves. Only in 1513, at the instigation of King Manoel I, were steps taken to ensure that baptism was made available; from 1514 it had to be offered to all imported or Portuguese-born slaves, except for those over ten who formally declined the offer. The order's effectiveness is questionable, but an attempt had been made. Moreover, Christian slaves could not be owned by Jews or Moslems (in theory impossible anyway after 1497, with the compulsory conversions of that year). An Italian visitor to Portugal in the 1530s remarked that blacks were enslaved because of their colour and Moslems because of their religion; but Christianity did have a certain cachet. Black Christians had the same opportunities as whites to indulge in religious practices, even establishing their own confraternities, usually dedicated to the Rosary. That at Lisbon, founded before 1494, claimed to speak on behalf of the black slaves. Some blacks even took orders or were associated with religious houses, but admission to the priesthood was extremely rare before 1518. In the hierarchy of attitudes, although blacks were considered inferior because of their colour their Christianity and consequent cultural assimilation to the Portuguese tended to place them above the Moslems, who were distrusted because of their religion.

Women

The most subtle problem of inclusion or exclusion has been left until almost the end. In this world of priests, where so much of life was dominated by men, how did women react to the church? Structurally excluded from performance of the major sacraments, and with their main outlet for an ordered acceptance requiring negation of their sexuality by enclosure in a nunnery, were women among the victims of the persecuting society?

Possibly they were, or became so. It has recently been claimed that the clericalisation of male monasticism in the twelfth and thirteenth century led to a reduction in the status of nuns, as they became one of many groups among 'the other'.[21] Women's participation in medieval heresy has sometimes been seen as a reaction against such changes, in the search for liberation through involvement in sects which rejected the patriarchalism of the existing religious structures. Whether that was so is questionable. While women could become perfect among the Cathars, it is clear that as Catharism became more structured opportunities for independent female activity declined, if Catharism was not anyway hostile to women by its rejection of reproduction. In Waldensianism the status of women remained similar to that of orthodox nuns. In Lollardy, although women were active and anti-heretical preachers claimed that a female priesthood had been created, their role may have been over-stated. Almost the only sect in which women had a dominant role was the Guglielmites of Milan; and even there there are hints of a strong male presence.

That may affirm the suppression of female spirituality; but the emphases perhaps need re-examination. In recent years an alternative approach has become increasingly obvious which, while existing alongside apparently misogynistic rantings, nevertheless affirmed women's role in religion. Part of the problem may be the search for stereotyping of women without noticing an equivalent stereotyping of men. The misogyny which is often encountered in medieval writings cannot be set aside; but it perhaps has to be tested. The easy linkages built into some approaches to it may be too simplistic: a presupposition that women were oppressed and repressed

---

[21] P. D. Johnson, *Equal in monastic profession: religious women in medieval France* (Chicago and London, 1991), pp. 257, 260–4.

leads to a search for evidence to support the interpretation. Most misogynistic tracts were written by churchmen, simply because church-men were the educated; but does that necessarily make Christianity antifeminist? Some aspects certainly were, especially among monks who were after all seeking to justify a celibate status which they felt to be under threat. But there is another linkage: the tracts were written by men, who accidentally were clerics. The misogyny may reflect problems of masculinity more than anything else (although admittedly the social structures within which masculinity had to be defined were reinforced and partially legitimated by interpretations of Christianity). Just as, on close examination, the tirades against clerical corruption are slowly dissolving as credible historical evidence, perhaps the anti-feminism of the medieval church is showing similar signs of melting. There may be a danger when approaching the status of medieval women of depending overmuch on interpretations derived from parts of St Paul's Epistles which only really gained ground in the sixteenth century; although the amalgamation of women with diabolic influences in witchcraft accusations, notably in the *Malleus malificarum*, shows the dangers which were appearing in the fifteenth.

For there is a positive side to the picture. Nunneries, for instance, have now been largely rehabilitated as places where some women were able to assert themselves irrespective of gender, or perhaps because gender was unimportant to them. Certainly nuns were quite ready to disobey prelates and claim independence. Moreover, as the nuns of Helfta demonstrate in the thirteenth century, and supported by many other instances, nuns readily assumed spiritual responsibilities. Such cases pose a question of definition: while nuns were physically women, were they gendered as women? Or was it the case that 'Nuns can be classified either as honorary males or as of neuter gender like all clergy'?[22] Modern answers to that question are unavoidably preconditioned, whatever form they take. Perceptions, actions, at the time would be modified by circumstances, by the particular activities in which any individual was engaged.

Beyond the nunneries, the great efflorescence of female piety and female sanctity from the thirteenth century onwards has been recognised in a reassessment of women's contribution to medieval spirituality. That is increasingly seen as positive, even if manipulated: many visionaries and saints relied on male amanuenses, perhaps even orchestrators. Yet it may be that 'we can add one more item to the growing list of religious assumptions widely shared . . . at the end of the Middle Ages: the

[22] M. T. Clanchy, *From memory to written record: England, 1066–1307* (2nd edn, Oxford, 1993), p. 252.

conviction that the privileged conduit for divine revelation was young, poor, and female.'[23]

Even women outside that category had a powerful role in medieval spirituality. As work progresses on book ownership, and on the processes of daily transmission of the basics of religion, so women become more prominent. Women increasingly appear as the prime readers of the devotional and instructional works of the period – it was no accident that a standard iconographical depiction was of St Anne teaching her daughter, the Virgin, to read. The medieval reader is increasingly seen as a woman, rather than a man. Moreover, Christianity, as in the pictures of Anne and the Virgin, becomes a matrilineal religion, its generational transmission part of the domestic routine which took spirituality away from the church and priestly control. The family, instructed by its mother, thus becomes another type of 'discourse community' among the many which made up medieval catholicism. (Writers on heresy have often stressed the processes of familial transmission there.)

A paradox ensues; for an awareness of women's religiosity is one thread in medieval 'antifeminism'. Women are portrayed as overly familiar with clerics, to whom they either reveal their husbands' secrets, or betray their beds; women are always trying to give away too much in charity, or in the wrong ways, or seeking to preserve their chastity by taking vows in opposition to their husbands. From another stand-point, preachers often seem to acknowledge women's spiritual role in the household, addressing them as the route whereby their familes were to be Christianised and their menfolk civilised. The reality of female participation in religion should perhaps be sought not in the strident antifeminism of tracts composed by men, but in the undertones of sermons and other evidence. Against the manifold denigrations of women in works like Alvaro Pelayo's *De planctu ecclesie* of *c.* 1330 must be set the seeming commonplace in a sermon of the Franciscan Berthold of Regensburg (d. 1272) that 'You women . . . go more readily to church than men do; speak your prayers more readily than men; go to sermons more readily than men'.[24] In heresy cases, the testimony of the orthodox is as impressive as that of the accused, as in Joanna Clifland's reply to Margery Baxter in the Norfolk trials in 1429, that daily 'immediately after her entry into the church she was accustomed, while kneeling before the cross, to say five Paternosters in

[23] D. Bornstein, 'The shrine of Santa Maria a Cigoli: female visionaries and clerical promoters', *Mélanges de l'École française de Rome: Moyen Age, Temps Modernes*, 98 (1986), p. 228.

[24] P. Biller, 'The common woman in the western church in the thirteenth and early fourteenth centuries', *Studies in church history*, 27 (1990), p. 140.

honour of the crucified, and as many *Ave Marias* in honour of the Blessed
Mary, Mother of Christ'.[25] Even a work as hostile to women as the
Malleus malificarum has its undertones. While seeking explanations of why
many witches are women, a search which doubtless accounts for the tone
of the discussion, there are also positive statements like the recommen-
dation that preachers should say much more about the devout women.

Men

The rehabilitation of women's role in the church and the reassessment of
their contribution to religious continuity and development has a corollary
which as yet has not been followed through, perhaps not fully
appreciated. Caroline Bynum has argued that women mystics 'seem to
have felt that they *qua* women were not only *also* but even *especially* saved
in the Incarnation', and that the idea that womanhood signifies Christ's
humanity was 'in some sense . . . literally true'.[26] If such attitudes were
shared generally among women, then the possible marginalisation of the
male, and more particularly of the masculine, becomes a real issue.
Among the rethinking which that demands is a re-examination of the
relationship between men and Christianity.[27]

Real questions can certainly be asked. Even though exclusively
depicted and almost exclusively discussed as male, how realistic as role
models were God the Father and Son? How did the 'ordinary male' relate
to an incarnate God lacking a biological father, and whose mother's
husband was marginalised – if not actually a cuckold – in an asexual
marriage? Where did men fit into a Holy Family which was emphatically
matrilinear and which, in many illustrations either ignored the men or
pointedly exiled them from the central group by putting the women and
children within a garden with the men outside its fence? How were men
to find themselves in Mary and Martha (the active and contemplative
lives), or Mary Magdalene (the repentant sinner)? Did men appreciate that
a consequence of contemporary theories of reproduction was that it was
the male generative force which actually transmitted the stigma of
Original Sin? One argument about the Reformation is that it asserted

[25] N. P. Tanner, *Heresy trials in the diocese of Norwich, 1428–31*, Camden society publications,
4th ser., 20 (1977), p. 44.

[26] C. W. Bynum, *Fragmentation and redemption: essays on gender and the human body in medieval
religion* (New York, 1992), pp. 150, 179.

[27] For a tentative attempt to address some of the issues, see R. Kieckhefer, 'Holiness and the
culture of devotion: remarks on some late medieval male saints', in *Images of sainthood in
medieval Europe*, ed. R. Blumenfeld-Kosinski and T. Szell (Ithaca and London, 1991),
pp. 288–305.

Figure 6 Religion for women? *Holy kinship*, painted by a follower of the Master of St Veronica, *c.* 1420. The women and children sit within an enclosure, the men outside. Neither Joseph nor Joachim (the two central males, Joseph on the right) has a nimbus as a sign of sainthood: that attribute is reserved for the women and the two principal children. Christ (on the Virgin's lap in the centre) and John the Baptist.

patriarchy within the church: perhaps it did so in reaction to a sense of exclusion. It may be significant that one strand of anti–ecclesial satire stressed the dangers of sexual links between wives and clerics: the lay males might here be expressing worries about spiritual complicity between women and the clergy from which they felt excluded.

In practical terms, men may have felt less attachment than women to some aspects of the church. While men were active – indeed, prominent – in parochial life, and readily joined in pilgrimages and many other contemporary devotions, their commitment to the ecclesial and sacerdotal church is sometimes questionable. Men are, after all, predominant among

the heretics and those who appear most doubtful of the validity of
Christianity; men are most frequently mentioned among those accused of
working on Sunday and holy days; men created the fraternities which
were almost separate facets of the church, free of the parochial structure
and therefore of sacerdotal authority. Possibly, then, men in the later
middle ages – and perhaps earlier – resented the female aspect of religion,
which was arguably derived from its Incarnational emphases, and sought
to recreate a Christianity more to their liking. If this is so, then the
problem of religion as a battleground between the genders may have been
increasingly intense in the fifteenth century. As men claimed a greater
stake in religion, and one which was almost necessarily patriarchal if
women's place was to be wrested from them, so the tensions increased.
The developments are complex; but two features of the period perhaps
show the changes. The first is the gradual development of the cult of St
Joseph, advocated by Gerson in the late fourteenth century, but only
slowly brought out of the shadows. The second is the shift in emphasis
from a Christianity of the Gospels, whose dominant features were the life
and death of Christ, to a theological and exegetical Christianity based on
Pauline texts. The conflict which could result has been most vigorously
identified by Colin Richmond, tempted 'to see the English Reformation
as an onslaught on those means of religious expression particularly dear to
women . . . Dare one assert that men had become envious of a religion
which women practised better than they did?' The Reformation can thus
be summarised as 'men taking on women' – and winning.[28]

A SUMMING UP

The processes of inclusion and exclusion impacted very really, if sometimes subtly and barely perceptibly, on the evolution of religion and
devotion in medieval Europe. Sometimes this was direct and evolutionary. Sometimes change was a reaction to challenges, as seems to apply
mainly to the expressions of extremism and nonconformity and the search
for a redefinition of the notion of a Christian community through drastic

[28] C. Richmond, 'The English gentry and religion, *c.* 1500', in *Religious belief and ecclesiastical
careers in late medieval England*, ed. C. Harper-Bill, Studies in the history of medieval
religion, 3 (Woodbridge, 1991), pp. 140–2. The article was written before the eruption
of the current spate of 'revisionism' on the English Reformation, which has produced
fundamental reinterpretations of the implementation of the religious changes in England
(see C. Haigh, *English Reformations: religion, politics, and society under the Tudors* (Oxford,
1993)). Richmond's comment clearly relates to the changes under Henry VIII; he may
not be summarising the views of all men. Despite revisionism, the implications of his
comment merit further reflection.

revolutionary action. Unavoidably, the nonconformists advanced the definition of conformity. It was fear of disorder and deviation which encouraged the definition of what was to be excluded as unacceptable and the identification of those who were to be rejected because they threatened to infect and corrupt the normality of orthodoxy. Admittedly – something which merits more attention than it can be given here – the conflicts around inclusion within or exclusion from the catholic church dragged in other factors. At times, the religious element appears decidedly secondary, as in the Albigensian crusade of the thirteenth century, or some of the proceedings against *conversos* in fifteenth-century Spain.

Nevertheless, the rejection of nonconformists as advocates of unacceptable ideas necessarily tightened the definition of catholicism. The process of defining the excluded, especially in matters of Christian doctrine, was part of the process of identifying the included. The cohesiveness of being among the included, the inclusiveness of the church as a safety net, had its own implications for the society which it enfolded. Despite the development of national and international rivalries throughout the later middle ages, and the creation of a strong sense of national identity and autonomy in some places, the essential unity of a church which was by definition catholic remained a powerful force. Even when the Great Schism wracked the church between 1378 and 1417, a striking feature of those years is not the extent to which the institution was divided, but the anxiety with which reunification was sought. This drive must, admittedly, be put in a proper perspective – many of Europe's inhabitants, if they actually had opinions on the crisis, were undecided on how to deal with it or fiercely partisan for their own pope, accepting the authoritative pronouncements of their local hierarchies apparently without demur. It would be idealistic to claim that the princes were concerned with much more than the political implications of the division: they only became actively involved in the reunification process when the schism threatened to become a political embarrassment, or there was the prospect of gaining international prestige by supporting the drive towards unity. Yet among the church hierarchs, especially among theologians, there was a strong sense of unease at the division, an awareness that the split was artificial and unChristian, and that the church's rightful status was as an entity which incorporated and included, rather than separated and excluded. The eventual resolution of the schism was more a matter of practical ecclesiastical politics than doctrinal and idealistic concerns; but the concerns were there nevertheless.

The message of order and inclusion, the message of social structure, was constantly enforced and reinforced by public demonstration and theoretical construction. At the heart was the old system of estates, the ideal of the social unity of those who worked, those who prayed, and those who fought, in which the prayers took precedence over the other groups but interdependence was the intended result. Even if the theory had become hopelessly fragmented over the centuries as attempts were made to integrate all those occupations which did not seem to fit, especially those involving money, the ideal of the tripartite structure was still proclaimed in sermons and elsewhere. Plays and other entertainments reinforced the message, as did processions. They were all social statements, all designed to maintain the unity of that society; but society's essential unity derived from its being recognised as part of a church whose underlying ethic was the interdependence inherent in the notion of *caritas*.

However, the unity of inclusion required an opposite, an antithesis. Here, what is striking about the excluded groups is how the development of a vocabulary of exclusion dissolved the distinctions between them as 'the other'. This especially applied when there were real oppositions, rather than mere social tensions. The demonic, the immoral, were the elements which were stressed, bringing all the oppositions down to common denominators. This is evident in the extension of the idea of leprosy from actual lepers to heretics, Jews, and Moslems – an extension which then rebounded back on the lepers. Jews were (unwittingly) agents of the Devil; witchcraft was Satanic; Islam was Antichrist. Heretics, witches, and lepers indulged in sexual orgies. All polluted, and were polluted. Most insidiously, charges of child murder became one of the generalised topoi. Heretics murdered the offspring of their orgiastic indulgence to provide a blasphemous communion; witches used unguents confected from murdered children to assist their Satanic purposes; Jews were repeatedly accused of ritual murder; lepers might be cured by the blood of a child. Moslems are notably absent from many of these generalisations: perhaps that reflects lack of contact with them more than anything else.

Such exclusions may not have been universally acknowledged; here the difficulties about the existence of possibly distinct 'learned' and 'popular' cultures are most intractable. Yet all together they did assist the creation of an identity, one which was explicitly Christian and catholic, and which was also insecure. The evolution of that insecurity across the centuries, alongside the expansion of Christianity within Europe and the search to extend it beyond, provides a cautionary tension in the era before the Reformation, raising questions about the rootedness and reality of Christianity in Europe between 1215 and 1515.

9

THE REALITY
OF RELIGION

—————— • ——————

Most of the issues considered so far have necessarily been treated fairly generally, identifying strands and threads in the religious and devotional development of Europe between the Fourth and Fifth Lateran Councils. In the process, dissonances and tensions within the overall structure have usually been played down, if not ignored completely. Anecdotal and incidental evidence has emphasised specific points and cases, which have then provided the basis for generalisations applied to the whole of Latin Christendom. That approach obviously holds many dangers. The major threat is that the trees are lost in the wood: emphasis on trends submerges the individuals. Yet real people had to fit religious and devotional practices into a context of frequent poverty and constant threats both natural and human, and had to establish personal priorities for the demands made on their emotional, spiritual, and physical resources by families, church, neighbours, governments, and other forces. The reality of the religion has to be assessed.

The totality of the medieval religious experience is crucial to any such evaluation. In some ways, it makes the task impossible: externals are usually all that are recorded. However, conformity does imply a *prima facie* acceptance that the ideals had validity; at least awareness that nonconformity was dangerous. The tension inherent in that awareness calls for a multi-stranded attempt at an evaluation. First, this must recognise the problem of definitions and assessments – a matter of both historiography and history, as the definitions and identifications must be formulated not in terms imposed by the twentieth century, but in those valid for the period under review. Secondly, it must seek to reconstruct the vitality and integrity of people's experiences as revealed in the sources. This requires a double perspective, one examining acceptance of and participation in religious practices, the other considering scepticism, doubt, and ignorance. That can only be done cursorily here: it presupposes that earlier chapters and their arguments can be taken as read. Finally, some conclusion can be offered on the devotional state of catholic Europe in 1515, a terminal date which evades extension into the Reformation, but cannot wipe it from the horizon.

THE NATURE OF RELIGIOUS EXPERIENCE

Labels

Addressing Moslem converts to Christianity after the fall of Granada, Hernando de Talavera advised them that to make their acceptance of the new religion unchallengeable by others

> it is necessary that you conform completely to the good and honest conversation of the good and honest Christian men and women, and this is also necessary in your clothes and shoes, and in shaving, and in your food, and in eating at tables, and in cooking the food in the way that it is normally cooked.[1]

To be truly a Christian was not merely a matter of internalised spirituality, but of external conformity. Small deviations from accepted social practice were sufficient to mark anyone as of uncertain faith, from the woman who invoked the Spirit rather than the Virgin in her labour, to the suspected Lollards whose refusal to follow customary practices at the elevation of the Host made others question their orthodoxy.

In such circumstances, to test 'reality' presupposes a definition of 'reality', presumes a universal standard against which convictions and practices can be measured. However, any standard adopted in a retrospective assessment such as this is likely to be anachronistic, if nothing else based on post-Reformation definitions of Christianity – from whatever standpoint – which may have little relevance to pre-Reformation approaches. Moreover, the techniques of testing are open to challenge. What evidence is to be used? If the way people practised religion, what criteria are to be adopted to define how people should have acted? Does failure to act appropriately mean that the religion was unreal, or that individuals had not lived up to its demands? Is such failure to be explained because the demands were unattainable, or because people did not care?

---

[1] A. MacKay, 'The Hispanic-*converso* predicament', *Transactions of the royal historical society*, 5th ser., 35 (1985), p. 171 n54.

How do we measure the extent to which people regretted their failure – a regret which may actually rehabilitate the religion as a reality?

The fact of hindsight, and a seeming reluctance to adopt what might be called a 'holistic' approach to religion and religious practices, here certainly complicates historians' perceptions and judgements, in ways which have already been addressed slightly differently when treating the role of magic in medieval catholicism.[2] The concern to isolate experiences, to dissect and compartmentalise facets of a life's totality, which is characteristic of modern historians' approaches to medieval religion, disrupts the unity of a lifetime and the integrity of a mentality. This particularly applies with attempts to differentiate between 'Christian' and 'unChristian' aspects of medieval religion. Here insistence on anachronistic judgements and categories – on definitions of pre-Reformation catholicism as 'pagan' or 'folkloric', being transformed into a real religion by Protestant or Tridentine Reformation – seem tantamount to spiritual Whiggery, using twentieth-century ideas of Christianity (and, often, of what Christianity 'ought' to be rather than as it is) which are, bluntly, irrelevant to the middle ages. This attitude has been rightly criticised as resting on an 'evolutionist presupposition, according to which populations live in a profound irrationality, in a magical world from which they little by little detach themselves, thanks to their elites, to arrive at rationality, which is more or less to be identified with the historian's ideology'.[3] Historically, a religion has to be assessed in its own terms, if they can be identified.

While pre-Christian survivals were integrated into the totality of pre-Reformation religious practices, at several levels, the mere fact of that integration militates against considering them as unChristian; nor can the beliefs be seen as the hang-overs of irrationality which denigrating them as 'superstition' implies. In the synthesis which was constantly evolving throughout Christian Europe, the end result was always a new form of Christianity. Admittedly, some at the time condemned some practices as superstitions – but those were usually activities which were seen as fundamentally anti-Christian, like belief in portents and fortune-telling. Even with these, though, there is a telling circumstantiality in the way in which the parents of Simon of Trent, ready to denounce the Jews for the death of their son, consulted a clairvoyante or fortune-teller (*vaticinatrice*) in the search for his body. Preachers like the fifteenth-century Pole, Stanislas of Skarbimierz, felt themselves surrounded by a vital and

---

[2] Above, pp. 184–8.

[3] J. Wirth, 'Against the acculturation thesis', in *Religion and society in early modern Europe, 1500–1800*, ed. K. von Greyerz (London, 1984), p. 77.

dynamic mélange of errors and superstitions which had to be fought to bring their flocks back to the fold; but while the shepherds battled against what they saw as misuse of Christianity, the flocks fought for the preservation of what they considered right uses. An anachronistic vocabulary of those who later attacked the religion cannot be used to evaluate it. Nor can a patronising intellectual stance based on ideas of 'rationality'. In its own terms, on its own premises, the religion was perfectly rational, from Biblical givens which were undeniably historical. Moreover, it had to fit into a historical structure whose end result was already known: on his island fastness of Patmos, John the Divine had seen the future, and the Christian world knew that it would work, knew how this transitory existence with its ephemeral concerns would receive its final consummation.

Vitality and change

Beyond the rejection of inappropriate labels, the search for the 'reality' of medieval Christianity must be accommodated within a real historical context, one of ineluctable change. This was not a static religion. In European terms, 'Christianity' in 1215 was very different from 'Christianity' in 1515. That had been acknowledged in the pastoral revolution of the thirteenth century, whose spread and impact might be considered the real Christianisation of Europe. The penetration of the Christian message into the various corners of Europe clearly could not occur at a steady pace; nor could all parts Europe be at the same stages of development. The regionalisation of practices, indeed the varying stages of conversion in parts of Europe, notably the east, necessarily meant that the depth of Christianisation varied greatly. While a jurisdictional and administrative model can be constructed which integrates all of the Latin church under the umbrella of papal authority from the thirteenth century onwards, the spirituality of the catholicism beneath that umbrella differed markedly from region to region. The cross-fertilisation of different Christianities between the regions is one of the key features of the period.

Acceptance of the different spiritualities must affect expectations on the 'reality' of religion. Moreover, what religion was for would also vary regionally, indeed, personally, and over time: what people expected of the saints would change; what they needed from God. Perceptions of sin had to evolve with society: there was little point in highlighting the sinfulness of usury in a moneyless economy; whereas greed and cupidity could be attacked more vociferously as economic development spread and brought its attendant social changes. It is just not possible to treat medieval Christianity as an unchanging, static monolith: the more closely the

religion which was lived in the period is examined, and the preconceptions imposed by the sources and post-Reformation prejudices
challenged and penetrated, the more complex but stimulating the picture
is. It is easy to see things as organised from the top, to be beguiled into
seeing the church as a structure in which the authorities dictated the
content and manifestations of religion. That, after all, is what the largely
administrative and jurisdictional sources cannot avoid conveying. The
Inquisition, control of canonisation, insistence on obedience, and
somewhat patronising stance towards lay theological investigation all
contribute to the same picture. But the idea of authoritarian control must
be questioned. It may be better to view the apex of the system more as
a sorcerer's apprentice, constantly battling to control fissiparous and
evolving spiritual demands, seeking to get a genie into a bottle but
without being quite sure what is actually happening. Spirituality could not
be imposed from the top – although attempts might be made to regiment
it. The church existed as an institution, but consisted of individuals at
every level of its structure, and the spiritual attitudes of those individuals
varied, evolved, and could be mutually contradictory. 'The church'
existed as an institution or conglomeration of institutions; 'Christianity'
existed as a faith; but Christians and their individual spiritualities were the
atoms with which both had to be constructed, and they were by no means
uniform or constant. Whether any pope other than Innocent III would
have legitimised the mendicants is a meaningless question; but the
possibility of their formal rejection and its implications for the development of the church cannot be discounted. Equally, at diocesan and even
parochial levels, the acceptance or rejection of particular strands of
spirituality was a matter for individuals, but with long-term after-effects.
On the other hand, the pressures for acceptance came largely from the
bottom: if one bishop rejected, his successor might not. If pressures
continued, and if those seeking a particular legitimisation were prepared
to explore all available avenues to secure it, they might prove successful
in the long-term. It took 350 years of campaigning, admittedly not
uninterrupted, to secure the canonisation of Osmund, the bishop of
Salisbury who died in 1099; in many other cases such persistence was lacking, perhaps because the interests affected were insufficiently coherent to
maintain the vitality of the campaigns. Most saints (official or unofficial),
most fraternities, most celebrations, most pilgrimages, depended on
acceptance and recognition by enough of that vast body which
constituted 'the church' to allow them to continue. Even if individual
holiness was accepted, a saint might prove ephemeral unless the cult was
maintained by particular associations, exemplified in the increased
popularity of St Sebastian against plague after 1350. Without active

participation, the religion or particular manifestations of it could not flourish. That also means that opposition, passive or active, could also be effective if sufficiently maintained, and might force the authorities to amend their definitions. This clearly affects some of the theological developments. Purgatory seems to have been a legitimisation of a pre-existing tendency. Views on usury and economic transactions had to be ameliorated if any of the attendant moral precepts were to be accepted. Rigidity, unless backed by repression, courted rejection.

The problem must be addressed from both ends of the system. As a vital religion, which sought to resolve problems and provide spiritual satisfaction, medieval Christianity was bound by the constraints of supply and demand. The church had to supply a satisfactory code of moral, religious, and spiritual obligations: one not so demanding that it repelled, nor so undemanding that it offered no challenges; not so complex that it was impractical or incomprehensible, nor so simplistic that it could not satisfy needs for self-assurance. This tied it to a form of spiritual market forces. It could not simply offer and await reaction; it had to respond to demand, to accept modifications to its own programme and definitions of manifestations of religion which derived from its flock. To that extent, medieval Christianity was consistently a demand-led religion, although the demands would vary from place to place, and subject to change over time in response to social and economic evolutions. This need to integrate a sense of 'market forces' gives additional validity to the perception of medieval religion as a form of spiritual economics, in which individuals invested effort, money, hopes, in return for rewards and benefits; producing an economy of salvation which ultimately embraced all who accepted the faith. But just as a macro-economy consists of a series of micro-economies, so too with medieval Christianity. That also appears as a collection of fragments, of 'discourse communities' in a series of complex relationships which may be in conflict or co-operation. Circles overlap – the catchment areas of shrines and fraternities, the calendars or liturgies, charitable practices, testamentary customs, and much more. Some extend to issues of real theology and doctrine: attitudes to the Immaculate Conception, penitential practices. Some, especially with shrines and pilgrimages, are highly localised, others more expansive, until eventually all are contained within that most inclusive of circles, the universal church, one, holy, catholic, and apostolic – but still struggling to prove that it is so. Some overlaps prove unacceptable, and are condemned as heresy once they produce conflict with a more encompassing circle. Others, like *conversos*, generate tensions which can only be resolved by action against a non-Christian community.

Faced with such issues, questions of authority arise: who stimulates, who legitimates, who rejects? Repression demands a top-down perspective simply because of the presumptions of the word; but if a local community found that the authority it had previously accepted was considered dubious by a higher level in the structure, that community might also reject its teachers. The complicity of parishioners and diocesans in checking the quality of the parochial clergy is an important feature in religious life which is easily overlooked, as are alliances between preachers and 'the poor' against exploiters. The interplay which made the actions and reactions of the audiences and recipients as vital an element in the development of devotional practices as the dictates and demands of the authorities again contributes to the vibrancy of the issues. Local pressure might itself repress by refusing recognition (as in certain cults); or might resist repression by exploiting the structures and appealing up the system.

This complex and evolving amalgam of post-Lateran IV catholicism necessarily produced changes in the overall awareness of religion, and an accumulative expansion of religious knowledge and devotional options. This is apparent even in the thirteenth century with the implementation of the pastoral revolution, which must have produced a dramatic but unquantifiable improvement in religious awareness. At the start of the century, in a sermon to the young, Jacques de Vitry had cited the inability of some among the old to recite their Our Fathers completely; presumably he expected them not to follow the bad habits of their elders. It is in this context that the mass of *pastoralia* produced after 1215 had its rationale. Although it is impossible to test how adequately the laity acquired their faith overall, in the absence of evidence to the contrary it seems fair to assume that they did. Even if it was rote learning, that was better than nothing; and whether it was that banal may even be questioned. Admittedly it was probably in Latin – although that under-estimates the scale of production of vernacular translations, and their memorisation. In any case, just because something was recited in one language does not preclude comprehension in another.

The chronological changes in awareness of religion, and therewith changes in the demands which the laity made of that religion, also changed expectations. Ignorance might be expected in the early thirteenth century, and therefore excused simply because people knew no better. But as the campaign of indoctrination gathered pace, and bore fruit, so the retention of apparently inconsistent attitudes became more of a problem, especially to the instructors. The grafting of the new Christianity onto the pre-existing mentality was not necessarily exclusive: the earlier mentality could still linger, and a wide range of practices be retained which would thereby be 'Christianised' as they became part of the totality of a new religious experience. The same applied to later converts from Judaism and Islam; except that Old Christians were less prepared to tolerate the retentions. Possibly this made the terrestrial efficacy of Christianity but one of a range of practical options for the organisation of earthly life; but for the instructors such retentions would be less acceptable. The evolution of the definition of religion is reflected in the changing attitude of the instructors to the persistence of unacceptable practices among Christians. In the thirteenth century, the attitude to the retention of magic seems to have been unsympathetic but not unduly condemnatory: it was a devilish delusion, but not automatically diabolic. By 1400, however, the attitude had transformed: from unwitting ensnarement belief in magic had become active complicity with the devil, presumably on the basis that the message had been rammed home sufficiently often for people not to be unaware of what they were doing.

Christianity's demands, and the increasing sophistication and sophistry of its intellectual statements and of the responses to them added further complications. Religion had to be an act of will; this carried the possibility of rejection, especially of a faith which seemed antithetical to reasoned argument. Insofar as there was a 'conversion' process in the expansion of Christianity, the claims made for it would be tested by the intended recipients. This applied as much to individual devotional practices and specific claims to sanctity as to the doctrinal formulae. Such testing offered the possibility of questioning, of doubt. Paradoxically, as Christianity became increasingly part of the cultural baggage of medieval society, it may have become more subject to questioning and uncertainty. Whether or not that occurred, the fact of questioning and the resulting implications, as themselves part of the reality of religious experience, must also be integrated into the final analysis.

LIVING FAITH

Individuals and experiences

Medieval people, like those of any age, rarely had to proclaim their individuality. Those who attracted attention were rarely the contented, the conformists: evidence on individual spiritual development is accordingly usually associated with the extremes of sainthood or dissidence, not with the ordinary. Among the sources quarried in the search for private spirituality, several – visitations records, heresy material left by inquisitors and other legal or anecdotal processes, and archives of the ecclesiastical courts – are by definition abnormal: they usually show how the ideal had become flawed, and the system failed. An opposite bias appears with the evidence for sanctity, although as with other inquests the investigation of miracles can provide insights into the normality of behaviour as well. Wills, although highly revealing, are subject to different reservations, but reservations none the less. All sources pose methodological questions, further complicating assessment. The authorities would not worry when the system was working as they intended; they might also be reluctant to ask whether it was actually working effectively, perhaps appreciating that close investigation of private beliefs could evoke more problems than it would solve. Usually the only clear evidence for a catholic life lived catholicly appears in hagiographical material, but that can rarely be taken at face value.

Nevertheless, it is not wholly impossible to gain some insight into the individual spiritual perceptions and activities of real people. Admittedly, individual lives present problems of typicality, too massive to address here. The evidence must simply be taken as it stands, and the issue of generalisation set aside. Obviously there would be overlaps, but precisely where they arise cannot be surmised with any assurance of validity. To attempt to demonstrate all the possibilities from across the whole of Europe would be folly; but a few, mainly English, examples will suffice to show the possibilities.

'Biographies' (the word must be placed in inverted commas) offer one type of source. Saints' lives obviously give an idealised version of events, but their very idealisation of the individual gives an idea of what a 'real Christian' should be doing. More mundane reality is provided by the references in funerary sermons. John Fisher's oration for Lady Margaret Beaufort in 1509 gives a good outline of her daily religious routine of masses and readings. That is very like the routine of Cecily, duchess of York, in the preceding century. More bizarre is Margery Kempe's *Book*, which is often considered the first English autobiography. This reveals much of her attitudes towards the church and religion, her idiosyncratic approach to God, and her day-to-day contact with the clergy. At the same time, reactions to her behaviour show her contemporaries' perceptions and actions in religious matters; with some accepting her as divinely inspired, others considering her diabolically directed, heretical, or simply a 'God-squad' killjoy. While some people sought greater devotion and contact, others were content with the Christianity they were accustomed to, and its undemanding integration into daily life.

Other evidence reinforces the information from life-stories. Extant accounts from a variety of sources indicate involvement in religious activity, ranging from parish accounts with their statements of receipts for tithes and donations to constructing buildings and other work, through to the personal records of individuals and details of household arrangements. The household material and domestic accounts are probably skewed, particularly towards the higher social levels. Moreover, households tended to be organised in writing on the basis of expectations rather than what might be achieved. Accounts run a kindred risk, but may be more personal in revealing something of the private choices in expenditure. With the personal material, its miscellaneous nature and relative scarcity make it somewhat troublesome as a source: usually it can give little more than incidental hints for purposes of generalisation, even if they do round out individuals. What it does show is that the demands of religion had to be meshed in among the other demands and pressures of daily life; and that private charity and devotional offerings were both haphazard and ritualised. Clearly, this material is abnormal: only the great left the sort of accounts which can actually be used, although lesser families in England like the Pastons and Stonors have left correspondence and some financial memoranda which add to the picture at a slightly lower level. But Elizabeth, Queen to Henry VII, and Lady Margaret Beaufort, his mother, are of rather a different level.

All this material suggests that the demands of devotion had to be met almost accidentally. The queen's accounts[4] have an almost ritualised element in their lists of offerings made at feasts, almost always of 5s., and presumably made through third parties on her behalf. Sometimes, also, they were made in arrears: on 9 June 1502 a lump sum payment of 20s. was made to the dean of her chapel for her offerings for the feasts of St George (23 April), St Mark (25 April), SS Philip and James (1 May), and the Invention of the Holy Cross (3 May). This was sandwiched between payments to one Henry Roper for cooking utensils purchased for the Queen of Scots, and to a London mercer for making a black cloak (for which the bill came to almost £5). On the other hand there are occasional, if erratic, indications of personal choice in the payments: 3s. 4d. to the anchoress of St Peter's at St Albans on 28 May; 5s. to the fraternity of Corpus Christi in St Sepulchre's, London, on 1 May, together with donations to nuns of the London Minoresses; 13s. 4d. to two friars for the indulgence offered on behalf of St Catherine's, Sinai (14 June); and so on. The devotional payments seem incidental, but were not necessarily so perceived. Their miscellaneous nature may actually attest a spontaneity and response to immediate concerns which is itself significant.

These royal accounts are necessarily somewhat aloof; but the idea of spontaneity is perhaps confirmed by the evidence provided by the Willoughby family, extensive landowners in Nottinghamshire and

---

[4] N. H. Nicolas, ed., *Privy purse expenses of Elizabeth of York; Wardrobe accounts of Edward the Fourth* (London, 1830), pp. 1–111.

Warwickshire. Most of their extant account books post-date 1515; but there is no reason to suppose that their evidence on spiritual concerns is invalidated by deriving from the 1520s rather than the 1510s.

Again, the material is miscellaneous, and extremely fragmented. Purchases of indulgences – sometimes the same indulgence bought year after year – are fairly noticeable. So also are payments to preachers, and incidental donations to friars, poor men, and charity-collectors. Offerings to shrines also figure. Obviously, accounts are not properly evidence of the intellectual and emotional response to the Christian message; but what does emerge is a Christianity which stimulated donations, which were treated as part of daily normality without having to be entered into a special 'account for God' (although such do appear in the records of Italian merchants of the time).

Also useful as evidence for individuals' attitudes are their book collections, and odd jottings of a religious nature. With books, the relevance is obvious: the accumulation of a library may well attest interests. However, while that may well be a test for modern readers, its application in the middle ages – before the advent of printing – is less obvious. Books as works of art, as ostentation, as precious objects in their own right, were rather different from the modern paperback. Possession is no guarantee of influence: books were acquired by gift and bequest as well as by commission and purchase, so that ownership may have had little to do with interests. Only where copies were deliberately requested or there are real signs of use, can interest be demonstrated. This might be most convincingly shown in the preparation of personal Books of Hours, from that commissioned from the Oxford scribe William de Brailes in the early thirteenth century, through to the Book prepared for Margaret Beaufort some three centuries later. The choice of prayers here often gives an insight on personal spiritual concerns.

Possibly more significant than production and ownership of full copies of texts in individual volumes was the late medieval practice of compiling selections of devotional material which were more reflective of personal concerns – manuscripts which would later be called commonplace books. Such collections clearly show something about their compilers, and are particularly revealing when the compilers can be identified. Thus, the Thornton manuscript, now in Lincoln cathedral library, offers an extensive accumulation of works of both didactic and devotional purpose, brought together by a fifteenth-century Lincolnshire gentleman. The volume – rather miscellaneous when considered purely as a run of texts – suggests that Thornton deliberately united material which he thought important, and which would assist his own development as a Christian. Many of the works are brief rules for living, others short prayers and lyrics, but all had devotional significance, suggesting an interiorised approach to religion which saw fulfillment of the demands of Christianity very much in terms of personal commitment to a virtuous life, and to acceptance of the demands of *caritas*.

Death-bed religion

Of all the personal records of individual relationships with God, undoubtedly the most important in purely quantitative terms are the wills which were left over the centuries by individuals scattered across western Europe. In certain circumstances they can be highly revealing. Both qualitatively and quantitatively, they provide the most useful source for the assessment of personal responses to the demands of the Christian pilgrimage. They offer the most immediate insights into human perceptions at a crucial point – the pivotal point between this life and the next, the bifurcation which determined whether the testator progressed to Heaven or to Hell. Unfortunately, as has already been noted,[5] they also pose as many questions as they answer: perhaps precisely because they are so useful, so many, and so critical.

To use two English wills here may seem insular, but English documents are among the best for this purpose: for whatever reason, English testamentary practices tend to incorporate much more 'spiritual' material than the continental records. Even so, the English wills which offer major insights into spirituality are also necessarily exceptional: the vast majority are nothing like as illuminating. For the poor, their lack of possessions in itself militates against being able to declare widespread spiritual choices which would permit the recreation of an individual spirituality. Even for the relatively wealthy, a will may actually say little explicitly; but the wider context against which it can be set adds to the illumination.

When Dame Jane Strangways wrote her will in 1500[6] she was a widow, living in the Dominican house at York (presumably as a boarder, but her exact status is unclear). She obviously had a real attachment to the house, desiring burial there should she die within a ten-mile radius of York; otherwise she was to be buried in the parish church of wherever she died. After providing for lights at her funeral, she left bequests to all four orders of friars in York, each house receiving 10s. for a trental of masses within a week of her burial. Other legacies went to the heads of the mendicant convents to attend her funeral, with doles for priests and other clergy who

---

[5] Above, pp. 212–13, 226–7.
[6] Translated in R. N. Swanson, *Catholic England: faith, religion, and observance before the Reformation* (Manchester, 1993), pp. 249–53.

were present. The repair of York Minster was to receive 26s. 8d.; 7 marks (£4 13s. 4d.) was left for a daily mass for her soul in York's Dominican priory (the celebrant friar was to have 2d., the rest being used for repairs). She also set up a temporary chantry, providing 7 marks a year for a priest to sing for herself, her parents, and all Christian souls for five years. The priest was to be 'honest . . . of good name and good reputation'.

Many other bequests showed Jane Strangways' spiritual concerns. She had considerable contact with the Carthusians of Mount Grace: her husband was buried there, and she left the house 10 marks to pray for his soul and her's, and to celebrate an obit within ten days of being asked to do so, with another twelve months after. Specific members of the Mount Grace community were also remembered: Dan Thurstan received 10s., as did Richard Methley. He is significant, as his extant writings place him firmly in the medieval English mystical tradition, and his mention offers a hint of Dame Jane's own spiritual feelings.

Beyond the Mount Grace connections, the links with the mendicants are this will's most striking feature. The Franciscans of Richmond (Yorkshire) were left 10s. for a trental, and another 10s. for repairs; while Friar French of that house received 40s. Detailed arrangements were made for an annual obit in York's Dominican priory, £20 being left to purchase lands worth 10s. a year to fund the project. This would be arranged through a trust, as technically the friars could not own property. The prior received a personal legacy of 20s. for prayers, and was named executor of the will, together with another priest, Henry Mortime. Mortime was also residuary legatee – precisely why is not explained, although he was to pray for her soul in recompense.

A few other bequests complete the tally of donations in a will dominated by attempts to purchase prayers. 10 marks were left to Norton priory (Cheshire) to purchase an obit for Dame Jane and her first husband, Roger Dutton. The first was to be sung within ten days of notification of her burial, the other twelve months later. Each inhabitant of the four leper houses in York received 1d., to pray for her soul. Her debts were to be paid 'as good conscience requires'. Each of her five god-daughters received 40s. towards marriage. A few other personal bequests to servants to pray for her soul complete the list – although suggesting that the concern for prayers had to be set alongside the concern for service, being conditional on the servants still being in her employ at her death. The donation of a silver piece, 'with Christ's blessing and mine', to her son Laurence Dutton was also conditional, on his doing nothing to disturb her executors. This again suggests that the devotional phrasing ought to be approached with some circumspection.

So Dame Jane Strangways disposed of her wealth in October 1500. In

March 1501 she added a codicil. Her affection for the York Dominicans remained, the prior receiving another legacy which included a pair of sheets to be made into surplices. But she may have quit their house, as the church of St Mary, Bishophill, 'where I lived at some time', was left a set of vestments in return for prayers. Most of the codicil's new bequests sought to secure *post mortem* prayers, from clerics: Sir Henry Morton was left a mass book, a chalice, and other mass impedimenta; James Best, a friar, was bequeathed a salary for a year; Sir Thomas, 'my priest', payment for one or two years (one at the least); and her kinsman Brian Ashton, if he would take it on, was to have a salary for two years.

As a widow, Jane Strangways had few familial obligations to reflect in her will. Traditional inheritance patterns need not operate, and although she presumably disposed of less than her husbands did, she enjoyed greater liberty in the distribution. She could concentrate on the afterlife, and her will's spiritual dimension is certainly striking. But while she may have been freer than most in disposing of her goods, even those active in the world were concerned to secure their souls. Thomas Kebell, a lawyer whose successful practice earned him a lifestyle of gentrified rural ease, made a very long will at his death in 1500.[7] Its preamble is unusual, eschewing the traditional invocation of Mary and the company of Heaven for a strong proclamation of faith, although whether it is actually Kebell's personal proclamation is less certain:

In the name of God, Amen. I, Thomas Kebell, . . . being whole in mind (thanks be to God), considering the instability of the world, and the certainty and necessity of death, to which I and every living creature am bound, and wishing to provide and arrange for the disposal of such goods as God has permitted me to have here on earth, ordain and make my testament and last will . . . First, I bequeath my soul to Almighty God my maker, my redeemer, my preserver from the many dangers to soul and body, and my singular relief, comfort, and aid in necessity, adversity, infirmity, poverty and all discomforts, humbly beseeching him to accept it in his mercy and grace . . .

He sought burial at his country establishment at Humberston (Norfolk), amongst his kindred, instructing his executors to arrange for the transfer of his body there, 'laying aside all vain pomp and glory of this world'. At his burial day, or as his executors saw fit, £20 was to be distributed among the poor. Arrangements were made to pay his mortuary, and donations to a few churches for repairs and forgotten tithes.

Concern for his soul pervades the next section, beginning with a fairly

---

[7] Swanson, *Catholic England*, pp. 244–9; in full, and with the additional documents cited later, in E. W. Ives, *The common lawyers of pre-Reformation England* (Cambridge, 1983), pp. 425–47.

laconic distribution of largesse to religious houses, centred in Leicester and London. These legacies ranged from 13s. 4d. to each house of friars in Leicester, to 40s. to the prioress and convent of Clerkenwell. There is no obvious predilection for one order or type of institution, although the white friars were the only London house specified among the mendicants: legacies went to male and female houses, mendicants and secular canons (the college of the Newark at Leicester), and to an almshouse.

Besides giving to religious houses, Kebell demanded prayers for his soul: 1,000 masses with as many recitations of *placebo* and *dirige* immediately after his death, at 4d. for each priest – or as many trentals as would equate to 1,000 masses, if his executors preferred. He also wanted a priest at Humberston for seven years, setting out a detailed programme of daily masses for himself and his family, of seven psalms and a litany on three days a week, with Our Lady's Psalter on the other three weekdays, and the psalms of the Passion on Sundays. The many individual legacies to relatives, servants, and friends generally carried the obligation to pray for him in return. His under-age son was the addressee of a lengthy admonition about behaviour, being urged to live a Christian life. Other bequests provide for chantries under his oversight, and for the disposal of goods for the sake of his soul and others' 'in deeds of alms and piety', at the discretion of his executors – although with special concern for his 'poor kinfolk and my neighbours and those places of religion in this region which are poor, or from which I have received fees'.

This will is informative about Kebell's concerns; further documents disposing of his lands and inventorying his goods add considerably more information. The arrangements for his lands include a residuary clause requiring revenues to be used to benefit the souls of himself and his relatives; but this is a last resort. The main spiritual provision is the arrangement of a chantry, or two. Kebell had been overseer of the chantry founded for his cousin Richard Hotoft, having received the lands for the foundation with the intent to provide a priest in perpetuity, but without their being legally amortised. This charge Kebell transmitted to his executors, instructing that if he had not sufficiently secured the covenant to ensure the chantry's continuity, they should do so. Kebell presumably hoped that this chantry would also serve for him – but he also provided that, if he died without issue, another priest would be appointed at Humberston to pray for himself and others, and that twelve poor men should be established there in an almshouse in perpetuity. These new foundations were both to be fully established in mortmain.

The will and the disposal of the lands equally show Kebell's concern for his soul, in proposals which seem very business-like. Despite the will's highly personal opening, and the admonition to his son, the devotional clauses suggest coolness. This is most striking in his chantry arrangements: only if the family died out was the chantry to be established; otherwise the prayers derived from Kebell's augmentation of the Hotoft chantry would suffice. (The augmentation was no novelty: many chantries were so treated over the centuries, and the status of second founder was as valid as that of originator.) Perhaps most striking is Kebell's sense of obligation to others: the list of those for whom his priests were to pray, even if anonymously included among 'those from whom I have received any kind of benefits, and especially for the souls of those whose benefits I have not deserved', is impressive. There is here, certainly, a sense of charity.

The inventory also reveals Kebell's personal concerns. The contents of the chapel were valued at a total of 29s., with nothing of particular value (the only vestment is described as 'sore worn', but at 13s. 4d. was still the most expensive item). That, however, gives a false impression, for the chief chapel furnishings appear elsewhere. The list of plate includes a chalice with paten and cover, worth 53s. 4d., and a paxbread, two cruets, and a sacring bell which, with a little pot, were valued at 79s. 2d. An altarcloth of arras was placed 'in the chamber over the parlour', and valued at £4; while other altar furnishings and two sets of vestments appeared under 'wearing gear'. The impressive list of books shows a concern with religious matters. A printed copy of Ludolf of Saxony's *De vita Christi* was in the chamber over the parlour; while the general list, alongside law books and Latin classics, included a Bible with Nicholas of Lyra's commentary, a printed book of Lenten sermons, a parchment glossed psalter, a manuscript *Tractus super vetus testamentum*, and works by Gregory the Great, Johannes Reuchlin, and Johannes Balbus. Taken altogether these suggest both an interest in Biblical studies, although some of the Biblical works may have been used by Kebell's chaplain, and an awareness of contemporary spiritual developments in their novelty and concern for a return to the old. That many of the works were printed shows how these new forms of spirituality were spreading immediately prior to the onset of the Reformation.

Such English evidence does have continental parallels. Roman wills of the thirteenth and fourteenth centuries match those of Joan Strangways and Thomas Kebell. In 1295 Pietro Saxonis scattered bequests among several Roman churches, with legacies to a number of regular institutions. Among the latter, his main beneficiaries were the Franciscans, the others being also mainly mendicants and new orders of the thirteenth century. He left money to be distributed among the recluses of the city: that, the emphasis on the mendicants, and his appointment of the new Celestinian establishment at Sant' Eusebio as a residuary legatee (jointly with a hospital, should his bodily heirs fail), does seem to illuminate his overall spirituality, placing him firmly in the currents of the century's ascetic developments. But his spirituality also had a physical focus: personal bequests were specifically made for the sake of his soul, and a bequest to San Salvatore in Santa Balbina was probably stimulated by its holding a portrait supposedly of the living Christ.

Rather different in its concerns is the will of Paola Savelli, of 1364. She again distributed widely, often to places containing sacred images, and to buy church ornaments. However, she also funded a vicarious pilgrimage for the sake of her soul; and concern with her soul reverberates through the demands for celebration of masses for herself and her first husband – but not her second!

Life-time religion

Although they may allow penetration of a testator's religious and devotional milieux, wills reflect a spirituality chronologically restricted by the time of their compilation – which, in England, usually means when close to death. Material disclosing the reality of religion during life is much more elusive; usually no more than incoherent and inconclusive fragments which may or may not contribute towards a larger picture. In individual cases an accumulation of evidence does sometimes offer a more rounded picture; but the fragments often must be combined not into an individualisation, but a generalisation, about the overall trends and features of spirituality at whatever level, time, and place is being reviewed.

The most significant source of information to supplement wills is usually correspondence. To stay in England, the letters of the Paston family of East Anglia in the fifteenth century, with its comments on pilgrimage, the references to negotiations to secure a domestic oratory, disputes about chantries, and discussions of ecclesiastical patronage, display the unavoidable intermingling of spiritual and other concerns. If enough letter collections survived for enough people of enough different social levels across Europe, a more definitive assessment of the reality of religious experience across the broad span of a lifetime might be possible. As it is, the cases where this can be done are few, and often problematical.

As with the wills, so with correspondence: the Pastons have their continental counterparts. The most informative range of material is probably that offered by the highly exceptional case of Francesco Datini of Prato (?1335–1410). His voluminous letters and related documents provide the raw material to analyse much of his life and activities. This material offers more of a challenge than wills do, and is more disconcerting. What is striking about the letters is the frequency of the spiritual and moral discussion, of the references to preparation for death, and of worries about sinfulness. Datini joined in pilgrimages, most notably those linked with the Bianchi movement of 1399; corresponded with the leading Dominican preacher Giovanni Dominici; attended sermons and masses galore; bewailed the sinfulness and exploitation of his wealth; made frequent charitable distributions; and repeatedly thought of judgement. Yet penetrating through to the reality of his spirituality is by no means straightforward: possibly more than with a will, the subjectivity of the interpreter interposes, because this is a personal spirituality, one in a state of development, and which has to be teased out of a mass of material which requires the context of a real life actually being lived – a wealthy merchant confronting the horrors of repeated plague, unavoidably involved in political and domestic concerns. Datini has his own real spirituality, but it cannot be pinned down. It may be merely pragmatic, although at times seems truly heartfelt. Possibly he did separate, but not divorce, his spiritual and worldly concerns: despite his constant protestations of sinfulness and disdain of the pleasures of this world, he did remarkably little to dissociate himself from them. Although the jollificatory nature of his participation in the Bianchi pilgrimages may have been over-stated, and it was probably less of a 'nine-days' picnic' than has sometimes been made out, it still did not entail major discomfort. Despite the years available to prepare for death, when it eventually came it apparently caught him unawares (but not unprepared – he had made a will during an outbreak of plague, but that was now revoked and replaced), and his friends thought that he resented its arrival.

The spirituality of Datini's correspondence seems to conflict with the business-like wording of his final will and its three codicils, drawn up at the end of July and beginning of August 1410, when he was on his deathbed.[8] His distribution of goods and wealth seems almost impersonal, despite the frequent invocations of the love of God, and the repeated references to the poor of Christ. The strictures associated with his foundation of a hospital for the poor seem also somewhat unspiritual, insisting that it and its possessions 'should be always private and not sacred, and in no way or for any reason be able to be called ecclesiastical, but be organised secularly, for the love of God, in perpetuity', and depriving the governors of any power 'to make it an oratory or any other sort of ecclesiastical place, or to do anything through which [it] might be called an ecclesiastical place'.

However, this may be to misread things. Clearly the distributions to the

---

[8] C. Guasti, ed., *Ser Lapo Mazzei: lettere di un notaro a un mercante del secolo XIV; con altre lettere e documenti* (2 vols., Florence, 1880), II, pp. 273–310.

churches and religious orders cannot be ignored. There is a pervading sense of charity in the will, brought home in his demand that all his slaves, wherever they were, should be freed 'for the love of God'. Conventionality in the dispositions does not undermine their personal nature, and the scale of the final hospital endowment is truly impressive. Moreover, even there, the lack of spirituality may in fact be a canny pragmatism: the insistence on continued lay governance was to prevent asset-stripping by a greedy cleric should it be considered an ecclesiastical benefice.

While Datini's spirituality cannot be dissected and assessed on a graduated scale, it would seem unreasonable to deny the reality of his religion. It was a major aspect of his life, possibly even a driving force. He was constantly aware of the contrast between what was expected of a 'true' Christian and the reality of his own experience – and seems to have regretted it. Beyond that it is impossible to go without becoming speculative. However, to be aware of the feelings of one who was actually among the audience at sermons, one of those rich whom the preachers were constantly denouncing for their theft from the poor, perhaps gives another perspective to the verbal flails from the pulpits. Datini identified himself among those so attacked, he evidently saw himself as a sinner. Yet life had to be lived.

Datini's case is individual, and exceptional because of the amount of material which survives; nevertheless he may not have been unusual. His correspondents seem to share his approaches to the spiritual life. The vignettes contained in the letters match the snatches of information given in so many other sources, without the justifiable doubts which may be attached to sermon *exempla*, but go on to validate those *exempla*. Insofar as all this material builds up to create an overall picture, there appears to be no justification for questioning an overall acceptance of the demands of the faith, no justification for challenging the almost universal participation – willing and intentional – in the devotional practices of the period. Even if people failed to meet all of Christianity's demands, it does not follow that they considered them inappropriate: if that test was universally applied, most devotees of any religion would fail.

DUBIUS IN FIDE INFIDELIS EST?

Scepticism: its existence and meaning

The attempt to assess the 'reality' of religion must also try to decide how far 'orthodoxy' was embedded in a wider context which might be considered religious, where Christianity co-existed with fairies and demons, where recourse to sacramentals had as much (if not more) daily significance as the sacraments. Even if fairies, ghosts, and magic had to be integrated into a Christian cosmos, that cosmos was still Christian, and to be taken seriously. But how seriously did people take their religion? Was there a whole-hearted acceptance of authoritarian pronouncements, or was there a deep-rooted scepticism, making most peoples' catholicism superficial and illusory? The distinction would not be between 'conviction' and 'superstition' – if such a distinction has any validity for this period beyond the declarations of the intelligentsia – but between on one side a catholicism which, for all its syncretism, its aberrations of sacramentals and accretions of pilgrimages and indulgences, was founded on a willing acceptance, and on the other a mere external conformity which says nothing about beliefs, extending to encompass active scepticism, and even downright rejection of catholicism.

Here several issues intertwine, but must be disentangled. For one thing, it is necessary to try to differentiate between 'impiety' and 'scepticism'. The former implies a deliberate refusal to adhere to the practical demands of a religion while maintaining a formal acceptance of its moral and theological stances. It may be the result of ignorance, but that is perhaps less certain. Scepticism, however, implies a more radical approach, a serious questioning of the fundamentals of a religion, and their outright denial or replacement by another set of ideas. Allocating individual incidents to one or the other category is often necessarily a subjective exercise; but if a subjective initial comment is permitted, it seems that impiety was virtually endemic, while scepticism was less common but still not infrequently voiced. Attitudes towards the two varied. Impiety had to be condemned, and thundered against from the pulpit; but in certain circumstances it was institutionalised, as in the carnivalesque celebrations associated with boy bishops. Scepticism had similarly to be condemned, but it also had to be eradicated because it offered a more serious and far-reaching threat to Christianity as a theological system.

Recognition of the dangers of scepticism was built into the canon law. The *Decretals* of Gregory IX, promulgated in 1234, reproduced a *dictum* ascribed to an unidentified Pope Stephen which was culled from earlier collections: 'Dubius in fide infidelis est' – 'One who doubts/questions/is uncertain in the faith is an infidel/faithless'.[9] In an era of vassalage, such faithlessness might also carry overtones of disloyalty, if not outright treason; but doubts, questions, and uncertainties were inherent in Christianity, largely because of the scale of its intellectual demands. In any case, the possibility of doubt and questioning was – and is – integral to

---

[9] E. L. Richter and E. Friedberg, eds., *Corpus iuris canonici* (2 vols., Leipzig, 1879–81), II, col. 778.

Christianity's continued development. As a speculative religion, it was necessarily subjected to processes of clarification and investigation. As an evolving religion, it had to be constantly assessed and reassessed in the light of its ability to solve contemporary questions. As a faith which required acceptance prior to understanding, its formulations might well prove incompatible with experience, and pose problems when a reconciliation of the two was attempted.

The ways in which Christianity did evolve, at all levels, attests the seriousness of the questioning to which it was subjected. Such evolution could only occur in response to doubt and uncertainty, in the search for a religion and spirituality which offered more satisfying responses than those previously available. Without that doubt, it would have stagnated. In this formulation, peasants' attempts to make sense of their religion are as valid as the scholastic investigations of the theologians: the same mental processes operate; it is only the tools and the acceptability of the process, and possibly the conclusions, which may differ.

Debate and questioning by the intelligentsia, those trained for the job, was clearly seen in a different light from similar expressions among the laity; but the scale of the questioning could not be controlled. Recognition of the possibility that doubts could be widely shared is suggested by the way in which an attack on the obscure heterodoxy of Amaury of Bène at Paris in 1210 became a purge of his supposed adherents in the surrounding region, although the reality of their links with him is questionable. Later assumptions of overlap between Wyclife's ideas and those of participants in the English Peasants' Revolt in 1381 show similar awareness. The extent of the questioning and uncertainty is rarely apparent, but the church authorities may have comprehended it, and appreciated that it could not be fully controlled or countered. Their response was to seek a better understanding of the demands of the religion through the *pastoralia* literature, although this often covered the moral and disciplinary demands rather than the intellectual. In that sphere, their concern was chiefly to try to prevent the questioning: the laity in their 'simplicity' should keep to their place and not try to tackle issues beyond their mental capacities. As Humbert of Romans put it, 'The laity ought not to rise up to look into the secrets of the faith . . . but adhere to them implicitly'.[10] Understanding was not necessary, merely acceptance and the intention to believe as the church believed – a form of words which also allowed individuals to question but fight against their questioning. There was also worry that preachers provoked uncertainty through their

---

[10] A. Murray, 'Religion among the poor in thirteenth-century France: the testimony of Humbert de Romans', *Traditio*, 30 (1974), p. 298 n70.

sermons, confusing the audiences by tackling issues too deep and theological for their safety. The 'simplicity' which led some people to the wrong conclusions was accepted, and to a degree tolerated: such people had only to be persuaded that they had been misguided. Their misguidedness was clearly distinguished (in theory, but practice may have been different) from the presumption and intellectual pride which produced the conclusions of heretics. Yet both sets of conclusions could be the result of the same process of questioning.

Christian dogmas are complex, the requirements of belief often contrary to human experience, yet set within a strongly human context. Possibly the greatest difficulty with Christianity is that essentially human context: the foci are not sufficiently unworldly to allow an uncritical suspension of disbelief. Many aspects could be subjected to experiential testing: resurrection, transubstantiation, the problem of evil, and so on, producing results which might well conflict with the official proclamations. When questioned, some people did claim to have thought out their unorthodoxies for themselves. This perhaps especially applied to peasants working in agriculture, who evolved naturalistic explanations of growth and decay in which God was not necessarily the prime mover. The nature of the personal crises which people faced, the spiritual struggles and intellectual challenges, make it hard not to accept as widespread what has been identified as 'a certain independence of mind and native skepticism' as a result of which 'unorthodox opinions . . . may well have arisen spontaneously from the cogitations of men and women searching for explanations that accorded with the realities of the life in which they were enmeshed'.[11]

How radically the questioning could penetrate is open to debate. That it could lead to formal atheism, a complete denial of the existence of the divinity, seems unlikely. The Bible's role as cultural foundation seriously undermined the possibility of really fundamental scepticism, certainly to the extent of atheism. It was possible to deny God verbally, but such denials were more often challenges *to* God than rejections of the existence of the Divinity. To reject God intellectually, and with conviction, required the substitution of a whole new cosmology from first principles. There is no sign that that actually happened. What scepticism there is rarely approaches the divinity except as forceful blasphemy; although it does challenge saints and specific devotional practices, the validity of the ecclesiastical structure and the power of the priests. The difficulty is to

---

[11] W. L. Wakefield, 'Some unorthodox popular ideas of the thirteenth century', *Mediaevalia et humanistica*, n.s. 4 (1973), p. 33.

judge why the scepticism was voiced. Were the outbursts fits of temper in domestic crises, or were individuals really thinking things through and reaching their own theological conclusions?

How historians respond to these issues is sometimes as intriguing as the contemporary response. For they seem obsessed with combining individual sceptics into heretical collectivities, especially notable with the Cathars and the Lollards. Even if the statements are not explicitly heretical, nevertheless they are used to adduce signs of the appropriate 'tendencies'. As ever, context is vitally important and, often, a statement's context is not recorded. The resulting assessments are therefore unavoidably tentative, and questionable.

The nature of doubt

The evidence for scepticism offers access to a substratum of medieval religion which demands, but denies, evaluation. By definition, a substratum only surfaces rarely, and allows access only by quarrying. It may actually surface more often than is usually noticed, because of the fragmented nature of historians' approaches to the history of spirituality, and their quest for 'popular religion'. That search rather ignores the theologians; yet their debates and disagreements may also serve as evidence of scepticism, dressed up in academic language but still questioning and challenging. The arguments about the Real Presence, the Immaculate Conception, and other issues, differ little in reality (but greatly in expression and sometimes in reaction) from parallel uncertainties voiced by those cited in inquisitorial proceedings. Joinville's tale in his *Life of St Louis* of the despairing French theologian who found the doctrine of transubstantiation unconvincing, and other anecdotal evidence, shows doubt at the highest levels. The nature of inquisitorial material, and particularly its patchy survival, precludes much in the way of quarrying; although it suggests that 'popular scepticism' was widely distributed in the mental geography of Europe. It certainly appears among those reported to the Inquisition in thirteenth-century Languedoc, late-fourteenth-century Savoy, and fifteenth-century Spain; it is indicated in some heresy cases in post-Wyclifite England, possibly even in codified form in the series of questions drawn up to identify 'Lollards'. The opportunities for scepticism were perhaps geographically dictated to an extent. Only where contacts with Jews and Moslems were common could the issue of the relative validity of the religions be a real one, open to discussion. That this happened in Spain is shown in Inquisition evidence gathered at Soria in the late 1400s, with one farmer bluntly asking, 'How does anyone know which of the three laws God loves best?'[12] The reaction to some of this questioning may have wider implications. When advanced in Spain by Old Christians it could be dismissed as ignorant simplicity; whereas if advanced by *conversos* the response would be much more hostile.

Overall, the evidence for the incidence of scepticism is impressive, inviting the assumption that there was much more which has eluded the records; but the overall impact may be legitimately doubted. The charges say little about the continuity of the doubting. Often they appear to derive from words said in very specific circumstances, blasphemy during games or arguments being common, and sometimes were clearly accusations rather than proof. Others may reflect a short-term uncertainty, removed by later awareness or even conviction. Among those examined by the Inquisition at Toulouse in the 1270s, for example, Ademarus Gelofi had tried to think through the idea of bodily resurrection, and reached the wrong conclusions, which he declared when examined that he had now rejected after being better informed. Bernardus Raymondi had also reached faulty conclusions – this time with the help of books – but again declared that the accusations related to ideas since abandoned under better instruction. The degree of emphasis to be given to one-off or short-term expressions of doubt and opposition can be debated. The immediate context of ale-house disagreements, local disputes with rapacious clerics, emotional traumas, and frustration, could all produce unthinking outbursts which might soon be regretted. Some of the reported denials of belief may have gained their force not from the verbal rejection of aspects of Christianity which brought them to the attention of the authorities, but from the fact that they were uttered in order to shock, and no more. Frequently the outcome of extreme frustration and exasperation, sometimes the outburst seemingly shocked and unnerved its utterer as much as its audience. In such circumstances, the outrages would be founded on a real acceptance of Christianity, albeit a Christianity which allowed God and the saints to be chastised and punished by blasphemy for provocation or indifference, just as divine chastisement threatened humans. To seek vengeance on God implicitly accepted His existence and power; a paradox epitomised in Humbert of Romans' succinct statement of the grumbling leper's attitude towards God: 'You have taken my body from me, and I will deprive you of my soul'.[13] It is hard not to sympathise, perhaps empathise, with the sacristan of Avila who, in what was seemingly a particularly sensitive self-defence

---

[12] J. H. Edwards, 'Religious faith and doubt in late medieval Spain', *Past and Present*, 120 (August, 1985), p. 17.

[13] Murray, 'Religion among the poor', p. 322 n212.

against blasphemy charges in 1525, admitted his words but added that 'none of this indicates that I am consciously rejecting the basic tenets of my faith'.[14]

The nature of the sources means that usually only the positive evidence about spirituality is recorded. Given the circumstances of their production, wills would be unlikely to denigrate religion, even if they did not reveal much about active spirituality. Most other evidence on religious and devotional practices is similarly skewed to emphasise conformity: records of fraternity membership, evidence of pilgrimage, miracle collections, devotional writings, and so on. The ideal can also be recreated from the instructional and spiritual literature of the time. Signs of aspirituality are rarer. Accusations of heresy can be placed in that category, but they may not reflect lack of spirituality, rather the deliberate choice of a distinctly different form. Some accusations in church courts, for blasphemy and non-attendance at church services, may equally not reflect aspirituality, but hostility to social requirements and controls; again they cannot be taken as tests of the importance of religion in an individual's life, or the degree of theological knowledge and spiritual awareness. Yet there is a problem here, for the heresy trials, and the clear signs of antipathy to some species of devotional activity, are generally treated as abnormal and odd: the church's own definitions of the spiritual norms are implicitly accepted; but these can only operate as means towards assessing the outsider, the rejected.

None of this denies the possibility of real doubt and scepticism. To blame the questioning on 'heresy' or the 'devil' was an obvious and simplistic response; what matters is that the possibility of doubt was acknowledged. The areas and occasions of doubt were regularly identified by preachers and others, seeking to reassure their listeners that full comprehension was not necessary, only acceptance that the church was not misleading them. That may be patronising, but certainly does not under-estimate people's ability and propensity to look for their own definitions of what Christianity entailed. In a sense, those conveying the message were engaged in damage-limitation. They seem to have recognised that anyone might at some point doubt or question, and not appreciate things fully – perhaps that is why they usually appear so reluctant to inquire deeply into people's beliefs. Certainly there was consistent awareness that souls were battlegrounds, with the formulation that unbelief was actually a test imposed by God (or the devil) to confirm

[14] M. Flynn, 'Betrayal of the soul in Spanish blasphemy', in *Religion, body and gender in early modern Spain*, ed. A. Saint-Saëns (San Francisco, 1991), p. 39.

belief, and the recognition that the point of most severe testing for faith was the deathbed, when despair and doubt had to be countered most vigorously, and faith confirmed to assure salvation.

Ignorance

Alongside the problem of doubt runs that of ignorance. That is even more difficult to assess than the questioning of religion: as it did not directly contravene the intellectual norms, it was less likely to be seen as a real threat. How widespread ignorance actually was also falls into the problems of treating Christianity as an evolving religion: the demands of 1215 were not those of 1515; as expectations of awareness changed, so would the definition of ignorance.

The charge that the laity were incompletely aware of the demands of their faith was almost a commonplace among the clergy. In some ways, it had to be: complacency was not to be encouraged, therefore there always had to be criticism. The validity of the charges, and their precise meaning, is more difficult to define. In some cases it is likely that the auditors were being attacked not for ignorance of their religion, but for a failure to fulfil obligations of which they were well aware – for impiety. Where clergy were failing in their duties, through negligence, or their own ignorance, the problems would be exacerbated. Again, however, assessment is problematic; and no definite conclusions can be drawn. The situation would vary from region to region, over time, and from priest to priest within a specific parish. Moreover, if the laity realised that they were not well served, they might act themselves to remedy the situation. An important factor here might be the mobility of the medieval population, and the contrast between town and country. In the latter, especially areas of semi-nomadic shepherding, access to the faith might be particularly weak, as Ramon Llull noted in his novel *Blanquerna*, making a point of the need to direct a semi-missionary effort at the shepherds (a situation which has striking parallels with the religion of the shepherds at Montaillou). Towns with several small but poverty-stricken parishes might not offer adequate spiritual care, others with a single parish might have too populous to permit proper oversight; in both cases a fluid and fluctuating population would probably allow many to slip through the net.

Among the most important developments which affected the laity was their increasing access to the church and its services. In the thirteenth century Humbert of Romans, one of the leading lights of the recently established Dominican Order whose function was explicitly to contribute to the pastoral revolution through preaching, complained about those who rarely attended church. Other preachers of the time echoed his suggestion that church-going was not exactly enthusiastic, Giordano da Pisa once receiving the blunt reply that church attendance on feast days was 'not the custom'.[15] There would always be some for whom that was the case; but the impression is that the problem of non-attendance had largely disappeared by the early sixteenth century. Visitation returns do report people who preferred to work or engage in commerce than go to church; but they appear rarely, and even rarer are charges of neglect of the annual confession and communion (which are sometimes countered by evidence that the accused had attended another church instead). The increasing geographical distribution of religion through the erection of rural chapels and the laity's assumption of responsibility for their maintenance, the domestication of religion in the spread of oratories and ownership of prayer books which themselves must have encouraged church attendance, and the integration of church services into the creation of a variety of group identities whose overlap contributed to the make-up of the individual, must all have conspired to increase the regularity of attendance. The self-policing which made those who did not conform into 'outsiders' would equally have made non-attendance a dangerous statement.

Concrete indications of ignorance are relatively rare, simply because the evidence of the testing does not survive. It is also worth stressing again that the formal demands were minimalist, so that the level of ignorance had to be dire before it became notable. There are occasional hints, some of the most striking coming from late medieval Spain. In 1501 some women of Quintana del Pidio expressed fears of falling into the hands of the Inquisition, precisely because it tested knowledge of the faith by demanding recitation of the four standard prayers (*Ave*, Creed, Our Father, and *Salve Regina*). Testimony offered in the investigation of fifteenth- and sixteenth-century Spanish visions also sometimes provides insights into the witnesses' knowledge of the general requirements of Christianity. From a twentieth-century perspective some replies reveal a disappointingly low standard. Most of those interrogated knew the basic texts, although sometimes with odd errors in the recitations; but few knew any more, and their personal devotions were largely restricted to repeated recitations of those prayers. Sometimes, indeed, even less was known. In 1518 Juan de Rabe of La Mota was questioned by the Inquisition about a vision he claimed to have experienced some four years before. During his questioning,

---

[15] A. Murray, 'Piety and impiety in thirteenth-century Italy', *Studies in church history*, 8 (1972), pp. 97–8.

He was asked . . . if he knew the Credo and the Salve Regina; he said he did not. And if he knew the Pater Noster and the Ave Maria; he said he did . . . He said the entire Ave Maria, and the Pater Noster he said in its entirety but he did not know it well . . . He said that he has confessed every year at Lent . . . and that every time . . . he received the most holy sacrament.

Asked if he knows the Ten Commandments and the Articles of Faith and the seven deadly sins and the five senses [which formed part of the general package of instruction in the pastoralia literature], he said that he did not know any of these in whole or in part. Asked . . . what . . . he confessed, if he did not know the deadly sins or the Ten Commandments or the five senses, he said that he confessed what he did know about. He was asked if pride or envy or lust or the killing of a man or insulting someone with offensive words was a sin, and to each of these he replied that he did not know. He was asked if theft was a sin, and he said that, God preserve us, theft was a very great sin.[16]

So much for three centuries of pastoral care! Such ignorance presumably reflects fundamental failure by the parish clergy, and was probably not unique. Yet it would stretch the evidence to say that equivalent ignorance was widespread – we cannot tell.

Ambiguity

Reaching a conclusion about scepticism and ignorance is the most difficult aspect of any analysis of medieval religion and devotion. Disciplinary records give almost the sole concrete evidence – although preachers often complained that their flocks were inattentive, saying that people were reluctant to attend services, prefering folktales and taverns to sermons and communion and being generally inattentive in using the church for worldly business rather than God's. But preachers had a high opinion of the value of preaching, which may not have accorded with their intended audience's devotional priorities (although sermons were popular, and famous preachers attracted huge audiences). Humbert of Romans complains about those who failed to pay attention when they were in church during a sermon; but his listed distractions include prayers, kneeling before images, and collecting holy water, which for the participants might be providing answers to more immediate concerns. Those wishing to sow unorthodoxy were equally rebuffed, as William Thorpe complained when his listeners at Shrewsbury in 1407 dashed off to see an elevation at the sound of a sacring bell. Court records – especially parochial visitations – offer instances of people not attending

---

[16] W. A. Christian, jr., *Apparitions in late medieval and Renaissance Spain* (Princeton, NJ, 1981), pp. 153–4

church because they preferred the tavern; ignoring services on Sundays and holy days in order to work and trade; ridiculing preachers and priests; and being generally disruptive. What is to be made of this? Was it heresy, or laziness, or scepticism, or poverty, need, and greed, which drove people to neglect their spiritual obligations?

Sometimes, as in evidence from late fifteenth-century Spain, there are signs of real objection to the church, almost an anti-Christian temperament. But that often centres on dealings with the clergy, rather than relationships with God. English evidence, especially charges against supposed or actual Lollards, similarly raises the problem of apparent scepticism and rejection which may be nothing more than a common-sense approach to events: if a saint's image could not keep itself warm and free of cobwebs in a cold and dusty church, why assume that it could work miracles? Such rationalisation is ambivalent: it does not deny the power of saints, merely how others approached them; so it could be considered as calling for a purer stance on religion. Satire, one of the dominant themes of late medieval literature, may similarly reflect a disenchantment with religion, but possibly more with its mechanics than its spiritual tenets. It may, equally, reflect spiritual vitality, and a concern for the removal of perceived abuses so as to reinvigorate the religion.

Doubt, uncertainty, were bound to be encountered in any religious quest. Yet mockery may also be an expression of seriousness. Criticism and scepticism certainly had a place in medieval religion, and challenges were offered to devotional practices because their validity and efficacy were queried – which drives discussion back to the point that medieval religion was largely demand-led in its structures and manifestations; and must again integrate the constant struggle by the authorities to curtail credulity. Yet, even with the onset of humanism in the fifteenth century, it seems unlikely that there were many – if any – actual atheists. The period's cosmological perceptions made atheism perhaps the most irrational of stances, opposing all received notions of creation, of human organisation, and of future destinations. Man could not survive unaided against the pressures of the world: God was necessary, if only as a scapegoat. Yet a capricious God, an arbitrary God, an indifferent God, a God who refused to be manipulated by his petitioners and devotees, might stimulate scepticism, repudiation, and ridicule as much as fear and devotion. As with heresy and orthodoxy, the dividing line was tenuous, and flexible. This is perhaps the most vital point in seeking to establish the 'reality' of religion. 'Believers' and 'sceptics' were not sheep and goats; were not distinct species. The balance within each individual 'religiosity' would vary, and constantly change, according to circumstances and immediate conviction. But for most of the millions who lived as

Christians in the communion of the catholic church between 1215 and
1515, the changes and the personal struggles associated with them are
totally unrecorded.

THINGS TO COME

Whether doubt and scepticism were increasing in the late fifteenth and
early sixteenth centuries cannot be assessed with any accuracy. What is
clear, above all, is that vocal opposition to the church's established
structures and beliefs was very much a minority affair, a situation which
highlights the problem of the status of Christianity on what – with
hindsight only – was the eve of a new sort of Reformation: one which
destroyed the unity of the Latin tradition by imposing and demanding
choices rather than merely extending the range of options within the
overall system. To bring that phenomenon into the equations is, perhaps,
to distort the perspective massively. That is why the formal termination of
this book is placed in 1515; but subsequent events cannot be completely
cast aside. How they actually fit in is, nevertheless, almost impossible to
say: to predict developments in religion and devotion at the time of the
Fifth Lateran Council would have been a thankless task.

If the centuries before 1515 are considered in their own right, and on
their own terms, then the picture is certainly not bleak. These had been
years of great vitality, of great expansion. Christianity had, necessarily,
changed massively. The waves of enthusiasm which had rippled out from
the Fourth Lateran Council onwards – whether the mendicants, the
Devotio moderna, the beguines, new definitions of sanctity, and the
manifold new devotions and devotional practices – had all and each left a
mark on the church and its members. That mark varied, according to time
and place, but it was ineradicably there. The religion had evolved, had
almost certainly become more widespread. By 1515 it was unavoidably
more a part of the cultural baggage of more people, and more deeply
embedded, than it had been in 1215. None of those waves of enthusiasm
had proved easy to channel; most – perhaps all – at some point had
produced conflict, at least tension, and sometimes even heresy. In the late
fifteenth century, it may be that other waves were breaking, or building
up: the back-to-basics Observantine movement in the regular orders, the
greater lay concern for controlling the clergy, the developments in
appreciations of purgatory, the elevation in the status of Marian and
Christocentric shrines, the move from an Incarnational to a Pauline
theology, the developing élitism of some of the clergy, possibly even the
gender tensions as men sought a redefinition of religion more to their
liking and a reduction of a perceived female domination of spirituality.

Clearly, there was hope for some major reform of the church – there always was – but in the early sixteenth century the impetus does seem to have been building up considerably. Not only were there the schemes for a widespread reconstruction of the ecclesiastical system put forward within the context of the Lateran meeting, there were also local ideas such as those of John Colet in England. This has the appearance of a process of 'top-down' reform, with Colet's advocacy including an appeal to hierocracy almost Hildebrandine in its assumptions. How such reformism would eventually have worked out – if it had been allowed to – is not clear. The frustrations and tensions in the late medieval church seem to focus primarily on disciplinary, moral and administrative issues. Assertion of local rights against papal centralisation or clerical authoritarianism seems to have been the common stance, with little sense of widespread alienation from the devotional regimes. If anything, there was a reluctance to abandon them in opposition to the purificatory demands of some of the would-be reformers.

To concentrate on such reformers would be to skew the issues. There was also considerable evolution elsewhere, among both clergy and laity. By 1515 all of western and central Europe was included within the catholic church: the need for mission within Europe seemed to have disappeared. New cults continued to rise, and old one declined; pilgrimage remained important; prayers for the dead still called forth massive investment. Religion remained at the core of social organisation in its moral demands, although the tensions between morality and reality were possibly becoming more obvious. Perhaps in some places the laity were becoming more demanding of their clergy, certainly the continued availability of priests and their dependence on the laity for employment gave the latter more control over the type of religion which they accepted. The hiring of chaplains, of chantry priests, may have contributed to a greater localisation of religion, and certainly greater lay independence of the hierarchical ecclesiastical structure. This was at its most developed in the fraternities, which offered a Christianity often unconstrained by the demands of parochial and other conformities.

However, it would be dangerous to overstress that separateness. Religion was still highly sacramental, dependent particularly on confession and communion as routes to salvation. To that extent, it was still priest-centred. But the role of the priest had changed significantly after 1215: from celebrant of remote rites before 1200 to pastoral minister in accordance with the demands of Lateran IV, to employee as the laity took charge of their own salvations. The change was not exclusive: priests still celebrated, still ministered, and those with benefices were in a position very different from that of a guild or parish chaplain. Nor was change constant or linear: attitudes would vary with circumstances. Nevertheless, the general trend was symptomatic of the overall evolution and increasing complexity of catholicism. Perhaps it was also a catholicism which had got out of control, with the fissiparous tendencies of a society lacking the means of imposing uniformity finding fruit in devotional localism and individuality.

There is another element which may need to be built in here: print. In religious terms, the advent of printing was possibly even more significant than the advent of the mendicants and their impact on religious life; there is certainly come equivalence. Print gave a new vitality to religious debates; gave a new range of spiritual outlets and opportunities; challenged clerical status and control. It also had to respond to market forces, it might convey heresy as much as orthodoxy. But it was also repressive, for it gave new rigidity to authority, allowing regimentation through texts and the stultification of the local. In 1515 its importance in the extension and imposition of a spiritual message remained to be appreciated, but its potential was evident in the printing of sermons almost as they were preached.

Does that mean that 'The Reformation' was unforeseeable in 1515? Probably. Does it mean that pre-Reformation religion was in fact vital and progressing (whatever progress is) rather than decadent and ready to fall? Almost certainly. However, the reformist pressures within the late medieval church should not be under-stated; they were clearly strong. The Fifth Lateran Council of 1512–17 was meant to accommodate them; but in the end failed. Those reformist pressures were not 'Protestant' but catholic, and no matter how different its appearance, the church which grew out of them would have been by definition as catholic as the one it replaced. But the Reformations got in the way, and we will never know what would have happened without them.

BIBLIOGRAPHY

This is intended to be only a select bibliography. Given that there are few notes, I have not included everything which would have appeared in a list of material cited for a fully annotated volume. The aim is to list the main sources on which I have drawn, and which will themselves offer further bibliographical guidance. The range of works which could and perhaps ought to appear here is massive, my major problems being where to start and where to stop. The most straightforward decision has been to include all the works mentioned in the footnotes. Beyond that I have been deliberately selective, a process which has been necessarily subjective.

Part I Primary sources

The aim in this listing is both to indicate the works referred to in the book (in Section A), and to indicate the range of additional material which is available by including in Section B a small selection of additional works. Some of these have been mentioned without being explicitly cited in the main text. There is no attempt to be comprehensive, and the list is confined to works available in modern English. The range of appropriate medieval texts available in translation is constantly increasing. Beyond those which appear here, several important English works are available in Penguin Classics editions, while the series of *Classics of western spirituality* offers translations of a wide range of major texts, among which the works of medieval mystical writers are particularly well represented. I have also included here a small number of works which give an indication of the non-literary aspects of medieval Christianity.

Section A

Aquinas, Thomas, *Summa theologica, vol. 34: charity (2ª2ªᵉ, 23–33)* (London and New York, 1975)

Barnum, P. H., ed., *Dives and pauper*, Early English text society, o.s. 275, 280 (1976–80)

Calvert, E., 'Extracts from a fifteenth century MS', *Transactions of the Shropshire archaeological and natural history society*, 2nd ser., 6 (1894), pp. 99–106

Cigman, G., ed., *Lollard sermons*, Early English text society, original ser., 294 (1989)

Dudley, Edmund (ed. D. M. Brodie), *The tree of commonwealth* (Cambridge, 1948)

García y García, A., ed., *Synodicon Hispanicum, I: Galicia* (Madrid, 1981)

Guasti, C., ed., *Ser Lapo Mazzei: lettere di un notaro a un mercante del secolo XIV; con altre lettere e documenti* (2 vols., Florence, 1880)

Kingsley, J., ed., *The poems of William Dunbar* (Oxford, 1979)

McCracken, H. N., ed., *The minor poems of John Lydgate*, II, Early English text society, original ser., 192 (1934)

Mills, C. A., ed., *Ye solace of pilgrimes: a description of Rome, circa AD 1450, by John Capgrave, an Austin friar of King's Lynn* (London, New York, Toronto, and Melbourne, 1911)

Nicolas, N. H., ed., *Privy purse expenses of Elizabeth of York; Wardrobe accounts of Edward the Fourth* (London, 1830)

Richter, E. L., and E. Friedberg, eds., *Corpus iuris canonici* (2 vols., Leipzig, 1879–81)

Sneyd, C. A., ed., *A relation, or rather a true account, of the island of England, with sundry particulars of these people and of the royal revenues under king Henry the seventh, about the year 1500*, Camden society publications, 1st ser., 37 (1847)

Strauss, G., ed., *Manifestations of discontent in Germany on the eve of the Reformation* (Bloomington and London, 1971)

Swanson, R. N., ed., *Catholic England: faith, religion, and observance before the Reformation* (Manchester, 1993)

Tanner, N. P., ed., *Heresy trials in the diocese of Norwich, 1428–31*, Camden society publications, 4th ser., 20 (1977)

Decrees of the ecumenical councils (2 vols., London, 1990)

Tierney, B., ed., *The crisis of church and state, 1050–1300* (Englewood Cliffs, NJ, 1964)

Wakefield, W. L., and A. P. Evans, eds., *Heresies of the high middle ages* (New York, 1968)

Woolley, R. M., ed., *The officium and miracula of Richard Rolle of Hampole* (London, 1919)

Zacour, N., ed., *Jews and Saracens in the consilia of Oldradus de Ponte*, Pontifical Institute of Mediaeval Studies: studies and texts, 100 (Toronto, 1990)

Section B

Alexander, J., and P. Binski, *Age of chivalry: art in Plantagenet England, 1200–1400* (London, 1987)

Arnould, A., and J. M. Massing, *Splendours of Flanders: late medieval art in Cambridge collections* (Cambridge, 1993)

Bokenham, Osbern (trans. S. Delany), *A legend of holy women: Osbern Bokenham, 'Legends of Holy Women'* (Notre Dame and London, 1992)

Brunn, E. zum, and G. Epinay-Burgard, eds., *Women mystics in medieval Europe* (New York, 1989)

Cawley, A. C., ed., *Everyman and medieval miracle plays* (2nd edn, London, 1974)

de Deguileville, Guillaume (trans. E. Clasby), *The pilgrimage of human life (La pelèrinage de la vie humaine)* (Hamden, CO, 1992)

Enghen, J. van, ed., *Devotio moderna: basic writings* (New York and Mahwah, 1988)

Innocent III, pope, *see* Lotario dei Segni

à Kempis, Thomas (trans. L. Shirley-Price), *The imitation of Christ* (Harmondsworth, 1952)

Laster, G. A., ed., *Three late medieval morality plays* (London and New York, 1981)

Llull, Ramon (trans. E. A. Peers), *Blanquerna: a thirteenth-century romance* (London, 1925)

Peters, E., ed., *Heresy and authority in medieval Europe: documents in translation* (London, 1980)

Petroff, E. A., ed., *Medieval women's visionary literature* (Oxford, 1986)

Segni, Lotario dei (Pope Innocent III), (trans. R. E. Lewis), *De miseria condicionis humane* (Athens, GA, 1978)

Voragine, Jacobus de (trans. W. L. Ryan), *The golden legend: readings on the saints* (2 vols., Princeton, NJ, 1993)

Warren, F. E., ed., *The Sarum manual in English*, Alcuin club collections, 11 (2 vols., London, Oxford, and Melbourne, 1913)

Wenzel, S., ed., *Fasciculus morum: a fourteenth-century preacher's handbook* (University Park and London, 1989)

Windeatt, B. A., ed., *The book of Margery Kempe* (Harmondsworth, 1985)

Part II Secondary works

This list gives all the secondary material cited in the notes, regardless of language, and a selection of the works which have made a significant contribution to the research for the text. With the latter I have concentrated on indicating material in English; but to confine the list solely to English works would had been counter-productive and overly restrictive. The coverage has therefore been stretched to include material in French. Other languages are sometimes represented in collections of articles, but that is accidental. Although much important material has been arbitrarily excluded by these choices, they do make the listing manageable. To save space, collections of essays are usually recorded as such if I have used more than two articles from the volume.

Almog, S., ed., *Antisemitism through the ages* (Oxford, 1988)

Amos, T. L., E. A. Green, and B. M. Kienzle, eds., *De ore domini: preacher and word in the middle ages*, Studies in medieval culture, 27 (Kalamazoo, 1989)

Ashley, K., and P. Sheingorn, eds., *Interpreting cultural symbols: Saint Anne in late medieval society* (Athens, GA, and London, 1990)

Aston, M., *Faith and fire: popular and unpopular religion, 1350–1600* (London and Rio Grande, 1993)

Asztalos, M., 'The faculty of theology', in *A history of the university in Europe, vol. I: universities in the middle ages*, ed. H. de Ridder-Symoens (Cambridge, 1992), pp. 409–41

Ault, W. O., 'Manor court and parish church in fifteenth-century England: a study of village by-laws', *Speculum*, 42 (1967), pp. 53–67

Avril, J., 'A propos du "proprius sacerdos": quelques réflexions sur les pouvoirs du prêtre de paroisse', in *Proceedings of the fifth international congress of medieval canon law: Salamanca, 21–25 September, 1976*, ed. S. Kuttner and K. Pennington, Monumenta iuris canonici, series C: subsidia, 6 (Vatican City, 1980), pp. 471–86

Banker, J. R., *Death in the community: memorialization and confraternities in an Italian commune in the late middle ages* (Athens, GA, and London, 1988)

Barber, M., 'Lepers, Jews, and Moslems: the plot to overthrow Christendom in 1321', *History*, 66 (1981), pp. 1–17

Barron, C. M., 'The parish fraternities of medieval London', in *The church in pre-Reformation society: essays in honour of F. R. H. du Boulay*, ed. C. M. Barron and C. Harper-Bill (Woodbridge, Suffolk, 1985), pp. 13–37

Batlle, C., 'Els Granollacs, metges de Barcelona (segle XV). De la cort del rei a la beneficència parroquial', in *La pobreza y la asistencia a los pobres en la Cataluña medieval; volumen miscelaneo de estudios y documentos*, ed. M. Riu, Anuario de estudios medievales, 9, 11 (2 vols., Barcelona, 1980–2), II, pp. 383–414

Bell, S. E., 'Medieval women book owners: arbiters of lay piety and ambassadors of culture', in *Women and power in the middle ages*, ed. M. Ehler and M. Kowaleski (Athens, GA, and London, 1988), pp. 149–87, also in *Sisters and workers in the middle ages*, ed. J. M. Bennett *et al.* (Chicago and London, 1989), pp. 135–61

Berger, D., 'Mission to the Jews and Jewish-Christian contacts in the polemical literature of the high middle ages', *American historical review*, 91 (1986), pp. 576–91

Bériac, F., '"Mourir au monde". Les *ordines* de séparation des lépreux en France au XVᵉ et XVIᵉ siècles', *Journal of medieval history*, 11 (1985), pp. 245–68

Biller, P., 'Words and the medieval notion of "religion"', *Journal of ecclesiastical history*, 36 (1985), pp. 351–69

Black, A., *Political thought, 1250–1450* (Cambridge, 1992)

Black, C. F., *Italian confraternities in the sixteenth century* (Cambridge, 1989)

Blickle, P., 'Communal Reformation and peasant piety: the peasant Reformation and its late medieval origins', *Central European history*, 20 (1987), pp. 216–28

Bolton, B. M., *The medieval Reformation* (London, 1987)

Bornstein, D.,'The shrine of Santa Maria a Cigoli: female visionaries and clerical promoters', *Mélanges de l'École française de Rome: Moyen-âge, Temps Modernes*, 98 (1986), pp. 219–28

'The uses of the body: the church and the cult of Santa Margharita de Cortona', *Church history*, 62 (1993), pp. 163–77

Bossy, J., 'The mass as a social institution, 1200–1700', *Past and present*, 100 (August 1983), pp. 29–61

Christianity in the west, 1400–1700 (Oxford, 1985)

'Prayers', *Transactions of the royal historical society*, 6th ser., 1 (1991), pp. 137–48

Boswell, J., *Christianity, social tolerance, and homosexuality: gay people in western Europe from the beginning of the Christian era to the fourteenth century* (Chicago and London, 1980)

Boyle, L. E., 'Montaillou revisited: *mentalité* and methodology', in *Pathways to medieval peasants*, ed. J. A. Raftis, Pontifical institute of mediaeval studies: Papers in mediaeval studies, 2 (Toronto, 1981), pp. 119–40

'The Fourth Lateran Council and manuals of popular theology', in *The popular literature of medieval England*, ed. T. J. Heffernan, Tennessee studies in literature, 28 (Knoxville, TN, 1985), pp. 30–43

Breshahan Menning, C., 'The Monte's "Monte": the early supporters of Florence's Monte de Pietà', *The sixteenth-century journal*, 23 (1992), pp. 661–76

Briscoe, M. G., 'How was the ars praedicandi taught in England?', in *The use of manuscripts in literary studies: essays in memory of Judson Boyle Allen*, ed. C. C. Morse, P. R. Doos, and M. C. Woods, Studies in medieval culture, 31 (Kalamazoo, 1992), pp. 41–59

'Artes praedicandi', in M. G. Briscoe and B. H. Jaye, *Artes praedicandi and Artes orandi*, Typologie des sources du moyen âge occidental, fasc. 61 (Turnhout, 1992), pp. 9–76

Brody, S. N., *The disease of the soul: leprosy in medieval literature* (Ithaca and London, 1974)

Brooke, C. N. L., 'Reflections on late medieval cults and devotions', in *Essays in honor of Edward B. King*, ed. R. G. Benson and E. W. Naylor (Sewanee, TN, 1991), pp. 33–45

Brooke, R., 'The lives of St Francis of Assisi', in *Latin biography*, ed. T. A. Dorey (London, 1967), pp. 177–98

Brooke, R. and C., *Popular religion in the middle ages: western Europe, 1000–1300* (London, 1984)

Brown, D. A., 'The Allelulia: a thirteenth-century peace movement', *Archivum franciscanum historicum*, 81 (1988), pp. 3–16

Burgess, C., 'Late medieval wills and pious convention: testamentary evidence reconsidered', in *Profit, piety, and the professions in later medieval England*, ed. M. A. Hicks (Gloucester, 1990), pp. 14–33

Burns, R. I., 'Renegades, adventurers, and sharp businessmen: the thirteenth-century Spaniard in the cause of Islam', *Catholic historical review*, 58 (1972), pp. 341–66

Moors and crusaders in Mediterranean Spain (London, 1978)

Bynum, C. W., 'Women mystics in the thirteenth century: the case of the nuns of Helfta', in C. W. Bynum, *Jesus as mother: studies in the spirituality of the high middle ages* (Berkeley, Los Angeles, and London, 1982), pp. 170–262

Fragmentation and redemption: essays on gender and the human body in medieval religion (New York, 1992)

Byrne, J. P., 'The merchant as penitent: Francesco di Marco Datini and the Bianchi movement of 1399', *Viator*, 20 (1989), pp. 219–31

Cameron, E., *The European Reformation* (Oxford, 1991)

Camille, M., *The Gothic idol: ideology and image-making in medieval art* (Cambridge, 1989)

Cheney, C. R., *English synodalia of the thirteenth century*, (Oxford, 1941)

Chenu, M. D., *Nature, man, and society in the twelfth century: essays on new theological perspectives in the Latin west* (Chicago and London, 1968)

Chiffoleau, J., *La comptabilité de l'au-delà: les hommes, la mort et la religion dans la région d'Avignon à la fin du Moyen Age (vers 1320–vers 1480)*, Collection de l'École française de Rome, 47 (Rome, 1980)

'Les testaments provençaux et contadins à la fin du moyen âge: richesse documentaire et problèmes d'exploitation', in *Sources of social history: private acts of the late middle ages*, ed. P. Brezzi and E. Lee, Pontifical institute of mediaeval studies: papers in mediaeval studies, 5 (Toronto, 1984), pp. 131–52

Chittolini, G., 'Civic religion and the countryside in late medieval Italy', in *City and countryside in late medieval and Renaissance Italy: essays presented to Philip Jones*, ed. T. Dean and C. Wickham (London and Ronceverte, 1990), pp. 69–80

Chomel, V., 'Droit de patronage et pratique religieuse dans l'archevêché de Narbonne au début du XVᵉ siècle', *Bibliothèque de l'école des chartes*, 115 (1957), pp. 58–137

Christian, W. A., jr., *Apparitions in late medieval and Renaissance Spain* (Princeton, NJ, 1981)

Chydenius, J., *The friendship of God and the two ends of man: a study in Christian humanism, 1100–1321*, Societas scientiarum fennica: commentationes humanarum litterarum, 68 (Helsinki, 1981)

Clanchy, M. T., *From memory to written record: England, 1066–1307* (2nd edn, Oxford, 1993)

Clay, R. M., *The hermits and anchorites of England* (London, 1914)

Cohen, E., '*In haec signa*: pilgrim-badge trade in southern France', *Journal of medieval history*, 2 (1976), pp. 193–214

Cohen, J., 'Scholarship and intolerance in the medieval academy: the study and evaluation of Judaism in European Christianity', *American historical review*, 91 (1986), pp. 592–613

'The mentality of the medieval Jewish apostate: Peter Alfonsi, Hermann of Cologne, and Pablo Christiani', in *Jewish apostasy in the modern world*, ed. T. M. Endelman (New York and London, 1987), pp. 20–47

Cohn, S. K., jr., *Death and property in Siena, 1205–1800: strategies for the afterlife* (Baltimore and London, 1988)

The cult of remembrance and the Black Death: six Renaissance cities in central Italy (Baltimore and London, 1992)

La communauté rurale/Rural communities, IV, *Recueils de la société Jean Bodin pour l'histoire comparative des institutions*, 43 (Paris, 1984)

Constable, G., 'The popularity of twelfth-century spiritual writers in the late middle ages', in *Renaissance studies in honor of Hans Baron*, ed. A. Molho and J. A. Tedeschi (Florence, IL, 1971), pp. 5–28

Coulet, N., *Les visites pastorales*, Typologie des sources du moyen âge occidental, fasc. 23 (Turnhout, 1977)

Davis, O., *God within: the mystical tradition of northern Europe* (London, 1988)

Dawson, C., *The Mongol mission* (London, 1955)

Deanesly, M., *The Lollard Bible and other medieval Biblical versions* (Cambridge, 1920)

Delaruelle, E., E.-R. Labande and P. Ourliac, *L'église au temps du grand schisme et de la crise conciliare* (2 vols., Paris, 1962–4)

Delumeau, J., *Catholicism between Luther and Voltaire: a new view of the Counter-Reformation* (London and Philadelphia, 1977)

La peur en occident, XIVe–XVIIIe siècles: une cité assiegée (Paris, 1978)

Sin and fear: the emergence of a western guilt culture, 13th–18th centuries (New York, 1990)

Donovan, C., *The de Brailes Hours: shaping the Book of Hours in thirteenth-century Oxford* (London, 1991)

Duffy, E., *The stripping of the altars: traditional religion in England, 1400–1580* (New Haven and London, 1992)

Dunn-Lardeau, B., ed., *Legenda aurea: sept siècles de diffusion: Actes du colloque international sur la Legenda aurea: texte latin et branches vernaculaires, à l'Université du Quebec à Montreal, 11–12 mai 1983*, Cahiers d'études médiévales, cahier spécial 2 (Montreal and Paris, 1986)

Dygo, M., 'The political role of the cult of the Virgin Mary in Teutonic Prussia in the fourteenth and fifteenth centuries', *Journal of medieval history*, 15 (1989), pp. 63–80

Dykema, P. A., and H. A. Oberman, eds., *Anticlericalism in late medieval and early modern Europe*, Studies in medieval and Reformation thought, 51 (Leiden, New York, and Cologne, 1993)

Edwards, J. H., 'Mission and inquisition among *conversos* and *moriscos* in Spain, 1250–1550', *Studies in church history*, 21 (1984), pp. 139–51

'Elijah and the Inquisition: Messianic prophecy among *conversos* in Spain, *c.* 1500', *Nottingham medieval studies*, 28 (1984), pp. 79–94

'Christian mission in the kingdom of Granada, 1492–1568', *Renaissance and modern studies*, 31 (1987), pp. 20–33

'Religious faith and doubt in late medieval Soria', *Past and present*, 120 (August, 1988), pp. 3–25

The Jews in Christian Europe, 1400–1700 (London and New York, 1988)

Eltis, D. A., 'Tensions between clergy and laity in some western German cities in the later middle ages', *Journal of ecclesiastical history*, 43 (1992), pp. 231–48

Emmerson, R. K., *Antichrist in the middle ages: a study of medieval apocalypticism, art, and literature* (Seattle, 1981)

L'encadrement religieux des fidèles au moyen-âge et jusqu'au Concile de Trent: la paroisse – le clergé, la pastorale – la devotion. Actes du 109e congrès national des sociétés savants, Dijon, 1984: section d'histoire médiévale et de philologie, tome 1 (Paris, 1985)

Enghen, J. van, 'The Christian middle ages as an historiographical problem', *American historical review*, 91 (1986), pp. 519–52

'Faith as a concept of order in medieval Christendom', in *Belief in history: innovative approaches to European and American religion*, ed. Thomas Kselman (Notre Dame and London, 1991), pp. 19–67

Evans, G. R., 'Exegesis and authority in the thirteenth century', in *Ad litteram: authoritative texts and their medieval readers*, ed. M. D. Jordan and K. Emery, jr. (Notre Dame, 1992), pp. 93–111

Faire croire: modalités de la diffusion et de la réception des messages religieux du XIIe au XVe siècles. Table ronde organisée par l'École française de Rome, en collaboration avec l'Institut d'histoire médiévale de l'Université de Padoue (Rome, 22–23 juin 1979), Collection de l'École française de Rome, 51 (Rome, 1981)

Fin du monde et signes du temps: visionnaires et prophètes en France méridionale (fin XIIIe–début XVe siècle), Cahiers de Fanjeaux, 27 (Toulouse, 1992)

Finucane, R. C., *Miracles and pilgrims: popular beliefs in medieval England* (London, 1977)

Flint, V. I. J., 'Christopher Columbus and the friars', in *Intellectual life in the middle ages: essays presented to Margaret Gibson*, ed. L. Smith and B. Ward (London and Rio Grande, 1992), pp. 295–310

Flynn, M., 'Betrayal of the soul in Spanish blasphemy', in *Religion, body, and gender in early modern Spain*, ed. A. Saint-Saëns (San Francisco, 1991), pp. 30–44

Fox, A., 'Facts and fallacies: reinterpreting English humanism', in A. Fox and J. Guy, *Reassessing the Henrician age: humanism, politics, and reform, 1500–1550* (Oxford, 1986), pp. 9–33

Ganshof, F., 'Pèlerinages expiatoires flamands à Saint-Gilles pendant le XIVe siècle', *Annales du midi*, 78 (1966), pp. 391–407

Gibson, G. McM., *The theater of devotion: East Anglian drama and society in the late middle ages* (Chicago and London, 1989)

Gonzalez-Casanovas, R., 'Preaching the gospel in *Barlaam* and *Blanquerna*: pious narrative and parable in medieval Spain', *Viator*, 24 (1993), pp. 215–31

Goodich, M., '*Ancilla Dei*: the servant as saint in the late middle ages', in *Women of the medieval world: essays in honor of John H. Mundy*, ed. J. Kirschner and S. E. Wemple (Oxford, 1985), pp. 119–36

Goodman, A., and A. MacKay, eds., *The impact of humanism on western Europe* (London, 1990)

Gurevich, A., *Medieval popular culture: problems of belief and perception*, Cambridge studies in oral and literate culture, 14 (Cambridge, 1988)

Haigh, C., *English Reformations: religion, politics, and society under the Tudors* (Oxford, 1993)

Halperin, C. J., 'The ideology of silence: prejudice and pragmatism on the medieval religious frontier', *Comparative studies in society and history*, 26 (1984), pp. 442–66

Hamesse, J., and X. Hermand, eds., *De l'homélie au sermon: histoire de la prédication médiévale. Actes du colloque international de Louvain-la-Neuve (9–11 juillet 1992)*, Université catholique de Louvain, publications de l'institut d'études médiévales: Textes, études, congrès, 14 (Louvain-la-Neuve, 1993)

Hamilton, B., *Religion in the medieval west* (London, 1986)

Heath, P., *Church and realm, 1272–1461* (London, 1989)

Henderson, J., 'Confraternities and the church in late medieval Florence', *Studies in church history*, 23 (1986), pp. 69–83

'Religious confraternities and death in early Renaissance Florence', in *Florence and Italy: essays in honour of Nicolai Rubinstein*, ed. P. Denley and C. Elam, Westfield publications in medieval studies, 2 (London, 1988), pp. 383–94

'The parish and the poor in Florence at the time of the Black Death: the case of S. Frediano', *Continuity and change*, 3 (1988), pp. 247–72

Herlihy, D., 'Tuscan names, 1200–1530', *Renaissance quarterly*, 41 (1988), pp. 561–82

Highfield, R., 'Christians, Jews, and Muslims in the same society: the fall of *convivencia* in medieval Spain', *Studies in church history*, 15 (1978), pp. 121–46

Holbrook, S. E., 'Margery Kempe and Wynkyn de Worde', in *The medieval mystical tradition in England: Exeter symposium IV. Papers read at Dartington Hall, July 1987*, ed. M. Glasscoe (Woodbridge, Suffolk, 1987), pp. 27–46

Housley, N. J., 'Politics and heresy in Italy: anti-heretical crusades, orders and confraternities, 1200–1500', *Journal of ecclesiastical history*, 33 (1982), pp. 193–208

Huizinga, J., *The waning of the Middle Ages* (London, 1965)

Ives, E. W., *The common lawyers of pre-Reformation England* (Cambridge, 1983)

Jacob, E. F., 'Christian humanism', in *Europe in the late middle ages*, ed. J. Hale, R. Highfield, and B. Smalley (London, 1965), pp. 437–65

Jacoby, D., 'Pèlerinage médiéval et sanctuaires de Terre Sainte: la perspective venitienne', *Ateneo veneto, anno CLXXIII (= xxiv, N.S.)*, 24 (1986), pp. 27–58, reprinted in his *Studies on the crusader states and on Venetian expansion* (London, 1989)

Jaye, B. H., 'Artes orandi', in M. G. Briscoe and B. H. Jaye, *Artes praedicandi and Artes orandi*, Typologie des sources du moyen âge occidental, fasc. 61 (Turnhout, 1992), pp. 77–118

Jeanne, D., 'La société rurale face à la lèpre à travers le registre de l'officialité de Cerisy de 1314 à 1377', *Annales de Normandie*, 43 (1993), pp. 91–106

Johnson, P. D., *Equal in monastic profession: religious women in medieval France* (Chicago and London, 1991)

Kaminsky, H., 'Chiliasm and the Hussite Revolution', in *Change in medieval society: Europe north of the Alps, 1050–1500*, ed. S. Thrupp (New York, 1964), pp. 249–78

Kedar, B. Z., *Crusade and mission: European approaches toward the Muslims* (Princeton, NJ, 1984)

Kedourie, E., ed., *Spain and the Jews: the Sephardi experience, 1492 and after* (London, 1992)

Kieckhefer, R., *European witch trials: their foundations in popular and learned eculture, 1300–1500* (London and Henley, 1976)

'Holiness and the culture of devotion: remarks on some late medieval male saints', in *Images of sainthood in medieval Europe*, ed. R. Blumenfeld-Kosinski and T. Szell (Ithaca and London, 1991), pp. 288–305

King, A. A., *Liturgies of the past* (London, 1959)

Klaiczay, G., *The uses of supernatural power: the transformation of popular religion in medieval and early-modern Europe* (Cambridge and Oxford, 1990)

Klapisch-Zuber, C., 'The name "remade": the transmission of given names in Florence in the fourteenth and fifteenth centuries', in C. Klapisch-Zuber, *Women, family, and ritual in Renaissance Italy* (Chicago and London, 1985), pp. 283–309

Kleinberg, A. M., *Prophets in their own country: living saints and the making of sainthood in the later middle ages*, Chicago and London, 1992

Lambert, M., *Medieval heresy: popular movements from the Gregorian Reform to the Reformation* (Oxford, 1992)

Lampe, G. W. H., ed., *The Cambridge history of the Bible, volume 2: the West from the Fathers to the Reformation* (Cambridge, 1969)

Långfors, A., '*Le miroir de vie et de mort* par Robert de l'Omme (1266): modèle d'un moralité wallonne du XVᵉ siècle', *Romania*, 47 (1921), pp. 511–31

Langmuir, G. I., *History, religion, and antisemitism* (Berkeley, Los Angeles, and Oxford, 1990)

Lea, H. C., *A history of auricular confession and indulgences in the Latin church, volume III: Indulgences* (Philadelphia, 1896)

Le Goff, J., *The birth of Purgatory* (London, 1984)

Lerner, R. E., 'Medieval prophecy and religious dissent', *Past and present*, 72 (August, 1976), pp. 3–24

'The Black Death and western European eschatalogical mentalities', *American historical review*, 86 (1981), pp. 533–52

Le Roy Ladurie, E., *Montaillou: Cathars and catholics in a French village, 1294–1324* (Harmondsworth, 1980)

Lesnick, D. R., 'Dominican preaching and the creation of capitalist ideology in late medieval Florence', *Memorie Domenicane*, n.s. 8–9 (1977–8), pp. 199–247

Preaching in medieval Florence: the social world of Franciscan and Dominican spirituality (Athens, GA, and London, 1989)

Lewis, B., and F. Niewöhner, eds., *Religionsgespräche im Mittelalter*, Wolfenbütteler Mittelalter-Studien, 4 (Wiesbaden, 1992)

L'Hermite-Leclercq, P., 'Reclus et recluses dans le sud-ouest de la France', in *La femme dans la vie religieuse du Languedoc (XIIIᵉ–XIVᵉ s.)*, Cahiers de Fanjeaux, 23 (1988), pp. 281–98

Limor, O., 'Missionary merchants: three medieval anti-Jewish works from Genoa', *Journal of medieval history*, 17 (1991), pp. 35–51

Little, L. K., 'Spiritual sanctions in Wales', in *Images of sainthood in medieval Europe*, ed. R. Blumenfeld-Kosinski and T. Szell (Ithaca and London, 1991), pp. 67–80

Llompart, G., 'El angel custodio en la Corona de Aragón en la Baja Edad Media (fiesta, teatro, iconografía)', in *Fiestas y liturgia: actas del coloquio celebrado en la Casa de Velázquez/Fêtes et liturgie: actes du colloque tenu à la Casa de Velázquez, 12/14-XII-1985*, (Madrid, 1988), pp. 249–69

Lunt, W. E., *Financial relations of the papacy with England, 1327–1534*, Publications of the Mediaeval Academy of America, 74 (Cambridge, MA, 1962)

McCue, J. F., 'The doctrine of transubstantiation from Berengar through the Council of Trent', in *Lutherans and Catholics in dialogue, III: the Eucharist as sacrifice* (Washington, DC, and New York, 1967), pp. 89–124

McCurry, C., 'Religious careers and religious devotion in thirteenth-century Metz', *Viator*, 9 (1978), pp. 325–33

McDonnell, E. W., *The beguines and beghards in medieval culture, with special emphasis on the Belgian scene* (New Brunswick, NJ, 1954)

MacKay, A., 'The Hispanic-*converso* predicament', *Transactions of the royal historical society*, 5th ser., 35 (1985), pp. 159–79

'The Lord of Hosts', in *Essays on hispanic themes in honour of Edward C. Riley*, ed. J. Lowe and P. Swanson (Edinburgh, 1989), pp. 41–50

'Religion, culture, and ideology on the late medieval Castilian-Granadan frontier', in *Medieval frontier societies*, ed. R. Bartlett and A. MacKay (Oxford, 1989), pp. 217–43

MacKenney, R., *Tradesmen and traders: the world of the guilds in Venice and Europe, c. 1250–c. 1650* (London and Sydney, 1987)

Macy, G., 'The dogma of transubstantiation in the middle ages', *Journal of ecclesiastical history*, 45 (1994), pp. 11–41

Manselli, R., 'La sinodo lucchese di Enrico del Carretto', in *Miscellanea Gilles Gérard Meersseman, Italia sacra*, 15–16 (2 vols., Padua, 1970), I, pp. 197–246

Martin, H., *Le métier de prédicateur en France septentrionale à la fin du moyen âge (1350–1520)* (Paris, 1988)

Michaud-Quantin, P., 'Les méthodes de la pastorale du XIIIᵉ au XVᵉ siècle', in *Methoden in Wissenschaft und Kunst des Mittelalters*, ed. A Zimmermann, Miscellanea medievalia: Veröffentlichungen des Thomas-Instituts des Universität zu Köln, 7 (Berlin, 1970), pp. 76–91

Miguel Rodriguez, J. C. de, *Los mudéjares de la corona de Castilla*, Cuadernos de investigacion medieval, 8 (Madrid, 1988)

Moeller, B., 'Religious life in Germany on the eve of the Reformation', in *Pre-Reformation Germany*, ed. G. Strauss (London, 1972), pp. 13–42

Montagnes, B., 'La repression des sacralités populaires en Languedoc au XVᵉ siècle', *Archivum fratrum predicatorum*, 52 (1982), pp. 154–85

Moore, R. I., *The formation of a persecuting society* (Oxford, 1987)

Le mouvement confraternel au Moyen Age: France, Italie, Suisse. Actes de la Table Ronde organisée par l'Université de Lausanne avec le concours de l'École française de Rome et de l'Unité associée 1011 du CNRS, 'L'institution ecclésiale à la fin du Moyen

Age', *Lausanne, 9–11 mai 1985*, Collection de l'École française de Rome, 97 (Rome, 1987)

Muldoon, J., *Popes, lawyers, and infidels: the church and the non-Christian world, 1250–1550* (Philadelphia, 1979)

Murray, A., 'Piety and impiety in thirteenth-century Italy', *Studies in church history*, 8 (1972), pp. 83–106

'Religion among the poor in thirteenth-century France: the testimony of Humbert de Romans', *Traditio*, 30 (1974), pp. 285–324

Nellhaus, T., 'Mementos of things to come: orality, literacy, and typology in the *Biblia pauperum*', in *Printing the written word: the social history of books circa 1450–1520*, ed. S. Hindman (Ithaca and London, 1991), pp. 292–321

Nicholas, D., 'Looking for the origins of the French Reformation', in *Power, culture and religion in France, c. 1350–c. 1520*, ed. C.T. Allmand (Woodbridge, Suffolk, 1989), pp. 131–44

Niles, P., 'Baptism and the naming of children in late medieval England', *Medieval prosopography*, 3 (1982), pp. 95–107

Nirenberg, D., 'Muslim-Jewish relations in the fourteenth-century Crown of Aragon', *Viator*, 24 (1993), pp. 249–68

Oakley, F., *The western church in the late middle ages* (Ithaca and London, 1979)

Oates, J. C. T., 'Richard Pynson and the Holy Blood of Hailes', *The Library*, 5th ser., 13 (1958), pp. 269–77

Odber de Baubeta, P. A., 'Towards a history of preaching in medieval Portugal', *Portuguese studies*, 7 (1991), pp. 1–18

O'Meara, C. F., 'Eucharistic theology and the house of God in late medieval and early Renaissance painting', in *Classica et mediaevalia: studies in honor of Joseph Szövérffy*, ed. I. Vaslef and H. Buschhausen, Medieval classics: texts and studies, 20 (Washington and Leyden, 1986), pp. 125–37

Origo, I., *The merchant of Prato: Francesco di Marco Datini* (rev. edn, London, 1963)

Orme, N., 'Bishop Grandison and popular religion', *Report and transactions of the Devonshire association for the advancement of science, literature, and art*, 124 (1992), pp. 107–18

Osheim, D. J., 'Conversion, *conversi*, and the Christian life in late medieval Tuscany', *Speculum*, 58 (1983), pp. 368–90

Owen, D. M., 'Bacon and eggs: Bishop Buckingham and superstition in Lincolnshire', *Studies in church history*, 8 (1972), pp. 139–42

Pantin, W. A., 'Instructions for a devout and literate layman', in *Medieval learning and literature: essays presented to Richard William Hunt*, ed. J. J. G. Alexander and M. T. Gibson (Oxford, 1976), pp. 398–422.

Pelikan, J., *The Christian tradition; a history of the development of doctrine, 3: the growth of medieval theology (600–1300)* (Chicago and London, 1978)

The Christian tradition; a history of the development of doctrine, 4: The Reformation of church and dogma (1300–1700) (Chicago and London, 1984)

Pfaff, R. W., *New liturgical feasts in later medieval England* (Oxford, 1970)

'Prescription and reality in the rubrics of Sarum rite service books', in *Intellectual life in the middle ages: essays presented to Margaret Gibson*, ed. L. Smith and B. Ward (London and Rio Grande, 1992), pp. 197–205

Pontal, O., 'Le rôle du synode diocesain et des statuts synodaux dans la formation du clergé', *Cahiers de Fanjeaux*, 7 (1972), pp. 337–59

Les statuts synodaux, Typologie des sources du moyen âge occidental, Fasc. 11, A-III.1* (Turnhout, 1975)

Post, R. R., *The modern devotion: confrontation with Reformation and humanism*, Studies in medieval and Reformation thought, 3 (Leiden, 1968)

Powell, J. M., ed., *Muslims under Latin rule, 1100–1300* (Princeton, NJ, 1990)

Pullan, B. R., *Rich and poor in Renaissance Venice: the social institutions of a catholic state* (Oxford, 1971)

Rafoth, B. A., 'A discourse community: where readers, writers, and texts come together', in *The social construction of written communication*, ed. B. A. Rafoth and D. L. Rubin (Norwood, NJ, 1988), pp. 131–46

'The concept of discourse community: descriptive and explanatory adequacy', in *A sense of audience in written communication*, ed. G. Kirsch and D. H. Roen, Written communication annual, 5 (Newbury Park, London, and New Delhi, 1990), pp. 140–53

Raitt, J., ed., *Christian spirituality, II: High middle ages and Reformation* (London, 1987)

Reeves, M., *Joachim of Fiore and the prophetic future* (London, 1976)

Reinburg, V., 'Liturgy and the laity in late medieval and Reformation France', *The sixteenth-century journal*, 23 (1992–3), pp. 526–47

Reynolds, S., 'Social mentalities and the case of medieval scepticism', *Transactions of the royal historical society*, 6th ser., 1 (1991), pp. 21–41

Rice, E. F., jr., 'Jacques Lefèvre d'Étaples and the medieval Christian mystics', in *Florilegium historiale: essays presented to Wallace K. Ferguson*, ed. J. G. Rowe and W. H. Stockdale (Toronto and Buffalo, 1971), pp. 89–124

Richard, J., *La papauté et les missions d'orient au moyen âge (XIIIᵉ–XVᵉ siècles)*, Collection de l'École française de Rome, 33 (Rome, 1977)

Richmond, C., 'The English gentry and religion, *c.* 1500', in *Religious belief and ecclesiastical careers in late medieval England*, ed. C. Harper-Bill, Studies in the history of medieval religion, 3 (Woodbridge, Suffolk, 1991), pp. 121–50

Romano, D., 'Charity and community in early Renaissance Venice', *Journal of urban history*, 11 (1984), pp. 63–81

Rubin, M., *Corpus Christi: the eucharist in late medieval culture* (Cambridge, 1991)

Rycraft, P., 'The late medieval Catalan death-bed', in *God and man in medieval Spain: essays in honour of J. R. L. Highfield*, ed. D. W. Lomax and D. Mackenzie (Warminster, 1989), pp. 117–28

Sargent, S. D., 'Saints' cults and naming patterns in Bavaria, 1400–1600', *Catholic historical review*, 76 (1990), pp. 673–96

Schmitt, J.-C., *Mort d'une hérésie: l'église et les clercs face aux béguines et aux béghards du Rhin supérieur du XIVᵉ au XVᵉ siècle* (Paris, 1978)

The holy greyhound: Guinefort, healer of children since the thirteenth century, Cambridge studies in oral and literate culture, 6 (Cambridge, 1983)

Scribner, R.W., 'Cosmic order and daily life: sacred and secular in pre-industrial German society', in R.W. Scribner, *Popular culture and popular movements in Reformation Germany* (London and Ronceverte, 1987), pp. 1–16

'Ritual and popular religion in catholic Germany at the time of the Reformation', in R. W. Scribner, *Popular culture and popular movements in Reformation Germany* (London and Ronceverte, 1987), pp. 17–47

Shaffern, R. W., 'Learned discussions of indulgences for the dead in the middle ages', *Church history*, 61 (1992), pp. 367–81

Shatzmiller, J., 'Jews "separated from the communion of the faithful in Christ" in the middle ages', in *Studies in medieval Jewish history and literature*, ed. I. Twersky, Harvard Judaic monographs, 2 (Cambridge, MS, and London, 1979), pp. 307–14

Shaw, J., 'The influence of canonical and episcopal reform on popular books of instruction', in *The popular literature of medieval England*, ed. T. J. Heffernan, Tennessee studies in literature, 28 (Knoxville, TN, 1985), pp. 44–60

Sheils, W. J., and D. Wood, eds., *Women in the church*, Studies in church history, 27 (Oxford, 1990)

Simons, W., and J. E. Ziegler, 'Phenomenal religion in the thirteenth century: Elizabeth of Spalbeek and the Passion cult', *Studies in church history*, 27 (1990), pp. 117–26

Spencer, B., 'Medieval pilgrim badges: some general observations illustrated mainly from English sources', in *Rotterdam papers: a contribution to medieval archaeology*, ed. J. G. N. Renaud (Rotterdam, 1968), pp. 137–54

'King Henry of Windsor and the London pilgrim', in *Collectanea Londiniensia: studies in London archaeology and history presented to Ralph Merrifield*, ed. J. Bird, H. Chapman, and J. Clark, London and Middlesex archaeological society, special papers, 2 (1978), pp. 234–64

Spencer, H. Leith, *English preaching in the late middle ages* (Oxford, 1993)

Stacey, R. C., 'The conversion of Jews to Christianity in thirteenth-century England', *Speculum*, 67 (1992), pp. 263–83

Sullivan, D., 'Nicholas of Cusa as reformer: the papal legation to the Germanies, 1451–1452', *Mediaeval studies*, 36 (1974), pp. 382–428

Sumption, J., *Pilgrimage: an image of mediaeval religion* (London, 1975)

Swanson, R. N., 'Problems of the priesthood in pre-Reformation England', *English historical review*, 105 (1990), pp. 845–69

Szarmach, P., ed., *An introduction to the medieval mystics of Europe* (Albany, NY, 1984)

Tanner, N. P., *The church in late medieval Norwich, 1370–1532*, Pontifical institute of mediaeval studies: Studies and texts, 66 (Toronto, 1984)

Tarvers, J. K., '"Thys ys my mystrys boke": English women as readers and writers in late medieval England', in *The uses of manuscripts in literary studies: essays in memory of Judson Boyce Allen*, ed. C. C. Morse, P. R. Doob, and M. C. Woods, Studies in medieval culture, 31 (Kalamazoo, 1992), pp. 305–27

Taylor, L., *Soldiers of Christ: preaching in late medieval and Reformation France* (Oxford and New York, 1992)

Tentler, T. N., *Sin and confession on the eve of the Reformation* (Princeton, NJ, 1977)

Thomson, J. A. F., *Popes and princes, 1417–1519* (London, 1980)

Tillinghast, P. E., 'An aborted Reformation: Germany and the papacy in the mid-fifteenth century', *Journal of medieval history*, 2 (1976), pp. 57–79

Toussaert, J., *Le sentiment religieux en Flandre à la fin du Moyen-Age* (Paris, 1963)

Trexler, R. C., 'Florentine religious experience: the sacred image', *Studies in the Renaissance*, 19 (1972), pp. 7–41

'Charity and the defense of urban élites in the Italian communes', in *The rich, the well born, and the powerful: elites and upper classes in history*, ed. F. C. Jaher (Urbana, Chicago, and London, 1973), pp. 64–109

The spiritual power: republican Florence under interdict, Studies in medieval and Reformation thought, 9 (Leiden, 1974)

Trinkaus, C., '*In our image and likeness*': humanity and divinity in Italian humanist thought (2 vols., London, 1970)

'Themes for a Renaissance anthropology', in *The Renaissance: essays in interpretation* (London and New York, 1982), pp. 83–125

Utterback, K. T., 'Worship in the church of your choice? Church attendance in mid-fourteenth century Barcelona', *Journal of medieval history*, 17 (1991), pp. 245–53

Vandenbroucke, F., 'New milieus, new problems: from the twelfth to the sixteenth century', in J. Leclercq, F. Vandenbroucke, and L. Bouyer, *A history of Christian spirituality, 2: the spirituality of the middle ages* (London, 1968), pp. 223–543.

Vauchez, A., *La sainteté en occident des derniers siècles du moyen âge, d'après les procès de canonisation et les document hagiographiques*, Bibliothèque des écoles françaises d'Athènes et de Rome, 241 (Rome, 1981)

Les laics au moyen âge: pratiques et expériences religieuses (Paris, 1987)

Verdon, T., and J. Henderson, eds., *Christianity and the Renaissance: image and religious imagination in the Quattrocento* (Syracuse, NY, 1990)

Verger, J., '"Studia" et universités', in *Le scuoli degli ordini mendicanti (secoli XIII–XIV), 11–14 ottobre 1976*, Convegni del Centro di studi sulla spiritualità medievale, 17 (Todi, 1978), pp. 173–203

Vodola, E., *Excommunication in the middle ages* (Berkeley, Los Angeles, and London, 1986)

Wakefield, W. L., 'Some unorthodox popular ideas of the thirteenth century', *Mediaevalia et humanistica*, n.s. 4 (1973), pp. 25–35

Walsh, M. W., 'Divine cuckold/Holy fool: the comic image of Joseph in the English "Troubles" play', in *England in the fourteenth century: proceedings of the 1985 Harlaxton symposium*, ed. M.W. Ormrod (Woodbridge, Suffolk, 1986), pp. 278–97

Warren, A. K., *Anchorites and their patrons in medieval England* (Berkeley, Los Angeles, and London, 1985)

Warner, M., *Alone of all her sex: the myth and the cult of the Virgin Mary* (London, 1976)

Webb, D. M., 'Penitence and peace-making in city and contado: the Bianchi of 1399', *Studies in church history*, 16 (1979), pp. 243–56

Wenzel, S., 'The Pilgrimage of Life as a late medieval genre', *Mediaeval Studies*, 35 (1973), pp. 370–88

Wessley, S., 'The thirteenth-century Guglielmites: salvation through women', in *Medieval women*, ed. D. Baker, Studies in church history: subsidia, 1 (Oxford, 1978), pp. 289–303

Westlake, H. F., *The parish guilds of medieval England* (London, 1919)

Wirth, J., 'Against the acculturation thesis', in *Religion and society in early modern Europe, 1500–1800*, ed. K. von Greyerz (London, 1984), pp. 66–78

Wood, D., ed., *Christianity and Judaism, Studies in church history*, 29 (Oxford, 1992)

Woodruff, C. E., 'The financial aspect of the cult of St Thomas of Canterbury, as recorded by a study of the monastic records', *Archaeologia Cantiana*, 44 (9132), pp. 13–32

Ziegler, J. E., *Sculpture of compassion: the Pietà and the beguines in the southern Low Countries, c. 1300–c. 1600*, Institut historique belge de Rome, études d'histoire de l'art/Belgisch historisch Instituut te Rome, Studies over Kunstgeschiedenis, 6 (Brussels and Rome, 1992)

Zika, C., 'Hosts, processions, and pilgrimages in fifteenth-century Germany', *Past and present*, 118 (February 1988), pp. 25–64

INDEX

Indexing is always difficult, particularly with a book like this. Some of what follows is necessarily cursory: fully differentiated entries for 'laity' and 'spirituality', for instance, would include virtually every page. Individuals with proper surnames appear under those surnames, those usually known as 'X of Y' are indexed under Christian names.

Cambridge Medieval Textbooks

Already published

Germany in the High Middle Ages *c.* 1050–1200
HORST FUHRMANN
Translated by Timothy Reuter

The Hundred Years War
England and France at war *c.* 1300–1450
CHRISTOPHER ALLMAND

Standards of Living in the Later Middle Ages:
Social Change in England, *c.* 1200–1520
CHRISTOPHER DYER

Magic in the Middle Ages
RICHARD KIECKHEFER

The Papacy 1073–1198: Continuity and Innovation
I. S. ROBINSON

Medieval Wales
DAVID WALKER

England in the Reign of Edward III
SCOTT WAUGH

The Norman Kingdom of Sicily
DONALD MATTHEW

Political Thought in Europe, 1250–1450
ANTHONY BLACK

The Church in Western Europe from the Tenth
to the Early Twelfth Century
GERD TELLENBACH
Translated by Timothy Reuter

The Medieval Spains
BERNARD F. REILLY

England in the Thirteenth Century
ALAN HARDING

Monastic and Religious Orders in Britain 1000–1300
JANET BURTON

Religion and Devotion in Europe *c.* 1215–*c.* 1515
R. N. SWANSON

Other titles are in preparation

Lightning Source UK Ltd.
Milton Keynes UK
UKOW04f0059060118
315648UK00001B/6/P